THE COMEDY OF REDEMPTION

The Comedy of Redemption:

CHRISTIAN FAITH AND COMIC VISION
IN FOUR AMERICAN NOVELISTS

RALPH C. WOOD

University of Notre Dame Press
Notre Dame, Indiana

Library of Congress Cataloging-in-Publication Data

Wood, Ralph C.
    The comedy of redemption.

    Includes index.
    1. American fiction—20th century—History and
criticism. 2. Christianity in literature. 3. Redemption
in literature. 4. Comic, The, in literature. 5. Barth,
Karl, 1886–1968, 6. Percy, Walker, 1916–   —Religion.
7. Updike, John—Religion. 8. O'Connor, Flannery—
Religion. 9. De Vries, Peter—Religion. 10. Religion and
literature. I. Title.
PS379.W65   1988   813'.54'09382   87-40613
ISBN 0-268-00767-5

Manufactured in the United States of America

FOR WARREN CARR

CONTENTS

PREFACE

John Cheever prefaces one of his novels by saying thanks to everybody. This is exactly my own sentiment. A book on the comedy of redemption could not have been written except in utter dependence upon the gifts of others, and thus in radical awareness that we receive infinitely more than we give. I cannot possibly pay all my debts in so brief a space as this, but I can at least offer more than a general thanksgiving.

This is a story that began, like most human stories, very early—with a small-town East Texas home and school and church. Belatedly, but no less gratefully, I have come to understand that they gave me what neither privilege nor ease could so well provide: undeserved love from my parents, unsophisticated tutelage from my teachers, unapologetic proclamation from my ministers. Whatever understanding of the Gospel of grace this book may evince thus begins at the beginning.

It was nourished along the way by mentors at both East Texas State and the University of Chicago. The decisive turn came in 1962, when a Roman Catholic professor introduced a Roman Catholic author to a Baptist undergraduate who came from a Texas county where there was not a single Catholic church. Dr. Paul Wells Barrus was the Catholic professor, Flannery O'Connor was the Catholic author, and I was the Baptist undergraduate. From the moment I first read *A Good Man Is Hard to Find*, I knew that I had been struck with revolutionary force by something at once hilariously funny, literarily excellent, and ecumenically Christian. That the work of this Baptist Southerner is published by a Catholic university press brings the story full circle.

For almost a quarter-century I have sought to probe the scandal of the comic redemption that first registered upon me as an undergraduate. Nearly a generation of my own Wake Forest University students has joined me in this enlivening task. Nothing gives me greater pleasure than to salute former pupils who, having once learned from me, are now my instructors. Richard Vance has read virtually every word of this wordy book, as perhaps only a pathologist could be motivated to do. Repeatedly he has cured me of my own stylistic and conceptual ills. Other former students have read smaller portions of the manuscript and commented helpfully on them: Cindy Caldwell, Ken Carter, Ken Cooper, David Green, Tim Hood, Araminta Johnston, David Kellogg, Jim McCoy, Suzanne Morrison, Nathan Parrish, Ann and Brewster Rawls, Ben Salt, Tom Steagald, Steve Walker, and especially John Sykes.

My colleagues in the Wake Forest departments of Religion and Philosophy have kept their resident Barthian appropriately humbled. They have reminded me that, if Christendom survived Tertullian in the third century, it can withstand Barth in the twentieth. Marcus Hester, Gregory Pritchard, and Charles Talbert have been particularly strong companions in faith as well as fine sparring partners in ideas. Edwin Wilson has served as an exceptionally encouraging provost, looking with unfailing kindness on all my requests for support. The president emeritus of Wake Forest, Dr. James Ralph Scales, has my lasting admiration for caring less about committee reports than about what his faculty was thinking and writing and teaching. I shall always treasure his witty cautionary note penned to an essay of mine on John Updike: "You will baptize anyone who writes elegantly."

Far from negligible has been the help given by Rick Matthews and John Baxley, who patiently nursed me through the many vicissitudes of computer life. Colleagues from other schools and universities have also given generously of their time to aid my efforts: Richard Brantley at Florida, Frank Burch-Brown at Virginia Polytechnic, Lawrence Cunningham at Florida State, Stanley Hauerwas at Duke, David Jasper at Durham, Kevin Lewis at South Carolina, James McClendon at Church Divinity School of the Pacific, Martin Marty at Chicago, James Moseley at Chapman, Theron Price at Furman, John Reist at Hillsdale, and Nathan Scott at Virginia.

I have also been fortunate to have audiences outside academe. Both the secular and religious communities of Winston-Salem, North Carolina, have given lively reception to my work. Nicholas Bragg and Marjorie Northrup have repeatedly invited me to lecture at Reynolda House, where I have always had a sympathetic hearing. Sunday School classes at St. Paul's Episcopal Church and the Wake Forest Baptist Church have demonstrated that lay theologians and critics often ask tougher questions and make more penetrating judgments than do our official scholars. It has been enormously invigorating to try out my texts and ideas on church members who know what both art and faith are truly about. They have been burned and bruised by life, graced and blessed by God, in ways that few undergraduates can understand. To face such thoughtful Christians on Sunday mornings has been the most splendid challenge of my career as teacher.

Institutions have been no less supportive than individuals. Wake Forest University granted me a Reynolds Research Leave for the beginning of this project, and a Fellowship for College Teachers awarded by the

National Endowment for the Humanities enabled me to complete the early research and writing. Both the *Christian Century* and the *Flannery O'Connor Bulletin* have published initial versions of what were later developed into full-length chapters here.

Thanks to the revisory powers of a word processor, my wife Suzanne has typed not a word of the manuscript. But she has borne, ever so redemptively, the far heavier burden that comes from having as her life-companion one who is "with book." Our children Kenneth and Harriet must also wonder what is comic or redemptive about a project that took their father back to his office night after night. Perhaps they will eventually understand that the prospect of returning home to them and their mother was one of the main mercies that sustained me through the long ordeal of writing and revising and rewriting.

Finally, an all too inadequate word of gratitude for the man to whom this work is dedicated, Warren Carr: eloquent and fearless proclaimer of the Gospel, pastor and counsellor without peer, friend and companion who enabled my own recovery of faith. He has taught me, in word as well as deed, in person even more than in precept, nearly everything I know about the divine comedy of our redemption. Karl Barth is the intellectual inspiration behind this essay in the theology of culture, but it was Warren Carr who first convinced me that eschatological grace issues in a very earthy humor and joy. We laugh not in order to stanch the tears, I have learned from him, but because God in Christ has wept and died and risen in our stead. I could not have been so well instructed in the comedy of the Gospel except by one who has written perhaps the only authentically Christian will. It officially bequeaths to his heirs something far more important than his modest worldly possessions; it also leaves them the scandalously immodest instructions to remember one thing only: "Nothing matters but the Resurrection."

Ralph C. Wood
Christmas 1987
Worrell House, London

INTRODUCTION

It is not obvious that Christian faith has an indissoluble connection with comic vision. Scripture records Jesus as having wept, but there is no mention of his laughter. "Holy Books never laugh," said Baudelaire, "to whatever nations they may belong." Not without cause has the Bible been called the world's least amusing book, a sober-sided tome whose black covers convey its essential mood and vision. A faith which has a cross as its central symbol can hardly be a laughing matter. In its patent unseriousness, its pointless frivolity, its japing mimicry, its clownish exuberance, comedy seems alien to the solemn reality of sin and salvation. It threatens to make a joke out of life itself and thus to render the God of life a prankster if not a monster.

Reinhold Niebuhr contends that there is no comedy in the redemption wrought at Calvary. The only people amused by the event of the cross are the brigands who gamble for Christ's clothes, the mockers who taunt the Savior unable to save himself, the scoffers who erect a scornful inscription to the thorn-crowned, gibbet-throned "king" of the Jews. It is not a scene that induces a sense of the comic. It is a picture, Niebuhr insists, of fearful evil transmuted by the grace of God into sober forgiveness.[1] If there be any merriment in faith, says Niebuhr, it can occur only in the outer courts of religion. Jubilation may surround but must never enter the sanctuary. For there, in the Holy of Holies where the crucified God atones for the sins of humanity, "laughter is swallowed up in prayer and humour filled with faith."[2]

Niebuhr is right, of course, about the sinful horror of Golgotha and the utter seriousness of the atonement achieved there. Yet he fails properly to distinguish between the cross itself and its effects—between Christ's suffering in our behalf and the life we are enjoined to live as a result of his sacrifice. The central contention of this study is that Jesus' death and resurrection render human existence comic in both its roots and its ramifications. Christian faith is comic, I will argue, in the profoundest sense of the word. It is about eschatological laughter and joy and hope. In the life, crucifixion, and final victory of Jesus, it discerns a decisive turning for the whole of human history. The Place of the Skull,

1

because sin and death have been conquered there, is the place past which there is no regression. The crucified and risen Lord commands his people to live in celebration of the victory he has won. This, I maintain, is the real dayspring of ethical life. Because God in Christ has reconciled the world unto himself, we are no longer free to regard ourselves and the world from a merely human point of view. The grim sobriety of the old aeon has been replaced with the gracious hilarity of God.

Such, in brief and paradoxical assertion, is my fundamental thesis. It needs not only to be argued and substantiated, but also to be set in relation to our contemporary situation. The recovery of a genuine Christian faith for the secular world depends, I believe, upon our rediscovery of what is deeply comic about the Gospel. The chief failure of the church in the late modern epoch is the failure to determine its proper relation to post-Enlightenment culture. Either it recoils in curdled contempt for secular reality as godless and nihilistic, or else it attempts to show that the best secular values are covertly Christian at their core. Rightist and leftist versions of Christian faith thus have an unamusing similarity. They are equally unable to discern those places and moments where the Gospel stands over against the world in critique and alongside the world in affirmation. Thus is the church left without any compelling word for addressing either society or itself. To recover the comic vision of our redemption in Christ is, I maintain, an important way to regain an authentic Christian witness to church and culture alike.

The opening chapters are devoted to a discussion of tragedy and comedy as theological no less than as literary categories. Special attention is given to the work of Reinhold Niebuhr. More than any other modern theologian, he has sought to establish the right relation between Christian faith and tragic vision. Niebuhr's Christian critique of tragedy is thoroughly convincing, as I will attempt to demonstrate. But while Niebuhr provides a clarifying Christian interpretation of tragedy, he fails to see the essential connection between Christianity and comedy. The theology of Karl Barth, I argue in the succeeding two chapters, discloses what is profoundly comic in God's reconciliation of the world unto himself in Jesus Christ. Against the common view that Barth is an anticultural theologian, I seek to demonstrate that his evangelical theology enables him vigorously to embrace the world of human creation. He is free to celebrate culture because he regards it as the arena rather than the vehicle of salvation. Especially in its comic expression, Barth reveals, culture can provide surprising parables of our divine redemption.

Then in the latter half of this study, I examine the work of four contemporary writers of fiction: Flannery O'Connor, Walker Percy, John Updike and Peter De Vries. They are all comic artists in the theological sense of the term, although their fiction echoes the laughter of the Gospel in radically different ways. A concluding chapter offers a brief comparative assessment of these four writers. There I suggest that the largest comic reflection of the Gospel may be found, often ironically and unintentionally, in fiction which is not overtly Christian.

Wags rightly make fun of unfunny books on humor. After a De Vriesian character named Dr. Didisheim gives a lecture on comedy, a listener responds by slapping him in the face with a *recipe* for custard pie. Such, alas, is the relation of theories about laughter to the real thing. If this study fails to elicit a sense of holy cheer, it is not the fault of the writers here explicated. They have provided me and my students an inexhaustible store of both laughter and pleasure. The failure lies rather with the idolatry that we commit in heavily sober thought, where we take ourselves and our projects all too seriously.

G. K. Chesterton was right to note that seriousness is often sinful because it is too obvious and natural. Gaiety can serve as the means of grace because it is supernaturally surprising. To take oneself and the world gravely, wrote Chesterton, is the trite thing to do. Solemnity, he said, flows out of us naturally, like the seepage of a fetid pool. Laughter, by contrast, requires a transcendent leap. "It is easy to be heavy: hard to be light. Satan fell by the force of gravity." The unfallen angels still fly, Chesterton added, because they take themselves so lightly.[3]

1

REINHOLD NIEBUHR AND THE TRAGIC VISION

To argue that the Gospel is fundamentally comic is not to deny the tragic element in either life or faith. A refusal to countenance the tragic vision renders the church's message shallow and banal. If human finitude and suffering are not taken seriously, Christ's triumph over evil becomes merely sentimental, and the life of faith degenerates into an idiotic optimism. With good cause does Chesterton's Father Brown—that pure-souled discerner of evil spirits and deeds—confess that he might himself be brought to commit murder. His target, he adds, would surely be some gleaming-gummed barker of happiness. "People like frequent laughter," Father Brown explains, "but I don't think they like a permanent smile. Cheerfulness without humour is a very trying thing."[1]

Chesterton's distinction between humor and cheer is exactly right. Cheer is a mere pumped-up eagerness and enthusiasm, a grinning obliviousness to the real sorrows and joys of life. Humor, by contrast, is a deep gladness of soul that does not blink the reality of evil and tragedy, but interprets them in the light of a higher and deeper comedy. The thesis argued here is that nothing other than the comedy of God's reconciliation of the world unto himself can sustain such humor, and that apart from this divine comedy the human story is a tragedy which silences all laughter and joy.

I. The Truth in Tragedy

Aristotle defined tragedy as the mimetic representation of those who are better than ourselves, comedy as the imitation of those who are worse. This distinction does not mean, as James M. Redfield rightly explains, that comedy deals with vicious and tragedy with virtuous characters. It means, instead, that "in comedy we are surprised by virtue and

4

success, in tragedy by vice and failure." Aristophanes' *Frogs* reveals Dionysus as a coward and fool who turns out to be unexpectedly brave and wise. In the *Iliad*, by contrast, Hector is undone by his very heroism: the same courage that makes him valorous in battle also makes him unwilling to retreat even when necessity demands it. His error (*hamartia*) is at once his own responsibility and yet something imposed upon him. He goes wrong because his virtue is inadequate to the demands of his situation. The tragic actor, says Redfield, "does the wrong thing at the very moment he is trying to do right."[2]

Tragedy is the profounder of the two genres, Redfield argues, because it tests the limits of morality and culture as comedy does not. "Through culture man has transformed his world and made it habitable, but this transformation is only partial. Primal disorder continually reasserts itself around man and within him." The tragic vision acknowledges our personal and cultural inability to fend off the darkness that arises from within and that falls upon us from without. Its lasting appeal lies, therefore, in its unblinkered truthfulness. Tragedy makes us confront the stark fact, says Redfield, that culture often enables us to avoid: "We might prefer to think that the world is on our side, that goodness will always be rewarded and vice punished, that virtue is a sufficient cause for happiness, that suffering is not real."[3] The tragic vision of life will not tolerate such self-delusion. It forces us painfully to acknowledge the truth that civilization and its virtues will not finally suffice in the face of life's terror.

Far from wanting to negate it, Christians must affirm what is right about the tragic vision at work in both classical and modern culture. As the highest achievement of human wisdom, it is not something which the Gospel glibly cancels and makes irrelevant. Belief in the transcendent God does not nullify moral ambiguity and tragedy; on the contrary, it actually increases our appreciation of them. To conform one's life to God's order is hardly to be assured of happiness and certainty. Especially in moral matters, as James M. Gustafson explains, true piety admits the inevitability of uncertainty and unhappiness:

> Conflicting values and claims, each of which can be ethically defended, cannot always be brought into harmony. Costs are involved in every complex choice: some proper interests cannot be met because others have been judged to be of greater merit; in many circumstances, some persons necessarily have to take risks, suffer, and even die because larger purposes require this. Tragedy, though not necessarily in an intense psychological form, is present in human moral and social life even as it seeks to consent to the divine governance. What is evil for some persons necessarily

occurs in the pursuit of what is good for others—not only good for other persons but for social causes and for the sake of nature itself. As Augustine pointed out, the order of nature and the order of utility for the human community do not coincide.[4]

This tragic perception of faith belongs not only to a theist like James Gustafson, but also to a Christocentric theologian like Stanley Hauerwas. To believe that we can know what is morally good and that we can act on the basis of such knowledge is, in Hauerwas's view, to commit the Pelagian heresy afresh. Every human act entails, on the contrary, the choice of both evils and goods. Nor is it only within the climactic moments of life—in the maintenance or dissolution of a marriage, in the abortion or preservation of fetal life, in the confession or denial of God before tyrants—that tragic choices must be faced. In even the smallest everyday exchanges, Hauerwas insists, we confront problems that are too complex for pure solutions. Only an honesty sustained by trust in the forgiving God can enable us to live amidst such ethical ambiguity and uncertainty, and thus to admit what Hauerwas calls the tragedy of "irresolvable moral conflict."[5]

The public realm is such a tightly knit fabric of interdependence that any moral act is bound to create the tragedy of painful and unintended results. To pluck but a single strand of the social web, even in obedience to the Gospel, is to make the whole network shimmer and perhaps also to shear. Hauerwas cites, as an example, the biblical prohibition against killing—and the concomitant willingness to die rather than to use force against one's enemies. Christians heeding this injunction are likely to entangle themselves and others in the knots of grief and pain, as Hauerwas wisely observes: "To live morally thus means that we must necessarily be willing to risk our own and others' lives for those values which we find necessary to maintain our life together. In certain crucial cases . . . we must be willing to let ourselves and others die rather than act against these goods."[6]

Faithfulness to Jesus Christ may serve, Hauerwas insists, to make the world a more perilous place even as it seeks to foster true peace. The Christian cannot expect to go through life serenely unopposed by the world. Radical fidelity to God requires that we surrender the very deceptions which often give the world its cohesion. Chief among them is the lie wherewith we convince ourselves that our social and political order is built on justice and equity, when it is usually constituted for our own security and thus at the expense of the weak and defenseless. To proclaim God as the sole Master of human life—and thus as our one real security—is to threaten the very foundation of human certainty and assurance. No wonder that the Gospel courts a certain violence, says Hauerwas, "since we do not give up our illusions without a struggle."[7]

II. Niebuhr on Myth and Tragedy

More than any other modern theologian, Reinhold Niebuhr has insisted that Christian faith must come to terms with the tragic vision of life. Though not a single and unitary thing, tragedy can be defined briefly as the notion that human misery has its chief source in life's own contradictions, and not chiefly in sin and rebellion. The tragic vision focuses upon the rending paradox that to create is also to destroy, to impose order is also to restrict freedom, and thus to do anything good is also to generate evil. Niebuhr is right to distinguish this tragic vision from what is often confused with it—namely, ordinary pathos. We often speak of the "tragic" victims of earthquakes and floods, of cancer and automobile accidents. Yet such hapless sufferers are not truly tragic so much as they are pitiable. They are the pathetic pawns of an absurd fate; they are blameless wretches who have been victimized by the slings and arrows of outrageous fortune.

Tragedy, says Niebuhr, entails a certain sense of guilt and blame: humanity is responsible for its sorry state even if it cannot escape it. We become guilty, in this tragic view, by the very fact of our existence. We break the seamless web of nature and disrupt the balance of life. Prometheus the defier of the gods and bringer of fire to humanity is the prime instance of this tragic truth that all good deeds have evil consequences:

> every achievement of human culture implies the HYBRIS which brings the wrath of Zeus upon the human agent. . . . But it is apparent that the power of Zeus is essentially that of the order of nature. Man becomes involved in evil by breaking the harmonies of nature and exceeding its ends.[8]

Niebuhr freely acknowledges that, even in the Greek view, only the exceptional man or woman is capable of such heroic guilt. In the run of human commonalty, pathos predominates. "Most men," say Niebuhr, "perish in weakness, frustration, and confusion." The Oedipus who pulls out his eyes in fury and grief over the truth that he was unable to see is the rare exception rather than the rule: "In true tragedy the hero defies the malignant power [in order] to assert the integrity of his soul. He suffers because he is strong and not because he is weak. He involves himself in guilt not by his vice but by his virtue."[9]

Niebuhr insists, as his book title indicates, that Christianity lies *beyond* tragedy. Biblical faith denies, in Niebuhr's opinion, the tragic assumption that evil is *necessarily* entailed in all free acts. Sin may be inevitable, as he never tired of iterating, but it is not necessary. Only because there is no inexorable link between creation and destruction can Christians call the world to repentance and proclaim hope for all people.

Neither God nor the world is to blame for our universal misery. Human suffering is not ontological but existential; it arises out of history rather than nature. The cross and the resurrection are symbols, for Niebuhr, of a divine hope that transcends the human tragedy:

> Christianity stands beyond tragedy. If there are tears for this man on the cross they cannot be the tears of "pity and terror." The cross does not reveal life at cross purposes with itself. On the contrary, it declares that what seems to be an inherent defect in life itself is really a contingent defect in the soul of each man, the defect of the sin which he commits in his freedom. If he can realise this fact, if he can weep for himself, if he can repent, he can also be saved. . . .
>
> . . . Repentance does not accuse life or God but accuses self. In that self-accusation lies the beginning of hope and salvation. If the defect lies in us and not in the character of life, life is not hopeless.[10]

To what extent, it must be asked, does Niebuhr believe that Christian faith overcomes tragedy? My contention is that Niebuhr's theology lies just barely beyond tragedy, and thus that it constitutes an inadequate tool for a theological interpretation of comic literature. Niebuhr has difficulty answering the problem of tragedy because he has an essentially mythical understanding of Christian faith. Niebuhr seizes upon the category of myth as a way of avoiding biblical literalism. Far from being the work of mere wishful thinking or unsophisticated religion, myth can be the means for conveying theological truth.

Myth is especially useful to Niebuhr's nondogmatic, American style of theology. He makes no radical distinction between divine revelation and human self-understanding, nor therefore between biblical and nonbiblical myth. In his view, the human penchant for myth making is a universal phenomenon. Biblical myths are thus a particular species of an all-inclusive genus. The Tower of Babel story does not differ in kind, for example, from the myth of Prometheus: they both convey universal insight into the problem of arrogance.[11] The central Niebuhrian distinction lies not between myth and revelation, as for Karl Barth, but between permanent and primitive myth. Primitive myth is but a pictorial and imaginative means for conveying an obvious truth which could be just as well discerned by abstract reason. Permanent myth offers, by contrast, a dialectical and paradoxical reading of human existence which mere thought cannot establish.

The biblical myths of creation and fall, salvation and judgment, are enduringly reliable because they convey the profoundest ultrarational truths about human existence. This criterion of permanency applies even to those biblical events which may be regarded as historical rather than mythical. The Christian ideal of love, Niebuhr declares, "is not true because the cross has revealed it. The cross justifies itself to human faith because it symbolizes an ideal which establishes points of relevance with the deepest experiences and insights of human life."[12]

Niebuhr's answer to the question of tragedy becomes problematic in his treatment of the resurrection. Can there be any real nontragic hope if Christ be not raised from the dead? Is there any evidence that evil is *already*—and not just "finally"—under the dominion of God? Niebuhr again finesses the difficulty by insisting that the resurrection is a religious myth rather than an actual occurrence. Like Rudolf Bultmann and a host of other theologians, Niebuhr regards it as the subjective experience of early Christians who "miraculously" recognized God's sovereignty at work even in Jesus' death. The disciples and evangelists thus *altered* the account of the crucifixion in order to reflect their conviction that Jesus had triumphed despite his defeat:

> The story of this triumph over death is thus shrouded in a mystery which places it in a different order of history than the story of the crucifixion. Yet the church as a fellowship of believers was obviously founded upon the conviction of the fact of the resurrection. This "fact" contained an alteration in the story through faith's apprehension of the significance of the story. To recognize that the Cross was something more than a noble tragedy and its victim something else than a good man who died for his ideals; to behold rather that this suffering was indicative of God's triumph over evil through a love which did not stop at involvement in the evil over which it triumphed; to see, in other words, the whole mystery of God's mercy disclosed is to know that the crucified Lord had triumphed over death. . . .[13]

The discerning eye of faith engenders the interpretive myth of resurrection. As Niebuhr wrote to his friend Norman Kemp-Smith, "I have not the slightest interest in the empty tomb or physical resurrection."[14] This explains why, as Richard Fox has shown, Niebuhr is far closer to the tragic view than he admits. To speak of faith as the conviction that human existence has ultimate meaning is to go but barely beyond tragedy. Niebuhr's kind of Christianity does not envision God as acting in history through the risen Lord to establish his eschatological kingdom. Everything hinges, instead, upon the human quest for a proximate earthly justice as it is symbolized in the life and death of Jesus. Such faith differs from tragic wisdom only in its insistence that the good will "ultimately" prevail. "To argue that Christianity was beyond tragedy because it regarded evil as 'finally' under the dominion of God," says Fox, "conceded vital ground to the tragic view, since the 'finally' was beyond history altogether."[15]

III. Niebuhr as a Negative Natural Theologian

Niebuhr does not deny, of course, the scandal of biblical revelation. He insists that there is a foolishness in faith that offends those who regard themselves as autonomously wise. Yet he softens the scandal by maintaining that the truth of faith does not stand "perpetually in contradiction to experience. On the contrary it illumines experience and is in turn validated by experience."[16] Niebuhr is obviously right: Christian faith would get no hearing if it made no connection with human experience—if there were nothing compellingly truthful about the kind of life it engenders, both communally and individually. Yet Niebuhr means more than this. There is a negative natural theology at work in his theology which discerns an unexpected reciprocity between human nature and divine grace. This surprising conjunction of the sacred and the secular makes Niebuhr finally unable to discern the comic disjunction between human despair and divine hope.

Niebuhr does not share the medieval confidence in the native human ability to ascend to God through the great "chain of being." Yet he does hold to an inverted form of natural theology, seeking to plumb the depths of human sinfulness as a reverse path to God. More noteworthy still is the fact that, for Niebuhr, this negative path to God is not limited to biblical faith alone. Whether in the story of Prometheus or Oedipus, many of the great pagan myths also teach us the *via negativa*. They attest to the human misery which God's grace seeks to heal. Not for Niebuhr the radical notion of Luther that the true horror of sin is revealed only in the rejection of Christ and the Gospel. Niebuhr believes—with Emil Brunner and against Karl Barth—that God's point of contact with humanity lies in its own terrible awareness of misery:

> No man, however deeply involved in sin, is able to regard the misery of sin as normal. Some memory of blessedness seems to linger in his soul; some echo of the law which he has violated seems to resound in his conscience.[17]

> It is this capacity for self-transcendence which gives rise to both the yearning after God and to the idolatrous worship of false gods. It leads both to the expectation of Christ and to the expectation of the false Christ, who will vindicate us, but not our neighbour. Neither the finiteness of the human mind nor the sinful corruption of the mind or the "ideological taint" in all human culture can completely efface the human capacity for the apprehension of true wisdom. . . . It is this residual virtue which emerges in true contrition.[18]

"Original righteousness" is the name that Niebuhr gives to this negative, Protestant version of natural law. There is a vestigial *capax dei* that enables us to comprehend the nature and depth of our vexation. What it reveals is the inexorability of the divine rule over nations and empires. Communities, like individuals, seek dominion over those who seem to threaten their security. Such, for Niebuhr, is the essence of injustice.

Yet he is confident that the ordering power of God will eventually redress the inequities of history. The weak and the oppressed are sooner or later endowed with a strength which works vengeance on their oppressors. These same artificers of justice are prone, alas, to the overweening pride which once tyrannized them. Thus do they come at last to commit the very evils from which they had once sought deliverance. Like Arnold Toynbee, Niebuhr envisions history as having a spiraling rather than either a repetitive or a progressive character. Not by the pattern of natural necessity does history change; its life derives from the power of the just God to overcome injustice. "Mankind does not destroy the law of life by violating it. It operates in history, if in no other way than by destroying those who violate it. Every empire which seeks to make itself the centre and law of existence is ultimately destroyed."[19]

Only in an ultimate sense is Niebuhr an optimist about the outcome of history, convinced as he is that injustice will not *finally* prevail. Yet Niebuhr tends to make the object of this hope little more than a naked metaphysical principle of transcendence—the lonely monotheistic God who stands above the chances and changes of time. His Christology is "low" to the same degree that his doctrine of God is "high." Jesus belongs, for Niebuhr, to the line of great Hebrew prophets who called Israel to solitary faith in the Alone. Nothing other than God—not our own spurious substitutes—can provide surety against the transience of time and place: "In a true religion, faith in the ultimate meaningfulness of existence, grounded in a God who transcends the caprices and contingencies of the physical order and who is capable of overcoming the chaos created by human sin, is the final security of the human spirit."[20]

Richard Fox has demonstrated the quintessential liberalism of Niebuhr's entire theological project. "By conceiving of Christianity as the most reasonable philosophy of life available to twentieth-century, skeptically minded people, by seeing himself (like Schleiermacher) as an apostle to the 'educated despisers' of religion, he had embraced the historic liberal mission of reconciling Christianity with the scientific world view."[21] Niebuhr himself confessed his hope to establish an intellectual and religious synthesis that would "reorient" contemporary culture.[22] What modern Western civilization requires, in Niebuhr's view, is a common basis for its political and social life—just as the Augustinian-Thomistic synthesis once provided a coherent vision for medieval culture.

We must learn, says Niebuhr, to combine and unite the seemingly opposed insights of the Renaissance and the Reformation. Their revolutionary religious and secular discoveries will tend, without such a synthesis, to contradict and defeat each other. A new vision of human nature and destiny built on these two great modern movements "would reach farther into the heights and depths of life than the medieval synthesis; and would yet be immune to the alternate moods of pessimism and optimism, of cynicism and sentimentality to which modern culture is now so prone."[23] The question remains whether such a synthesis can go significantly beyond the tragic vision, or whether it will approximate, once again, the ancient dialectic in which human nature and destiny have always been caught.

IV. The Dialectic of Sin and Faith

Niebuhr undertakes his unifying synthesis in the conviction that biblical religion confirms the best secular wisdom because they are both dialectical in essence. Indeed, Niebuhr interprets the reality of God in the same terms wherewith he perceives the human phenomenon: each in its own way is a set of unified opposites held together by means of a tense dialectical balance. The dialectical character of Niebuhr's theology is most discernible in his reading of the Fall. With Augustine and the classical Reformers, Niebuhr argues that sin originates with humanity's own perversion of God's good creation. The essential defect lies in us and not in the world.

Greek tragedy and Christian faith are agreed, Niebuhr believes, in their mutual conviction that the sin of pride inevitably attaches to the noblest human achievements. They are disagreed, however, about the necessity of this sinful *hubris*. For the Greek tragedians, evil and destruction are inexorably linked to every good and creative act. For Niebuhr the Christian theologian, the fact that sinful distortions and perversions accompany every act of human freedom does not make sin a requisite concomitant of freedom. In perhaps the most celebrated passage of Niebuhr's *magnum opus*, he declares that sin is inevitable but not necessary: "The Christian doctrine of original sin . . . is a dialectical truth which does justice to the fact that man's self-love is inevitable but not in such a way as to fit into the category of natural necessity. It is within and by his freedom that man sins."[24]

From Søren Kierkegaard's *The Concept of Dread* Niebuhr derives his notion that "sin presupposes itself." In a mind-tangling paradox, Niebuhr declares that "man could not be tempted if he had not already sinned."[25] With such strange language does Niebuhr attempt to explain the strange fact that in humanity alone does the natural order transcend itself. Our overleaping self-consciousness gives us the possibility of becoming something more than the sum total of the antecedent causes and conditions that go into our making. Alone among all the species, we are able either to plunge beneath ourselves into willful bestiality, or else to rise above ourselves in pseudo-angelic pride. Humanity sits astride a high and narrow ridge dividing the abysses of arrogance and sensuality that stretch down on either side. We suffer thus from a perpetual vertigo of the spirit. The dizziness of freedom is indeed a perennial allurement to evil: to stand in the uniquely human place is also most surely to fall. Our very liberty beguiles us into seeking false security amidst a perilous world—when, in fact, God alone is the one sure source and end of life.

For Reinhold Niebuhr the central paradox of human existence—glimpsed by the Greeks but fully understood only in Scripture—is that good and evil have their origin in a common source. They both spring from the unparalleled human ability to leap beyond animality in irrepressible longing for either a true or a false infinite. We humans exist apart from all other creatures in having the freedom either to surrender ourselves in fidelity to the God who is our only assurance, or else to exalt ourselves in a vain effort "to overcome contingency by raising what is contingent to absolute and unlimited dimensions."[26] Hence Niebuhr's characteristic claim that "injustice flows from the same source from which justice comes, from the historical organization of life."[27]

Without social and political institutions, life would remain an anarchy of competing interests. But with them comes the temptation to absolutize some relative good such as nation or race, culture or class. We sin, therefore, not because we are finite and dependent, but because we are anxious and unwilling to trust God as our sole security. In one of his few disputes with Paul Tillich—whom Niebuhr thought too Greek in his equation of actualized and fallen existence—he insists that we are miserable and alienated creatures "not because we are egos but because we are egotists."[28]

There is deep truth in this argument. It is at once psychologically profound and religiously persuasive. Like few other theologians, Niebuhr provides a coherent explanation of evil while preserving its essential mystery and seriousness. Yet the inescapable fact is that Niebuhr's theology here again stands but barely—if at all—beyond tragedy. Niebuhr sounds more Sophoclean than scriptural in declaring that "sin posits itself," that "to be tempted means in a sense to have sinned," and thus that "temptation is a state of anxiety from which sin flows inevitably."[29] The problem is evident in the logic of Niebuhr's last phrase: to be human is to be anxious, to be anxious is to be tempted, and to be tempted is inevitably to sin. The force of this argument is not only to make God responsible for evil—in so creating humanity as to insure its inevitable sinfulness—but also to make God extremely limited in his power to overcome the world's misery.

Niebuhr holds out, of course, the bare theoretical potential for our species to use its finite freedom other than it invariably and sinfully does:

> [Anxiety] must not be identified with sin because there is always the ideal possibility that faith would purge anxiety of the tendency toward sinful self-assertion. The ideal possibility is that faith in the ultimate security of God's love would overcome the immediate insecurities of nature and history. . . . Ideally anxiety is overcome by faith but a life totally without anxiety would lack freedom and not require faith.[30]

Yet Niebuhr does not cite a single case wherein this "ideal possibility" has been made actual. There is none who is perfectly faithful, not even Jesus. We cannot assert, says Niebuhr, "the sinlessness of every individual act of any actually historical character." The most that can be said of Jesus is that in him "there is a remarkable coincidence and consistency of doctrine, of purpose and of act."[31] Anxiety led even Jesus—one must presume—to commit individual acts of sin, although the totality of his life must not be called sinful in the same way that our own lives are sinful. Jesus thus differs from other human beings in degree rather than kind. He more fully overcame the temptation inherent in our anxious condition, Niebuhr implies, than does the vast preponderance of our species.

The upshot of the matter is that Niebuhr makes the ground of faith the same as the ground of sin. Trust in God does not arise from the sovereignly free bestowal of God's grace so much as from our rightful use of the anxiety inherent in being creatures at once finite and free. Sin and faith both spring from humanity's dialectical condition as created by God. Good and evil have the same origin if not the same cause. It follows that, in Niebuhr's view, freedom can issue in sin and still be called freedom. Here he stands against the tradition of both Augustine and the Reformers. They argue that to choose a life of concupiscence and pride is to prove the bondage of the will, not its liberty. Niebuhr claims, by contrast, that "freedom becomes an accomplice of sin," and that "where there is freedom there is sin."[32] He cannot say that freedom is the enemy of sin, and that where there is freedom there is always faith.

Niebuhr rightly interprets Jesus' injunction to "Be not anxious" as having no meaning apart from its subsequent condition: "for your heavenly father knoweth that ye have need of these things." But Niebuhr does not read such blessed assurance as enabling a gracious freedom from anxiety. He sees it, instead, as another instance of the impossible ideal that cannot be accomplished on earth: "The freedom from anxiety which [Jesus] enjoins is a possibility only if perfect trust in divine security has been achieved."[33]

The only place where God's voice can be unambiguously heard and heeded is in the vexed human conscience. Self-transcending humanity is able to name its own disease even if it cannot pronounce its own cure:

> The ultimate proof of the freedom of the human spirit is its own recognition that its will is not free to choose between good and evil. For in the highest reaches of the freedom of the spirit, the self discovers in contemplation and restrospect that previous actions have invariably confused the ultimate reality and value, which the self as spirit senses, with the immediate necessities of the self.[34]

There is no denying that such reflexive self-analysis is a powerful cultural and religious reality. It becomes, indeed, the basis for Niebuhr's civic theology. It is a theology which is able to speak to the great secular public because it speaks no scandalously unnatural word, holds out no radically eschatological hope. Reinhold Niebuhr's call to transcendent faith is universal because humanity is universally capable of recognizing its own entrapment.

V. The Limits of a Civic Theology

Dietrich Bonhoeffer toured the United States for the first time in 1930–31, spending much of his time at Union Seminary in New York, where Reinhold Niebuhr had recently joined the faculty. Though positively impressed by many things on the American scene, Bonhoeffer was disturbed by the dogmatic and christological barrenness of American theology. He called it "Protestantism without Reformation." Bonhoeffer warned that the church's freedom from state interference can lead to delusion. So long as it is allowed liberty both to conduct its own affairs and to influence the state, the church may falsely assume itself to be free. True church liberty, Bonhoeffer insists, is not a gift from secular society but the work of God's Word in the world. It is not a political achievement but a theological gift that is christologically given and received: "The freedom of the church is not where it has [government-provided] possibilities, but only where the Gospel really and in its own power makes room for itself on earth, even and precisely when no such possibilities are offered to it."[35] American Christianity is in frightful danger of secularization, Bonhoeffer prophetically cautioned, exactly because of the church's "enthusiastic claim . . . to universal influence on the world."[36]

Reinhold Niebuhr was the prime mover in this churchly influence on secular politics. His transcendent theism was the clamant need of the historical hour. With the courage of an ancient prophet, he set his tongue and pen against the sentimental and optimistic idols of the age. Rather than turning his criticism upon the easy targets represented by political and theological conservatism, Niebuhr sought instead to discomfit his own fellow liberals. They needed a sobering dash of what Niebuhr called Christian realism. He freely supplied it by reminding the enlightened leaders of his time that human evil is truly pernicious rather than merely moralistic. Evil is most perverse, Niebuhr never wearied of repeating, when we are at our best rather than our worst. It is when we have done genuine good, whether as individuals or societies, that we stand in greatest peril. For it is then that we are blinded to what is always self-serving even in our most sacrificial acts.

Niebuhr's civic theology had extraordinary influence over the life and thought of many liberal intellectuals and government leaders, perhaps the preponderance of whom did not share his Christian faith. Hans Morgenthau is a typical example of secular sympathy for Niebuhr's work. Morgenthau called Niebuhr "the greatest living political philosopher of America, perhaps the only creative political philosopher since Calhoun."[37] Niebuhr was able to appeal to the civic conscience because he understood the faith of the churches as concerned primarily for the well-being of society in general—and for the American commonweal in particular.

The Kingdom of God has, in Niebuhr's interpretation, few if any concerns that are unique to itself. This is what makes him a liberal theologian at heart, no matter how fierce his criticisms of political liberalism and the Social Gospel, no matter how drastically reconstructed his estimate of human sin and divine grace. Niebuhr seeks to provide a Christian interpretation of Western culture that, as Karl Löwith has acutely observed, ignores the gaping discontinuity be tween secular history and the Reign of God as proclaimed and enacted by Jesus:

> Nothing in the New Testament warrants a conception of the new events that constituted early Christianity as the beginning of a new epoch of secular developments within a continuous process. For the early Christians the history of this world had rather come to an end, and Jesus himself was seen by them not as a world-historical link in the chain of historical happenings but as the unique redeemer. What really begins with the appearance of Jesus Christ is not a new epoch of secular history, called "Christian," but the beginning of an end. The Christian times are Christian only insofar as they are the last time. Because the Kingdom of God, moreover, is not to be realized in a continuous process of historical development, the eschatological history of salvation also cannot impart a new and progressive meaning to the history of the world, which is fulfilled by having reached its term. The "meaning" of the history of this world is fulfilled against itself because the story of salvation,

as embodied in Jesus Christ, redeems and dismantles, as it were, the hopeless history of the world. In the perspective of the New Testament the history of the world entered into the eschatological substance of its unworldly message only insofar as the first generations after Christ were still involved in it, but without being of it.[38]

Niebuhr's failure to discern this discontinuity led him, as Stanley Hauerwas has observed, to "an understanding of justice and its attainment that [does] not require any direct theological rationale."[39] Niebuhr reduces the central Christian events to mythic-symbolic representations of eternal norms that transcend the limits of history. He surrenders the historical particularity of Jesus' earthly career as the basis for Christian existence. The Gospel becomes a superior vision of reality that makes largely negative sense of the world by bringing all human achievement under the critique of transcendent faith. Niebuhr interprets the Kingdom of God as an ideal possibility more than an eschatological reality whose preliminary manifestation is already visible in the Christian community.

The universal message of self-abnegation and forgiveness has no special seat in either the synagogue or the church. One does not look primarily to them for evidence of the Light that comes into the world. Niebuhr does not envision the faithful community as embodying and making unique witness to a way of life that stands as a radical alternative to even the noblest ways of the world. Niebuhr seeks to address the nation with a universal word, rather than to speak the church's own particular Word of salvation in Christ. To his large civic audience he speaks a very somber word indeed. It is the sobering message that, while the cross resolves the injustices of history from God's side, there can be no eschatological confidence that world history has already ended and a new age has begun. God's suffering love is sinfully defeated in history. Its only triumph consists in the knowledge that such love is *ultimately* vindicated:

> The love which enters history as suffering love, must remain suffering love in history. Since this love is the very law of history it may have its tentative triumphs even in history; for human history cannot stand in complete contradiction to itself. Yet history does stand in actual contradiction to the law of love; and Jesus anticipates the growth of evil as well as the growth of good in history. . . .
>
> In thus conceiving history after Christ as an interim between the disclosure of its true meaning and the fulfillment of that meaning, between revelation of divine sovereignty and the full establishment of that sovereignty, a continued element of inner contradiction in history is accepted as its perennial characteristic. Sin is overcome in principle but not in fact.[40]

A critic like Löwith prefers old-fashioned tragedy to such abstract, transhistorical hope. Why, asks Löwith, "should not the contradictions and ambiguities of our historical enterprise have to be endured with mature resignation instead of [being] overcome and resolved 'ultimately'?"[41] Niebuhr's reiterated emphasis on the dialectic of divine offering and human acceptance obviates any drastic stress on God's sovereign and irreversible victory over the world. The Lord has not gone up with a shout—to use a biblical metaphor—but with the muted sound of partial triumph amidst continuing defeat. Jesus is not for Niebuhr the *Christus Victor* whose death and resurrection, having mastered evil, enable the faithful to live gladly, even triumphantly, in the face of sin and mortality. He is, instead, the Suffering Servant who enjoins a humble sense of our own sin and the world's limits. Faith, in Niebuhr's estimate, is the willingness to live

> in a dimension of meaning in which the urgencies of the struggle [against our foes] are subordinated to a sense of awe before the vastness of the historical drama in which we are jointly involved; to a sense of modesty about the virtue, wisdom and power available to us for the resolution of its perplexities; to a sense of contrition about the common frailties and foibles which lie at the foundation of both the enemy's demonry and our [own] vanities; to a sense of gratitude for the divine mercies which are promised to those who humble themselves.[42]

There is an almost tragic sobriety about such Niebuhrian faith. It is a majestically humane alternative to what usually passes as human wisdom. So valiant a faith inspired Reinhold Niebuhr to demand justice for coal miners in the American Midwest, for blacks in the American South, and for the victims of American militarism in Vietnam. There is not another American thinker who can compare with Niebuhr in the profundity and seriousness of his vision. America was his parish, and he served it nobly. The question remains, however, whether the chief aim of the Gospel is to provide a civic theology, a vision that will guide the nation to a more just and moral life. It is clear that Niebuhr answered in the affirmative. He perceived the task of theology as providing a sobering ethical realism to a naively idealistic culture. He developed, therefore, a theology of neither comedy nor tragedy but of irony.

VI. Niebuhr as Ironist

What issues from this somber Niebuhrian vision of sin is a deeply ironic understanding of faith. It is an ironic faith because its fundamental act is to perceive the incongruity of our pretensions to wisdom and virtue. Nothing other than self-transcendent vision can provide this ironic perspective on ourselves. Seen in the light of God's own wisdom and virtue, even the noblest human achievements are revealed to be contradictory and self-interested. Humor is the name Niebuhr sometimes gives to this irony that produces religious contrition and humility. It is an indispensable ingredient of life because it also serves as a social unguent, oiling the troublous machinery of human existence with the lubricant of laughter.

> Humour is a proof of the capacity of the self to gain a vantage point from which it is able to look at itself. The sense of humour is thus a by-product of self-transcendence. People with a sense of humour do not take themselves too seriously. They are able to "stand off" from themselves, see themselves in perspective, and recognize the ludicrous and absurd aspects of their pretensions. All of us ought to be ready to laugh at ourselves because all of us are a little funny in our foibles, conceits and pretensions. What is funny about us is precisely that we take ourselves too seriously. We are rather insignficant little bundles of energy and vitality in a vast organization of life. But we pretend that we are the very center of that organization. This pretension is ludicrous; and its absurdity increases with our lack of awareness of it. The less we are able to laugh at ourselves the more it becomes necessary and inevitable that others laugh at us.[43]

Yet there are serious limits set upon such ironic faith. It can warn against the sin of gravity but it cannot alert to the hope of gaiety. Laughter can serve as "a prelude to the sense of contrition" and a "vestibule to the temple of confession"[44] but as nothing more positive. Humor can criticize the self, says Niebuhr, only on the self's own terms. It cannot judge with the sin-negating sobriety of God. Our humor is gentle; God's is derisory. We chuckle at our faults while God, says Niebuhr in echo of the Psalmist, sits in his heavens and laughs our folly to scorn:

> The knowledge that we are sinners, and that inordinate desires spring from a heart inordinately devoted to itself, is a religious knowledge which, in a sense, is never achieved except in prayer. There we experience with St. Paul that "he who judges us is the Lord." There is no laughter in that experience. There is only pain. . . .
>   . . . The saintliest men frequently have a humourous glint in their eyes. They retain the capacity to laugh at both themselves and others. They do not laugh in their prayers because it is a solemn experience to be judged of God and to stand under the scrutiny of Him from whom no secrets are hid. . . . To know oneself a sinner, to have no illusions about the self, and no inclination to appear better than we are, either in the sight of man or God, and to know oneself for-

given and released from sin, is the occasion for a new joy. This joy expresses itself in an exuberance of which laughter is not the only, but is certainly one, expression.[45]

Irony provides no sure entry to faith because it can also lead to bitterness and hatred. To the Pharisees who regarded themselves as the purest religionists of their day, Jesus' ironic exaltation of the publican must not have seemed amusing at all. The irony of Christ, rather than converting their self-confident righteousness into humble faith, may have angrily confirmed them in it. Like all the other products of religious self-transcendence, therefore, irony is double-edged. It can issue in both faith and unbelief. In either case, the fundamental decision remains ours, as we respond in repentant self-negation to the thunderous Nay of God's judgment. "It is because man is inevitably involved in this primal sin [of pride]," writes Niebuhr in a typical passage, "that he is bound to meet God first of all as judge, who humbles his pride and brings his vain imagination to nought."[46]

God's grace must be met by our own contrite response if it is to have efficacy. Niebuhr is radically Christian in his contention that such repentance buds forth from the tree of the cross. What happens at Calvary reveals that sin is truly heinous because it injures God himself. It violates the divine order and thus the God who orders all things. Such sin wreaks upon us the wrath of God. Only as we discern our sinful helplessness in the blinding light of the divine fury can we repent in dust and ashes: "Without this despair," Niebuhr solemnly warns, "there is no possibility of the contrition which appropriates the divine forgiveness."[47] Divine grace thus stands in dialectical and reciprocal relation to our human willingness to receive and enact it. God's initiating goodness proffers forgiveness, but we must decide to appropriate it for ourselves: "Both affirmations—that only God in Christ can break and reconstruct the sinful self, and that the self must 'open the door' and is capable of doing so—are equally true; and they are unqualifiedly true, each on its own level."[48]

We must repent in order to know God, and we must know God in order to repent. This astringent word needs perennially to be heard, especially among a people whose single cultural inheritance, as Lionel Trilling long ago reminded us, is the liberal tradition. Our American faith, said Trilling, is rooted in the power of simplification and the rational organization of life. What the critic of American culture must provide, says Trilling, is the "imagination of variousness and possibility, which implies the awareness of complexity and difficulty."[49] Trilling might just as well have said that the prophet of the American experience will recall us to the ironic faith which our native optimism and sentimentality are likely to ignore. Reinhold Niebuhr ably and admirably answered this summons. He is our premier theologian of "complexity and difficulty," of the dialectic bind wherein all things human are inevitably caught, and thus of a necessary humility before the vast cosmic powers that circle without and the worm of self-interest that turns within.

> The real situation is that man, as a part of the natural world, brings his years to an end like a tale that is told; and that man as a free spirit finds the brevity of his years incongruous and his death an irrationality; and that man as a unity of body and spirit can neither by taking thought reduce the dimension of his life to the limit of nature, nor yet raise it to the dimension of pure spirit. Either his incomplete and frustrated life is completed by a power greater than his own, or it is not completed.
>
> Faith is therefore the final triumph over incongruity, the final assertion of the meaningfulness of existence. There is no other triumph and will be none, no matter how much human knowledge is enlarged. Faith is the final assertion of the freedom of the human spirit, but also the final acceptance of the weakness of man and the final solution for the problem of life through the disavowal of any final solutions in the power of man.[50]

To scorn this call to theological irony would be an act of gross vanity and ingratitude. Yet we best honor Niebuhr's accomplishment by also contesting its weaknesses and limits. The chief of these, as I have sought to demonstrate, is his reluctance to acknowledge the real scandal of the Gospel in all of its particularity and finality. Niebuhr the antiliberal is, paradoxically, the quintessential liberal. He seeks to universalize Christian faith as a call to a timelessly valid repentance that puts absolute trust in God alone. This naked and negative monotheism threatens to rob Christian faith of its rich concreteness, severing the Gospel from the historically particular community called the church. Yet it is precisely the historically grounded determinants of Christian faith which enable it to provide a comic alternative to the inherent selfishness and sadness of worldly life. The primary task of God's people, as Stanley Hauerwas declares, "is not to make the world the kingdom, but rather to witness to the power of God to transform our lives" in joyful service to his eschatological reign of grace.[51]

In the counterview to be argued in the succeeding chapters, there will be no denying the fact that the world continues to dwell in terrible contradiction to God's glad reconciliation of the world unto himself. The emphasis will lie, instead, on the powerlessness of human sin to destroy the reality and finality of what God in Christ has already achieved. In his death and resurrection, history has experienced its essential crisis. The end of the world is not about to happen; it has already happened. The kingdom has been established and God's lordship over our existence has been made firm. The church is called to be both the herald and the embodiment of this unexampled Good News. It lives by the comic faith that the darkness is not to be feared because the Light has overcome it, that losing battles can be fought gladly because the ultimate victory has already been won, that we can sport and dance like merry tumblers of the Lord because Christ is the Clown who has borne our griefs and carried our sorrows.

2

COMIC VISION AND CHRISTIAN FAITH

While the faith that springs from the resurrection is obviously not tragic, neither is it obviously comic. The way of the cross is hardly a rollicking journey, and the cost of our redemption remains nothing less than absolute. It exacted of God the sacrifice of his only Son. What is not obvious, however, is not necessarily untrue. Much that is vital to Christian faith is far from being apparent and self-evident. The Gospel totally revolutionizes ordinary human understanding. It announces God's own surprising—indeed, utterly unanticipated—turning of human life away from its native calamity toward hope and joy and freedom. This news is radically *good* for being what "neither eye hath seen nor ear heard" but what God alone has prepared for humanity (I Cor. 2:9).

I contend that this unexampled message of redemption in Christ finds a larger reflection and analogue in comic than in tragic art. The human urge to laugh—and especially the artistic transmutation of laughter into comic vision—may reveal more about the human condition and situation than do the pity and terror of tragedy. The comic conviction that we humans are more often clowns than heroes, that even the worst perplexity is liable also to be funny, that life can sometimes be catastrophically happy—in all of these comic moments, there are reverberations of the divine comedy wrought in Jesus and the Jews. Yet there is no easy linkage between comic vision and Christian faith. Indeed, there are real theological difficulties inherent in comedy, and these must honestly be faced.

I. Comedy as Sheer Vitalistic Energy

What does the Pauline injunction—"Rejoice in the Lord always; again I will say, Rejoice" (Phil. 4:4)—have in common with comic exuberance and vitality? Little, it would seem. Despite the repeated biblical commands for believers to take joy in their salvation, Christians have not been noted for their comic sense of life. The grim visage and the dour spirit are all too characteristic of the people upon whom Light has broken and to whom the happiest of tidings have been spoken. The ideal of the sour saint is all too much a part of the Christian tradition. Friedrich Nietzsche made a deadly accurate thrust when he said that "the redeemed ought to look more like it."

Yet the faithful are not altogether wrong in their suspicions of comedy. Much of human jubilation arises from mere animal high spirits. Perhaps it was such suspicion that prompted Ambrose to wonder why a Christian should ever seek occasion for laughter. The human penchant for merrymaking seems to be rooted in a vitalistic denial of the transcendent and redeeming God. Molière came thus to regard the artistic use of comedy as the chief weapon in his arsenal of unbelief. "Once you stop passively succumbing to laughter as to a sneeze," he wrote, "once you make serious use of it to render this earth supportable, you set up competition against religion. . . ."[1]

Christian mistrust of the comic vision springs perhaps from its rootage in the ancient spring festivals celebrating the earth's renewal and replenishment. Like tragedy, comedy seems to have been born out of religious ceremonies devoted to the death and resurrection of such fertility gods as Comus and Dionysus. As F. M. Cornford explains, this annual ritual drama set the forces of decay and death over against the powers of fecundity and rebirth. After a pitched battle of the antagonistic gods, the victor would marry his elect queen and a great festal procession of Comus, replete with phallic emblems, would be held. Finally, the old god who had been deposed and buried would be resurrected amidst a scene of ribald rejoicing.

Cornford contends that these same fertility rituals gave rise, paradoxically, to both tragic and comic art. In tragedy, the sexual high jinks and obscenities disappear, except for the satyr plays at the end of the Aeschylean and Sophoclean trilogies. The emphasis came to rest, instead, on the tragic death of the god. His resurrection was preserved, albeit only faintly, in the scenes of inward recognition and outward apotheosis. Comic drama, by contrast, retained not only the phallic element and the stress on joyful rebirth; but, most significantly, it exalted the fertility marriage to a new eminence. "From that day to this," Cornford observes, "not only has a marriage been the canonical end of Comedy, but this whole form of art, together with other romantic forms which it has influenced, has been marked through its history by an erotic tone. "[2]

From the very beginning, destruction no less than creation has been central to the comic vision. Theodore Gaster maintains, for example, that the *komos* at the end of Aristophanes' plays is not, as Cornford argues, a relic of the bridal procession following the original Sacred Marriage. He contends that it is nothing other than a drunken binge and a wanton "night on the town." The verb *epi komon* means to engage in such bawdy revelry, which can be as physically destructive as it is sexually celebrative. At the end of Aristophanes' *Clouds*, says Gaster, "the *komos* is represented by burning down the house of Socrates, for this is simply an amusing twist to the common, well-attested habit of revelers . . . setting fire to the doors of accomodating ladies!"[3]

The violence and eroticism of comedy has been a source of considerable consternation to Christians, and not only because of the apocalyptic asceticism intrinsic to Christian faith. Comic licentiousness and exuberance are suspect because they implicitly deny that there is any reality beyond earthly reality. Comic art and ritual immerse their celebrants in the heedless flux of natural life. They aim at sheer obliviousness to—if not outright denial of—the God who originates and sustains life from beyond itself. Augustine is not being merely priggish when he describes, with deep revulsion, the obscene rites performed in honor of the god Liber and the Great Mother. His justifiable fear is that such raucous and perverted sensuality—"daily rehearsed in song and dance in the theatre"—deifies mere animal spiritedness while denying the true Maker and Savior of the world. "As for us," Augustine writes, "what we are looking for is a soul which puts its trust in true religion and does not worship the world as god, but praises the world as the work of God and for the sake of God."[4]

Susanne K. Langer has explored, with great philosophical acuity, the undeniable connection between comic art and heedless vitality. Langer is agreed with Henri Bergson that comedy arises from the world's inherent contradiction. There is a stunning gap, says Langer, between the teleological bent shared by all organic life and the mechanical pointlessness of the inorganic world. Laughter is promoted, in Bergson's famous definition, by "something mechanical encrusted on the living." The comic spirit issues, in Langer's similar view, from the instinctual biological need of all living things to persist within a lifeless world. By variation and adaptation, by generating more life and seizing still more opportunities, by sexual passion and action, do all living things participate in what Langer calls the "basic rhythm" of animal vitality: "a brainy opportunism in the face of an essentially dreadful universe."[5]

The human species, being uniquely able to anticipate and thus to fear its own end, seeks all available means for seizing "*as much life as possible* between birth and death."[6] Comedy springs, therefore, from humanity's deep and ineluctable need to affirm life—"by wit, luck, personal power, or even humorous, or ironical, or philosophical acceptance of mischance." Comedy aims thus to allay and assuage the vagaries of fortune, fending off calamity by means of laughter. Yet comic action has more than a merely negative purpose. It also celebrates human adroitness and ingenuity in recovering our lost equilibrium:

> Comedy is an art form that arises naturally wherever people are gathered to celebrate life, in spring festivals, triumphs, birthdays, weddings, or initiations. For it expresses the elementary strains and resolutions of animate nature, the animal drives that persist even in human nature, the delight man takes in his special mental gifts that make him the lord of creation; it is an image of human vitality holding its own in the world amid surprises of unplanned coincidence. The most obvious occasions for the performance of comedies are thanks or challenges to fortune.[7]

The near-animal vitalism of the comic spirit accounts, in Langer's view, for the episodic and often circular character of comic art. Comic characters do not undergo fierce moral struggle and development, for the simple reason that their lives are not pointed toward a tragic and fated end. The comic quest is never concluded. It ends, instead, with the promise of boundless life to be lived "happily ever after." Comedy's perpetually opening future accounts, in Langer's estimate, for the preeminence of comic art and vision in Asiatic culture:

> both Hindu and Buddhist regard life as an episode in the much longer career of the soul which has to accomplish many incarnations before it reaches its goal, nirvana. Its struggles in the world do not exhaust it; in fact they are scarcely worth recording except in entertainment theater, "comedy" in our sense—satire, farce, and dialogue. The characters whose fortunes are seriously interesting are the eternal gods; and for them there is no death, no limit of potentialities, hence no fate to be fulfilled. There is only the balanced rhythm of sentience and emotion, upholding itself amid the changes of material nature.[8]

The episodic and circular character of comedy also makes it morally subversive. It is not the shocks of fortune alone that serve to overthrow the tenuous balance of organic life; so do the restraints and requirements of social existence also call into question our animal exuberance. Freud was not the first to note the deep conflict between civilization and the libidinal life. Comedy, as the expression of the primitive desire to live a self-regarding existence, makes japing mockery of the moral principles that preserve society against the otherwise uncontrolled passions. The clowns and fools of comedy are not, as is often thought, the mere butt of the comedian's humor. They are sympathetic spirits who embody our own secret and silent urges. The buffoon's amorality, says Langer, is not something accidental but essential. The buffoon is nothing less than "the personified *élan vital;* his chance adventures and misadventures, without much plot, though often with bizarre implications, his absurd expectations and disappointments, in fact his whole improvised existence has the rhythm of primitive, savage, if not animalian life, coping with a world that is forever taking new uncalculated turns, frustrating but exciting."[9]

Perhaps it is the implicit amoralism of comedy that has led to its devaluation as an art form. Aristotle, as we have seen, was the first to depreciate comedy. It aims, he declares in a famous passage from the *Poetics*, "at representing men as worse, tragedy as better than in actual life." Aristotle contends that comedy imitates not those who are truly malignant in their moral character, but those who are ludicrous in their physical ugliness and spiritual eccentricity. Comedy lacks the ethical grandeur of tragedy, in Aristotle's view, because it tends to reduce humanity to animal need. Instead of lifting characters above their ordinary condition, through ennobling pain and suffering, comedy confines them to their foolish entrapment in mere mortality.

This negative regard for the comic vision is shared by even so sympathetic an interpreter of comedy as Langer. In her view, comedy finally trivializes the human struggle for meaning and purpose in life. It allows no real possibility for either lasting defeat or permanent victory: there is only the circling comic dance in syncopation with the ongoing rhythm of organic life. Comic calamities, says Langer, "are not real disasters, but embarrassment and loss of face. That is why comedy is 'light' compared to tragedy."[10] This also explains why tragedy is the "mature" form of art which even high cultures do not always attain, while comedy (as a presumably "immature" medium) is the property of virtually every civilization.[11]

Cornford makes exactly the same observation. He calls tragedy a true phenomenon, an exception to the prevailing pattern.[12] It requires the self-reflexive consciousness that few cultures possess. Unlike Langer, he sees comedy as having moral import; yet he agrees that it lacks the ethical profundity of tragedy: "The *Sophrosyne* of Comedy is the spirit of genial sanity, in all its range from the flicker of lightning reason and the flash of wit, through the large humour of common sense, down to the antics of the fool, making ironical play with every form of absurdity. Its antagonist is pretense, assumption, arrogance, conceit, all the less serious and tragic species of imposture."[13]

The clear implication is that comedy, as the celebration of life's organic vitality, can deal only with those lesser evils which stand in the way of animal exuberance. It must avoid, according to this reading, such profound enemies as *hubris* and mortality, alienation and despair. Yet there is a species of comedy that does have metaphysical aspirations. It is the much-controverted *humour noir*. This so-called black comedy is not content with playful and cheering common sense. By means of the very self-reflexivity which is the usual province of tragedy, it offers anti-religious answers to the grand religious questions.

II. Comedy as Covert Nihilism

Laughter's deep eructations need not always spring from the vitality of the world's ongoing process. They may have their real source in the uniquely human capacity for self-transcendence. Far from being the product of organic life laughing at its immurement within inorganic existence, comedy may register a distinctly human protest against the metaphysical contradiction implicit in self-conscious existence. Comedy, in this reading of it, becomes the supremely spiritual art, something not at all akin to mere animal vitality. Instead of binding humanity to its finitude, as Aristotle and the classic tradition insist, comedy may be the ultimate evidence of the mind's self-reflexivity: its ability to bend back upon itself in moral self-criticism and irony.

This metaphysical interpretation of comedy is made especially acute in the work of the so-called black humorists. According to the advocates of this darkened comedy, humanity awakens from its slumbering animality only to confront cosmic nothingness: the blankness and emptiness of the unanswering heavens. Whereas the tragedian attempts to depict either a noble human resignation or an elevating human defiance of the *néant*, the black humorist breaks into bitter peals of laughter. This darker kind of comedy sees no way of reconciling the human cry for meaning with the ultimate meaninglessness of the cosmos. Humanity's self-transcending freedom is not something admirable and salutary, in this view, but a bad joke at best and a horrid mistake at worst. Our self-contradictory situation deserves not the warm-spirited guffaws of affirmative laughter but the howling cachinnations of despair.

The scope of this study does not include the literature of such black humorists as Samuel Beckett and Eugene Ionesco in France, of Italo Calvino and Luigi Pirandello in Italy, or of Kurt Vonnegut and John Hawkes on the American scene. Yet the import of such disconsolate comedy is not to be dismissed. How to maintain the worthiness of life once human consciousness has bent back upon itself in comic subversion is an acute problem. Even if the black humorists do not solve the difficulty, they are to be saluted for pointing up its unavoidable reality. Their radical emphasis on the spiritual absurdity of the human condition overturns the ancient estimate of comedy as a playful tribute to common sense. They deny the received idea of comedy as described by Robert M. Torrance: "The prevalent conception of comedy in the classical European tradition, from Aristotle to Bergson, in effect postulated normal patterns of human behavior from which the comic was a deviation worthy of ridicule and contempt. It remained a socially oriented conception in which the consensus of civilized men presided as arbiter and the comic character was viewed as butt or scapegoat, not hero."[14]

Molière, perhaps more than any other modern writer, first understood the moral and spiritual subversiveness of comedy. It is "an unearthly undertaking," he declared, "to make respectable folk laugh."[15] The problem is not merely that we are stuffy and priggish people seeking always to protect our own self-interest. It is our very virtues that ensnare us, as we have seen Reinhold Niebuhr endlessly iterate. Our sincerity and earnestness and responsibility—even when these traits are not at all self-regarding—often obviate real self-criticism. They collapse the spiritual self-distance that enables irony. We remain at home with ourselves and the world when what we really need is to be healthily estranged. "To take a person seriously," Ramon Fernandez wisely observes, "is only to be at one with him; to take a person comedically is to be, so to speak, at two with him."[16]

The enormous appeal of comedy lies in its power to generate this double attitude of both sympathy and criticism. The dual thrust of humor enables the audience not only to laugh at the foolishness exposed in the comic victim, but also to deride its own stupidities. Yet, as Molière discerned, the distance between the audience and the comic culprit must not be too great, lest the ties of sympathy be fatally severed. Satire tends toward such a mocking denial of the malefactor's humanity, and farce abandons all semblance of fellow-feeling, resorting instead to "the bald statement of comic ideas."[17] Molière seeks, by contrast, to dress his most ridiculous characters in the lineaments of sympathy, so that even a hypocrite like Tartuffe is oddly respected and honored.

Yet an insoluble difficulty remains. The laughter which pulverizes dead propriety and decorum is itself dependent upon the norms it attacks. Were they not securely fixed, the comedian would have nothing to dismantle. Comedy aims at demolishing the grand social and moral domain created by human rationality. It brandishes before us the illogicalities which convention ignores: the strange sanity of an insane asylum in Percy's *Love in the Ruins*, the awful truthfulness of a murderer in O'Connor's "A Good Man Is Hard to Find," the human faithfulness of a lecher and adulterer in Updike's Rabbit Angstrom novels, the backslidden unbelief of an atheist in De Vries's *The Mackerel Plaza*. Yet how can comedy do anything more than unmask the absurdity of all claims to final truth and authority—whether these be made by religion or the state or the regnant worldview of the academy? Can comedy transcend, in short, its own essential negativity?

Molière discovered the terrible limits of comedy, Fernandez argues, when he came to write *The Misanthrope*. There he sought to have comedy perform the ultimate acrobatics of self-reflexivity, folding back upon itself in self-scorn, ridiculing not only the stupidity of society, but chiefly Molière's own honesty and reasonableness. The mocker of cant and hypocrisy must thus mock the mocker. In the character of Alceste, therefore, Moliere creates a figure who has thrown off all social constraints whatsoever, a man indulging himself in the pleasure "of flatly defying the entire species in lieu of paying it off by the circuitous method of having it stumble into comic snares."[18] The experiment, though enormously successful, remains profoundly ambiguous in its results. Molière does indeed make marvelous fun of his own waspish immoderation. Yet the effect of such self-ridicule is, at least potentially, to confirm his audience in its original prejudice and complacency. Critics of society, his playgoers can now say, are but vain and self-righteous prigs. Alceste, the satiric reformer, ends by making his own unintentionally ironic contribution "toward keeping the world exactly the way it is."[19]

The final circularity of the comic vision may account for Molière's stoic weariness of spirit, his notoriously taciturn and morose demeanor. The twin epithets applied to Molière reveal how potentially self-cancelling and nihilistic are the dialectics of comedy—how, indeed, they seem but the opposite faces of a single coin. "Molière, the God of Laughter," he was called; but also "Molière, who is no laugher."[20] Humanly speaking, there is no Archimedean point whereupon one might fix the fulcrum of laughter, thus dislodging the world from its sad deformity and catastrophe. Comedy remains powerlessly encased within the same world it seeks to correct and transform. It threatens—even more fearfully than tragedy—to fling us into a vortex that dissolves all distinctions, into an infinite regress of mockery mocking the mocker, until every thing becomes equally ridiculous and life is reduced to a madhouse of mirrors. The comic paradoxes nihilistically multiply, until we are finally brought around to the banal truism that we laugh in order not to weep.

Fernandez sums up this fearful dialectic which seems to make comedy and tragedy coinciding and self-negating opposites: "There are no feelings, no situations, that are inherently ridiculous as compared to others that are not. Tragic emotion and comic emotion can spring from causes of precisely the same category and with the same title to respect."[21] This near-identity of the comic and the tragic explains, perhaps, why anthropologists have traced the human smile to a simian baring of the teeth in order to ward off enemies. The grin and the grimace are often indistinguishable. Laughter is frequently born of deep pain. "Life is much too important to be taken seriously," said Oscar Wilde in comic recoil from a world that he had meant to charm but that had answered his enchantments with hostility and scorn. Thus is humor often prompted by a mean-spirited desire to repay the world's cruelty with a cruelty all its own. Comedy hovers, therefore, over a moral and metaphysical void.

So long as we are confined to our own human resources, comedy (like tragedy) dangles over the abyss. Its potential nihilism is definitively overcome only in the divine comedy. Yet the Gospel is not some high and ethereal gnosis that stands aloof from the comic and tragic visions of life. God's reconciliation of the world unto himself has its echo and reflection in the human no less than the natural order. It finds a greater analogue in comedy, I maintain, than in tragedy. Comedy's proverbial "lightness" makes it less prone to human presumption than tragedy is, and thus more open to divine corrective and completion. The Gospel itself is comic, I will argue, in the singularity of the hope and joy it announces to the world. What makes the biblical message stand apart from every human truth is its undialectical character. It declares not two words but one: not a tragicomic opposition between the Nay of judgment and the Yea of mercy, but the unilateral and uncompromising comedy of God's grace.

III. The Comedy of Redemption

Karl Löwith has observed that radical atheism is a uniquely Christian phenomenon. The pagans of the ancient world were not atheists at all; they believed not in no God but in *many* gods. It was the early Christians who were regarded as atheists: "they believed in only one single God transcending the universe and the city-state, that is, everything that the ancients had consecrated." Modern atheism arises only with the collapse of belief in the redeeming God of the Jews and Jesus:

> the feeling that the world is thoroughly godless and godforsaken presupposes belief in a transcendent Creator-God who cares for his creatures.... If the Christian belief in a God who is as distinct from the world as a creator is from his creatures and yet is the source of every being is once discarded, the world becomes emancipated and profane as it never was for the pagans. If the universe is neither eternal and divine, as it was for the ancients, nor transient but created, as it is for the Christians, there remains only one aspect: the sheer contingency of its mere "existence."[22]

From Molière forward, modern comedy has acknowledged the frightful contingency of a creation without a creator. The redeeming irony of our radically secular situation is that we may be able to acknowledge the scandal of the Gospel as the so-called ages of faith are not. Goethe, for example, was rightly offended by the Pauline declaration that God has "made foolish the wisdom of the world" (I Cor. 1:20). Nietzsche was appropriately scandalized at the notion that "if any one is in Christ, he is a new creation" (II Cor. 5:17). They both saw how totally outrageous is the claim that something divinely and comically fresh has broken the perpetual round of colliding and coinciding contraries. Without the God who makes the old pass away and, behold, all things to become new, we are left with the Eternal Return, the infinite sameness-in-variety of nature and culture. Falstaff's heedless vitality must alternate endlessly with Prince Hal's demand for personal and social order. Charlie Chaplin's affable Tramp must remain a sardonic clown, a sad comedian who grants no quarter to ultimate hope or victory. Secular comedians must, like Bertrand Russell, stake their lives on the solid rock of unyielding despair. They are compelled to take their stand, as G. K. Chesterton said of the proverbial atheist, on the premise that miracles *cannot* happen.

The scandalous Christian affirmation is that the ultimate miracle has, in fact, occurred. What Christian faith confesses is that God, in the Jews and Jesus, has perpetrated the most outrageous of tricks, a joke to end all jokes, a surprise beyond all surprises. He has upset our tragicomic equilibrium. He has thrown over our own calculus of good and evil, which metes our rewards to the righteous and punishments to the wicked. He refuses to become the cosmic projection of our own values. The redeeming God will not tolerate the all-too-human extension of our binary consciousness into ultimate terms. In Israel and Christ he acts unilaterally to deliver the human race from its dialectical enslavement. "By grace are you saved" is the comic declaration that—whether we like it or not, whether we even accept it or not—God has reclaimed us as his own. We have been repossessed as the property of the God who wants us gladly to give back our lives to him in faith and to the world in service. We have been made citizens, in sum, of a singular Kingdom which admits of no duplicity.

Faith, in this reading, is the supremely comic act. It takes joy in the fact that God enjoys his people. It freely owns the fact that we are owned. The believer is permitted no frowning disdain on the world's passing parade. The central command and privilege of the faithful life is to dwell in gladness and trust rather than fear and distrust. Christians are enjoined, like liberated King David, to play and dance and sing before the ark of our redemption—rejoicing in the Lord always, becoming unabashed fools for Christ's sake. The merriment of faith does not blithely disregard the sinful ambivalence wherein all things remain bound. It does not blink the awful reality. On the contrary, faith discerns human captivity all the more acutely for knowing that the shackles have been broken and the prison door flung wide. It is unbelief that constitutes the ultimate lack of humor. Sin is the refusal to be cheered by God's unstinting largesse. It is the glum unwillingness to celebrate the divine comedy.

What this radically comic faith will not countenance is the notion that we can once again shut and bar the gate of God's grace, closing ourselves into that windowless chamber called hell. Christian faith is nowhere more comic than in this eschatological confidence. No matter how grim the immediate prospect, no matter how great the likelihood of being calcined in a nuclear bonfire, the Gospel announces that history's final destiny has been graciously fixed. The preliminary fulfillment of God's purpose in actual history assures the transhistorical outcome. This gracious fact puts the believer in a position of exquisite but joyful tension, as Löwith notes: "Being relaxed in his present experience and straining toward the future, [the Christian] enjoys what he is anxiously waiting and striving for."[23]

Nothing other than bitter unbelief could have prompted Voltaire to call God the comedian whose audience is afraid to laugh. Viewed on its own terms, the world does appear to be a botched job, the work of a cosmic bungler, the product, if not of an imbecile, then surely of a graceless dialectician. Its tragicomic oppositions inspire chuckles only as means of stanching tears. Seen, however, from the perspective of Good Friday and Easter Sunday, the world is the arena of God's redemptive activity. And God himself is the comedian who *wants* his audience to laugh—to rejoice in and thus to be transformed by the Good News. Karl Barth, almost alone in modern theology, has convincingly argued (albeit indirectly) for a comic reading of the Gospel. To his work, therefore, we now turn.

3

KARL BARTH AS A THEOLOGIAN OF THE DIVINE COMEDY

It may seem a trifle late and not a little comic to propose a return to Karl Barth. His theology is now as thoroughly out of fashion as it was once *de rigeur*. Barth's work was applauded because it seemed to provide the hammer wherewith disillusioned liberals could smash the crystal bauble of culture-religion inherited from the Victorian age. Now that academic theology has marched bravely backward into the nineteenth century again, Barth appears altogether as irrelevant as he was once current. My conviction is that both the early admirers and the late despisers have got Barth wrong. The Barth of the Romans commentary insisted so strongly on the infinite qualitative distance separating God and humanity—thus setting Christ and culture in absolute disjunction—that few people bothered to notice his later recantation of these views. Both enthusiasts and detractors miss, therefore, the real burden of Barth's mature theology. His aim is not to pummel secularized modernity with the fist of the transcendent God, but to recall the world to the great glad tidings that God has unilaterally reconciled the world unto himself in Jesus Christ.

The thesis here argued is that Barth's reading of the Gospel is fundamentally comic, and that the comedy of our redemption is what scandalizes both secularists and believers. Biblical faith derives from the radically undialectical revelation of God himself. It is not a tragicomic business of laughing in order to disguise the tears. For while, humanly speaking, it may be true that earthly creativity issues always in destruction, the action of God does not entail such sad consequences. In granting to us nothing less than himself, God presents the world with an unmixed blessing; its underside is not laden with evil. The Gospel is an unalloyed comedy, I maintain, because it proclaims a happier outcome to life than humanity itself might dream or wish. It envisions nothing less than the unqualified triumph of God's own Kingdom.

The news heralded in Christ is not the *partially* good proposition that God's grace is enchained by our own decision for or against it. Faith and doubt, life and death, hope and despair—these are not the stark alternatives between which we must make our desperate choices. The Gospel as Barth reads it is the comic proclamation that God himself has already made the first and final decision about our immediate welfare and final worth. We are not thrust into fearful existentialist straits. Whether we elect to follow Christ can never be as important a matter as the fact that he has chosen us. Martin Luther is not altogether correct, therefore, when he says that we lie like wretched beggars before the Lord's table. At the heavenly banquet spread before all whom the King has driven in from the highways and hedges, we are indeed guests of divine honor. We can do absolutely nothing for ourselves because everything has already been done for us. Not a solitary duty remains, but the most enormous privilege of all—namely, to rejoice and be glad in our redemption, to live it out in thankful service to the world and in comic celebration of the God who is its Savior.

I. The Gospel as a Singular Message of Joy

Many analysts of Barth's work regard him as a narrow and negative theologian, a thinker more renowned for refutation than affirmation. I maintain, on the contrary, that Barth's theology is overwhelmingly positive, and that it is characterized by an enormous gaiety. Nor does its *hilaritas* spring merely from Barth's natively ebullient spirit: it arises from the Gospel's own irrepressible gladness. More remarkable still is that Barth is a humorous and happy theologian not in spite of his Calvinism but because of it. The doctrine for which the stern John Calvin is most celebrated and castigated—the dread decree of election—becomes, in Barth, the basis for his theology of joy and celebration. Barth insists that Calvin was quite right to conceive of God as making an aboriginal decision about the world—not only *whether* to bring it into being at all, but also (and chiefly) *how* he should be disposed toward it. Except as God elects from the outset both to create and redeem, says Barth, the cosmos must be understood as an inexorable process rather than a gracious personal order. Only in such a primordial determination of all things is the biblical God properly acknowledged. We are left otherwise with a God whom Barth describes as a mere "world-principle self-developing and self-evolving in infinite sequence."[1]

Few of Calvin's critics have acknowledged his desire to keep faith with the God of Scripture. His predestinarian theology is commonly thought to be monstrous, as if Calvin were a virtual sadist who projected his own curdled imagination into cosmic terms. From John Milton's enraged willingness to dwell in hell rather than believe in Calvin's "horrible decree," to Max Weber's philanthropic protest against its "pathetic inhumanity," the cry of fury has gone virtually unabated. Barth has little patience with these high-minded objections. They are all wrong-headed in their assumption that the God of Abraham, Isaac, and Jacob is a well-tempered university deity who must abide by the noblest dictates of human conscience. Barth knows all too well that the Lord of Hosts is a jealous God who will not tolerate the apostasy of his people. Rather than aligning his thoughts with theirs (cf. Isa. 55:8-9), he tramples the human idea of equity and desert. Instead of consuming Israel in the fire of his wrath, meting out the justice that its rebellion merits, God hears Moses's plea that he remain the God of the Covenant. The prophet changes Yahweh's mind by reminding him who he is. He is not an all-too-human wielder of the destruction Israel so fully deserves: he is the God who is gracious to whom he will be gracious, who has mercy on whom he will have mercy, no matter how little our worth, or how great our sin.[2]

It is not Calvin's insistence on God's sovereignty which troubles Barth. He is bothered, instead, by Calvin's inclination to speak of God's electing activity apart from Jesus Christ. Calvin's error lies in the attempt to determine the aboriginal destiny of things apart from him who is the Logos made flesh: "The electing God of Calvin is a *Deus nudus absconditus*. It is not the *Deus revelatus* who is as such the *deus absconditus*, the eternal God."[3] This untrinitarian separation of God's electing activity from his self-revelation in Christ results in a fatal parallelism, Barth insists, between the divine Yes and the divine No. God's act of election becomes a virtually symmetrical decision, an almost mathematical balancing of his acceptance with his rejection. It is not Weberian or Miltonic sentiment, therefore, that prompts Barth's protest against the predestining of all humankind either to salvation or damnation. He objects to Calvin's notion of the double decree for christological reasons instead: it denies the asymmetrical revelation of the Incarnate Lord. Worse still, it turns God into an absolute and unconditioned deity, thus denying the self-conditioned God of Jesus Christ.[4]

Despite his immense reverence for Calvin, Barth could not in good faith repeat his master's insistence on double predestination—one decree for the elect minority, and another for the overwhelming mass of the rejected majority. Gradually the truth sprang upon Barth that the biblical God is never of two minds but always of one. He is not duplicitous but completely single-minded. Over and again Barth finds that the main New Testament emphasis lies upon Jesus Christ as the sole elected and rejected Son of God. The real focus of God's decision lies not on humanity, Barth says, but on the One in whom all are damned for their murderous mistrust, but also the same One in whom all are finally reconciled to the God whom they have slain. Barth confesses that, in writing his massive *Church Dogmatics*, he came to recognize and to spell out what is implied in God's utterly singular and gracious decision "with a joy of discovery I experienced in perhaps no other volume."[5]

The decree of single rather than double election does not imply, for Barth, any mechanistic notion of divine determinism—as if God proceeded with a plan such as Napoleon devised (disastrously!) before invading Russia. Human history is not the fatalistic effoliation of an eternal scheme. The utter singularity of the divine decision means, instead, that the entire cosmos is the theater of God's glory, the arena where he seeks unambiguously to display his mercy and goodness:

> In the beginning, before time and space as we know them, before there was any reality distinct from God which could be the object of the love of God or the setting of His acts of freedom, God anticipated and determined within Himself (in the power of His love and freedom, of His knowing and willing) that the goal and meaning of all His dealings with the as yet non-existent universe should be the fact that in His Son He would be gracious towards man, uniting Himself with him.[6]

It is in light of this christological understanding of election that Barth reads the entirety of Scripture. He regards the covenant made with Israel and consummated in Jesus not merely as the Bible's grand theme, but as the ever-narrowing focus of God's scandalously particular revelation. It begins with the creation of Adam as humanity-in-general, continues in Noah and Abraham as the specially called out, and reaches a high point in Jacob-Israel as the father of God's uniquely destined people. Even the period of the kings is characterized by this elective pruning and magnetic centering. From David and Solomon right down to the "pitiful ex-king Jeconiah,"[7] the divine election moves toward a point of absolute reference. Finally, Zerubbabel the invader reveals what the holy empire could not: God remains the King of his people even when his temple is destroyed and the Jews are forced to occupy Palestine without an earthly sanctuary.

At the very last comes the largest irony of all, the final and absolute reversal of human expectation and desert. Jesus the despised and rejected Messiah assumes the Davidic seat now transferred to Golgotha. At this the most minute focus of God's determination to make and keep covenant with humanity—at the cross-hairs where all things are centered—the divine mercy finds its widest reach. From the throne of shame, the crucified Son reaches out to embrace and reconcile the entire world unto God. The executed Savior drags the whole vast Roman imperium, says Barth, into an unwitting collusion with Israel both in its sin and in its redemption.

Far from being a dreadful and horrible decree, the doctrine of God's singular election of Jesus Christ is what Barth calls the Gospel *in nuce*, the evangel whose tidings are not a mixed message of joy and woe. Here in this one Man the ultimate horror of the human rejection of grace is overcome in God's own rejection of sin:

> To be a man means to be so situated in God's presence as Jesus is, that is, to be the Bearer of the wrath of God. It belongs to us, that end on the gallows. Yet that is not the final thing, neither man's rebellion nor God's wrath. But the deepest mystery of God is this, that God Himself in the man Jesus does not avoid taking the place of sinful man and being . . . that which man is, a rebel, and bearing the suffering of such a one, to be Himself the entire guilt and the entire reconciliation! . . . And so the limit [of human evil and divine wrath] becomes visible, *total help* over against *total guilt*. This is the last thing, as it is also the first, that God is present and His kindness is unending.[8]

Barth is a theologian of the *comic* Gospel in just this sense: he is determined to leave happily undialectical and graciously unbalanced that which God himself has set out of kilter. It is the ultimate ingratitude and unfaithfulness to make the God of Jesus Christ into a dialectical deity—a God who is as much darkness as light, as full of wrath as mercy, and thus as bent on damning as on saving. To locate such a duality in God himself is to seek divine justification for the human either/or. A duplicitous God would be but a grand projection of our existential ambiguity into cosmic terms. It would be possible to maneuver oneself onto the right side of a God who both elects and rejects, who both rewards and punishes, in symmetrical fashion. We humans prefer the heavy yoke of a moralistic savior who insists that we must all pull our own load. The Gospel proclaims, by contrast, the Christ whose burden is gay and light because he has already borne our griefs and carried our sorrows, thus enabling us gladly to bear each other's burdens. God's unambiguous Yes pronounced upon us in Jesus Christ is therefore the unaccountable mystery. The wonder of biblical faith is not that God hides himself in namelessness and obscurity, but that he freely grants to humanity nothing less than himself.

II. The Meaning of Evil as Revealed by Radical Grace

There could be nothing more ludicrously wrong than the old allegation that Barth is a dour pessimist. Robert McAfee Brown contends that Barth stands in far greater danger of one day being declared a heretic of optimism.[9] A Barthian reading of the Christian revelation may seem blithely unrealistic about evil and thus falsely joyous about faith. Barth may lead to a summery confidence about life that ignores the wintry facts of tragedy, sin, and despair. The enormous merit of Reinhold Niebuhr's theology is that it scrupulously attends to the moral and political calamities that dominate modern experience. The peril implicit in such an approach is, as we have seen, that it tends to make the negativities of life more than a constituent part of mortal existence—to make them contrapuntal necessities within the music of divine grace. Without death, no life; without tragedy, no comedy; without sin, no mercy; without evil, no good; without nonbeing, no being. This is the logical tendency of Niebuhr's dialectical way of thinking.

Apart from its intrinsic merit, Barth's theology is immensely important for its resolute resistance to such a dialectical rendering of Christian faith. His work tacks steadily against the prevailing winds of the *Zeitgeist*. In his view, even the slightest parallelism of sin and grace would lethally subvert the glad tidings of the Gospel. Any counterpoint of good and evil ends by committing the error which Barth wants most assiduously to avoid: the positive valuation of sin, and thus the devaluation of what God has wrought in Christ. Rather than taking his theological bearings from the sadness of modern life, therefore, Barth seeks to answer it with an undiminished emphasis on the Gospel's comedy and joyfulness.

Barth begins his treatise on sin and evil by noting that, properly speaking, the demonic is not an article of faith. Nowhere in the creeds do Christians confess their belief in the devil. "Credo in Deus," the faithful repeat, but not "Credo in diabolus." Barth admits the peril of giving evil a consistent meaning and definition, since sin entails the breaking of all order and logic. Here, more than anywhere else, theologians must acknowledge "the necessary brokenness" of their efforts, their radical inability to comprehend and systematize the truth. "All theology is *theologia viatorum*," Barth declares. "It can never satisfy the natural aspiration of human thought and utterance for completeness and compactness. It does not exhibit its object but can only indicate it, and in so doing it owes the truth to the self-witness of the theme and not to its own resources."[10]

The difficulty is compounded by Barth's unwillingness to grant evil even the logic which Augustine accords it. To understand sin as *privatio boni* is rightly to deny it any positive character, but it is also to give evil a logic that Barth denies. The bishop of Hippo makes enormous good sense when he says that evil is a parasite living off its host, a perversion of an essentially wholesome creation, an idolizing of the world's beauty as if it were not transient but permanent, and thus a mistaking of the creation for the Creator. What such a humane and reasonable account of evil ignores, in Barth's view, is the real horror of sin: its inexplicability. Augustine might have learned this lesson from his experience with the pear tree, which he and his young friends stripped of its luscious fruit for no discernible reason other than the joy of sheer destruction. The true terror of evil, Barth argues, lies precisely in its irrationality and absurdity.

The commonplace assumption is that, even in this late hour of human calamity when the good seems ever more vaporous, we can still name the beast of evil. Hans Jonas voices the truism concisely: "Perhaps we cannot know what the *summum bonum* is, but we can surely know, when presented with it, what a *malum* is. We recognize evil even when ignorant of the good."[11] It is this seemingly obvious truth which Barth disputes. He contends that the real meaning of evil cannot be known apart from Jesus Christ. Sin enters the field of human vision not with Herod or Attila or Nero, not with Hitler or Stalin, not at Auschwitz or Dresden or Hiroshima, but solely on Golgotha. There on the cross is exhibited the one sin which is the measure of all other sins. There in the rejection and crucifixion of Jesus is the full desperation of human existence made manifest. Completely helpless humanity spurned the divine Help, greeted God's entrustment of himself with a deadly distrust, and thus answered his great Yea with its murderous Nay:

> The serious and terrible nature of human corruption, the depth of the abyss into which man is about to fall, . . . can be measured by the fact that the love of God could react and reply to this event only by His giving, His giving up, of Jesus Christ Himself to overcome and remove it in a way to redeem man, fulfilling the judgment upon [sin] in such a way that the Judge allowed himself to be judged and caused the man of sin to be put to death in His own person.[12]

The mistaken notion that true evil can be known independently of God's revelation is the real gravamen of the infamous *Nein!* Barth shouted at Emil Brunner. Barth does not deny, of course, that human wretchedness cries out for deliverance. But he denies that our ingrained misery has the creative power to discover its real source in our deep distrust of God himself. Against Brunner, Barth argues that it is the subtlest form of reverse Prometheanism to believe that natural human despair provides a negative propadeutic for the Gospel. He quotes Luther on our native inability to discern ourselves truly as sinners—the confession of sin being "a rare thing and a hard one."[13] Only God in Christ is able to disclose to us the total calamity of our condition:

> For what [Luther asks] is sin? Is it not theft and murder and adultery and the like? Yes, these are sins, but they are not the chief sin. . . .

This sin is not to believe in Jesus Christ. The world knows nothing of this sin: it has to be taught by the Holy Ghost.[14]

Sin must be understood first and last as the human repudiation of the covenant-making and covenant-keeping God. Any other regard for evil ends, Barth maintains, by granting it an independent and positive status within God's good creation. It is this quasi-Pelagian estimate of sin that Barth combats. If evil is merely a latent human possibility, it becomes inevitably a good possibility as well as an evil one. Leibniz and his tribe lie lurking behind the door of this misconception of evil, ready to make it a mere metaphysical imperfection, indeed a necessity permitted by God in order for human beings to be free and rational creatures. Good and evil enter thus into a mutual reciprocity wherein one is required for the other, and the two become inseparable halves of a greater whole.

Against this dialectical vision of evil's paradoxical goodness, Barth relentlessly insists that God's creation is good without any admixture of error or evil. The popular motto "E tenebris lux" is, theologically, a terribly mistaken notion. God does not bring day out of night. The formless void is neither a primeval darkness wherefrom God fashions light, nor an aboriginal chaos which God orders into a cosmos. Nowhere in Scripture, Barth reminds us, do we find the words "Let there be darkness" but only "Let there be light." The *tohu-wabohu* of Genesis 1:2 is literally a "desert-ocean"—an absurd thing, a caricature and mockery of the real world which God creates, a virtual antiuniverse. Hence Barth's much-controverted contention that evil is *das Nichtige*, an awful Nothingness. It is the "impossible possibility" which God refuses to bring into being, creating instead his totally good world. Evil "exists," therefore, only as that which God rejects, the thing which he declines to create, and thus as a preterition having no positive and proper existence.

John Hick has assailed the anthropomorphism implicit in Barth's vision of God as a Maker who, like any other, must choose among the possible worlds he is able to create. "Might we not more properly think of God as able, if He wished, to create a good universe that is not accompanied by the threatening shadow of rejected evil?"[15] Barth is not troubled by anthropomorphism, if only because the Bible is so full of it! The point of such human comparisons—as of Barth's own "analogies of faith"—is to declare that the biblical God creates, not out of any inherent necessity, but from the same gracious will that later calls and sustains Israel without regard to its desert. Hence Barth's conclusion that, for the cosmos to be truly good, God must face and reject the monstrous possibility of an evil universe.

Yet in so considering and rejecting the hideous alternative, God concedes evil at least a negative and putative existence. Barth's waggish critics are thus oddly right: his God is so sovereign that, even when he says No, something happens. The sinister world God refuses to create comes to have a terrible presence, even though God does not make or ordain it. Against all Pelagianism, Barth is willing to insist on God's prime responsibility for everything that exists, including evil. Were God not to allow his creatures such self-annulling and thus false opportunity of rebellion, the universe would not be the good product of God's free love: "Without this possibility of defection or of evil, creation would not be distinct from God and therefore not really his creation."[16] Yet Barth escapes the monistic charge that God is the author of sin by insisting that the status granted to evil is essentially unreal, for all its terrifying effect in the world. Nothingness exists, says Barth in a paradoxical formulation, "only by the fact that it is that which God does not will."[17] Indeed, the whole aim of God's activity in the world is to negate Nothingness. "It is God's *opus proprium*, the work of His right hand, which alone renders pointless and superfluous His *opus alienum*, the work of His left."[18]

Such a confession may seem to reveal Barth as the supreme supralapsarian—a theologian who envisions God as smashing with his right hand what he has permitted with his left, the cosmos itself being but an exhibition of this divine shadowboxing. Barth knows, with Luther, that there is considerable biblical evidence for believing God to be the *Deus absconditus*. Isaiah 45:7 has God declare: "I form the light, and create darkness; I make peace and create evil; I the Lord do all these things." Deuteronomy 32:39 is even more chillingly succinct: "I kill, and I make alive." Rather than denying the existence of these scriptural claims, Barth interprets them to mean that, while death and evil are tyrants over humanity, they have no sovereignty over God. His real activity is to be found in his creation, reconciliation, and redemption of the world in Christ. God's strange nonwilling of evil does not give him a dark and sinister side. On the contrary, we understand the terror of evil only because God is not himself a dialectical interplay of opposites—only because the intrinsically negative reality of evil "does not exist side by side with Him or above Him, but under Him":

> Yahweh is the boundary of death, as death is the boundary of man. . . . [This fact] rules out the view that in the matter of life and death, Yahweh wears a Janus head, as though in mysterious ambivalence and neutrality He were both the God of life and the God of death. He is the Lord of death, but this does not mean that He affirms it. As the Creator He affirms life and only life. . . . His control over death is exercised for the sake of life and not for the sake of death.[19]

III. Creation's "Shadow-Side" and the "Impossible Possibility"

Evil is so very deceptive because it disguises itself behind the catastrophes and calamities which are endemic to mortal life. Suffering and disaster become the occasion for the denial and distrust of God because they seem to deny his goodness—because they seem, in fact, to affirm the demonic fatedness of human existence. Barth contends that "the slings and arrows of outrageous fortune" are, instead, the shadow-side of God's good creation. They are not the work of the Evil One from whom Jesus instructs his disciples to pray for deliverance. All mortal things exist within the gracious polarities attested by Ecclesiastes and summarized by Barth:

> In creation there is not only a Yes but also a No; not only a height but also an abyss; not only clarity but also obscurity; not only progress and continuation but also impediment and limitation; not only growth but also decay; not only opulence but also indigence; not only beauty but also ashes; not only beginning but also end; not only value but also worthlessness. . . . It is true that individual creatures and men experience these things in most unequal measure, their lots being assigned by a justice which is curious or very much concealed. Yet it is irrefutable that creation and creature are good even in the fact that all that is exists in this contrast and antithesis. [20]

This oft-quoted passage would seem to make Barth a dialectician in the same fashion as Niebuhr: the apostle of an earthly ambiguity in which all things are paradoxically caught, and of a religious faith which seeks to endure life's duality without idolatry. Quite to the contrary, Barth insists that the trials and vicissitudes endemic to mortal existence are not to be confused with true evil. The Epistle of James can declare the blessedness of "the man who endures temptation" because creation contains its own intrinsically good terminus, not because there is a dialectical interplay between being and nonbeing, between sin and grace. This sense of life's proper limits are, for Barth, the heart of the plea in Psalm 39 for God to "let me know my end, and what is the measure of my days; let me know how fleeting my life is!"[21]

The positive character of creation's shadow side was no mere theoretical notion for Karl Barth. He lived it as consistently as he taught it. When his own twenty-year-old son Matthias was killed in a mountain-hiking accident, Barth was unwilling to make a stoic garden of his sorrow, planting a willow tree in its center and watering it daily with his tears. Such sweet melancholy would have signalled, for Barth, the unfaithful reception of a gift freely given and just as freely taken. So to accept a seemingly meaningless death is to believe that which cannot be demonstrated, as Barth himself implicitly confessed in choosing to preach the funeral sermon on I Corinthians 13:12a: "For now we see in a mirror dimly, but then face to face." It was not stoic serenity, therefore, but eschatological confidence that enabled Barth to affirm the goodness even of this death which had grieved him more deeply than any other. "We all felt that [Matthias'] life, during which he had always gone his own particular way, was so complete that we did not really dare to lament."[22]

The counterside of this proposition that God's creation remains good even in its shadowy unclarity is the denial that good is generated out of evil. Barth resists the Faustian notion that evil is the matrix wherein good is properly born, and that the deep crevices of sin and anguish are a necessary counterpart to the lofty places of grace and peace. Not for him the Keatsian idea of life as "a vale of soul-making." The danger inherent in the tragic vision is that evil, first being necessary to good, soon becomes good in itself, and finally is regarded as God's own creation. Nor will it do to say, with C. S. Lewis, that God permits suffering in order to make it the means for drawing us unto himself. Lewis goes so far even as to describe pain as God's "megaphone to rouse a deaf world."[23] Thus to regard physical anguish as but a call to godly awareness would trivialize agony and turn God into a monster.

Just as it is a deadly act of self-deception to confuse the shadow side of God's beneficent order with genuine evil, so is it equally wrong to deny that suffering and death can become the demonic "wages of sin." Human disease and illness are not, in Barth's view, the inevitable and necessary counterparts of vitality and wholeness. If sickness were thus intrinsically linked to health, there would be no real motive for combatting it. Jesus is filled with real repugnance, Barth maintains, when he approaches the grave of Lazarus. Death is an offense to him because it is a sign of the threat which evil poses against God's creation, and of the chaos into which humanity has already plunged.

Such, in Barth's estimate, is the view of sickness shared by Job, the Psalms, and the Synoptics. They regard it as God's subjection of humankind to "the power of nothingness in virtue of . . . sin." Illness thus represents "the inevitable encroachment of the realm of death upon the living space squandered and forfeited by man." Jesus' miracles of healing and exorcism and resurrection must be understood in this light. They point to a Kingdom which grants death no dominion, but excludes it as the disorder wrought by the demonic powers.[24] Evil has no *proper* place, therefore, in God's world. The shadow side of the good creation seems evil only because *das Nichtige* turns it into an occasion for unbelief. Death's "sting" comes from the terrible Nothingness which sinfully encroaches upon human life. This is not to say that we humans would not suffer and die were we not sinful, but that our suffering and dying derive their horror from our fall. "Our creatureliness is a curse," Barth declares in his very first work, "only in virtue of our sin."[25]

If evil is the *Nihil* which God declines to create, how does it enter human life? Barth is unsparingly honest in his admission that this is the darkest of all mysteries. Sin, in his view, is the ultimate absurdity and irrationality. There is no *reason* for sin. Thus is Barth compelled to stretch language to the breaking point in order to describe sin. He calls it the "impossible possibility." What he means by this stark paradox is that good and evil are not set before humanity as if they were equal God-given possibilities. The forbidden fruit does not hang in luscious temptation to human self-determination; nor is it a secret test of our faithfulness. The interdicted tree containing the knowledge of good and evil serves but to mark the limits of what humanity can know and determine on its own. The serpent is present, of course, but there is no indication that he is sent by God. On the contrary, the J-writer is quite justified in depicting God as having been caught off guard by the first couple's act. Yahweh *ought* to be surprised, for he has prepared no place for evil in his world. Sin has no objective or natural right to exist within God's good creation.

Barth vehemently denies the popular conception of Adam and Eve as primordial existentialists choosing bravely between secure acquiescence and perilous defiance of the divine will. He will have nothing of Milton's Promethean Satan declaring in heroic perversion, "Evil, be thou my good." Such a notion is the essence of the Pelagian heresy. Against it, Barth insists with Augustine that there is only one *real* choice open to humanity. "Freedom to decide means freedom to decide towards the Only One for whom God's creature can decide, for the affirmation of Him who has created it, for the accomplishment of His will: that is, for obedience."[26] To choose evil is not to act freely but to prove that one is bound in shackles and chains:

> The decisive point is whether freedom in the Christian sense is identical with the freedom of Hercules: choice between two ways at a crossroads. This is a heathen notion of freedom. Is it freedom to decide for the devil? The only freedom that means something is the freedom to be myself as I am created by God. God did not create a neutral creature, but *His* creature. He placed him in a garden that he might build it up; his freedom is to do that. When man began to discern good and evil [for himself], this knowledge was the beginning of sin. Man should not have asked this question about good and evil, but should have remained in true created freedom. We are confused by the political idea of freedom. What is the light in the Statue of Liberty? Freedom to choose good and evil? What light would that be? Light is light and not darkness. If it

shines, *darkness is done away with*, not proposed for choice! Being a slave of Christ means being free.[27]

It is a notorious fact, of course, that humanity is not free but enslaved. We make the choice which is no choice. The "impossible" occurs. Yet it happens not with any Niebuhrian inevitability, and still less with any tragic necessity. Though the serpent is "the subtlest beast of the field," the match with him could and should have been won. Never by solitary human volition, one must admit, might such an adversary have been overcome. Yet the aboriginal couple is not alone in Eden. God has already instructed them in the meaning of trust and faithfulness. Disobedience was and is the truly unnatural act. Faith, in Barth's understanding of it, is always the *real* alternative. It is never "a high and difficult but a near and easy command—the requirement of gratitude which is natural to man because the God who requires it is beside him, is covenanted to him in His mercy, has identified Himself with him and has freed and bound him to do His will."[28]

Our antique parents listened not to the voice of God but to the promptings of the snake. With sardonic acuity, Barth labels him the "first ethical philosopher." Called upon to define sin succinctly, Barth is said to have replied with the single word "ethics." Asked to extrapolate the meaning of *original* sin, Barth is supposed to have answered: "a Ph.D. in ethics." The serpent seeks to supply Adam and Eve with an ethical criterion for taking the measure of God, instead of encouraging them to remain the subjects of God's own gracious assessment. He urges them to travel the high and noble road of human self-determination. The Satanic allurement is thus to a "deeper" and more "humane" life than "mere" faithfulness allows. His appeal is "to genuine morality, to the freedom of a knowledge which distinguishes and an activity which elects. . . ."[29] Such, for Barth, is the perennial character of sin: in the name of seemingly good and worthy ends, humankind chooses its own righteousness over God's. Whether in the most miniscule personal acts or in the most grandiose corporate structures, we refuse to trust the God who from the foundation of the world has entrusted himself to us. This is why evil is falsity and illogic; why the fall is not fortunate but disastrous; why sin cannot be comprehended as a mistaking or perversion of the good; why the descent into chaos and disorder and unmeaning is an "impossible possibility."

What makes Barth's phrase more than a play with words is his conviction that God renders evil "impossible" both by his gracious act of creation and by his yet more remarkable redemption of the world. The real miracle, says Barth, is that God should have been offended by sin in the first place. Nothingness has power only over the created order; it is impotent against God's own self-sufficient life. God could have remained serenely indifferent and unaffected by sin. The wonder of God's grace is that he elects not to keep himself detached and aloof from the human plight, but that he enters this fray in his own self-surrendering Person.

To say that God redeems the world is to acknowledge that he does not smash evil by sheer fiat, obliterating it by brute might. Such are the tactics of evil itself. As the parody and ape of God, the demonic seeks to rule by domination—by the desire to subordinate and subjugate everything to its own selfish will. Jesus' crucifixion exposes the prepotency of evil in all of its futility. By seeking not to possess but to surrender himself, offering his life in adoration to God and in service to his fellows, Jesus abolishes the satanic pretense to coercion and control.[30]

Over and again Barth contends that God's power is never mere *potentia*, the naked force which can do any-and-everything, squaring the circle and making two plus two equal five. The strength of God is always *potestas*, the ordering and redeeming power which works through human agency, and ultimately through the Man who is also God.[31] God does not compel us, therefore, to accept his acceptance of us. He neither prevents our disobedience nor compels our obedience. But he does sovereignly, and of his own gracious accord, reject our rejection of him. He renders it null and bootless, refusing to allow humanity to turn his mercy into wrath:

> The intention of disobedience is to deny that God is really God and really love. If disobedience were a real possibility, if men could effectively and unambiguously disobey the living God, then they could evoke His complete destruction [of them] as the response of His justice. But this complete rejection would ... imply that God is limited to the extent that He must exclude disobedience from His presence. ... And in demonstrating that there are limits to God's love and reality the [disobedient] man would have justified his own disobedience.[32]

Far from annihilating evil and thus excluding it from his presence, God subjects himself to it. Nothing other could break sin's terrible thrall. Beyond all human conceiving, and further still past all human deserving, God willingly offers himself to be "offended and humiliated, attacked and injured by nothingness."[33] Though God could make evil an "easy match," he refuses to do so. Acting not out of external compulsion but from his own uncoerced goodness, God offers himself in our human stead:

> Where His creature stands or succumbs, He comes and exposes Himself to the threat of the assault; to the confrontation with nothingness which the creature cannot escape and in which it

falls as an easy prey. God is not too great, nor is He ashamed, to enter this situation which is not only threatened but already corrupted, to confess Himself the Friend and Fellow of the sinful creature which is not only subject to the assault but broken by it, to acknowledge Himself the Neighbour of the sinful creature stricken and smitten by its own fault.[34]

Ronald Goetz has observed that the ancient heresy of divine impassibility—the notion that God cannot undergo change and therefore cannot suffer—has become a theological commonplace in the twentieth century. Yet Karl Barth is one of the few theologians who, as Goetz notes, has made theopaschitism central to his entire theology.[35] God in Christ suffers not only the penalty of sin, says Barth, but also the pain of creaturely life: "The real goodness of the real God is that the contradiction of creation has not remained alien to Himself. Primarily and supremely He has made it His own, and only then caused it to be reflected in the life of the creature. His rejoicing and sorrow preceded ours."[36] God rules the world not by visible might, therefore, but by suffering love. His invisible sovereignty can be discerned, as Goetz remarks, only through the eyes of faith: "God's reality is so unobtrusive that it is possible to fail to see that a God even exists."[37]

The cross is the throne of God's kingdom only because suffering love has been empowered by Christ's victory over sin, death, and the demonic. The weakness and humiliation of God are not of the same order as his resurrection and exaltation. "In the person of Jesus Christ God has not definitively, let alone eternally, but only transiently shared the pain and death of creation."[38] Barth speaks thus of the "the asymmetry and disproportion" of Christ's death and resurrection: "Christ dieth no more. He lives eternally."[39] The unique achievement of Barth's theology consists, I believe, in this rediscovery of the Gospel's gracious unilaterality. There is a joyous imbalance between humanity's sin and God's love. Good and evil do not stand on the same plane, issue from the same source, or serve as necessary concomitants to each other. The Christian proclamation is not, therefore, a message of joy *and* sadness. It is the comic announcement that the tragic duality and the sinful curse of human existence have been once and for all overcome.

IV. The Christian Life as Eschatological Rejoicing

While Karl Barth is certainly no Pelagian who makes salvation depend on our subjective appropriation of grace, neither does he hold to an old-fashioned "objective" soteriology wherein God alters humanity's metaphysical status while leaving its existential condition unaffected. Joseph Bettis has put the matter clearly: "The work of Christ is not some ontological reorganization or historical reorientation which men are called on to acknowledge. Grace is not the cosmological restructuring of the universe, but is God's participation in human history which allows men, through the fellowship of the Church, to participate in the divine life."[40]

It would seem, however, that very few people enter this transformed life with God. Even—perhaps especially—within the church, there are few who can be said to live the reconciled life fully rather than meagerly. How, then, can we speak of human redemption as a triumphant comic fact? As we have heard Nietzsche reminding us, the redeemed do not *look* redeemed. George Lindbeck notes that Luther himself had to admit that "we do not have our goodness *in re*, but *in fide et spe*." This faith and this hope make salvation always, as Lindbeck observes, a matter of eschatological expectation rather than existential realization: "Believers have by grace just begun to learn of the one in whom alone is salvation, but in moral and religious quality they are like other human beings, worse than some and better than others."[41] The disconsolate character of modern life has led the Italian novelist Ignazio Silone to declare that history seems fixed at Good Friday, as if the Easter event had never occurred. Yet Barth insists that the grace of God glows in the darkness of sinful rejection. The glory of God is still evident in human lostness—in the wretchedness which results when we refuse to take joy and hope in the divine comedy. The great glad fact obtains despite our denial of it. Humanity cannot put asunder what God in Christ hath joined together: himself and the world he would redeem.

This is not to suggest that Barth is a universalist, not at least in the naive sense of the word. He repeatedly rejects the sentimental notion that God is too benevolent and kindhearted to consign anyone to perdition. The idea of *apokatastasis*—the guaranteed restoration of all things at the end of time—is heretical for Barth because it ignores the New Testament warnings against eternal condemnation. These threats of a final lostness are too stark to be ignored, especially in an age that seems bent on self-annihilation. Many are called but few are chosen. Two men shall be in the field, two women at the well; one shall be taken and the other left. Dives writhes in flames. The damned are cast into an outer darkness full of "weeping and gnashing of teeth." It is a frightful place where, in the terrifying language of the King James Version, "the worm dieth not, the fire is not quenched" (Mark 9:44), and "the smoke of their torment ascendeth up for ever and ever" (Rev. 14:11).

With characteristic originality, Barth insists that none of these biblical images of hell can compare with the reality of evil which Jesus experiences on the cross. His bearing of Israel's sin—and not only Israel's but the evil of humanity entire—shows how onerous is the weight of evil, how horrendous the repudiation of God. What may have seemed a

mere peccadillo in Adam and Eve's attempt to fend for themselves is revealed to be, in fact, the most heinous of offenses. That God himself has
borne our sorrows and carried our sins is what makes his wrath so fearsome. Even if the world may seem to escape the condemnation of God
now, it cannot flee forever. There will be a terrible division of the sheep
from the goats, those on God's right hand from those on his left. And the
sundering shall occur even more fiercely within than without:

> God's grace and God's right are the measure by which the whole of
> humanity and each man will be measured. *Venturus judicare*: God
> knows everything that exists and happens. Then we may very well
> be terrified, and to that extent those [biblical] visions of the Last
> Judgment are not simply meaningless. That which is not of God's
> grace and right cannot exist. Infinitely much human as well as
> Christian "greatness" perhaps plunges there into the outermost
> darkness. That there is such a divine No is indeed included in this
> *judicare*.[42]

Nowhere does Barth seek to soften the severity of this divine reck-
oning with humankind. Though his theology has an undeniably universalist bent, he refuses to say that God's fearful Nay will not be absolute.
"To the man who persistently tries to change the truth into untruth,"
Barth solemnly observes, "God does not owe eternal patience and therefore deliverance." The hope that God will spare us from ultimate condemnation remains exactly so—a hope and not a certainty. Christians
pray for what they must never assume: "the supremely unexpected withdrawal of the final threat."[43] Were humanity assured of universal excul-
pation, God's real intention for the world would be eclipsed. He desires
not merely to salvage the shards of humanity at the very last; God wants
to enter into redeeming fellowship with his people even—indeed, especially—now.

When pressed to announce whether he believed in the actual existence of hell, Barth is said to have playfully dodged a direct answer. One
can believe in the reality of hell, Barth is supposed to have declared, without believing it is occupied. He added, in a more sardonic vein, that an inhabited hell would be populated exclusively by Christians. The worst
judgment falls on believers who have been given God's grace, Barth
suggests, and yet who enact it so very poorly. The point of these witty re-
torts is that, for all the terror of God's wrath, Christians do not live in
trembling fear of death and judgment. The Christ who comes, Barth
liked to say, is the One who has already come. Just as God in Christ once
judged us with unalloyed mercy, so the Christian hopes and trusts that
grace will once again abound. "Jesus Christ's return to judge the quick
and the dead," Barth declared to a group of young German seminarians
just after their country had committed unprecedented atrocities, "is ti-

dings of joy."[44] Even if God pursues his creature to the depths of hell, we are still held there by divine grace:

> Indeed, it is just as the One who is so palpably against us that He is so much more mightily for us. If the fire of His wrath scorches us, it is because it is the fire of His wrathful love and not His wrathful hate. Man has always stood up to the hatred of the gods. But God is not one of these gods of hatred. Man cannot stand up to His wrath because it is the wrath of His love. The reason why His curse falls so hard upon us is that it is surrounded by the rainbow of His covenant. It is the dark side of the blessing with which He has blessed us and wills to bless us. Those whom He loves He chastens. Those whom He will find and have for Himself He pursues to the remotest corner where their backs are to the wall and they can no longer escape from Him. From those to whom He wills to be all in all, he strips everything else.[45]

This is Barth's characteristically positive message. He refuses to dwell on the possibility of our final lostness because such a negative word is not the central Christian declaration. The great pealing bell of the Gospel rings out the joyous tidings that no longer are there distinctions between Jew and Greek, slave and free, male and female (Gal. 3:28)— neither in the evil they commit nor the grace they receive: "Since all have sinned and fall short of the glory of God, they are justified by his grace as a gift, through redemption which is in Christ Jesus" (Rom. 3:23). The happily unjust fact is that God has not counted our sins and trespasses against us. He has, instead, "consigned all men to disobedience that he might have mercy on all" (Rom. 11:32). It is a stunning paradox that God's furious indictment of sin rests on his prior reconciliation of the world unto himself. The biblical judgment, Barth writes, "accuses [man] by showing that all the charges against him have been dropped. It threatens him by showing him that he is out of danger."[46]

Barth argues for the radical prevenience of God's grace even within texts which would seem to controvert it. With dauntless bravado, for example, he tackles the so-called two-way schema of Deuteronomy 30. It would appear that Yahweh is compelling Israel to decide between life and death, good and evil. Blessings moral and material are promised to Israel if it chooses aright, while curses and destruction are threatened if it commits apostasy. In the face of such an apparently moralistic conception of the Two Ways, Barth notes pointedly that God grants Israel not two choices but one—not an existential either/or but the singular injunction to "Choose life." Any other decision would be no decision at all, but rather slavery and self-deception. Just as God has kept faith with Israel when it elected evil and death, so must Israel "make a right choice, i.e., one which in analogy to that of Yahweh means life and not death, blessing and not cursing, the service of its own God and not that of alien deities."[47]

Not even the most "Pelagian" of passages deters Barth from his insistence that it is God's grace which enables every movement of the human will toward him. Revelation 3:20 would appear to make the ultimate appeal to our own unfettered decision: "Behold I stand at the door and knock; if anyone hears my voice and opens the door, I will come in to him and eat with him, and he with me." For Barth, however, the important fact is that Christ does the summoning. Jesus does insistently knock at the threshold of our lives, offering to whoever shall open the door his gracious presence and succor. Yet who would think of unlatching the door, asks Barth, were there not first this thunderous or (as the case may be) this gentle rapping? Though we are indeed his necessary respondents, Jesus himself creates the condition for response. He is not a meek supplicant unable to enter except as we deign him worthy. As Barth jauntily observes, "The risen Christ passes through closed doors."[48]

The singleness of the choice set before us, far from negating the significance of human decisions, actually enhances them. No human action can be considered merely neutral in its import. God's primordial decision to give himself to the world means, instead, that we are constantly compelled to decide about him. Never, of course, do we choose merely within the isolation of our own subjectivity, but always in relation to our entire communal history and character. That God has elected us before and whether we elect him is the one great fact. It undermines all moralistic notions of personal and social behavior. It replaces the grim calculus of good and bad deeds with an ethics of gladness and gratitude for God's irreversible redemption of the world. To be the chosen of God is to be truly able to choose. It lifts the terrible yoke of human self-justification and self-sufficiency, and frees us to live in the confidence that God alone determines our ultimate worth:

> We either praise or blaspheme God's great love. This is what differentiates between good and evil in our lives. And the differentiation is made in the fact that God is gracious to us in Jesus Christ. This [fact of] His will with us and His act for us is the law of our lives both as a whole and in each detailed moment. It is this because He is the Lord of our lives, because we belong to Him, because we belonged to Him before we existed and will always belong to Him—to no one else, and certainly not to ourselves. What we were and are and will be stands or falls by whether it is righteous or not in His sight. And the conclusion that we are righteous or not in His sight, and therefore [whether we] stand or fall, is not for us to make but for Him.[49]

The action wherewith we praise God's great love—and it is a lifelong choice, not a series of discrete decisions—is itself a gift. Barth takes with unrelenting seriousness the declaration of Jesus that the Spirit blows where it wills. He goes so far, in fact, as to say that "Christians are those breathed upon by Christ."[50] Believers seek to acknowledge their redemption in word and deed, owning the fact that they are owned. We can persist, of course, in the mad notion that we belong to ourselves. Such self-deceit is the essence of evil, and nowhere does Barth underestimate the demonry of our massive presumption and ingratitude. Yet unbelief is not to be given the same regard as faith. Christ and the devil are not contraries set in equal opposition. The cross and resurrection constitute an irreversible comic triumph:

> How can we make clear the victory of Christ? In this way: when speaking of sin, demons, darkness, by *not* speaking of them in too tragic a manner—like the German theologians, all so serious. The further north you go in Germany, the more they are concerned with the realm of darkness. And if you move into the Scandinavian countries, all is darkness: God against Satan, and *vice versa*! . . . But because there must be room for the victory of Christ, you cannot be so anxious and pitiful and sad. . . . We cannot deny the reality of evil and the Nothingness, but in and with Christ we are above these mysteries. It is not wise to be too serious. We must be serious, of course; life is hard. But we are not to take Satan as a reality in the same sense that Jesus is real.[51]

The peculiar failing of Christians is to regard God's own self-surrender as a thing to be seized or spurned like any other benefaction. Faith is the utter gift of God, Barth insists, the one offer that cannot be refused. God's victory over evil is at once so costly and so free that it cannot be reduced to a mere offer held out for us either to accept or to reject. Faith is not a momentous existential decision to cast one's vote on the right side. Against those who would make salvation a matter of our own grave choice, Barth is supposed to have said, "We are not asked to extend the right hand of fellowship to the Lord God Almighty." Faith is the humble and humorous acknowledgment that we can escape God's grace no more than we can walk out of our shadow or select our parents. It is the replacement of the tragic claim that we are more sinned against than sinning with the comic confession that we receive infinitely—*infinitely*—more than we give.

In response to so wondrous and comic a deliverance, the Christian life can be nothing other than a joyful celebration, an endless delight over what God has wrought in Christ. Belief in the redeeming God yields no quarter to the grim visage and the humorless doubt. Believers are not permitted to sit like "melancholy owls" in frowning disdain for the transient scene below. The central Christian command and privilege is to live in gratitude and gladness, not in fear and suspicion:

> If you have heard the Easter message, you can no longer run around with a tragic face and lead the humorless existence of a man who has no hope. One thing still holds, and only this thing is really serious, that Jesus is the Victor. A seriousness that would look back past this, like Lot's wife, is not *Christian* seriousness. It may be burning behind—and truly it is burning—but we have to look not at [the encroaching flames], but at the other fact, that we are invited and summoned to take seriously the victory of God's glory in this man Jesus and to be joyful in Him.[52]

This joy is not natural to humanity. The Gospel is a scandal to human reason and morality whenever they are used to manipulate God, demanding that he become *humanly* equitable and comprehensible. "Blessed is he who takes no offense in me," declares the Jesus of Matthew 11:6. The gift of salvation remains an offense in the age of the Holocaust and the bomb no more than in first-century Palestine or the High Middle Ages. Scientific discovery and historical criticism may have given piquancy to modern doubt, but they do not alter the fundamental scandal. In all ages people have been humorlessly appalled that God should send rain and sun upon the just and unjust alike, that he should prefer Abel and Jacob over Cain and Esau, that he should pay the laborer who comes to work in the late afternoon the same wage as the one who starts at dawn, that he should hide himself from Jeremiah and put Job in unutterable misery, that he should harden the great Egyptian pharaoh and choose the lowly Jews as his own people, that he should assume flesh and blood in the person of so unimpressive as figure as Jesus of Nazareth. We are scandalized, above all, that "while we were yet sinners Christ died for us" (Rom. 5:8).

The opposite of offense is gaiety and gladness over God's redemption of the world in Jesus Christ. The Philippian call to "rejoice always" is, in Barth's view, a summons for the Christian "continually to hold himself ready for joy." "The man who hears and takes to heart the biblical message," Barth declares, "is not only permitted but plainly forbidden to be anything but merry."[53] Christian joyfulness means nothing less than a constant seeking of "opportunities for gratitude."[54] These occasions are not always obvious. Joy is often to be found in the strangest of places, even amidst sorrow. Our capacity for enjoyment, Barth wisely observes, is measured by our capacity for suffering. Real "joy before the Lord" is nothing else than the willingness to play the part one has been assigned by God rather than longing wistfully for another place or role:

> For the power of God . . . is the power of Jesus Christ, and therefore the power of the Lamb as well as the Lion, of the cross as well as the resurrection, of humiliation as well as exaltation, of death as well as life. . . . The power which comes from him is the capacity to be high or low, rich or poor, wise or foolish. It is the capacity for success or failure, for moving with the current or against it, for standing in the ranks or for solitariness. For some it will always be only the one, for others only the other, but usually it will be both for all of us in rapid alteration. In each case, however, it will be true capacity, the good gift of God, ascribed to each as needed in His service. God demands one service to be rendered in light, another which can be performed only in shadow. This is why He distributes this varied ability according to His good-pleasure. Either way, it is grace, being for each of us exactly that which God causes to be allotted to us.[55]

Comic serenity amidst a tragic world requires, above all else, an eschatological vision. The world must no longer be viewed with a human outlook but from the perspective of what God in Christ has irreversibly accomplished. The comedy of divine redemption holds that the game of life has been forever fixed in favor of reconciliation and rejoicing, against anger and alienation. The glad Gospel proclaims the news that God has determined not to let humanity dwell in the closed shell of its own sadness. Though still caught in the sinful oscillation and tragic ambivalence of life, we have also been transported beyond condemnation and bitterness into the joy of life eternal. The tidings of redemption and release are comic because they announce that the strife is over, the victory won, the contest ended, the enemy checkmated. No matter how furiously the forces of evil continue to manuever and attack, even at times seeming to be triumphant, the Easter message declares that the Evil One will never succeed. In fact, he is already defeated.

Far from being the unfunniest of books, as the old canard has it, the Bible contains the one ultimate cause for laughter and rejoicing. Its joy is not cheap and easy but something deep-seated and lasting. Indeed, it often comes reluctantly. "We may as well admit it," Barth says of the believer, "he has got something to laugh at, and he just cannot help laughing, even though he does not feel like it."[56] The divine comedy is not a hollow denial of the gathering darkness. Christians can honestly acknowledge the shadow of death because they have seen how thoroughly God has dispersed its darkness:

> The binding seriousness of the covenant relationship between Yahweh and His people, the gloom of the indictment continually brought against this people, the terror of the divine judgment pro-

claimed and executed on them, the final call to repentance with which John the Baptist introduces the New Testament, and at the heart of the New Testament the darkness of the day on which the Son of God is nailed to the cross—all these do not signify a suppression of the joy to which there is constant reference, nor of the summons to rejoice, but it seems rather as if this joy and summons arise from these dark places, and that what is declared from this centre is glad tidings. Why? Because God the Creator and Lord of life acts and speaks here, taking the lost cause of man out of his hand, making it His own, intervening majestically, mercifully and wisely for him.[57]

If we are thus freed for singing and playing and dancing before the ark of our redemption, there can be no fatal suspicion of culture, much less any accusation and condemnation of it. God in Christ has reconciled the entire world unto himself, however little we recognize or celebrate our already accomplished happiness. The God whose essence is Immanuel must be with humanity in culture no less than in the church and the synagogue. I contend that there is a fuller echo and parable of God's earthly presence in the comedy wherewith the culture takes itself lightly than in the tragedy whereby it regards itself gravely. Barth's theology of culture reveals why, I will seek to show, the Gospel can be distantly overheard in certain kinds of literary comedy.

4

BARTH'S EVANGELICAL
THEOLOGY OF CULTURE

It is a commonplace to say that Karl Barth's work is Christocentric. It is even more conventional to dismiss his theology as antihumanistic. The aim of this chapter is to show that, while the former is incontestably true, the latter is demonstrably false. Barth's theology of culture, far from being misanthropic, has a profound regard for humanity and all its works. Yet it is not built upon our native longing for God. Barth makes a radically evangelical estimate of human creation, rooting it in the Gospel's own unapologetic claim that God in Christ has shown himself to be ineluctably for us rather than against us. In beginning with the Gospel rather than the world, Barth is able to make a fairer estimate of both biblical faith and secular culture than does the Christian humanist who, having sought natural evidence for God within the world, then makes it serve as the foundation for revealed faith. Barth's unique accomplishment, I will argue, is to have genuinely honored human achievement without conflating its truth with the Gospel's own suprahuman gladness. There is a radical incommensurability, Barth never wearied of repeating, between God's glad tidings and our own common sense.

I. The Gospel That Cannot Be Synthesized with Culture

Barth's massive theological reconstruction of Christian faith is nothing other than an attempt to honor the biblical insistence that God's revelation of himself in the Jews and Jesus is unique, absolute, incomparable. The Messiah of Israel is not one light among many, not even the best and brightest light that has ever shone, but the one and only Light of the world (John 8:12). As the single Illuminer of every human life, Jesus Christ requires no acolytes. He alone is the Radiance who has dispersed the gathering gloom, the Effulgence in whose glory every creature is rendered incandescent. The task of theology and church alike is neither to trim the wick nor to replenish the oil, but to let the Lamp shine—chasing shadows, exposing lies, revealing truth, brightening the path of life.

So to insist on the finality of God's self-disclosure in Jesus is, inevitably, to give offense. Barth insists, however, that the Gospel scandalizes Christians no less than secularists. The uncompromising precedence of divine revelation over all human potentiality sets both believer and pagan on the same footing—namely, in radical dependence on this "one truth which is superior to both of them."[1] The Christian, Barth declares, "must of necessity be far more concerned with his own unbelief than with that of other people, with whom he can only know himself to stand in all too strong a solidarity."[2] What offends Christian and secularist alike is the refusal of this unique Word to be synthesized with other human words. The Gospel resists all attempts to join God's transcendent revelation with our own immanent creations and discoveries. It can be chained to neither philosophy nor psychology, to neither the arts nor the world religions, not even to politics or the church. "There is no legitimate place," Barth asserts, "for projects in the planning and devising of which Jesus Christ can be given a particular niche in co-ordination with those of other events, powers, forms and truths. Such projects are irrelevant and unfruitful because as the one Word of God He wholly escapes every conceivable synthesis envisaged in them."[3]

The stunning import of the First Commandment, in Barth's interpretation, is not that it forbids apostasy through obeisance to false gods, but that it prohibits the dilution of Yahwism through combined reverence for other divinities. "Israel can look to him alone," Yahweh demands, "or not at all." God directs his wrath and jealousy less at atheism and idolatry, Barth wryly observes, than at "the fatal little word 'and'." Whether in the subjection of the church to the state among German Christians, or in the synthesis of faith and reason among religious humanists, this tiny conjunction remains the dire enemy of God. With three deceptive little letters, we would link together what God has driven apart: his singular and incomparable revelation, on the one hand, and our relative and self-serving truths, on the other. The way of Christian calamity, Barth believes, lies precisely in such combinations of the Gospel with other things:

> This combining of the Word of Jesus Christ with the authority and contents of other supposed revelations and truths of God has been and is the weak point . . . at almost every stage in the history of the Christian Church. The prophecy of Jesus Christ has never been flatly denied [in Christendom], but fresh attempts have continually been made to list it with other principles, ideas and forces . . . which are also regarded and lauded as divine, restricting [the Gos-

pel's] authority to what it can signify in coordination with them, and therefore to what remains when their authority is granted.[4]

The problem with all worldly illuminations is not that they are false but that they cannot master our minds and wills to the service of God. Far from wanting to belittle these human insights, Barth insists that they are the product of God's good creation. The world would not be God's were it not full of truth and beauty and goodness. Yet, as Kierkegaard says of all immanent revelations, these earthly glories are self-conditioned. They issue from the world's radical contingency, and are thus derivative rather than original. Their truth springs from no absolute source and has no final force. Great though the splendors of music and poetry and philosophy may be, they remain ultimately at our own disposal, to manipulate and control them as we will. No earthly reality—not even the threat of atomic annihilation—has the power to convert our hearts and conform our minds to the will of God. "We have experienced the most frightful things," Barth writes in the aftermath of the Holocaust, "but man is not broken by the lords who are not the Lord. Intrepidly he passes through the ruins and asserts himself against the earthly powers."[5]

Jesus Christ alone has the authority to bind human life decisively to God because he alone speaks an unequivocal Word to us. The biblical annunciation stands apart from every human message because it is unilateral and irreversible in character. As Barth says of the resurrection, it is not an event about which we make absolute claims but an event which makes absolute demands upon us: "The content of the Easter witness, the Easter event, was not that the disciples found the tomb empty or that they saw [Christ] go up to heaven, but that when they had lost him through death they were sought and found by Him as the Resurrected."[6] Every human happening, by contrast, is a reflection of our own—and the world's—essential duplicity. As our great poets and thinkers tell us, we are creatures of a double nature: both spirit and flesh, both animal and angel, a thinking reed (Blaise Pascal), a questing genital (Walker Percy), the only beast who both smokes and laughs (W. H. Auden).

In the life, death, and resurrection of Jesus Christ alone is this doubleness overcome. Binary though the world may be, the Gospel of God is not. It does not mete out punishments to the evil and rewards to the good. It does not balance the Nay of God's judgment with the Yea of his mercy. The Word of God is first and forever Yes:

> Do I make my plans like a worldly man [asks the Apostle], ready to say Yes and No at once? As surely as God is faithful, our word to you has not been Yes and No. For the Son of God, whom we preached among you, Silvanus and Timothy and I, was not Yes and No: but in him it is always Yes. For all the promises of God find

their Yes in him. That is why we utter the Amen through him, to the glory of God (II Cor. 1:17-20).

Such thunderous biblical affirmations enable Barth to put a profoundly positive construction, as we have seen, on the dread doctrine of election. What in Calvin remains a "horrible decree"—precisely because it is an equivocal business of both affirming and negating—becomes in Barth a univocal word of gladness and triumph. The Gospel is to be understood not dialectically but undialectically. It is not a message compounded of both "joy and terror, salvation and damnation." It is—in what may be the single most joyous passage of the entire *Church Dogmatics*—the annunciation that God has graciously reclaimed humanity for himself:

> [The Word of God] does not proclaim in the same breath both good and evil, both help and destruction, both life and death. It does, of course, throw a shadow. We cannot overlook or ignore this aspect of the matter. In itself, however, it is light and not darkness. We cannot, therefore, speak of the latter aspect in the same breath. In any case, even under this aspect, the final word is never that of warning, of judgment, of punishment, of a barrier erected, of a grave opened. We cannot speak of it without mentioning these things. The Yes cannot be heard unless the No is also heard. But the No is said for the sake of the Yes and not for its own sake. In substance, therefore, the first and last word is Yes and not No.[7]

Nothing less than this uncompromising christological affirmation lies at the base of Barth's work. It is extremely unfortunate that so positive a reading of the Gospel should have been so largely ignored, and that Barth should have become renowned as a despiser of culture and a hater of humanism. The truth of the matter is exactly the reverse. Barth can look favorably upon the glory and beauty of human creation and discovery because, and only because, he does not seek to squeeze salvation from the turnip of culture. Redemption is the free gift of God already provided in Jesus Christ, who liberates his people to enjoy a world which they are not to regard as the final reality. Barth is able to acclaim the worth of all human stories because he knows that the saga of God's Reign is not the supreme fiction but "the only interesting story ever told." He is an enthusiastic reader of other books because he is convinced that the Bible is a book like none other:

> *By grace you have been saved!* . . . The prophets and the apostles wrote a very strange book called the Bible, for the very purpose of testifying to this fact before mankind. The Bible alone contains this sentence. We do not read it in Kant or Schopenhauer, or any

book of natural or secular history, and certainly not in any novel, but in the Bible alone.[8]

II. Scripture as God's Narrative of Redemption

Karl Barth has no interest whatsoever in defending Scripture as the inerrant, infallible Word of God. For all its appeal to ancient orthodoxy, fundamentalism is a modern phenomenon, as Barth repeatedly notes. It is a vain attempt to answer scientific objections to Scripture by elevating the Bible to scientific reliability and perfection. Yet neither does Barth share modern liberalism's estimate of the Bible as an account of religious experience among ancient Israelites and early Christians. In this liberal view, Scripture has continuing authority because of its power to evoke transforming faith in its modern readers and hearers.[9] For Barth, the Bible is a book of neither objective propositions and concepts nor subjective experiences and symbols. The propositionalist idea of Scripture makes its truthfulness depend, as George Lindbeck has shown, upon its cognitive correspondence with some ideal realm to which the Bible supposedly refers.[10] The symbolic-experiential reading of Scripture regards it, not altogether differently, as an expression of the Ultimacy experienced in common by all religions.[11] In either case, Scripture is understood as pointing to something either above or below the biblical story itself.

Against both the liberal and conservative views of Scripture, Barth regards the Bible as God's own story—a virtual nonfiction novel recounting God's redemptive dealings with his people. This means, as David Ford has convincingly demonstrated, that Barth has a narrative understanding of God's self-revelation in the Jews and Jesus. Ford shows that, especially in the later volumes of the *Church Dogmatics*, Barth moved away from the I-Thou personal encounter as his chief metaphor of God's earthly activity, and towards an increasingly community- and story-oriented understanding of the divine self-disclosure. It is Barth's claim, Ford argues, "that God chooses to bring people to faith through certain stories; that this [intention] does not depend on [our] being able to verify the stories historically or affirm them as inerrant; but that it does depend on [our] following the stories carefully and trusting that their subject, who is still alive in them, is rendered adequately for God's purposes."[12]

The resurrection is what makes Jesus Christ the central figure in the New Testament narratives. It is the event toward which the gospel stories move and the viewpoint from which they are narrated. The strangeness of their ending, far from being a detriment to their credibility, is all in its favor. The meaning of the resurrection lies not in what a redactor or historian can reconstruct, but in the risen Christ who confirms the story's truth by his living presence. Van A. Harvey has complained that Barth's reading of the resurrection as a quasi-historical event occurring in space and time requires the believer "to surrender the autonomy of critical judgment" and thus to commit a *sacrificium intellectum*. Barth fails, in Harvey's estimate, "to state what constitutes the reality of historical events and what would constitute sufficient grounds for believing in a resurrection."[13] What Harvey ignores is the startling fact that the resurrection itself—and not Karl Barth!—requires us to sacrifice our belief in the self-enclosed causality of the scientific worldview. That there are no adequate historical grounds for believing in Jesus' resurrection is exactly its miraculous point.

This also explains why—against Rudolf Bultmann and his followers—Barth sees the passion and resurrection narratives as focused not upon the disciples' responsive faith, but upon the risen and active Christ. The evangelists' accounts are not ordinary histories, says Barth, because Jesus is not a dead savior who must be recalled from the distant past; he is the living and present Lord. Nor are the Gospels ordinary fictions. As in no novel, the main Character is acting and speaking through the story itself: "He does not need first to be spoken of. Existing in that history, living and ruling and speaking and working as the One who exists in that history, He speaks for Himself whenever He is spoken of and His story is told and heard. It is not He that needs proclamation but proclamation that needs him."[14]

This uncompromising insistence on the living Christ who speaks through Scripture frees Barth from the late modern obsession with the "hermeneutical gap" separating our time from the prescientific world of the Scriptures. Barth seeks, in fact, to turn the historical-critical method upon its head. Instead of having the subject interrogate its object, as in post-Enlightenment interpretation of Scripture, Barth regards the Bible as the object which puts us subjects under scrutiny and investigation. As James Robinson has observed, Barth makes a deeply anti-Cartesian move. The so-called higher criticism of Scripture assumes, with Descartes, that "everything must give account of itself, state its cause, to the investigating subject to which it is answerable." Nothing can exist for itself; everything must be accountable to our objectifying investigation. The result, notes Robinson, is a strange kind of subjectivity: "The objective world, since it is defined by a science that understands reality as answerable to the inquiring subject, is a world seen from the viewpoint of the investigating subject, the subject's world view."[15]

The Cartesian presumption is implicit in G. W. H. Lampe's declaration that the resurrected Christ "was never seen by Caiaphas or Pilate or the Jerusalem mob. It would be childish to think that there could be some dramatic confrontation between the risen Lord and his enemies.

For God says 'Yes' to the man who is willing to trust him. He cannot speak to those whose hatred and complacency makes faith and trust impossible."[16] To whom else does God speak, one might ask in reply, if not to his hateful and complacent people? The resurrection may be regarded as miraculous, *contra* Lampe, because it attests to what God does *without* our willing assent. He breaks through the crust of sin and rejection, and thus resuscitates—through him whom he raised from the dead—the entire death-bent world. This, in Barth's view, is what gives the resurrection narratives their nonmythical character. They are not a mythical alteration of historical fact but an astonished accounting of God's own wondrous deed: his unexpected reversal of the dead end to which human life would otherwise be doomed.

The question is not whether the event of Jesus' resurrection is historical in the sense that Lincoln's Gettysburg Address is historical. If one takes God's transcendence seriously, then his activity within the world—and especially his unequivocal presence in this act—is by necessity a miraculous occurrence. No divine deed can ever be proved by the canons of scientific verification. The resurrection is an event that *creates* the whole history of salvation rather than an event that *is created* by either religious or secular history. The real issue, therefore, is whether God raised the dead Christ in such a way as to counter all human expectation and desert, thus making possible the faith and trust that are humanly impossible.

"Flesh and blood has not revealed this to you" (Matt. 16:17) is a saying that applies to the resurrection no less than to Peter's recognition of Jesus as the Christ. It points up the truth of Rachel Trickett's observation that, for the Gospel narrators, Jesus' bodily resurrection "is the *raison d'etre* of the narrative." They vouch for its transnatural reality not in order to make believers murder their minds, but to stress the radicality and unilaterality of the deed which God has done. He has conquered death in every sense, breaking open the closed shell of our sinful self-absorption and breathing new, indeed everlasting, life into the world. In the biblical order of things, therefore, it is resurrection which precedes and faith which follows—not the reverse:

> The evangelists are concerned to verify the story of the empty tomb, countering the anxious arguments of the high priests and of subsequent doubters. The resurrection appearances of Luke and John are emphatic in their underlining of the physical side of it: Thomas's declaration of his doubt and its resolution; the disciples on the Emmaus road seeing Jesus break bread and knowing him in that action. Only John's account of the appearance of Jesus by the lake of Galilee has about it a sort of eeriness which seems to exist in the no man's land between actuality and dream. Yet in all of

these accounts the sense of mystery and the sense of reality are both strongly and simultaneously present. Jesus' injunction for Mary Magdalene not to touch him seems as natural as his sudden appearance in the upper room to answer Thomas's demand seems mysterious.[17]

Because none other than Christ himself addresses us in the biblical narratives, its hearers are not first of all asked to *translate* the scriptural images and categories into modern equivalents that make them "relevant" to their own time and place. We are summoned, instead, to *participate* in the biblical world by entering imaginatively into its story. One's encounter with the Gospel is not engendered by anything intrinsic to human nature; it is something enabled by the biblical narrative itself. The scriptural stories *shape* the Christian's self and world far more than they *express* the experience of the Numinous that all religions have in common. To borrow from George Lindbeck, one must say that the public narrative produces the private encounter, and not the other way around: "To become a Christian involves learning the story of Israel and of Jesus well enough to interpret and experience oneself and one's world in its terms."[18] Barth himself states the matter even more acutely:

> The history of Christ is not an explanation of my life and the life of the Church, *after the event*. It is not one possible idea thanks to which my life may be given a certain interpretation. It is not a revelation of a certain number of abstract truths that may fortunately apply to the life of the Christian and of the Church. No! Rather, it constitutes the very history of both the Christian and the Church. . . .
>
> Either we understand God as the master and subject of this history, or we do not understand this history at all. Thus the question we have to answer now is not: "Can I admit that all this occurred?" but: "Where do I stand vis-à-vis God the master? Do I live 'with' God? Do I live in keeping with God's deeds?" And since we know these deeds mainly and primarily through the Scripture, the question of faith is first a question of reading the Bible. One cannot pray without reading the Bible, without getting a knowledge of the divine history directed by God wherein we discover what we need: faith in God the rector and sovereign and living master of Christ's history which "comprehends," that is, embodies, sums up, locates and fulfills our own history.[19]

The meaning of the biblical history does not lie, for Barth, in some transtextual realm above or below it but in the story itself. It bothers Barth not at all that the Gospels make witness to Jesus from a standpoint "beyond the temporal limits of his life; that they saw and attested Him in the contexts of events which took place after His death and which they described as His resurrection and ascension and the impartation of His Holy Spirit to the community." To understand Jesus' earthly career apart from these postcrucifixion events would be to misunderstand it. "Neutrality of this kind is illegitimate when it is a matter of expounding the witness to Jesus in the New Testament as the witness to the Kingdom of God drawn near in him."[20] For Barth, therefore, Jesus has no identity other than the one rendered in the biblical narratives. Their picture of Jesus, as David Kelsey observes, is not something "inferred from the details of the story. It *is* the story."[21] The Gospels are thus significant in themselves and need no external support or justification. What they mean is what they tell.

Yet they "tell" not in the fashion of myths so much as of sagas. Barth does not deny, of course, that Scripture contains many mythic elements borrowed from other cultures. He admits, for instance, that Babylonian creation myths are probably the source of Genesis 1 and 2. Yet they are put to decidedly nonmythic uses. Though myth has the guise of history, says Barth, it aims to convey timeless truths which are common to people everywhere and which can be expressed without recourse to narrated historical events. "At best a myth may be a parallel to exact science; that is, myth has to do with viewing what has always existed and will always exist. . . . Myth considers the world as it were from its frontier, but always the world which already exists." The Babylonian creation myths seek thus to explain the perennial problem of the world's growth and decay, its beginning and ending. The Genesis narratives are concerned, by contrast, with God's merciful election of Israel. They have the character of saga rather than myth, for saga depicts quasi-historical happenings that cannot be reduced to general truths. Sagas recount events that are historylike in their uniqueness and unrepeatability. The Genesis creation sagas are concerned, in Barth's view, to establish the unique Day of the Covenant. The six days all point to this final day of Sabbath rest wherein Israel witnesses the salvation that comes from Yahweh alone.[22]

Barth does not canonize saga as a uniquely revelatory genre. He makes use of it to illumine the biblical stories because, like them, sagas do not depend upon historical verification for their credibility. Sagas cannot be "proved" because they often narrate events that occurred in the remote and historically unrecoverable past. They transcend scientific objectivity by employing poetry and imagination to recount "the kind of history which escapes ordinary analogies and cannot therefore be verified historically, but is real history all the same."[23] By *poetry* Barth does not mean anything merely personal and invented, but rather something intuitively sensed rather than inductively observed. One cannot understand even the battle of Waterloo, says Barth, by means of a merely objective idea of history.[24] A right reading of the biblical stories will not seek, therefore, to translate them into the categories of ancient myth or modern history, but to repeat the sagas in such a way as to preserve their own mysterious kind of historicity. Speaking of the strange presence of angels within the biblical narratives, Barth makes a prescient remark regarding the saga character of all Scripture:

> The whole history of the Bible, while it intends to be and is real spatio-temporal history, has a constant bias toward the sphere where it cannot be verified by the ordinary analogies of world history but can be seen and grasped only imaginatively and represented in the form of poetry. How can it be otherwise when it is the history of the work and revelation of God, which as such, as the history of the action of the Lordship of heaven and earth, although it can also take place in the comparatively narrow sphere of the historically verifiable occurrence, is not confined to the sphere of earthly analogies?[25]

Although the secular and divine histories remain discontinuous, Barth has an almost Hegelian confidence in their final unity. As Thomas W. Ogletree has shown, Barth's basic assumption is "that history has a single, unified content which is wholly determinative throughout all the richness and variety of its development." There is, for Barth, a serene objectivity about history's redemptive character. What God accomplishes in his people and their Messiah "stands in history but does not stem from history." It is given, says Ogletree, "quite apart from our particular response to it. Our own action toward it can only have the character of an acknowledgement of it or of a subsequent decision to participate freely and responsibly in it." Hence the wondrous—if hidden—concord between world history and salvation history. This gracious divine action remains the center of things and history becomes its circumference. It "is the basis and unity of world occurrence in general." There is an awful disjunction between the two realms only because of human faithlessness. Yet this secular denial of God's purpose for history does not silence the call to interpret all of history in light of the biblical story. We do so, says Ogletree quoting Barth, in the assurance that "we shall find . . . it . . . concretely confirmed."[26]

Whereas secular history hides God's covenant purpose, the Bible reveals it. Scripture has God not only as its subject and content but also, in a very real sense, its author: "God creates in the foreknowledge that his works are to function as meaning-bearers in the covenant, and so that story (and not science or comparative religion or common sense) is the court of appeal for the meaning of the saga's terminology."[27] Barth takes the story of Jesus Christ as what Ford calls "the all-inclusive story of world history."[28] Since the whole of human history and culture is contained within this divine history, the believer can discern typological and figurative correspondences to this history both inside and outside Scripture. God's election of Israel and Christ is the largest pattern to be discerned in the Bible. By revealing what the real world is like, this story summons its readers and hearers to participate in the world by conforming their stories to it, as Lindbeck explains:

> Typology does not make scriptural contents into metaphors for extrascriptural realities, but the other way around. It does not suggest, as is often said in our day, that believers find their stories in the Bible, but rather that they make the story of the Bible their own story. The cross is not to be viewed as a representation of suffering nor the messianic kingdom as a symbol of hope for the future; rather, suffering should be cruciform, and hopes for the future messianic.[29]

Scripture has final authority, for Barth as also for Lindbeck, because it renders the agency and thus the character of God.

III. Parables of the Kingdom beyond the Bounds of the Church

The heart of Barth's evangelical theology of culture is to be found in the biblical story of God's transcendent graciousness. Against all humanisms based upon a supposedly "natural" reciprocity between human seeking and divine giving, Barth insists that the sovereign goodness of God disclosed in Jesus Christ is the real fundament upon which all of life is built. It alone accords dignity and honor, freedom and responsibility to human existence. God can bestow these good gifts only upon a world that exists freely apart from himself. The miracle consummated in the Jews and Jesus is that the all-sufficient God should have given the cosmos its own independent existence. The real mind-tangling paradox is not that the world yields evidence of God, but that God grants the gracious reality of the world. More wondrous still is the mutuality which God in Christ has established between himself and the world. Just as humanity would not be truly human without the independence God accords it, neither would God be truly God without the glory rendered to him by humankind. The priority belongs, of course, wholly to God: he gives, we receive. Yet the Giver does not belittle, much less obliterate, the receiver. On the contrary, God places humanity at the highest place in the created order—namely, as a joyful witness to the good God:

> We must stress—even if it seems "dangerous"—that the glory of God and the glory of man, although different, actually coincide. There is no other glory of God (this is a free decision of His will) than that which comes about in man's existence. And there is no

other glory of man than that which he may have in glorifying God. Likewise, God's beatitude coincides with man's happiness. Man's happiness is to make God's beatitude appear in his [own] life, and God's happiness consists in giving himself to man in the form of human happiness.[30]

Because God has engendered this gracious accord between himself and the world, Christians are freed to discern what Barth calls "parables of the Kingdom." These analogues of the Gospel are not to be understood as mere "illustrations." God's redemptive action is not illuminated by secular examples so much as it clarifies the world's own obscurity. Nor is it proper, in Barth's view, to speak of the church as the extension of the Incarnation. Such a prolongation or continuation of Jesus's life and death would deny their unique and unrepeatable character: "It is finished." "What happened once for all," says Barth, "possesses in what now happens on earth a correspondence, a reflection; not a repetition but a likeness."[31] The church seeks, therefore, to make its own life reflect the reconciliation wrought in Christ, just as it also seeks to detect secular similitudes of God's grace at work in the world. Christians can never assume that the cause of redemption is solely their own. "The community is not Atlas," Barth candidly confesses, "bearing the burden of the whole world on its shoulders." God raises up witnesses to his purpose even amidst godlessness, and it is the church's duty and honor to "find itself enlightened, gladdened and encouraged" by these secular corroborations of divine redemption.[32]

It is possible to discern such parables of grace only when the Gospel is not set in equipoise with secular truth. God's immanent presence within creation always depends, for Barth, on his transcendent sovereignty over it. Far from being antimodernist, Barth welcomes the radical distinction between church and culture which Western secularization has accomplished. There was something deeply pernicious, in his view, about the old *corpus Christianum* that once obtained in both Catholic and Protestant cultures. Not for Karl Barth the motto of Hilaire Belloc: "Europe is the Faith and the Faith is Europe." Such a collapse of Christ and Christian culture threatens to conflate the laws and customs of the old aeon with the radically new requirements of the age to come. This spurious fusion of "throne and altar"—of secular politics and so-called Christian religion—needed to be broken up. Just as the world was finally able to disentangle itself from the church, so did the church gain a salutary distance from the world.[33] When everyone belonged to Christendom by birth, as Søren Kierkegaard endlessly complained, there was no need to become a Christian, and thus to encounter the Gospel of Christ in all of its transforming and renewing power.

This new and dynamic *diastasis* with culture does not mean that the church looks upon the world with either benign neglect or callous contempt. Barth is untiring in his insistence that the church is set in distinction from culture only in order to stand first and last for it. Christians must always acknowledge how deeply they belong to the world even as they refuse to put their final trust in it. Not indifference and hostility, therefore, but solidarity and sympathy are the only appropriate responses of the church to culture.[34] The Christian must be willing to discern the redemptive activity of God even in the most furious unbelief. No matter how vehement the secular denial of God, says Barth, God refuses to deny the *saeculum*:

> Man may be hostile to the Gospel of God, but this Gospel is not hostile to him. The fact that he is closed to it does not alter the further fact that it is open to him. . . . No Prometheanism can be effectively maintained against Jesus Christ. . . . there is no secular sphere abandoned by Him or withdrawn from His control, even where from the human standpoint it seems to approximate most dangerously to the pure and absolute form of utter godlessness.[35]

Barth's deliberate reference to Soviet Communism cannot be missed. His refusal to anathematize it is based not upon a naive estimate of Soviet aggression, but upon his unshakeable assurance that God is reconciling the world unto himself in atheist no less than in so-called religious cultures.

The secular sphere is, in fact, as full of these analogies of grace as are the Bible, the church, and the synagogue. Were they not, God would be reduced to lordship over merely the biblical world, and the Gospel would remain a powerless and irrelevant message. Not to discern these parables of the Kingdom is to be worse than blind; it is to deny that God has subjected all the cosmic powers to his gracious will. Yet, as Barth notes, such signs of the Kingdom have no especially religious subject matter. Jesus' own parables, for instance, do not possess any intrinsic human interest. The people who act and speak in these stories—"the peasant on the land, the owner of the vineyard and his workers, the father and his sons, the capitalist and his stewards, the shepherd and his sheep, the king and his banquet, the children on the streets, the bridesmaids at the marriage"—do not normally comport themselves in the way Jesus depicts them. The purpose of his analogies is not to engender a sudden "shock of recognition" which will deepen our understanding of the human, all-too-human, world. Instead, Jesus likens his parabolic characters and events to that which eye has not seen nor ear heard— namely, the Kingdom of heaven.[36]

The explosive implication of this claim is that there are attestations of God's saving will that lie *extra muros ecclesiae*.[37] So great a Gospel cannot be contained within the walls of the church. Although the

Christian community is custodian of the Good News, it does not determine the bounds of God's activity. The church can never presume to
specify the limits of the Power which can raise up children to Abraham
from the very paving stones. Nor does God wait for the world's readiness
before he acts. Outside the church no less than within it, the sovereign
strength of the Gospel is at work. The church's task is not single, therefore, but double. It must listen to echoes of the Gospel *from* the world
even as it announces the glad tidings *to* the world. Christians are not
only doers of the Word, one might say in reply to the Epistle of James, but
hearers also. "In the narrow corner in which we have our place and task,"
writes Barth, "we cannot but eavesdrop on the world at large. We have
ears to hear the voice of the Good Shepherd even there too, distinguishing it from other clamant voices."[38]

The real basis for Barth's theology of culture lies in his conviction
that "the world derives unknowingly, while the Church derives know-
ingly from Jesus Christ, from His work."[39] Even if the secular world refuses to acknowledge the true God, it remains his property nonetheless.
It will not suffice, therefore, to declare with Augustine that the virtues of
the pagans are to Christians but splendid vices. The insights of the secular mind also derive from God's truth, says Barth, no matter how complacently their divine origin may be denied. Because these extracanonical
and extraecclesiastical witnesses to the Gospel serve to benefit the
world, the church must freely and gratefully honor them. The church's
nonparochial mission requires it to hold the secular world to its own
highest standards, not allowing it (for example) to be satisfied with a
shabby humanism or a banal psychology.[40] George Lindbeck extends
this idea to include even the religious world. Other faiths make their
own distinctive contribution to the purposes of God. "The missionary
task of Christians," writes Lindbeck, "may at times be to encourage
Marxists to become better Marxists, Jews and Muslims to become better
Jews and Muslims, Buddhists to become better Buddhists." He admits,
of course, that Christian norms will decisively shape our notion of what
constitutes the best Marxism, Buddhism, etc.[41]

As examples of such secular attestations of the Gospel, Barth cites
the scientist's sense of both order and puzzlement in viewing the natural
world; the scholar's sober investigation and enthusiastic espousal of the
truth; the politician's insistence that the community take precedence
over the individual; the reformer's angry disquiet over injustice and resolute will to rectify it; the stoic's fearlessness in the face of death; and
the humanitarian's care for the needy without regard to their desert.[42]
Not all cats are grey, says Barth, in the dark night of human history. One
of the church's chief political and cultural tasks is to distinguish, among
the many claimants to truth, the better from the worse. "To what enterprises have they summoned [people]?" asks Barth. "Have they led to

greater freedom or greater bondage? Have they uplifted them a little, or thrust them deeper into the mire? Have they united them or divided them? Have they built up or thrown down, gathered or scattered, quickened or slain?"[43]

The fact that there are these positive parables of the kingdom outside the church does not lead Barth to embrace what Karl Rahner calls "anonymous Christianity." For Barth, being Christian is the antithesis of being anonymous: it is to bear Christ's name. Christians are those who claim this name because they have first been claimed by Christ, because the Holy Spirit has "breathed" upon them.[44] Only because they have first been shown the truth in Christ can Christians discern secular analogies of faith. Nor do these parables of the kingdom have any saving power in themselves. However much the church may be comforted or indicted by such earthly analogues of grace, they can never transcend their relativity and incompleteness to attain the status of divine truth. They lack, says Barth, "the constancy and universality of [God's] self-revelation as it takes place and is to be sought in Holy Scripture."[45]

No matter how full an echo of the Kingdom one may hear in politics or science or art, the Gospel remains a radical alternative to the best worldly possibilities. Indeed, it is heresies and schisms, sects and cults, that result when definitive authority is accorded to extracanonical disclosures of the truth. Hence Barth's extreme hesitance to cite concrete examples and particular instances wherein Christ is witnessed beyond the bounds of the church. Though he freely confesses that Christian teachers and preachers must discern secular similitudes of grace, these must not be confused with the Gospel itself.

Perhaps Barth's extreme caution arises from his fear of repeating the awful mistake made by nineteenth-century liberalism. It had regarded socialist politics as the advance guard of God's kingdom, finding in progressive German civilization a thorough analogue of the Gospel. Protestant liberals were utterly powerless, therefore, to make any radical Christian critique of German militarism at the outbreak of the First War. Though Barth remained a lifelong socialist, he knew—all too painfully—that socialism had proved to be an extremely poor parable of the Gospel:

> None of the major socialist parties in Europe opposed the war. The German Social Democratic Party, the acknowledged leader of them all, presented . . . the most shocking spectacle. Its parliamentary representation voted unanimously for the government motion for war credits. Even more disturbing was the attitude of rank-and-file German socialists, who appeared to share in the nationalistic fervor evoked by the news of the war. Soon, prominent socialist leaders volunteered for war duty, and the party of Marx, Engels, and

Liebknecht would, at least during the first two years of the conflict, show loyalty to the Kaiser hardly exceeded by that of the most hidebound Prussian Junkers.[46]

Yet there is one notable instance wherein Barth overcomes his usual reticence about specifying secular analogues of the kingdom—namely, in his high estimate of Mozart's music.

IV. Mozart as a Musician of Life's Gracious Imbalance

For the last twenty years of his life, Barth began and ended every day by listening to the work of Wolfgang Amadeus Mozart. Barth's study contained a picture of Mozart that was hung—as Barth always pointed out—at a slightly higher level than Calvin's. Barth's aphorisms about Mozart are widely celebrated. Mozart, says Barth, is content to play while Bach is determined to preach. The angels may perform Bach when they are before the throne of God, Barth speculates, but when gathered unto themselves it's always Mozart. "If I ever get to heaven," Barth declares, "I shall first ask after Mozart, and only then after Augustine and Aquinas, Luther and Calvin and Schleiermacher." "In relation to [Mozart]," Barth observes wickedly, "Bach is merely John the Baptist and Beethoven is Origen, if not the Shepherd of Hermas."[47]

Barth is no mere lover of Mozart. He hears in Mozart's work nothing less than a musical witness to God's redeemed creation. Mozart's "singing and sounding," as Barth calls it, echoes God's own gracious ordering of the world. It constitutes for Barth a parabolic correspondence to the Gospel so original that it is not discernible in any other genius of culture. Mozart's "childlike knowledge of the center of things" certainly did not derive from Goethe's "wide-open eyes for nature, history and [the] arts." Mozart perceived what the better-read and better-educated fail to see, what the "connoisseurs of the world and men" do not discern.[48] Not even the church Fathers and Reformers enable Barth to hear what sings forth from Mozart's "golden sounds and melodies"—namely, "parables of the kingdom revealed in the gospel of God's free grace." Without this musical echo of God's goodness, Barth adds in a remarkable tribute to Mozart, "I could not think of what moves me personally in theology, in politics."[49]

It is not the fabled "sunniness" of Mozart's music that enabled Barth to understand afresh the motive force of all theological work. It is, instead, Mozart's avoidance of that deadly balance and coincidence of opposites which characterize much of modern theology and nearly the whole of modern culture. To envision the cosmos as an equipoise of contraries—light and dark, earth and sky, laughter and weeping, heaven and hell—is finally to discern how they cancel each other. This binary view of the world ends ultimately in neutrality and indifference, if not in madness and suicide. That the creation is full of great contrariety there is no doubt, but the Gospel is not such a *coincidentia oppositorum*. For Barth, on the contrary, God's activity in history is bent on transforming the interplay of life's light and shadow so as to make the former always take precedence over the latter. Mozart's music is wondrously redemptive, in Barth's hearing of it, because it reveals this gracious imbalance at the core of things:

> [Mozart] . . . heard, and causes those who have ears to hear, even today, what we shall not see until the end of time—the whole context of providence. As though in the light of this end, he heard the harmony of creation to which the shadow also belongs but in which the shadow is not darkness, deficiency is not defeat, sadness cannot become despair, trouble cannot degenerate into tragedy and infinite melancholy is not ultimately forced to claim undisputed sway. Thus the cheerfulness in this harmony is not without its limits. But the light shines all the more brightly because it breaks forth from the shadow. The sweetness is also bitter and cannot therefore cloy. Life does not fear death but knows it well. . . . Mozart saw this light no more than we do, but he heard the whole world of creation enveloped by this light. Hence it was fundamentally in order that he should not hear a middle or neutral note but the positive far more strongly than the negative. He heard the negative only in and with the positive.[50]

Even in the works of his most radiant keys—in the serenades and divertimenti, in *Figaro* and *Così fan' tutte*—Mozart is no sanguine optimist. Yet neither do the darker pieces set in minor modes ever descend to self-pitying melancholy. In the overture and finale of *Don Giovanni*, in the large and small G Minor Symphonies, in the D Minor Piano Concerto, even in the "Dissonant" Quartet—in none of these, says Barth, is life perceived as a lugubrious dialectic of opposites. They are filled, instead, with a joyous sense of the world's wondrous imbalance:

> The sun shines but does not dazzle the eyes, nor demolish nor scorch. Heaven arches above the earth but does not press upon or crush or swallow it. And so earth remains earth, but without being forced to hold its own against heaven in titanic revolt. In the same way darkness, chaos, death and hell render themselves conspicuous but are not allowed to prevail even for a moment. Mozart makes music, knowing everything from a mysterious center. . . .
>
> What [happens] in this center is . . . a splendid annulment of balance, a *turn* in the strength of which the light rises and the shadow winks but does not disappear; happiness outdistances sor-

row without extinguishing it and the "Yes" rings louder than the still-existing "No." Notice the *reversal* of the great dark and little bright experiences of Mozart's life! "The rays of the sun *disperse* the night"—that's what you hear at the end of the *Magic Flute*. The play may or must still proceed or start from the beginning. But it is a play in which some Height or Depth is winning or has already won. This directs and characterizes it. One will never perceive equilibrium, and for that reason uncertainty or doubt, in Mozart's music. This is true of his operas as well as of his incidental music. Is not each *Kyrie* or *Miserere*, even if it begins at the lowest depth, carried by the trust that the prayer for grace has in fact been answered?[51]

Thomas Merton attributes Mozart's musical mastery to a mystical innocence that instinctively intuited the cosmic harmony. He criticizes Barth for his cerebral denial of this supposed heart-knowledge: "Though you have grown up to become a theologian," he exhorts Barth, "Christ remains a child in you. Your books (and mine) matter less than we think! There is in us a Mozart who will be our salvation."[52] Merton has missed Barth's point altogether. Barth finds Mozart's music wondrously liberating precisely because it contains nothing inwardly mystical, nothing of that romantic *Sehnsucht* which mystics confuse with transcendent grace. Like Cardinal Newman, Barth believes that "mysticism begins in mist and ends in schism." What moves Barth is the serene objectivity of Mozart's music—its unexampled freedom from mere subjectivity. Nothing in Mozart's biography, Barth argues, can account for his unsurpassed musical ability to encircle life's sadness with a deep and abiding joy. "Mozart often laughed," Barth declares, "but certainly not because there was much for him to laugh about. Rather he laughed (and that is something absolutely different) because he was allowed and able to laugh in spite of all."[53]

It was Mozart's unsurpassed gift to have been what Barth calls an impersonal instrument of the "sounding universe." Having listened to a redemptive harmony not of his own making, Mozart was intent on letting his music resound with it. Hence the virtual absence of any subjective element in Mozart's work, and hence also the stark divide between the unhappy events of Mozart's private life and the proverbial gaiety incarnate in his music. Barth cites Mozart's own assertion that "the emotions, strong or not, never should be expressed *ad nauseam* and that music, even in the most horrible situation, never must offend the ears but must please them nevertheless. In other words, music must always remain music."[54] Nothing less than a deep theological humility can explain, in Barth's view, Mozart's splendid self-transcendence over his personal interests:

Mozart's music, in contrast to that of Bach, has no message and, in contrast to that of Beethoven, involves no personal confession. His music does not give any rules, even less does it reveal the composer himself. . . . Mozart does not wish to say anything at all; he just sings and sounds. So he does not intrude a thing upon the hearer, he does not ask decisions or comments of him, he just lets him alone. You start to enjoy him the moment you allow him to act like that. . . . He does not want to proclaim the praise of God either. However, he does just that: in the very humbleness in which he is, so to speak, nothing more than an instrument himself. In this way he lets us hear what he clearly hears, namely, everything which from God's creation presses upon him, rises in him, and wants to spring from him.[55]

Barth is untroubled by the objection that Mozart did not intend his music, at least not his secular work, to resound with the praise of God's prevenient grace. That Mozart lived an often miserable life; that he accused Protesants of being unable to comprehend the meaning of *Agnus Dei, qui tollis peccata mundi*; that he was a Freemason of little moral and intellectual distinction—all of this is, for Barth, nothing to the theological point. On the contrary, it establishes his thesis ever more strongly: Mozart was a man who, however great his personal bondage, became utterly free in his service to Dame Music. Against Ulrich Zwingli's notion that certain people have a special direct access to God, Barth asserts that "God had a special access to this human being."[56]

V. Barth as a Humanist Christian

I maintain that Barth has uncovered not only the essence of Mozart's music but also the heart of a genuinely evangelical theology of culture. He has demonstrated what surprising echoes of the Gospel can be heard within human creation whenever it is not made the basis for faith in God. The less we look to culture for salvation, the more we may find corroborations of the Gospel there in its midst. Instead of leading away from the secular world, an evangelical theology of culture affirms our solidarity with it—not only, or even chiefly, in our common alienation from God; but mainly in the gift of redemption which Christ has brought to all humanity. Believers can freely and gratefully cast their lot with the world in the confidence that, as Calvin said, it is the theater of God's glory. Were God not at work in culture—beyond the bounds of the church—there would be hope for neither ourselves nor our secular brothers and sisters. Yet once we have been enabled to hear the euphony of the Gospel, we can detect its repercussions everywhere.

Barth's theology always moves from the Gospel to the world, and never the other way around. We cannot begin with Mozart or Shake-speare or Michelangelo, and then proceed to find the God of Jesus Christ hidden in their work. Only by first hearing God's unique and saving Word spoken in Christ can we later catch its worldly resonances. This is not to deny the intrinsic value of Mozart's music or of culture in general; it is merely to claim that they cannot serve as the groundwork for the knowledge of God. Barth himself confesses that he could not have heard the overtones of redemption in Mozart had he not first heard the music of salvation in the Gospel itself. "From this [Mozartian] place," Barth de-clared in the last year of his life, "I have heard a harmony which Mozart obviously heard first before he composed it, and for me this has always agreed with what I have heard from a very different place than he did."[57]

This means that Christian attention remains primarily focussed upon God's own direct self-revelation in Jesus Christ as recounted in Scripture and as proclaimed in the church. Its worldly echoes will always remain subordinate to the original Word. Even an artist possessed of a Christian sensibility must take care not to fabricate a surrogate for the Gospel itself. Barth remained extremely dubious about artistic represen-tations of God's decisive and unrepeatable self-disclosure in Christ. Since the Incarnation is history's unique and all-determining event, he asserts, it "does not permit itself to be fixed in an image."[58] How should we presume, Barth asks, to create an image of God once he "has pre-sented His likeness Himself? A well-intentioned business," Barth con-cludes somewhat scornfully, "this entire 'spectacle' of Christian art, well-intentioned but impotent, since God himself has made his own image."[59]

The Christian community at worship must be even more careful not to conflate divine self-revelation and human self-understanding, and thus to confuse the church with the concert hall or the art museum. Barth advocated, for example, a weekly celebration of the Lord's Supper to accompany the oral proclamation of the Word. And he preferred a small ensemble of wind instruments—rather than a pipe organ—to sup-port the congregational singing. "Singing is the highest form of human expression," Barth declared, and organ music should not be employed "to conceal the feebleness with which the community discharges the minisitry of the vox humana committed to it."[60] Barth was no less adamant in his opposition to a new stained glass window for the cathe-dral in Basel.[61] Faith comes by hearing, Barth insisted with the Apostle Paul. Static works designed for the eye distract the listening community, he believed, from the ministry of preaching:

> Even the most excellent of plastic arts does not have the means to display Jesus Christ in His truth, i.e., in His unity as true Son of God and Son of Man. There will necessarily be either on the one

side, as in the great Italians, an abstract and docetic over-emphasis on His deity, or on the other, as in Rembrandt, an equally abstract, ebionite over-emphasis on His humanity, so that even with the best of intentions error will be promoted.[62]

Barth must not be construed as an austere Calvinist whose fear of violating the Second Commandment blinded him to the power of religious art. Despite his low estimate of the visual arts as a means of worship, there was at least one painting that served as a constant guide for Barth's own theological life. He kept a reproduction of Grünewald's Isenheim Altarpiece over his desk as a double reminder. The gnarled fingers of the crucified Christ, grasping vainly after the God who has abandoned him, reminded Barth of what anguishing cost has been paid for our redemption. Barth also found the position taken by John the Baptist to be instructive. He stands anachronistically at the foot of the cross, gesturing with his giant index finger at the hanged Lord. For Barth, this is the proper stance of every Christian—pointing not to oneself and one's own experience, but witnessing to the One who is alone worthy to receive all praise and glory. *Illum oportet crescere, me autem minui*—"He must increase but I must decrease"—is not only the byword of the Baptist; Barth regards it as the calling of every believer to increase the honor of God, even as one's own importance is diminished. "The prophet, the man of God, the seer and hearer, ceases to be, as that to which he unwaveringly points begins to be."[63]

The upshot of the matter is that the realm of human culture, even if it be not our final home, can neither be foreign country to Christians. We cannot look upon it with suspicion and fear. For all its monstrous corruption and inhumanity, the world cannot be regarded with gnostic disdain. "What is culture itself," asks Barth, "except the attempt of man to be man and thus to hold the good gift of his humanity in honor and to put it to work?"[64] Thus it is that the church must maintain a dual attitude toward culture: not only addressing a redemptive word to it, and thus judging its failure to become the realm of grace which God intends it to be; but also discerning the extent to which it has already received God's reconciling and redeeming mercy, and is therefore able to reflect the Glory that gleams through it, often unawares.

This is why Barth must be called a humanist Christian rather than a Christian humanist. In the latter formulation, the noun always overwhelms the adjective. Hence Barth's refusal to set a so-called Christian humanism in opposition to scientific, existentialist, Marxist, or other humanisms. Because they are all abstract programs, says Barth, Christian faith must not seek to compete or to compare itself with them. The Gospel, Barth insists, differs from all humanisms not in degree but in kind. It "is neither a principle, nor a system, nor a point of view, nor a moral philosophy. It is spirit and life, a good message of God's presence and work in Jesus Christ. It does not form some Front or Party either, not even for the sake of a certain conception of man. It forms congregations, and these exist for service among all men."[65]

The body of Christ is built upon the *evangelium* that precedes all other wisdom and truth. Yet precisely because this word entails an unprecedented Good News, Barth's estimate of culture remains quintessentially positive and joyful. The life of faith is animated by the command to "regard no one from a human point of view" (II Cor. 5:16). Barth interprets this gracious injunction to mean that, because God in Christ has demonstrated himself to be the only true Humanist, his people are linked in fundamental solidarity with their fellows: "On the basis of the eternal will of God we have to think of *every human being*, even the oddest, most villainous or miserable, as one to whom Jesus Christ is Brother and God is Father; and we have to deal with him on this assumption."[66] It is an assumption that holds no less firmly when the Christian approaches the realm of culture.

Karl Barth himself is our example in deed no less than word. Especially in his later years, he declared himself to be ever more a man of the church and ever more a man of the world. He became in fact what he sought to be in principle: "a joyful partisan of the good God." He remained an inveterate frequenter of pubs and cabarets, a friend of the poet Zuckmayer and the playwright Durrenmatt, a reader of Dorothy Sayers's radio plays and detective novels, a careful student of the American Civil War, and a lover of his pipe. He returned, in his old age, to his early enthusiasm for Goethe—that pure genius of Enlightenment humanism. And, as long as his health permitted, he continued to ride horses, to hike in the Swiss Alps, and yet not to grieve too long when one of his sons was killed while mountain climbing.

At a memorial service held at the University of Toronto shortly after Barth's death in December, 1968, Martin Rumscheidt called the great Basler "the happiest theologian of our age." Rumscheidt reminded the audience that, even during his very last term of teaching, Barth never wavered in his conviction that Nietzsche is wrong and that "*Theologie ist eine fröliche Wissenschaft.*"[67] Theology is the gayest of sciences because Christian faith is the most joyful tidings ever received or borne by our human kind. At Barth's funeral in Basel, the congregation sang his favorite hymn, "Now Thank We All Our God." He was especially fond of the second verse and its ringing affirmation of "*der ewig reiche Gott.*" It is for this reason that Barth's theology of culture will perdure despite its current eclipse: because he lifted his voice not chiefly in praise of humanity, but gladly to the Son of "the eternally bounteous God" in whom humanity is infinitely cheered.

The remainder of this book is devoted to the analysis of four contemporary American novelists in whose work the Gospel is comically echoed. Not so much in tragic art, where culture regards itself most somberly, but in the laughter that refuses to take the world's sadness as final may we discern secular parables of the Good News. There we shall find repercussions of the tidings that God himself has acted to make the world's sin ultimately unserious. Amidst a laughter neither grim nor silly, we can overhear something of the Gospel's own rejoicing. We shall detect—sometimes clearly, often obscurely—the same *turning* which Barth catches in Mozart's music. We shall hear a laughter which moves painfully past a great mound of misery, and yet finally around a corner which, because God in Christ has turned it, the world shall never turn again.

5

FLANNERY O'CONNOR
AS A SATIRIST
OF THE NEGATIVE WAY

The fiction of Flannery O'Connor affords a fitting comic subject for theological analysis. She is a comedian in both the literary and religious senses of the word. The most memorable scenes and lines in her work are nearly all comic. In "Good Country People," for example, the narrator observes flatly that "Mrs. Hopewell had no bad qualities of her own but she was able to use other people's in such a constructive way that she never felt the lack." So wry a judgment serves not only to take us inside the mind of an extraordinarily complacent woman; it also reveals that O'Connor's humor never exists for its own sake. Her comedy always has a moral bite. Like a latter-day Swift, she lampoons the vices and follies of our age, especially our self-contentment.

Yet O'Connor is not primarily a moralist seeking to slap the world to its senses and to reform its vagrant ways. Her comic vision is far more theological than it is ethical. She cares more about belief than morality, even while appreciating their necessary relation. The murder and mayhem committed by O'Connor's protagonists would seem to make them worthier of execution than of salvation. Almost without exception—and to the reader's immense surprise—the criminals and egotists who populate her fiction are made into reluctant recipients of grace; indeed, they are redeemed. This does not mean that they become paragons of courage and self-sacrifice. O'Connor's heroes are marked, on the contrary, by their failure more than their success. They are blessedly unable to suffice unto themselves, graciously incapable of denying their redemption. Their secular defeat is thus their religious victory; their human loss is their divine gain.

The theological key to Flannery O'Connor's comedy lies in her thoroughly Catholic (and specifically Thomistic) conviction that grace does not destroy but completes and perfects nature. She seeks to recover, amidst the secular absence of God, the divine presence that is sacramentally at work in every living thing. Yet her natural theology is rooted in a radically negative vision of God's activity in the world. "Grace must wound," says O'Connor, "before it can heal. It must be dark and divisive before it can be warm and binding." The reason for this bleak judgment is not difficult to discern. O'Connor regards the modern age as unprecedented in its apostasy, and therefore as blinded to the positive presence of God's grace within the human and natural order. A classic natural theology built on our native desire for God is, in O'Connor's view, no longer possible. Our world is too far gone down the path of self-abandonment to permit anything so hopeful and positive as a traditional Christian humanism. Nothing less than a startled shock of self-recognition can awaken her characters to their desperate condition. They must approach the throne of grace through the rear door of a frustrated self-sufficiency, never through the vestibule of a native desire for God.

The Catholic character of O'Connor's negative natural theology must not be underestimated. Even in its fallen state, humanity has a magnetic allurement to the grace of God. Modern godlessness cannot extinguish it. Not for her John Calvin's conviction that, apart from God's intervening grace, the human heart remains a perpetual factory for the making of idols. O'Connor's characters remain obsessed with God even in their denial of the Holy. They are imbued with a longing for the Transcendent that, despite their vigorous attempts to rid themselves of it, cannot finally be suppressed. The aim of O'Connor's fiction is to plumb the depths of contemporary unbelief and to reveal, even there, the human restlessness that only the divine rest can still.

It is this paradox that explains why O'Connor's work, for all its slam-bang humor, often ceases to be funny in the obvious sense. Her characters confront their inadequacy far too painfully, and face deaths far too gruesome, for ordinary comedy. Yet precisely amidst inward pain and outward death does O'Connor locate a deeper kind of comedy. She is a satirist of the negative way only because she believes that, in our time at least, an anguishing self-knowledge is the prime requisite for recognizing the Gospel of God. Nothing less than this glad grace is what most of her protagonists find. Albeit reluctantly, they come to hear the Voice that will not be silenced, to drink the Water that alone slakes human thirst, to eat the Bread beside which all other food is as stones. If only with their last dying breath, they beseech that Mercy whose asking is already, as Pascal said, a receiving, whose seeking means its finding.

The aim of this chapter is to explore the deep biographical roots of Flannery O'Connor's comic vision, to examine the regional character of her theology no less than of her humor, and thus finally to demonstrate what she discovered to be universally Catholic in her narrowly Protestant milieu. It must be observed, at the same time, that there is a deep negativity at work in O'Connor's vision. She has a quasi-dualist tendency to envision good and evil as set over against each other in a pitched antagonism of equals. At its worst, I will attempt to show, her fiction is animated by a baleful desire to lash modernity for its unbelief, and thus to depict this late stage of human history as uniquely damned and devoid of grace. At its best, however, O'Connor's work overcomes this incipient dualism. She discerns that the Kingdom of Heaven is not borne violently away by frustrated atheists; it is gratuitously given to the unsuspecting children of God.

I. The High Cost of Dying

Readers are sometimes shocked at the grotesque quality of Flannery O'Connor's fiction. Her *dramatis personae* include a character who multilates himself with barbed wire, quicklime, and broken glass; another who steals a wooden leg from a crippled woman and leaves her stranded in a hayloft; and still another who drowns the imbecile child he was commissioned to baptize. Such macabre creations give psychologists a virtual charter for invidious judgments about their creator. Even the most generous and sympathetic of readers may rightly wonder about the author of such grotesques. The British novelist and critic Evelyn Waugh is said to have remarked—in the prefeminist days when such a comment was considered an accolade—that O'Connor's stories could not have been written by a woman. And yet the woman we meet in O'Connor's letters is at once gentle and genial. Though crusty in her social and theological opinions, she is the very opposite of an ogre. Yet there are not two Flannery O'Connors, but one: her life and work constitute, in fact, a remarkable integrity. She practiced in ordinary existence the same comic faith that she envisioned so extraordinarily in her fiction.

O'Connor's faith is all the more impressive for having been hammered out on the anvil of sickness and confinement. Her angular and unapologetic belief is nicely figured in the response she made to a reader who was angered by O'Connor's Christian concerns. She wrote O'Connor to object that Jesus would have been forever forgotten had he died at age eighty of athlete's foot. O'Connor replied to her critic that she was orthodox without knowing it. Jesus did not aim at "a long and happy life," O'Connor implies. He lived preeminently for the accomplishment of his divine mission, even if it meant a passionately brief existence. It is possible to say without sacrilege that so did Flannery O'Connor live.

She agreed with Samuel Johnson that nothing can so wonderfully concentrate the mind as the verdict of death. From age twenty-five until the end came fourteen years later, O'Connor lived with the almost certain knowledge that she would die young. The same lupus erythematosus that had killed her father was eventually to kill her. Knowing perhaps that she would not be able to complete her life work in leisurely fashion, she wrote with an especial intensity, making certain that no one mistook the radicality of her vision. In this regard at least, O'Connor can be compared to the poet Gerard Manley Hopkins, another Catholic writer whose short life issued in a slender but impassioned body of art.

O'Connor's correspondence bears impressive witness to the spiritual struggle that she transmuted into fiction. Her comic vision of reality was the source of her life no less than her art. So discerning and incisive are O'Connor's letters that they have been compared to Keats's. Even if such an estimate be extravagant, *The Habit of Being* must be read in tandem with her fiction in order to comprehend the unity of her art, her faith, and her life. The letters reveal a woman whose devout Christian faith was anything but a crutch that enabled her to limp through life. Against the callow view that Flannery O'Connor became religious after she became ill, her correspondence discloses the opposite: her faith was sorely tested by her long battle with the disease that eventually killed her.

Never does O'Connor roll her eyes heavenward in glib affirmation that her illness is another of God's "good and perfect" gifts. To one of her last letters she adds this poignant postscript: "Prayers requested. I am sick of being sick."[1] O'Connor's struggle with lupus was a destiny so harsh that she could be reconciled to it only partially. Even in acceptance, her voice remains ironic and realistic: "I can with one eye squinted take it all as a blessing. What you have to measure out, you come to observe closer, or so I tell myself."[2] The squinted eye and the qualified affirmation point to an unsentimental faith. So great was her revulsion for treacly piety that she went to Lourdes more in dread than in hope. "I am one of those people," she quips, "who could die for his religion easier than take a bath for it."[3] Only reluctantly did O'Connor agree to wash in the Lourdes waters and to drink from the common cup shared by *les malades*. The real miracle of the place, she commented later, is that it does not "bring on epidemics."[4]

O'Connor's tough-minded faith will not countenance the notion that religion is an easy comfort for the weak and the troubled and the sick. To a skeptic friend inclined so to think, she replies with arresting candor: "There are some of us who have to pay for our faith every step of the way. . . ."[5] The idea of costly grace is a theme that runs throughout O'Connor's work. Belief in God is never something obvious and natural. Her characters are redeemed after much suffering and usually in the face of death. Yet it is not God but themselves that they are finally made to doubt. An anguished self-recognition is always the means of their salvation. Yet this radical turning of the will—away from the self and toward

God—is itself enabled by grace. O'Connor agrees with Augustine that faith is a gift rather than an acquisition. Nor is it primarily an emotion, a Lawrentian palpitation of the solar plexus. Only its objective effects are discernible, and they remain an unaccountable mystery: "When I ask myself how I believe, I have no satisfactory answer, no assurance at all, no feeling at all. I can only say . . . Lord, I believe, help my unbelief. And all I can say about my love of God is, Lord, help me in my lack of it."[6]

The mystery of faith's utter givenness enabled O'Connor to regard her disease as a strange blessing. Without it, she came to see, her life might have been a massive act of presumption. Through the confinement that illness forced upon her, she was able to prepare for the death which, in her Catholic view, is the most important occasion that life offers a Christian: "I have never been anywhere but sick," she writes to the anonymous "A." "In a sense sickness is a place, more instructive than a long trip to Europe, and it's always a place where there's no company, where nobody can follow. Sickness before death is a very appropriate thing and I think those that don't have it miss one of God's mercies."[7]

O'Connor never wavered in her conviction that life is providentially ordered. In an unpublished letter written in 1964 to a Catholic lay volunteer disappointed by her work in South America, O'Connor counsels her to discern God's will even in the midst of uninviting conditions. She concludes with a testament that is all the more remarkable for having been made in the face of her own suffering and approaching death: "I have never been anywhere in my life that it wasn't the place I was supposed to be—no matter how it looked at the time."[8]

Death is a brother to Flannery O'Connor's imagination, as she liked to say. Yet the reason for this kinship is more than biographical. Death is central to O'Connor's fiction because she regarded it as the terminus that compels us to fix the shape of our souls—whether we shall keep our lives for our own vain use, or whether we shall give them back in gratitude to God. Our attitude toward death is thus the criterion not only of life beyond the grave, but for our present existence as well: "You do not write the best you can for the sake of art," she declares, "but for the sake of returning your talent increased to the invisible God to use or not use as he sees fit. Resignation to the will of God does not mean that you stop resisting evil or obstacles, it means that you leave the outcome out of your personal considerations. It is the most concern coupled with the least concern."[9]

Disease and the prospect of death forced Flannery O'Connor to face an enemy far more insidious than physical disability. The real death sentence was not her illness, she confesses, so much as it was the return to her native Georgia that it required. O'Connor had worked hard to establish her own independent existence as a writer, living first in Iowa and then later in New York and Connecticut. Such liberty of life and work was ended with the news that she would have to come back home. O'Connor admits her deep initial dread: "This is a Return I have faced and when I faced it I was roped and tied and resigned to death, and largely because I thought it would be the end of any creation, any writing, any WORK from me."[10]

The dread of returning home again springs from a deeper origin than mere rebellion against her small-town Georgia beginnings. On the contrary, her fictional subject matter was to be invariably Southern. She once remarked that, were she to live in Japan and to write about Oriental characters, they would all talk like Gene Talmadge, the Georgia cracker politician and populist hater of all things intellectual. Yet it is evident that O'Connor wanted to write about the South from a critical vantage point beyond it. She desired the cultural stimulus of Northern and urban life. Far more, she wanted to be freed from Southern small-mindedness. Nowhere is its oppressiveness more evident than in the story called "Good Country People." There a veritable avalanche of banality and triteness falls upon Hulga Hopewell, a crippled intellectual who lives at home with her mother. With mindless complacency, for instance, Hulga's mother observes that "It's very good we aren't all alike." A farm woman named Mrs. Freeman replies with a comic adage that exceeds even Mrs. Hopewell's in its self-satisfaction: "Some people," she says, "are more alike than others."[11]

It does not take a shrewd Freudian to discern that much of Flannery O'Connor's dread of returning home had to do with her mother. There are too many stories about sickly intellectuals living resentfully at home with their parents—usually their mothers—for there to be no autobiographical element in this pattern. Neither is it difficult to establish that Regina Cline O'Connor and her daughter were at the polar antipodes of character types: the mother an affable, outgoing, hard-working widow who operated a dairy farm and purchased herd bulls with equal acumen; the daughter a reflective, inward-turning, book-reading artist whose prime focus was upon the unseen realm of the spirit.

Flannery O'Connor could usually accept this clash of personalities with a droll sense of irony. She liked to say, for example, that her function at her mother's tea parties was to cover the stain on the sofa. But there were also times when she would burst forth in fury at her mother's failure to comprehend the daughter's literary vocation. Once after Mrs. O'Connor had expressed doubt whether Flannery were making the best use of her talents, seeing that so few people could read her books with enjoyment, the writer poured out her wrath to a friend: "This always leaves me shaking and speechless, raising my blood pressure 140 degrees, etc. All I can ever say is, if you have to ask you'll never understand."[12]

So splenetic a confession may seem to justify the psychoanalytic view that Flannery O'Connor suffered from an Electra complex—that she hated her mother, that she sought to commit matricide in her fiction, and that her violent depictions of death reveal a deep sexual frustration underlying the entirety of her work.[13] O'Connor's letters lay to permanent rest such reductionist suspicions, but not without acknowledging their partial truth. It is clear that O'Connor's illness ended whatever hopes she may have had for marriage. When an Atlanta woman complained that there is no "love" in O'Connor's books, the author candidly agreed. "You can't write about love when you haven't had it, least wise the [romantic] kind she's talking about. I never had any." "Marriages are always a shock to me,"[14] she writes in strange response to a friend who had announced her engagement. This is not to say that O'Connor herself did not desire married love. There is no literary evidence that she was either a determined spinster or a closet lesbian. It was her illness and confinement, not her scorn for men, that left her unmarried. In one of her most affecting letters, O'Connor confesses her early discovery that she was not meant to be an *isolé*. She traces her need for intimate friendship to her father's affectionate nature. But whereas he wanted such close relationships and found them, O'Connor confesses, "I wanted them and didn't."[15] In this simple but wrenching declaration lies the essential disappointment of Flannery O'Connor's life.

Great must have been the temptation to both rancor and self-pity. No wonder that so many of her characters succumb to it. Yet the enticement O'Connor admits in her fiction is the one she avoided in her life. Unlike her parent-hating Hulga Hopewells and Asbury Foxes, she remained truly devoted to her mother. Nor did her filial piety issue from a mere grudging sense of obligation. O'Connor's affection for her mother ran all the deeper because she knew that, despite sharing the local view of Flannery's work as grim and nasty, Mrs. O'Connor supported her daughter without stint. Hence the author's bemused observation of the mother's slow progress through *The Violent Bear It Away*: "All the time she is reading," writes the daughter, "I know she would like to be in the yard digging. I think the reason I am a short story writer is so my mother can read my work in one sitting."[16]

Having no notable mastery of the world herself, O'Connor admired her mother's savoir-faire. When a Catholic visitor to the O'Connor farm joined Flannery for a late-afternoon veneration of the Host, she shared his amusement at Mrs. O'Connor's parting declaration upon depositing daughter and guest in front of the parish church: "Y'all go pray while I buy the groceries."[17] Nor is the writer put off by her mother's strictures against a companion who fancied herself a mystic. The friend had stretched herself out upon the cold November ground, staring up at the sky in the hope, she said, of getting a more "sacramental" perspective on the world. Mrs. O'Connor admonished the guest to get up from there in a hurry, lest she catch a death of cold: "Can't you look at things standing up?" In two days' time the visitor had indeed fallen ill, prompting Flannery to remark approvingly, "You can't get ahead of mother."[18]

This comic affirmation of both her mother and her confinement makes Flannery O'Connor's personal triumph so very impressive. Even when the end was at hand, she resisted all self-pity. She would not countenance the notion that her pain was to be compared with Christ's. "I haven't suffered to speak of in my life and I don't know any more about the redemption than anybody else."[19] Such humility enabled her to discern humor even in her adversity. Rendered weak and giddy by the loss of blood, and thinking herself to be dying, O'Connor reports that she heard the idiotic lines of a folk song rather than the celestial choruses of Palestrina: "Wooden boxes without topses, They were shoes for Clementine."[20] A nurse who looked and talked like Ruby Turpin in "Revelation"—life thus imitating art—caused O'Connor to laugh so hard that she could not decide "whether the Lord is giving me a reward or a punishment."[21] The high cost of dying thus proved to be a strange kind of bargain. Despite her early dread of returning to Milledgeville, convinced that she would be a productive writer only at several removes from home, O'Connor came to pay splendid tribute to her mother and her town: "The best of my writing has been done here."[22]

II. A Roman Catholic in the Protestant South

Flannery O'Connor did not conceive of herself as a Catholic writer in the narrow sense. She strove, on the contrary, to embody an ecumenical vision in her art. Like C. S. Lewis' "mere" Christianity, O'Connor's faith is based on the bedrock beliefs shared by all Christians: the uniqueness of Jesus as the incarnate Son of God and Lord of all reality, the radical sinfulness and hopelessness of humanity apart from Christ's saving grace, the final authority of the Scriptures as testaments to God's reconciling action in history, and the indispensable importance of the church as the body of Christ wherein the Holy Spirit gathers the faithful and summons the world to its redemption. O'Connor's grand, all-inclusive Christian vision accounts for the near-absence of overtly Catholic characters and situations in her fiction. Priests and nuns make brief appearances in "The Enduring Chill," "The Displaced Person," and "A Temple of the Holy Ghost." Only in the last of these stories is the main character a professed Catholic, and her schoolgirl struggle with pride knows no denominational bounds. Unlike a fellow Catholic writer such as J. F. Powers, O'Connor never appeals to an "inside" audience who would need to know about rosaries and novenas, monasteries and abbeys, popes and encyclicals.

Though once the most notoriously anti-Catholic region of the country, the South served strangely to reinforce O'Connor's Catholic ecumenism. She was drawn to the Bible Belt for the same reason that H. L. Mencken was repelled by it—because most Southerners still take seriously the God whom the smart secular world has largely dismissed. O'Connor's affection for the primitive Protestantism of her region runs deep. Her God-drunk, self-ordained, wool-hat prophets are not the objects of her scornful satire, as early reviewers thought; they are figures whose concern with ultimate matters O'Connor profoundly shares. Hazel Motes and Francis Marion Tarwater may be grotesque and reluctant servants of God, but they are servants of God nonetheless.

O'Connor agrees with Gustave Weigl's judgment that Catholics are doctrinally closer to their bigoted enemies than to their enlightened friends. So close is the kinship between Catholic orthodoxy and Protestant fundamentalism that O'Connor sees the one as the successor to the other. "The day may come," she prophesies, "when Catholics will be the ones who maintain the spiritual traditions of the South."[23] Hence the surprising accord between O'Connor's Catholic Christianity and her Southern Protestant milieu. "The only thing that keeps me from being a regional writer," she declares in a letter, "is being a Catholic, and the only thing that keeps me from being a Catholic writer (in the small sense) is being a Southerner."[24]

O'Connor's regard for her Protestant region is nowhere better evinced than in her explanation for the prevalence of freaks in Southern fiction. Southern authors write about grotesques, O'Connor notes wryly, because they can still recognize a freak when they see one. Nothing less than an ultimate criterion can enable one to detect fundamental distortions and perversions of human nature. Though the South is surely not a Christ-centered region—witness the Southern treatment of Negroes—O'Connor insists that it is "most certainly Christ-haunted."[25] Southerners share Hazel Motes's inability to rid himself of "the wild ragged figure" of the Nazarene who moves "from tree to tree in the back of his mind, . . . motioning for him to turn around and come off into the dark where he was not sure of his footing, where he might be walking on water and not know it and then suddenly know it and drown."[26]

This startling image suggests that the summons to belief is a perilous thing. It alerts us to the danger no less than to the wonder of our deliverance from damnation. The forgiveness of sins engenders a water-walking faith that is able to traverse both the river of despondency and the lake of woe. So great a salvation, as the Book of Hebrews calls it, also creates unprecedented peril: to neglect it is to fall into the abyss of divine abandonment called hell. God's grace, far from being a thing of easy comfort, puts its recipients at ultimate risk. It is this sense of both divine danger and deliverance that, according to Flannery O'Connor, Southern Protestants have been blessedly unable to escape. Even the Southerner whose faith is uncertain still fears, she says, "that he may have been formed in the image and likeness of God."[27]

O'Connor's profound affinity for Southern Protestant Christianity in no way lessened the intensity of her Catholic vision. We learn from her letters that, throughout her adult life, she attended Mass frequently, said her daily prayers out of the Missal, and read from the theology of Thomas Aquinas for twenty minutes every night before bed. Her deeply sacramental Catholicism made her critical, therefore, of the fierce faith that she otherwise admired. Without the sacraments, she lamented, Southern Protestants have nothing to guide their belief or curb their heresies. What remains is only "a do-it-yourself religion . . . which I as a Catholic find painful and touching and grimly comic."[28] Yet it was finally sympathy and not disdain that O'Connor felt for these untutored and unsacramental cousins in Christ. She wrote to a fellow Catholic that her theological differences with literal-minded Southern Protestants were "on the nature of the church, not on the nature of God or our obligation to him."[29]

The most significant accord between O'Connor's Catholic orthodoxy and Southern fundamentalist faith is to be found in their common understanding of the divine activity in its relation to human freedom. They share the mutual conviction that God's prevenient grace can become efficacious only with our freely willed acceptance of it. There is a synergistic union between the divine self-offering and our human acceptance of it: "God rescues us from ourselves, if we want him to."[30] Conversion is the name for this all-determining decision. For the backwoods prophet or the small-town Protestant preacher, the call to repentance and salvation is addressed primarily to the unconverted. For O'Connor the Catholic, it is the already-baptized Christian who must constantly be converted to absolute reliance on the mercy of God. "All voluntary baptisms are a miracle," she writes, "and stop my mouth as much as if I had just seen Lazarus walk out of the tomb." She explains why: "I suppose it's because I know that [baptism] had to be given me before the age of reason, or I wouldn't have used any reason to find it."[31] Yet the Catholic O'Connor agrees with the revivalist Protestant that grace is far from irresistible, and that the saints persevere only by faith's constant renewal through drastic decision.

For the Catholic O'Connor no less than for the Protestant evangelist, the inevitability of death provides the inescapable summons to this final choice. In their encounter with life's ultimate limit, her characters are made to discern how their own souls are weighed in the divine balances and their eternal destinies finally fixed. The stakes are not merely high; they are absolute. In that last earthly assize, O'Connor believes, we return to God the gifts that we have multiplied by faith, thus trusting that he will receive us into his glory; or else we admit to having squandered our talent and wasted our substance, thus facing the pain of absolute loss. In "A Good Man Is Hard to Find," the murderous Misfit speaks the comic truth when he says (of the self-regarding Grandmother he has just killed) that "she would of been a good woman . . . if it had been somebody there to shoot her every minute of her life."[32] Had death been perennially present to remind the Grandmother of her total dependence on God, she would have trusted in his grace rather than her own gentility.

The conviction that the ultimate issue of our lives depends on our own reception or rejection of God's grace is the central premise of Flannery O'Connor's work. In one of her very last book reviews, she declares that the chief mission of the church is to ensure "salvation for every person who does not refuse it."[33] More arresting still is her insistence that "man [is] so free that with his last breath he can say *No*."[34] In unison with the entire Catholic tradition, O'Connor affirms that the efficacy of God's grace depends, in a radical way, upon our own receiving or rejecting of it. Henri de Lubac's work is a typical example of the synergistic theology which O'Connor espouses:

> If God had willed to save us without our own co-operation, Christ's sacrifice by itself would have sufficed. But does not the very existence of our Saviour presuppose a lengthy period of collaboration on man's part? Moreover, salvation on such terms would not have been worthy of the persons God willed us to be. God did not desire to save mankind as a wreck is salvaged; he meant to raise up within it a life, his own life. The law of redemption is here a reproduction of the law of creation: man's co-operation was always necessary if his exalted destiny was to be reached, and his co-operation is necessary now for his redemption. Christ did not come to take our place—or rather this aspect of substitution refers only to the first stage of his work—but to enable us to raise ourselves through him to God.[35]

For all her stress upon our human cooperation with divine grace, Flannery O'Connor cannot be construed as a Pelagian. Not one of her characters makes an autonomous decision for or against the grace of God—as if the summons to belief were something one could take up or lay aside at one's own convenience. With Augustine and the central tradition of Western theology, she knows that the act of faith is itself enabled by prevenient grace. Indeed, the divine pressure weighs so heavily upon a character like Francis Marion Tarwater (in *The Violent Bear It Away*) that his will appears to have been coerced. The boy makes a final defiance of God by drowning the imbecile child he had been commissioned to baptize. Yet even as Tarwater immerses the child in the waters of death, he finds himself—to his surprise and fury—uttering the baptismal formula.

Against his most fundamental freedom of will, it may seem, he has been made to do the will of God. For O'Connor, this imperious urgency at work on young Tarwater is but the universal presence of God that pervades all of human and natural life. It may encircle but it does not cancel his freedom. Indeed, it is the boy's deeper and truer will that, in performing the baptism, triumphs over his merely superficial (but still murderous) self-will.

From the classic Catholic tradition of natural theology, O'Connor derives her unswerving conviction that humanity is inevitably inclined toward God. Original sin and the Edenic Fall have distorted and perverted, but not extinguished, humanity's God-hungering and God-thirsting nature. Hence O'Connor's allegiance to the ancient theology of *exitus et reditus*—the inexorable procession of all things from God, and their equally ineluctable return to him. God is at once the Archer and the Target of all creation. The cosmos is the arrow which God flings primordially out of himself and eschatologically back unto himself. The arc of God's grace describes a gigantic circle wherein the divine goodness encompasses everything. Sin is the free deflection of life's true trajectory, causing the will to turn in upon itself (*incurvatus in se*) in hideous parody of the divine circularity. Salvation, by contrast, is to will what God wills. By the grace made available through Christ, we are enjoined to align our lives with the pattern of the universe itself.

To conform the sinful human economy to the graceful heavenly order is to undertake a gradual and disciplined process of obedience and sacrifice. It is a lifelong penance for the individual, and a history-long endeavor for the race. As the creek-preacher says in O'Connor's story called "The River," the blood of Jesus is a great Stream "full of pain itself, pain itself, moving toward the Kingdom of Christ, to be washed away, slow, you people, slow as this here old red river water around my feet."[36] The vain little schoolgirl in "A Temple of the Holy Ghost" embodies the problem of patient faith more comically: "She could never be a saint, but she thought she could be a martyr if they killed her quick."[37]

So to speak is to declare the real difference between Flannery O'Connor's Catholicism and the Protestantism of the classic Reformers. For both Luther and Calvin, salvation is the divine assurance *from* which the forgiven sinner lives by grace. For O'Connor, by contrast, it is the goal *toward* which the struggling soul journeys in fear and trembling. The quandary of salvation gives her stories their real plot interest. One comes to expect that, sooner or later, the protagonists will be laid low by the whammy of grace. Yet their response—embittered like Hulga Hopewell's, astonished like Ruby Turpin's, grateful like O. E. Parker's—is never predictable. The one sure thing is that divine grace must first manifest itself destructively before its recipients can respond to it positively. The fact that God's mercy shatters before it rebuilds gives Flannery O'Connor a deep affinity with Southern fundamentalist Protestantism; it also causes her to modify classic Catholic thought into her own kind of negative natural theology.

III. A Negative Natural Theology

Flannery O'Connor is a strange mixture of pre- and post-Vatican II Catholicism. Like many of her main theological mentors, especially Jacques Maritain, she has an almost intemperate regard for the modern world as an unrelieved spiritual wasteland. She shares with such antithetical writers as T. S. Eliot and C. S. Lewis the conviction that modernity represents a surrender of the grand medieval synthesis of biblical faith and classical culture. Yet, despite this disdain for modernity, O'Connor accepts the post-Vatican II conviction that the Christian must discern the workings of grace even in secular culture, and thus that modern Catholic theology must be done no longer from "above"—in pre-Vatican II style—but from "below." God does not impose his grace upon the world as a divine invader; he operates within the world as its deepest life. Her fiction assents to Karl Rahner's expression of what has become the nearly unanimous conviction of post-Vatican II theology: "God in his free grace, from the very beginning and always and everywhere, has communicated himself to his creation as its innermost energy and works in the world from the inside out."[38]

Everything human is potentially divine. All matter is sacred. The divine descent in Christ is met by an equally determined human ascent in longing for God. Hence O'Connor's enthusiasm for the work of Teilhard de Chardin, especially his conviction that the natural order itself is a sacramental reality that reveals the godward urgency and movement of every living thing. Asked to name the most important book published in the three decades prior to 1960, O'Connor nominated Père Teilhard's *The Phenomenon of Man*. She describes his work as "a scientific expression of what the poet attempts to do: penetrate matter until spirit is revealed in it."[39]

Teilhard's daring attempt to reconcile Darwinian evolution with Christian revelation demands comparison, in her view, with Thomas Aquinas's magnificent reconciliation of biblical revelation and Aristotelian reason. They both stand within the Christian humanist tradition that sees grace as completing and perfecting nature. O'Connor applauds Teilhard for his denial that the Christian life consists in an ascetic escape from the material world of the senses. Rather than being "purified" of matter, believers are summoned to sanctify and supernaturalize the concrete existence they have been given by God. The world is not a finished order which God beholds and acts upon from afar, but a continuing process in which human beings are called to become cocreators with

God. Humanity, she quotes Teilhard as saying, "is very far from being fully created, neither in its individual developments nor, above all, in the collective terminus toward which it is directed. . . ."[40]

In Teilhard's view, Jesus Christ is the definitive historical manifestation of this transcendent *telos*, the Omega point toward which the entire evolutionary process is moving. His suffering love reveals the cosmic purpose that unites all things into a stupendous wholeness. Teilhard can thus speak of Christianity, almost ecstatically, as "nothing more than a 'phylum of love' within nature."[41] With even greater cheerfulness, he is able to envision evil and suffering as endemic to the creative process and not as an absurd disruption of it:

> Indeed, if we regard the march of the world from this standpoint (i.e., not that of its progress but that of its risks and the effort it requires) we soon see, under the veil of security and harmony which—viewed from on high—envelop the rise of man, a particular type of cosmos in which evil appears necessarily and as abundantly as you like in the course of evolution—not by accident (which would not much matter) but through the very structure of the system. A universe which is involuted and interiorised, but at the same time and by the same token a universe which labours, which sins, and which suffers.[42]

Teilhard's Christianized Hegelianism issues in a breezy optimism about the human prospect. It is summarized in the watchword which O'Connor borrowed as the title for one of her stories: "Remain true to yourselves, but move ever upward toward greater consciousness and greater love! At the summit you will find yourselves united with those who, from every direction, have made the same ascent. *For everything that rises must converge!*"[43] Readers of Flannery O'Connor's fiction may find difficulty reconciling its dreadful violence with the Teilhardian conviction that human life constitutes "a movement of convergence in which races, people and nations consolidate one another and complete one another by mutual fecundation."[44] O'Connor's story with a Teilhardian title concerns a human convergence that is far from fecundating. The protagonist Julian is filled with a moral arrogance that converges violently with his mother's racial pretension to produce her anguishing death and his own wrenching condemnation. O'Connor's stories do not seem at all consonant, therefore, with Teilhard's vision of an ever-increasing renovation of the earth through a new scientific mysticism. They envision, on the contrary, an enduring struggle of good against evil that can be temporarily won with the intervention of transcendent grace, but that shall finally end only with an apocalyptic closure.

This apparent contradiction can be at least partially resolved by recalling that, in O'Connor's original endorsement of Teilhard, she likened his view of the world to a poet's. Thinking surely of her vocation as a writer, she remarked that "the poet, whose sight is essentially prophetic, will at once recognize in this immense [Teilhardian] vision his own."[45] From Thomas Aquinas by way of Jacques Maritain, O'Connor derived the notion that poet and prophet are united not by the ethical purity of their lives but by the keenness of their spiritual sight. "The prophetic vision," she declares in a letter, "is a quality of the imagination."[46]

The artist and the religious seer are linked by their penetrating perception of what nature and history signify. "The prophet," she says, "is a realist of distances." Prophetic vision "is a matter of seeing near things with their extensions of meaning and thus of seeing far things close up."[47] Poets possess this prophetic insight, she believes, because they fathom their own inward depths, tapping what O'Connor calls "the underground springs" of the spirit. The artist makes "a descent through the darkness of the familiar into a world where, like the blind man cured in the gospels, he sees men as if they were trees but walking."[48]

This passage reveals, as clearly as anything in all of Flannery O'Connor's work, the intensity of her Catholic humanism. To plumb the depths of human and natural life is, in her view, to discover the irrepressible instinct for God that animates the entire cosmos. If human life were not fatally perverted, there would be a fundamental accord between Christ and culture. By their very nature, all things human are expressions of the Holy. The divine condescension in Christ is intended to be united with the human aspiration for ultimacy to form a magnificent synergism between heaven and earth. It is not surprising, therefore, that O'Connor should have marked—with obvious approval—this passage from Teilhard's *The Divine Milieu*:

> By virtue of the creation and still more of the Incarnation, *nothing is profane* here below on earth to him who knows how to see. On the contrary, everything is sacred to him who in every creature distinguishes the particle of the elected being that is subjected to the attraction of Christ in the process of consummation.[49]

Yet while Teilhard remains highly positive about the prospect of human cooperation with the divine purpose, O'Connor is decidedly negative. Her dark estimate of human sinfulness is closer to Augustine than to Teilhard. O'Connor shares with the Bishop of Hippo the conviction that humanity has inverted its divine allurement and turned its natural magnetism for God perversely upon itself. Yet even this denial of God constitutes a strange affirmation of the divine reality. The Misfit (in "A Good Man Is Hard to Find") is obsessed with the very Christ whom he cannot believe. He complains that "Jesus thown ever thing off balance." Christ "was the only One that ever raised the dead," he protests, " . . . and

He shouldn't have done it."[50] The Misfit will not accept his devine re-demption because it would exact too great a toll in service to a Master other than himself. If Jesus "done what He said," he bitterly concludes, "then it's nothing for you to do but thow away everything and follow Him, and if He didn't, then it's nothing for you to do but enjoy the few minutes you got left the best way you can—by killing somebody or burn-ing down his house or doing some other meanness to him."[51]

Such cornpone nihilism is a demonstration of O'Connor's Augus-tinian conviction that all human acts, even murder and mayhem, are prompted by a strange love for God. O'Connor agrees with Jacques Mar-itain that the most heinous deed is the expression of a twisted urge for the Holy: "For the will goes by nature to the good as such, to pure good-ness. From the moment it acts, it acts for a final end which can only be a good that fulfills it absolutely . . . . Thus every will, even the most per-verse, desires God without knowing it. Although a will can choose other final ends, opt for other loves, it is still and always God that it desires under aberrant forms and contrary to its own choice."[52]

Only in this special Augustinian sense does O'Connor affirm Teilhard's discernment of a historical and biological movement of all things toward God. Her poetic eye, unlike his, finds at the core of human life a desperate repudiation of the grace that seeks to redeem the world. Yet even this willful refusal to believe and trust God provides O'Connor inherent evidence that humanity does not exist desperately unto itself. Were there "nothing but nothing," as Hulga Hopewell insists in "Good Country People," the world's angry unbelievers and complacent Chris-tians would not be so anxiously self-justifying. "If there were no God," says Chesterton, "there would be no atheists." We would be happily con-tent in our unbelief and half-belief. That we cannot rest at ease in our false Zion is proof, for O'Connor, that God is alive and at work—albeit negatively and subversively—in modern secularity no less than in ear-lier so-called "ages of faith."

This conviction that God manifests himself in absence as well as presence marks O'Connor's kinship with modern theologies done from "below" rather than "above." One does not need to begin with God's self-revelation in Christ in order to discover divine grace permeating all of creation. The divine Reality pushes up through everything, but most especially through the human spirit. Christ serves to confirm and clarify what God is already and everywhere doing in the world—namely, offer-ing himself to humankind in gracious self-surrender. In accord with such post-Vatican II theologians as Karl Rahner and Hans Küng, O'Con-nor insists that anyone who lives with an attitude of fundamental trust—toward both the neighbor and the world—lives implicitly by grace. By the same token, anyone whose life constitutes a massive act of distrust thereby denies the grace of God. In an age of apostasy, it is the latter response that O'Connor is compelled to remark. Unlike Rahner, she is not concerned chiefly with those "anonymous Christians" who heroically bear the weight of glory that presses so mercifully upon them. Hers is a *negative* natural theology determined to reveal how reluctant is our willingness to shoulder the yoke that is easy and the burden that is light. As her stories attempt literarily to demonstrate, it is the devil who "teaches most of the lessons that lead to self-knowledge."[53]

IV. The Necessity of Satiric Wrath

O'Connor's near obsession with apostasy gives her work much of its polemical character. She is convinced that our century is uniquely damned in its denial of the Holy. "If you live today," O'Connor writes to the anonymous "A," "you breathe in nihilism. In or out of the Church, it's the gas you breathe."[54] Our age's unprecedented unbelief makes her doubt whether "anything so sane" as Christian humanism is any longer possible.[55] There can be no supernatural completion and perfection of a human culture that has become grimly unnatural. Unlike ancient Terence and modern Whitman, neither of whom found anything human alien to them, O'Connor confesses that she is "alien to a great deal."[56] In one of her most nearly misanthropic declarations, she compares us moderns to poultry which, through genetic manipulation, has been shorn of its wings in order to produce more tender-breasted white meat. This new soft-chested species O'Connor describes as "a generation of wingless chickens, which I suppose is what Nietzsche meant when he said God was dead."[57] Lest such belligerency seem too harsh, one needs only to hear the voice of Jacques Maritain to understand that O'Connor is not alone in her fury:

> If I am anti-modern, it is not by personal taste, certainly, but because modern self-complacency, the offspring of the anti-Christian revolution, obliges me to be so by its spirit; because it itself makes opposition to the human patrimony its distinctive characteristic, [because it] hates and despises the past and adores itself, and because I hate and despise this very hating and despising and this spiritual impurity. . . .[58]

Like Maritain, O'Connor believes in what Dante calls *buona ira*, the salutary wrath which seeks to laugh folly to scorn. Unlike Kierkegaard and Percy, she makes a direct assault on her secularist readers— whether they be churchgoing unbelievers like Ruby Turpin or more conventional atheists such as Hulga Hopewell. Her art also runs counter to Kierkegaard and Percy in its attempt to serve as a medium of divine revelation. Not by preaching and the sacraments alone can, in O'Connor's view, the Christian faith be conveyed. She believes that the literary imagination, when rightly used, can also be a vehicle of saving grace. In her view, therefore, the church has no exclusive purchase on proclamation of the Gospel. On the contrary, O'Connor wants her fiction to serve as a propadeutic to the Gospel, making belief once again believable amidst this unbelieving age.[59] This task cannot be accomplished, she insists, by demonstrating the shared values that unite secular and religious people, nor by offering winsome portraits of the spiritual life. Indeed, the word *Christian* itself has lost most of its original force. "It has come to mean anyone with a golden heart. And a golden heart," O'Connor adds starchily, "is a positive interference in the writing of fiction."[60]

O'Connor contends that a modern secular audience needs prophetic confrontation rather than priestly comfort. "You have to push as hard," she declares, "as the age that pushes against you."[61] A writer with her concerns must make a baleful rather than a cheering witness. The reader must be shown how desperate life is apart from grace, how impossible it is to live without mercy, and thus how necessary it is to face the reality of God. In one of her most arresting declarations, O'Connor says that violent attack is the only means of approaching an unsympathetic audience: "You have to make your vision apparent by shock—to the hard of hearing you shout, and for the almost blind you draw large and startling figures."[62]

The grotesque is the artistic means O'Connor employs for this necessary act of theological aggression. Having little use for literary realism, she is drawn, instead, to the fiction of Poe and Hawthorne with its unblinkered acknowledgement that human life is besieged by the "power of blackness." Through willful exaggeration of both plot and character, O'Connor seeks to demonstrate the disfiguring effects of evil. Her fiction thus constitutes a veritable gallery of the maimed and misshapen: a self-blinded preacher and child-drowning prophet, a cretinous deaf mute and a one-armed con man, a wooden-legged philosopher and a club-footed delinquent. In wanting so outrageously to mirror our fallen condition, O'Connor does not desire merely to horrify her audience. She seeks also to show her freaks and invalids on their way to health and wholeness—indeed, to salvation. They all undergo fearful awakenings to the grace they have tried to deny. And they thus begin, if only minimally, to live the life of faith.

Yet the question remains whether, in her concern to trace the lineaments of evil, O'Connor does not become dualist in her theology and macabre in her art. She has such great respect for the satanic that, like Milton, she has been accused of belonging to the devil's party unawares. This allegation was first made by the novelist John Hawkes, who argues that O'Connor's stark images—a cat-faced baby, a woman who resembles a cedar fence post, a grandfather with Jesus hidden in his head like a stinger—reveal her secret nihilism. Her characters are real, Hawkes insists, only in their stunning ugliness and perversity. And when she allows the devil to speak, especially in *The Violent Bear It Away*, his sarcastic countrified voice sounds identical to O'Connor's own.[63]

O'Connor replies, not without heat, that she is able to perceive the demonic because she has first discerned the Holy. In her view, nothingness has meaning only in relation to a final plentitude, evil only as a perversion of the good, ugliness only as a disfigurement of beauty. Without such transcendent criteria, O'Connor argues, she would indeed fall prey to the fascination of abomination, an engrossment with the macabre for its own sake. To mitre and sceptre Satan—as Hawkes accuses her of having secretly done—is not to take him seriously at all, but to turn him into a Mephistophelean imp of the perverse, "an impeccable literary spirit whom [Hawkes] makes responsible for all good literature."[64] Satan can be clearly and realistically apprehended, O'Connor insists, only as God unmasks his deceit and deflects him to "ends other than his own." It is not the triumph of the demonic, therefore, that chiefly interests her. She is primarily concerned about its defeat: "More than in the Devil I am interested in the indication of Grace, the moment when you know that Grace has been offered and accepted. . . ."[65]

These clear statements of authorial intention might once have sufficed as definitive guides for interpreting O'Connor's work. Yet postmodern literary criticism denies the premise that an author is the best critic of her own work. Especially in its "deconstructionist" phase, this criticism argues that every piece of literature has a counterintention to the one put forth by the author, and that the aim of the wise reader is thus to discern how the work of art undermines itself. It is not the creative act of the author's mind alone that counts. The subversive power of language overtakes the writer's intention and suborns it to purposes of its own. Being itself a binary system of signs and countersigns, language has meaning only in light of what it does not mean. Lurking beneath every thing signified by speech is also the thing *not* signified. Every statement implies its counterstatement, every affirmation its refutation. No longer, therefore, is the literary work to be regarded as a finished thing with a specifiable meaning determined by the author's intention. It is, instead, an irreducibly ambiguous and multivalent text whose inner void the critic must lay bare, revealing thereby "the illusoriness of meaning, the impossibility of truth and the deceitful guiles of all discourse."[66]

The French critic André Bleikasten has performed such a "deconstruction" of Flannery O'Connor's fiction. O'Connor tries but inevitably fails, he argues, to overcome the reversibility and plurisignificance of all literature. She is a dishonest writer, Bleikasten maintains, for being so orthodox a Christian. "He who knows, or thinks he knows, the answers even before the questions have been asked, may be sincere as a person but compromises his honesty as a writer."[67] Bleikasten is unimpressed with O'Connor's claim that her orthodoxy enables her to discern the demonic only as it is unmasked by grace. He argues that her work is unintentionally dualistic, that the voice summoning her characters belongs indistinguishably to God *and* Satan, and thus that the demonic triumphs in the same act whereby her characters are seemingly brought to faith.

> In O'Connor, grace is not effusion but aggression. It is God's violence responding to Satan's violence, divine counterterror fighting the mutiny of evil. The operations of the divine and the demonic are so disturbingly alike that the concept of God suggested by her work is in the last resort hardly more assuring than her Devil.[68]

Unlike Hawkes, Bleikasten does not argue that O'Connor is a closet atheist, but that her fiction asserts, against her will, the demonic truth she attempts to deny. O'Connor sets out to reveal how wondrously her characters are freed by the grace of God, only to demonstrate inadvertently how fully they are enslaved to domineering parent figures. Bleikasten charges O'Connor with the same "heresy" that Jean-Paul Sartre finds at work in the fiction of François Mauriac. Like Sartre, Bleikasten insists that the putative divine reality has no place in fiction because such transcendent truth would deny the inexorable relativity and indeterminacy of human life. The autonomy of Flannery O'Connor's characters is violated, argues Bleikasten, because their free will is overwhelmed by the divine will:

> O'Connor's heroes are indeed sleepers: they traverse life in a dreamlike state, and with the sense of impotence and anxiety experienced in nightmares. They go through the motions of revolt, but their violent gestures toward independence are all doomed to dissolve into unreality. They are nothing more than the starts and bounds of a hooked fish. Tarwater and Motes both act out scenarios written beforehand by someone else.[69]

Bleikasten concludes that O'Connor is a misanthrope whose "theology holds nothing but scorn for everything human." She is a Christian whose belief in God's incarnate goodness has been corroded by "a very modern sense of the absurd." Hers is thus a fallen world visited by a grace so horrific as to be indistinguishable from "the vertigo of the *nada* and the encounter with death."[70]

For all the wrongheadedness of his interpretation, Bleikasten (like Hawkes before him) has struck an exposed nerve in O'Connor's work. There is, in fact, an implicit and deeply troubling dualism in her fiction. The demonic and the divine assault O'Connor's characters with comparable violence. I contend that this near duality of the Holy and the

Satanic derives not from O'Connor's unwitting concession to modern absurdity, as Bleikasten argues, but from her deepest theological convictions—namely, that God's Word is first wrath before it is forgiveness, a divisive No before it is a binding Yes, an evisceration before it is a restoration. Her fiction is premised, as we have seen, on the necessity of satiric attack. She wants to shake modernity by the nape of its neck, to knock flat the barred door of secular denial and misunderstanding. Such truculence is not, I maintain, a violation of secular propriety and civility—much less of literary ambiguity and plurisignificance—so much as it is a misreading of the Gospel's undialectical comedy of grace. O'Connor the Christian writer does not always discern that God's resounding Yea always precedes and follows his devastating Nay. In her better fictional moments, however, she acknowledges the glad Pascalian truth that we seek God only because—in Israel and Christ—he has already found us.

V. Dualism Defeated and Comedy Triumphant:
The Violent Bear It Away

It must be conceded that O'Connor's public statements are often quasi-dualistic, and that her fiction at times suspends characters between the virtually equal powers of God and Satan. "Our salvation," she declares, "is a drama played out with the devil, a devil who is not simply generalized evil, but an evil intelligence determined on its own supremacy."[71] Like other advocates of the Fortunate Fall, O'Connor insists that the Incarnation would be meaningless apart from sin, death, and the devil. Life would lack moral complexity and artistic interest if evil did not exist. "Drama usually bases itself on the bedrock of original sin, whether the writer thinks in theological terms or not. . . . For this reason," O'Connor explains, "the greatest dramas naturally involve the salvation or loss of the soul. Where there is no belief in the soul, there is very little drama."[72]

In the modern world, O'Connor contends, the outcome of this struggle for the spirit's ultimate allegiance remains very much in doubt, if not surely lost. She agrees with C. S. Lewis that Western culture after the Enlightenment is "enemy-occupied territory." "Christianity," Lewis writes, "agrees with Dualism that this universe is at war. But it does not think this is a war between independent powers. It thinks it is a civil war, a rebellion, and that we are living in a part of the universe occupied by the rebel."[73] O'Connor speaks of modernity in similar terms—as "territory held largely by the devil."[74] For her as for Lewis, it would seem, Satan is not only the "prince of this world" but also its very king.

This incipient dualism is especially noticeable in *The Violent Bear It Away*. Francis Marion Tarwater is compelled to decide between two stark metaphysical alternatives: either his Satanic inner "friend" who urges him to throw off his prophetic calling and live solely for himself, or else the God who has summoned him to proclaim the Mercy that hurries terribly near. Young Tarwater is stretched between these quasi-dualistic alternatives outwardly no less than inwardly. He must also decide between the two figures who vie for his spiritual loyalty: Rayber the atheist school psychologist, and Old Tarwater the untutored man of God. Like Dante, O'Connor regards hell as the inversion of purgatory if not also of paradise. The divine and the demonic are twin destinies which bear down upon all of her characters, compelling them to an either/or moment of truth. They are pushed toward either a radical act of obedience and faith, or an equally drastic choice of defiance and unbelief.

O'Connor does not share the Protestant Reformers' confidence that predestining grace also becomes efficacious and sanctifying grace. "The doctrine of double predestination," she observes, "is a strictly Protestant phenomenon." She complains that it destroys human freedom, cuts the nerve of moral choice, and thus renders life dramatically uninteresting. "I don't think literature would be possible in a determined world."[75] Freedom derives, in her view, from our occupancy of the middle ground between antithetical alternatives. Were the demonic not a positive possibility, we humans would remain the puppets of God. Not for nothing does O'Connor place the following quotation from Cyril of Jerusalem as the headnote to her first collection of stories: "The dragon is by the side of the road, watching those who pass. Beware lest he devour you. We go to the father of souls, but it is necessary to pass by the dragon."

Nowhere is O'Connor's idea of demonically-induced freedom more forcefully demonstrated than in the character of Rayber. As a school counselor trained in modern psychology, he is the compleat secular humanist. He insists that all metaphysical claims can be traced to psychological origins. Working from such premises, he has made a reductionistic analysis of his elderly uncle and backwoods prophet named Tarwater. Rayber's conclusion is predictable enough: the old man, lacking any sense of his own importance, projected his desire for worldly significance into theological terms and "called himself."[76] This despite the fact that the aging prophet has lived anything but a life of religious ease, having suffered isolation, persecution, and wrenching self-doubt in obedience to his prophetic calling.

Rayber has a reductionist regard for religion because he is convinced that the universe is without order and meaning. His imbecile son Bishop provides conclusive proof that the universe is absurd. If there is a God, Rayber cynically reasons, then Bishop is surely formed in his image. Yet Rayber is no mere atheist. Given Flannery O'Connor's view that every human being has an irrepressible longing for God, it is not surprising that Rayber should be a reverse mystic laboring to suppress his hunger for the Bread of Life. In order to silence his secret desire for grace, Rayber becomes a monk of the secular life. Taking hell with the same violence wherewith others seize heaven, Rayber refuses all worldly comforts lest they soften his stiff will to unbelief: "He slept in a narrow iron bed, worked sitting in a straight-backed chair, ate frugally, spoke little, and cultivated the dullest of friends."[77]

Rayber's suppressed thirst for the Water of Life manifests itself in an unaccountable love for his "useless" son Bishop. This cretinous child is the chink in Rayber's secularist armor, the single entry point for an "irrational" desire to care for something other than himself. Rayber's regard for Bishop is an opening, moreover, to a "horrifying love" that spreads outward to encompass the whole cosmos:

> Anything that [Rayber] looked at could bring it on. . . . It could be a stick or a stone, the line of a shadow, the absurd old man's walk of a starling crossing the sidewalk. If, without thinking, he lent himself to it, he would feel suddenly a morbid surge of the love that terrified him—powerful enough to throw him to the ground in an act of idiot praise.[78]

Flannery O'Connor is often chided, especially by humanists, for her unsympathetic portrait of Rayber. Like Sheppard in "The Lame Shall Enter First," he is portrayed as a coldly inhuman secularist, and thus as a travesty of the many compassionate souls who do not believe in God. No one, to my knowledge, has pointed out that there is also a theological objection to O'Connor's characterization of Rayber. O'Connor misses the real essence of the secularist mind by depicting him as a stymied mystic. Atheists are rarely characterized by their terror at love's morbidity, as Rayber calls it. His mystical kind of love for the whole earth often becomes the ideal surrogate for true belief in the transcendent and redeeming God. O'Connor would have done better to portray Rayber not as a suppressed mystic but as the advocate of Dover Beachism. The chief secular substitute for transcendent faith lies, I believe, in an Arnoldian absolutizing of human affection.

O'Connor's quasi-dualist theology is also evident in her dramatization of Rayber's final life-defining decision, his defiance of the soul's natural appetite for grace. He keeps it in abeyance by staying astride the narrow ridge between the "idiocy" of religious belief and the emptiness of metaphysical nihilism. Yet, as an either/or existentialist, Rayber vows to elect nothingness rather than God if he is ever compelled to make the bitter choice. Such a decision is forced upon him when Young Tarwater drowns Rayber's retarded child. Rigidly faithful to his terrible pledge, Rayber steels himself in unconcern upon hearing his son's dying scream.

He fights against the grace of God, says O'Connor, and "wins."[79] Rayber's physical collapse would seem, therefore, to be a descent into that spiritual vacuity—the pain of eternal loss—which he has freely chosen as his eternal lot. Yet O'Connor holds out the extratextual hope that Rayber's breakdown, like Mrs. McIntyre's at the end of "The Displaced Person," may reveal "that he is not going to be able to sustain his choice."[80]

It was Augustine who first questioned the validity of a "freedom" that chooses sin rather than faith. If one enslaves oneself to evil, he asks, what does it mean to say that one acts freely? The truly free choice, Augustine concludes, is the choice of obedience and trust in God. "What kind of liberty, I ask, can the bondslave possess, except when it pleases him to sin? Accordingly, he who is the servant of sin is free [only] to sin. And hence he will not be free to do right, until, being freed from sin, he shall begin to be the servant of righteousness. And this is true liberty. . . ."[81]

Sin, in this reading of it, is not something we commit by the plain fiat of willed decision. As the metaphor of the Fall suggests, we plummet into evil while charging ahead in the name of good. We are in direst danger, Reinhold Niebuhr says, not when we are at our moral worst but when we are at our moral best—when we have done the good and right thing, and then think well of ourselves for having done it. The sinister subtlety of sin lies more in its ethical high-mindedness than in its defiant wickedness. Seldom is it anything so obvious as a fist-shaking denial of God or an overt contest between the counterforces of good and evil. Milton's Satan is not a full-fledged sinner so much as he is a late-adolescent sprite when, like Rayber, he apostrophizes Evil, abjuring it to "be thou my good."

Flannery O'Connor falls prey to such a misreading of sin, at least in part, because of her overreaction to the modernist heresy. So great is the vehemence of contemporary unbelief that it must be answered, in her view, with an equally vehement faith. In *The Violent Bear It Away* she reveals how Young Tarwater comes finally to see the futility of unbelief, and thus to seize the brass ring of his redemption with the same vigor that Rayber uses to spurn it. O'Connor thus interprets Jesus' saying in Matthew 11:12 ("From the days of John the Baptist until now, the kingdom of heaven suffereth violence, and the violent bear it away") as the summons to an inward penitential violence of affirmation that makes atonement for modernity's colossal indifference to the things of God.[82] Grace no longer completes and perfects nature; it must be wrenched by force from the unnatural thralldom of modern apostasy.

This reading does its own violence to the biblical text—if not to its literal sense, then surely to its gracious message. Seldom if ever does Scripture depict the Kingdom as an either/or possibility to be commandeered with truculent acceptance or rejection. Modern Catholic commentators are eager to qualify the old interpretation of this passage as a call for Christians to be as violent in their seizure of the Kingdom as the Reign of God demands. The Greek word for "snatching" or "carrying off" (*harpazousin*) is a term used to describe the taking of plunder—not for receiving the heavenly prize.[83] The "violent" ones referred to in Matthew 11:12 can hardly be regarded as the followers of Christ. W. G. Kümmel argues, on the contrary, that they are the Satanic forces who assault God's Kingdom in attempting to rob humanity of it.[84] In nearly all of Jesus' parables, Kümmel contends, the Reign of God "comes certainly and without human effort."[85] We do not take it by force, and it does not impose itself violently upon us. On the contrary, it arrives surprisingly, graciously, even comically.

Flannery O'Connor acknowledges this glad fact in the conclusion to *The Violent Bear It Away*. When Francis Marion Tarwater returns to the remote farm where he committed his initial act of repudiation—having burned down the house with the intention of cremating his dead uncle inside it—he does not encounter the dread judgment he so fully expects and deserves. The farm house does indeed lie in ashes, but the corn crop has been freshly laid by. More remarkable still is the newly mounded grave with a crude cross planted at the head of it. Young Tarwater thus learns that that his attempt to incinerate his great-uncle had been thwarted by a black farm worker named Buford. He had dragged the huge old prophet from the burning building and given him the reverent burial he had requested. This radical bestowal of grace lifts from the rebel youth an otherwise onerous burden of guilt and despair. Tarwater's suppressed longing for God is not what saves him from spiritual destruction; he is freed by an utterly unbidden and unmerited gift of grace.

The boy prophet is delivered from calamity only after he is first sodomized by a man dressed in lavender. In horror at the evil which has both literally and figuratively raped him, Young Tarwater at last identifies the inner "friend" who has been urging him to throw off his holy calling. It is Satan himself, "the sounder of hearts," as O'Connor calls him in "The Lame Shall Enter First."[86] Once again she dramatizes her dubious notion that nothing less than demonic illumination can enable the dawning of true spiritual light. Furious at the violation he has suffered, Tarwater purges the Satanic presence with fire, setting the woods ablaze in a violent repudiation of the evil he has committed.

In the end, however, it is not the vision of evil and its fiery purgation that springs Tarwater free. He is released from sin's thrall by another vision altogether. Albeit reluctantly, he comes to see that the stark cross over Old Tarwater's grave is not a knife driven into the heart of the sinful world. This treelike emblem of Christian faith has roots, Tarwater discerns, to encompass all the dead and branches to shelter all the living. The fire the boy has set also betokens the ardor of God's forgiveness rather than the heat of his destruction:

> He knew that this was the fire that had encircled Daniel, that had raised Elijah from the earth, that had spoken to Moses and would in the instant speak to him. He threw himself to the ground and with his face against the dirt of the grave, he heard the command. GO WARN THE CHILDREN OF GOD OF THE TERRIBLE SPEED OF MERCY.[87]

No longer is there a dread either/or set before Young Tarwater. He faces only a single positive choice—to heed the sacred summons that his great-uncle had bequeathed to him and that his bitter fury has been powerless to cancel. Despite the novel's title, and perhaps even contrary to O'Connor's intention, Tarwater does not violently bear away the Kingdom of God. His citizenship in that City not made with hands is granted to him as a total gratuity. It lays claim to him ever so much more than he seizes hold of it. He has no need, therefore, to make Hazel Motes's wretched self-immolation at the end of *Wise Blood*. No human payment is sufficiently generous to acknowledge the divine largesse. This deliverance costs Tarwater less than nothing because, as sheer grace, it is completely free.

So incomparable a gift may, in the receiving of it, exact of Tarwater his very life. As O'Connor observes in a letter, the boy prophet is setting his face toward a modern Jerusalem, and there "the children of God . . . will dispatch him pretty quick."[88] Yet even if Tarwater dies rather than lives to accomplish his mission, it is the mission that counts more than the sacrificial death. His calling is to awaken sleeping sinners to the joyful news that they are the children of God. This is a message of hope to be happily proclaimed, not a minatory word to be hurled like a stone against a depraved secular world. Tarwater announces a Mercy that hurries graciously near. Its speed is terrible only in the Gospel sense that Jeremy Taylor voiced in the seventeenth century: "[God] threatens terrible things if we will not be happy."[89]

At its best, Flannery O'Connor's fiction announces these comic tidings. Her satiric anger at modern apostasy tempts her to an almost dualistic regard for evil as the concomitant of good. Her stories end, characteristically, in horrifying moments of grace that leave her characters devastated as much as they are renewed and reborn. Only as the power of God literally kills them are they made alive to the reality of their redemption. Yet in the ending of *The Violent Bear It Away*, as in several other works written near the end of her life, O'Connor largely overcomes this dualistic tendency in her work. Especially in her stories dealing with the irony and paradox of Southern racial relations—"The Artificial Nigger," "The Enduring Chill," and "Revelation"—we are shown a splendid comic vision of the grace that does not lead to perpetual grief so much as to infinite rejoicing.

6

FLANNERY O'CONNOR AS A COMEDIAN OF POSITIVE GRACE

In her concern for the grand religious questions, Flannery O'Connor may seem to have ignored the clamant social issue of her own time and especially of her own place—namely, the race question. Her publishing career (1952–64) spans the same decade that brought the Supreme Court decision banning segregated education; the defiance of that ruling in the public schools of Little Rock and New Orleans, and at the universities of Alabama and Mississippi; the black bus and lunch counter boycotts in Montgomery and Greensboro; the bombing of Negro Baptist churches in Birmingham; the slaying of civil rights workers in Mississippi and Alabama; the harassment of Clarence Jordan's interracial Koinonia Farms in O'Connor's own native state; the rise of Martin Luther King, Jr., as the nation's chief civil rights leader; and the massive protest march of blacks and whites from Selma to Montgomery. Although she did not live to witness the murder of Dr. King and the attendant racial riots of 1968, O'Connor had more than enough raw evidence to indicate that the single greatest moral imperative of her age was the liberation of black people from their American, and particularly their Southern, bondage.

Yet Flannery O'Connor did not respond to this racial crisis in the accepted literary ways—signing manifestoes, inviting black writers to her home, joining public demonstrations. Not did she take up the case against segregation in her fiction. Eudora Welty, by contrast, wrote a furious response to the senseless slaying of Medgar Evers, the Negro dentist and Mississippi civil rights leader. In an *Atlantic* short-story entitled "Where Is the Voice Coming From?" Welty excoriated Governor Ross Barnett and other Mississippi officials. It was their legal recalcitrance, Welty suggests, that inspired racist goons to murder Evers. One could cite similar examples of literary courage in the work of other Southern writers, especially Robert Penn Warren and William Styron. From every quarter of civilized thought and opinion, there arose a cry of protest against Southern race prejudice and violence. That Flannery O'Connor did not join this nearly unanimous chorus of condemnation is a fact that must be accounted for if her fiction is to be regarded as redemptive in the truly comic sense.

O'Connor's racial views must not be sanitized. She was nobody's liberal in matters social and political. Even if liberalism cannot be made the prescribed norm for fiction, neither can literary creativity atone for retrograde racial attitudes. Nor is there any antiseptically pure criticism that is able to skirt the moral implications of art. It is not ideas alone which have ethical and political consequences; so do works of fiction. To ask whether Flannery O'Connor is a racist writer is not, therefore, to raise an extraliterary question. Indeed, the real test of her comic vision lies precisely here—whether she penetrated to the heart of the racial issue that vexed her age, or whether she retreated into an oblivious laughter. I contend that, far from dodging the racial question, O'Connor analyzed it acutely. She discerned those spiritual subtleties that the gross moralism of the time was prone to ignore. Convinced as she was that God's grace overthrows all our conventional judgments and expectations, O'Connor turned her critical eye on the enlightened rather than the benighted. There she detected what the age was eager to deny—that the sins of the supposedly righteous were altogether as egregious as the evils of the obviously wicked.

The fact not previously noted is that O'Connor's most convincing comic stories all have to do with race relations. In dealing with the subject about which she may have seemed illiberal, she became a truly redemptive writer. Instead of furiously satirizing contemporary unbelief, she proved herself a comedian of positive grace. In "The Artificial Nigger," she discloses that white prejudice and black suffering have not only a causal but also a curative relation. Negro anguish is not only *produced by* racial hatred; it can, when redemptively borne, be a *cure for* that very malice. In "The Enduring Chill," O'Connor reveals again how surprisingly the moral categories can be reversed. By the strange paradox of human sin and divine grace, racists can become generous while liberals remain mean-spirited. In "Revelation," O'Connor shows how Ruby Turpin's racial pride is not only a violation of the Negroes she pretends to love, but also of the faith which she complacently professes. Anything less than the mercy of God would petrify her racial pride into an embittered recalcitrance. All of the protagonists in these stories discover—as rarely happens in O'Connor's work—that God's grace is not first and last a devastating negation but an edifying affirmation. Only the cooling succor of divine mercy can reveal the real heat of God's wrath. So unbounded is the forgiveness bestowed upon these characters that, in the light of God's clemency alone, do they discern the hugeness of their sin.

I. The Complex Irony of Racial Manners

Flannery O'Connor did not share, as we have noted, the official liberalism of the American literary and intellectual establishment. The chief liberal concern of her day was to break the shackles of racial discrimination that had held Southern blacks in ancient thrall. That this was not also O'Connor's main aim does not for a moment imply any sympathy with the White Citizens Councils organized to preserve "segregation forever"—as their sloganeers liked so immodestly to claim. But she does refuse to endorse the easy moralizing that the racial revolution afforded many liberal politicians and religionists. Thus does she describe the civil rights workers—who descended upon the South after leaving behind great bastions of unofficial segregation in their own Northern cities—as possessing a "moral energy that increases in direct proportion to the distance from home."[1]

It should come as no surprise that O'Connor has little sympathy for John Howard Griffin's celebrated journey across the South impersonating a Negro, thus revealing the evils of racial hatred while gathering material for his much-controverted book of 1960, *Black Like Me*. O'Connor says that Griffin would be welcome to visit her in Milledgeville, but only if he did not appear "in blackface."[2] One's racial identity is not something, in O'Connor's view, that can be put off and on with either an actor's skill or dermatological devices; it is the given fact of one's existence. "If I had been one of them white ladies Griffin sat down by on the bus," O'Connor writes with countrified acerbity, "I would have got up PDQ preferring to sit by a genuine Negro."[3]

O'Connor's regard for the black writer James Baldwin may cause even more consternation. To a friend wanting to bring him to the O'Connor farm for a visit, O'Connor replies that she would be willing to see Baldwin in New York but not in Milledgeville: "I observe the traditions of the society I feed on—it's only fair. Might as well expect a mule to fly as me to see James Baldwin in Georgia."[4] This seems a peculiarly uncourageous declaration on O'Connor's part—as if she were bound by social convention, and as if her fiction were not a sustained satire of other evils endemic to her native milieu.

Perhaps the real reason O'Connor did not want to see Baldwin is that she thought him a poseur. He uses his deserved reputation as a writer, she argues, to engage in public attitudinizing. "Baldwin can tell us what it feels like to be a Negro in Harlem but he tries to tell us everything else too." It is Baldwin's moral posturing, not his racial identity, that O'Connor will not abide. She admires Martin Luther King, by contrast, for his spiritual integrity, for his willingness to do "what he can do and has to do." For O'Connor there is but a single standard of civility and decency that measures blacks and whites alike. "My question is usually, would this person be endurable if white? If Baldwin were white nobody would stand him for a minute." She confesses that she prefers Cassius Clay, despite his conversion to Islam and his taking the name Mohammed Ali. Brashness befits a boxer, one must presume, as it does not become a writer. "Cassius is too good for the Muslims."[5]

Such angular opinions might make one conclude that O'Connor was an unreformed apologist for all things Southern. Quite to the contrary, she was never enthralled by what W. J. Cash calls "the moonlight, magnolias, and mint-julep" version of Southern history. Far from thinking the Civil War (or the Late Unpleasantness, as diehard Southerners still call it) to be a glorious defense of traditional values, O'Connor regarded it as a supremely boring subject. Nor did she read *I'll Take My Stand*, the Southern manifesto of the Vanderbilt Fugitives, until late in her short life. Even then, she did not accept their agrarian dream of a medievalized South freed from the supposed evils of machine production and a market economy.

Yet O'Connor did share the Agrarians' contempt for Menckenism—the notion that the postwar South was a cultural and religious backwater whose benighted condition was best revealed in the Scopes trial. Like Allen Tate and Andrew Lytle, she scorned the received liberal dogma that the "Southern problem" constituted the chief national ailment. According to such conventional wisdom, the entire Republic could have been assured progress and prosperity if only the South could have conquered its inveterate poverty, illiteracy, and racism. The Southern problem, in this view, is its alienation from mainline America. The problem with the South, O'Connor replies crustily, is that "it is not alienated enough, that every day we are getting more and more like the rest of the country, that we are being forced out not only of our many sins, but of our few virtues as well."[6]

The South's "many sins" are revealed preeminently in its racial injustice. That O'Connor does not devote more of her literary energy to limning the evils of Southern racism may signify a certain moral complacency on her part. It may also mark, on the contrary, her kinship with Hawthorne, Melville, James and other American writers who have been troubled by the nation's subtler sin—namely, spiritual naivety. One needs only to read a literary critic like R. W. B. Lewis (*The American Adam*), a historian like C. Vann Woodward (*The Burden of Southern History*), or a theologian like Reinhold Niebuhr (*The Children of Light and the Children of Darkness*) to discern that there is, in fact, a shadowy underside to the sunny American optimism about human nature and destiny.

Our nearly boundless natural resources, the moralistic character of our religious life, the vastness of our geographical space, the newness of our political institutions—all of these often combine to inspire Americans with the naive conviction that every human problem has a human solution. Many of our best writers and thinkers and preachers are convinced, on the contrary, that this wondrous freedom to right old wrongs and to seek a perpetual freshness of life constitutes, paradoxically, a pernicious problem of its own. It makes Americans prone to underestimate the crookedness of human character, to ignore the tragedy of human existence, and thus to fall prey to fatuous schemes for human health and happiness.

Flannery O'Connor belongs to this dissident tradition in American thought and letters. Her chief concern lies not with bigots who demean and degrade Negroes. She is exercised, instead, about the naive righteousness which besets enlightened people like herself and her readers. It was a more courageous act, in O'Connor's opinion, to write about liberal self-satisfaction than about racist injustice. In this regard she shares the concerns of the medical psychologist Robert Coles. He came to the South during the sixties in order to witness the effects of the racial revolution on children. What at first perplexed Coles is that the worst victims of racial and social injustice—poor whites and blacks alike—often cared more about Jesus and the Bible than they sought their own political liberation. Gradually he came to discover that the same people who had their eyes set on heaven also had their feet planted more securely on the earth than did many of their secular counterparts.[7]

Coles cites the testimony of a black woman who, fifteen years later, recalled the Mississippi Summer Project of 1964. She reveals, with arresting candor, the surprising truth that deliverers can be as arrogant as oppressors, that secular liberators can be as complacent as the most bigoted racists, and that idealist utopias which ignore the facts of sin and redemption can be as repressive as the old systems of discrimination and segregation:

> You'd tell your faith to the civil rights folks, and they'd look down at the ground, and they'd wait you out, with a bad, bad look in their eyes, and their mouths turned down, and they'd be scratching the back of their necks, until you've stopped talking, so they could start talking. And boy, did they talk! I told one white boy from up there in Massachusetts that he's going to be a minister of Christ the Lord one of these days, when he sees the light. But he didn't like what I said, no he didn't. He just went on, telling me what should be, and telling me about the heaven we're going to have here in this country, if we'd only turn everything around.
>
> Well, there's no heaven but in Heaven. And if you don't know

that, you don't know much. That's what I believe. Of course, you can't tell some people much. They want to tell *you everything.* That's how it goes: they come here to help us, but oh, if we don't bow and scrape to their every idea, then they lose patience with us, and I declare, you see them looking at you no different than the sheriff, and the people at the post office, and like that. Scratch some of the white civil rights people and you have the plantation owners. Scratch some of the black civil rights people, and you have white talkers. . . .

. . . Some of these people who came down here, they believed in men, not angels; and sure enough, they didn't believe in God. It's their choice, but it might have been nice if they'd said to me: it's your choice. Instead, they felt sorry for us. Jesus Christ didn't feel sorry for the people He went and attended to. He loved them. He healed them out of love. He wanted them on their feet and the equal of other people. He didn't want them to pray to other people. He wanted them to thank God. On your knees to him; "yes, sir," and "yes, ma'm" to the white folks, and hello to your colored brethren, but to God Almighty, it's a prayer, and it's please dear Lord, please, and I've failed again. There's a big difference between Him and us, that's for sure.[8]

This anonymous black woman from Mississippi is worth citing at length because she detects, in her marvelously unsophisticated way, the same ironies that Flannery O'Connor seeks to uncover in her fiction. Against the intellectual and moral grain of her cultured audience, O'Connor reveals an evil—ethical self-righteousness—that is far subtler than injustice and far deeper than prejudice. The further irony is that Southern religion and Southern manners—the two things that seemed to be the worst buttresses of the evil order—are potentially liberating and ennobling as their secular replacements are not.

Among the South's "few virtues," Flannery O'Connor regarded its sense of manners as chief. There is something immensely salutary, she believed, about the South's proverbial graciousness and politeness, its civility and propriety. Manners are not, of course, the equivalent of morals. Suavity of appearance and correctness of deportment may mask, in fact, a terrible cruelty of mind and heart. At their best, she insists, manners are a secular acknowledgement of original sin. They are a means of setting limits upon the vagaries of our fallen condition and the depredations of human self-interest. To behave courteously, therefore, is to accord fundamental respect to those one does not perhaps like, to preserve a necessary distance between people who are divided by preference and experience, and to assure privacy even among the closest of companions.

Given her high regard for the venerable Southern sense of manners,

O'Connor is predictably gradualist in her attitude toward racial integration. She did not believe that the past could be erased and history remade from the start. She thus feared that the old injustice done to Negroes would be overcome only at the loss of the civility which had helped to assuage the original evil. Yet she hoped that, slowly and patiently, Southern blacks and whites would discover, through a newly developed social propriety, a means for living together in mutuality no less than equality:

> The uneducated Southern Negro is not the clown he's made out to be. He's a man of very elaborate manners and great formality, which he uses superbly for his own protection and to insure his own privacy. . . . The South has survived in the past because its manners, however lopsided or inadequate they may have been, provided enough social discipline to hold us together and give us an identity. Now those old manners are obsolete, but the new manners will have to be based on what was best in the old ones—in their real basis of charity and necessity. In practice, the Southerner seldom underestimates his own capacity for evil. For the rest of the country, the race problem is settled when the Negro has his rights, but for the Southerner, whether he's white or colored, that's only the beginning.[9]

This paradox—that the evil system of segregation was ameliorated by an admirable civility and formality among both blacks and whites—is the background to Flannery O'Connor's stories that deal with race relations. They are not moralistic accounts of blacks breaking free from the fetters of racist injustice, nor of whites being condemned for their inability to accept the brave new world of racial equality. They are stories about the grace that makes clowns of us all, liberals no less than reactionaries, the old no less than the young, the genteel no less than the uncouth. In these works, unlike much of O'Connor's other fiction, her characters are not turned into mere fools; they are made fools for Christ.

Their foolishness is exposed only in order that they might acquire that jesting kind of freedom the early followers of Saint Francis embodied; they were called *le jongleur de Dieu*. These first Franciscans were the merry jugglers and tumblers of God because they had seen the whole world upside down, as if standing on their heads. From their topsy-turvy perspective, the world no longer appeared to be an immovable mass, rocklike and self-sufficient. It was now seen as a fragile orb, something delicately floating and literally dependent, hanging like a ball by the thread of God's grace. G. K. Chesterton observes that, once he had been revolutionized by the call to evangelical poverty, Francis could no longer take pride in his native Assisi as the city too strong to be thrown down. Instead, "he would be thankful to God Almighty that it had not been dropped; he would be thankful to God for not dropping the whole cosmos like a vast crystal to be shattered into falling stars."[10] It is such a joyfully revolutionized perspective that Nelson and Mr. Head acquire at the end of "The Artificial Nigger." There they discover that white mockery and black endurance can form an emblem of the crucifixion itself, and thus of a forgiveness that transcends mere equity.

II. The Redemptive Grace of Black Suffering: "The Artificial Nigger"

"The Artificial Nigger" seems, at first, to be a story about the origins of Southern race hatred. A child named Nelson is being reared by his Grandfather Head in the north Georgia hills where Negroes are a rare sight. Mr. Head has duly warned the boy that "niggers" are alien creatures whom, sooner or later, he must learn to "handle." Yet Mr. Head wants Nelson to acquire this mastery only under one condition: that the child's dependence upon his foster parent be fixed rather than broken. The grandfather has thus prepared to take the boy on a trip to Atlanta in order to teach him this lesson of total reliance. Mr. Head tells young Nelson that Negroes are identifiable by their blackness, not warning him that Negro skin color includes the various shades of brown. Hence the grandfather's perverse delight when the boy fails to detect his first "nigger." On a train bound for the city, young Nelson encounters a Negro who is not only light-skinned but dignified in gait and mien. He is hardly a forbidding figure. Asked by his grandfather what he has seen, the child replies with naive truthfulness that he has met "a man."[11] It is our universal and indivisible humanity that characterizes us, O'Connor would seem to argue, and not the petty distinctions of race and class.

Such an obvious humanitarian gospel Flannery O'Connor has absolutely no interest in perpetuating. She aims at subtler and deeper truth—the truth, namely, that original sin divides not only the races but also the nearest of kin. Though united in their scorn for Negroes, Nelson and Mr. Head are set against each other in an Adamic struggle of wills, each seeking to dominate the other. They share a spiritually fallen nature, and not an innocent Rousseauian humanity corrupted by artificial social distinctions. In their mad struggle for power over each other, therefore, they lose their way amidst the maze of city streets, circling about in a veritable Inferno of frustration. Dantesque images abound, as this perverted Vergil proves a poor guide for this would-be pilgrim.

Perhaps for the first time in his life, young Nelson is made to feel hopeless and homeless and parentless—in the ultimate no less than the immediate sense of these words. Gladly would he cast himself upon anyone who might show him mercy. A huge Negro woman looming up at a doorsill thus becomes for Nelson—all his racial stereotypes notwithstanding—a virtual Madonna:

He stood drinking in every detail of her. His eyes traveled up from her great knees to her forehead and then made a triangular path from the glistening sweat on her neck down and across her tremendous bosom and over her bare arm back to where her fingers lay hidden in her hair. He suddenly wanted her to reach down and pick him up and draw him against her and then he wanted to feel her breath upon his face. He wanted to look down and down into her eyes while she held him tighter and tighter. He had never had such a feeling before.[12]

That this is an erotic and maternal longing no less than a religious desire, O'Connor is not reluctant to reveal. Her sacramental imagination is unembarrassed at discovering the Holy in the profoundest recesses of human need. Yet Nelson is far too recalcitrant, even as a child, to acknowledge the motions of grace that course through him. To admit his terrible insufficiency, especially to a despised Negro, would put Nelson at a fearsome disadvantage against his grandfather. They are engaged in a contest of wills that, at all costs, Nelson wants to win. Old Mr. Head has brought him to Atlanta in order to break his desire for an independent life, to prove to the child what an inhospitable place the city is, and thus to make him return to their rural home in total submission.

In order to subdue Nelson completely, the grandfather plays a wicked trick on him. He hides himself from Nelson when, in exhaustion, the child falls asleep beside the city street. He hopes that, upon awakening in desperation, Nelson will be made forever thankful for the "rescue" the grandfather plans miraculously to perform. Instead, Nelson is driven wild with fear upon finding himself literally alone. In his fright and fury, he flattens an elderly grocery-carrying woman, who screams for the police and threatens to sue the skulking Mr. Head when he sheepishly appears at the scene.

Then follows the pernicious act of betrayal that threatens to lock grandfather and grandson in permanent alienation. Mr. Head denies to the gathering crowd that he has any relation to Nelson: "This is not my boy," he said. "I never seen him before."[13] Discerning how deeply he has wounded the child, how egregiously he has abrogated his own duty, the grandfather is rent with guilt. He is ready, like Nelson standing before the black Madonna, to admit his awful fault and his terrible need of rescue. But Nelson will have nothing of it: "His mind had frozen around his grandfather's treachery as if he were trying to preserve it intact to present at the final judgment." It matters not to Nelson that his grandfather has abjectly admitted his plight: "Oh Gawd I'm lost! Oh hep me Gawd I'm lost."[14] Now that the boy has the upper hand in their struggle for dominance, nothing can make him yield.

Such is O'Connor's vision of sin's hellish circle. The will-to-power replicates itself endlessly, every act of hostility generating still another, until the warring parties are locked in self-perpetuating hatred. The fundamental alienation dividing Nelson and Mr. Head makes them emblems of sin's unbreakable grip: the wrong one has suffered becomes the occasion for committing a worse wrong of one's own. Nelson prizes, paradoxically, his grandfather's treachery. It becomes his weapon for beating the old man into submission. This involuted personal distrust is the primordial ground and root, O'Connor suggests, of that social distrust which issues in racial hatred. Grandfather and grandson are bent on the same control of the other—each wanting to depend upon no one but himself—that leads one race to seek dominance over another. Whether at the racial or personal level, sin is fundamentally a denial of community.

Self-transcending evil can be broken only by transcendent Goodness. Yet the grace of God can be bidden no more than the wind can be ordered to change direction: it bloweth where it listeth. Nelson and Mr. Head thus undergo a liberation that occurs apart from any will or work of their own. It happens as, still lost and angrily unreconciled, they come upon a Black Sambo figurine standing on the lawn of an elegant suburban house. This particular symbol of black servility and white domination is doubly degrading. It is neither carrying a lantern nor grasping a horse's reins but holding a piece of watermelon. Unaccountably, the statue has not been kept in decent repair. Instead of looking like one of the carefree, watermelon-eating "darkies" that Southerners once believed Negroes to be, this black man lurches helplessly forward. One eye is chipped, and the watermelon has turned brown:

> It was not possible to tell if the artificial Negro were meant to be young or old; he looked too miserable to be either. He was meant to look happy because his mouth was stretched up at the corners but the chipped eye and the angle he was cocked at gave him a wild look of misery instead.[15]

Nelson and Mr. Head find themselves transfixed before this broken tribute to Southern racial arrogance. "They stood gazing at the artificial Negro as if they were faced with some great mystery, some monument to another's victory that brought them together in their common defeat. They could both feel it dissolving their differences like an action of mercy."[16] Though meant to signal the triumph of whites over blacks, this pathetic figurine unites a young boy and an old man in admission of their shared defeat. The miserable Sambo has this mysterious power because its patient wretchedness attests to something more startling than human injustice. It points to a suffering that has been willingly, patiently borne. Though Nelson and Mr. Head have perhaps never seen a crucifix, the old man recognizes its secular counterpart immediately:

Mr. Head stood very still and felt the action of mercy touch him again but this time he knew that there were no words in the world that could name it. He understood that [mercy] grows out of agony, which is not denied to any man and which is given in strange ways to children. He understood it was all a man could carry into death to give his Maker and he suddenly burned with shame that he had so little of it to take with him. He stood appalled, judging himself with the thoroughness of God, while the action of mercy covered his pride like a flame and consumed it. He had never thought himself a great sinner before but he saw now that his true depravity had been hidden from him lest it cause him despair. He realized that he was forgiven for sins from the beginning of time, when he had conceived in his own heart the sin of Adam, until the present, when he had denied poor Nelson. He saw that no sin was too monstrous for him to claim as his own, and since God loved in proportion as He forgave, he felt ready at that instant to enter Paradise.[17]

This is one of the most controverted passages in all of Flannery O'Connor's work. It has met both literary and theological opposition. Critics who value "showing" over "telling" complain that O'Connor has condescended to *explain* what the action of mercy means, when she should have been content simply to *dramatize* it. Secular readers object, on the other hand, to the use of overt theological language in a work of fiction that, up to this point, has had no expressed concern with religious matters. Both of these criticisms are misplaced. Though deliberately avoiding confessional language, O'Connor has made it clear from the beginning that Nelson and Mr. Head are engaged in a struggle whose proportions are absolute, and that their lostness is more metaphysical than geographical. For O'Connor to make explicit what has previously been implicit is, far from being an act of deceit, a deed of commendable clarification. "What I had in mind to suggest with the artificial nigger," O'Connor explains in a letter, "was the redemptive quality of the Negro's suffering for us all."[18] At the risk of sounding homiletical, therefore, O'Connor has her narrator voice her own concerns.

Yet it is not only literary clarity that O'Connor seeks to provide. Authorial judgment is necessary for a profounder reason. The bestowal of divine mercy, being transcendently given and humanly unearned, cannot be narrated in strictly literary terms. The grace of God—as surprising gift rather than earnest acquisition—comes as an action *upon* a character even more than it is a movement *within* a character. O'Connor's problem arises not from the fact that the forgivness of sin is too inward and invisible to admit of outward analogue, but that it is too unanticipated and undeserved to fit within the accepted categories of human motivation. Nelson and Mr. Head have been blessed beyond all adequacy of human showing *or* telling.

Neither in art nor in life is the mercy of God a ready panacea for all ills. O'Connor refuses thus to sentimentalize this scene by having young boy and old man fall upon their knees in a saccharine makeup of their differences. On the contrary, Mr. Head tries to brush off his experience of mercy with a wisecrack about white folks now having so few Negroes around that they need an artificial one to remind them of what they look like. The boy also lapses into platitudes about the city's being a place that he is glad to have visited once but that he hopes never to see again. Neither Nelson nor his grandfather has plumbed the significance of the Suffering Servant who has encountered them in the decaying lawn statue. In their unrepentant racism, they perhaps still regard Negroes as alien creatures who must be "mastered" by their white "superiors." They are very far, therefore, from being permanently humbled by their vision of Negro suffering as an earthly metaphor of their divine redemption.

Yet something unalterable *has* happened to them. Neither man nor boy will be able to exorcise the image of the bent and harrowed Sambo who stopped them in their repetitive cycle of sin and who opened them to the way of reconciliation. They have encountered the grace that dissolves all personal and racial hatred. A grandfather and a grandson who were bound for the hell of self-perpetuating spite have been placed before the paradisal gates of forgiveness. So great a turning, even if they do not fully comprehend or gladly seize it, remains irreversible. Past that particular entrance to damnation, Nelson and Mr. Head shall not have to travel again. Every conversion, said C. S. Lewis, begins with a blessed defeat. Comically and blessedly, if also embryonically and minimally, their conversion has begun.

III. Why Smart People Can't See Straight: "The Enduring Chill"

The mark of a Christian satirist like Flannery O'Connor is the willingness to turn her comic wrath upon herself, lampooning the foolishness of her own kind. To direct one's scathing wit at one's own failures and foibles is to discern the beam in one's own eye rather than searching for motes in the eyes of others. O'Connor's most stunning stories are therefore devastating self-studies. Julian of "Everything That Rises Must Converge," Hulga Hopewell of "Good Country People," and Asbury Fox of "The Enduring Chill" are all literary versions of herself. Yet they are deliberate theological confessions rather than unwitting psychological disclosures. To a friend wanting to read her stories as inadvertent autobiographies, O'Connor replies wisely—if also tartly—that real fiction discloses "something about life colored by the writer, not about the writer colored by life."[19]

O'Connor knows, of course, that one's experiences give one's life its essential hue. Her simple but oft-neglected point is that art constitutes far more than a transcription of either outward events or inward attitudes; it is a literary transformation of merely personal or private experience into something significant and publically apprehensible. Art is a means of seeing, O'Connor repeatedly affirms. Like Joseph Conrad, she wants to make the reader perceive the world in all its wonder and mystery. The plainness and directness of O'Connor's style—unlike the orotund rhetoric that characterizes so much Southern fiction—is an attempt to give us a clear perspective, to make art a lens through which we can see things afresh.

O'Connor's parent-hating invalids and ne'er-do-well nihilists are not, it should be clear, the author's unintentional self-portraits. On the contrary, they are revelations of the soured self that must have been Flannery O'Connor's perpetual temptation. Given her consignment both to an early death and to living within the narrow world she had meant to escape, O'Connor was surely tempted to become, like so many of her protagonists, an arrant ingrate scorning her mother, her past, and her God. The miracle of her life is that she escaped this bitter condition. The comedy of her characters' lives is that they too are brought—albeit painfully—to overcome the demonry of filial ingratitude. They are made to discover the fact that reverence for one's parents can be the beginning of wisdom.

Like Fyodor Dostoevski, O'Connor finds keen theological significance in the relation of children to their fathers and mothers. These immediate and ineluctable sources of our lives are also the emblems of our ultimate Parent. We are immediately joined to our fathers and mothers, O'Connor believes, as we are originally and finally related to God. Not because of their intrinsic goodness are human parents the surrogates of God. They may, in fact, be quite unworthy of our devotion. Yet they remain our progenitors in the most irrefragable way: in every sense of the word, they have *produced* us. We owe to them, therefore, a fundamental fealty, whatever their limits and however small their desert. To deny this proximate obligation, O'Connor agrees with Dostoevski, is to make an ultimate denial as well. Parricide—even in its subtlest spiritual expression—is always deicide.

O'Connor's sons and daughters have many nonphysical means for slaying their parents, but the chief of them is racial: they reject the parent's retrograde scorn for Negroes by demonstrating their own moral enlightenment. For a white Southerner steeped in racial prejudice and discrimination, sometimes even in racial hatred, it is a tremendous liberation to discover that black people are one's equals rather than one's inferiors. For a white Alabamian or Texan to accord Negroes their rightful place, both personally and politically, is to be freed from a terrible burden of guilt and wrong. Yet with every moral advance there are attendant evils. The worst of them is to take pride in one's own moral advancement. The sin of false righteousness becomes especially pernicious when it is linked with filial ingratitude. What begins as a genuine deliverance from racial prejudice often becomes the occasion, in O'Connor's fiction, for an egregious denial of one's most fundamental origins and obligations. Many of O'Connor's emancipated sons and daughters fall prey to this subtle evil, ending in a worse state than the moral myopia from which they have escaped. Only as they are made to repent their spurious goodness do they discover a strange set of paradoxes: that enlightened children may become mean-spirited in their ethical liberation, while benighted parents may remain generous despite their racism.

O'Connor gives this comic reversal of conventional truth its most persuasive fictional embodiment in "The Enduring Chill." Like "Everything That Rises Must Converge"—a story with a similar theme—it reflects Flannery O'Connor's own situation. The narrative concerns a twenty-five-year-old son named Asbury Fox who, against his literary ambition, has been forced by sickness to return from New York City and to live in his small-town Southern home under his mother's care. Yet it is unlike "Everything That Rises" in being a much more redemptively comic story. The humor here is, on the whole, benign rather than malign; and the reader is not so much appalled as cheered by Asbury's comeuppance. Whereas the arrogant Julian is virtually annihilated by grace, Asbury's false pride is conquered—until the final doom is lowered upon him—by needling humor rather than scathing satire.

Most of O'Connor's stories are narrated in straightforward chronological fashion: from a decisive beginning, through a complicated middle, to a conclusive end. But in this story, as in "Judgement Day," she resorts to a series of complex flashbacks that serve to reinforce both the comedy and the theology (if one may so speak) of the plot. Asbury has come home from New York City to his native Timberboro with the intention of dying. He wants to make a searing indictment of his mother and his town by yielding up his life as a sensitive lamb sacrificed on the altar of their aesthetic crudity and racial narrow-mindedness.

We learn from one of these narrative recollections that Asbury has written a Kafkaesque letter to his mother, accusing her of having squelched his talent with her busy-bodied interference. Though he claims to have forgiven her this slaughter of his art, he hopes that the letter (when read after his death) will chill her into the awful and enduring truth about herself:

If reading it would be painful to her, writing it had sometimes been unbearable to him—for in order to face her, he had had to face himself. "I came here to escape the slave's atmosphere of home," he had written, "to find freedom, to liberate my imagination, to take it like a hawk from its cage and set it 'whirling off into the widening gyre' (Yeats) and what did I find? It was incapable of flight. It was some bird you had domesticated, sitting huffy in its pen, refusing to come out!" The next words were underscored twice. "I have no talent. I can't create. I have nothing but the desire for these things. Why didn't you kill that too? Woman, why did you pinion me?"[20]

The verbal irony here is too heavy-handed. Asbury's self-pitying assertions are all totally counter to the truth: he has not faced the facts about himself; his home life was not enslaving; and his talent was not crushed beneath the rock of his mother's insensitivity. Yet Asbury is so totally deluded about himself and his world that his pretense is more funny than monstrous. Unlike Julian sitting in his mental bubble—a demon of righteousness peering out in search of moral evil that he can pounce upon—Asbury is a mere ninny. In so depicting his literary preciosity, O'Connor has discerned what she elsewhere ignores: the fact that evil is silly before it is serious. It deserves not the blows of iron-fisted satire so much as the needle prick of wit. "The best way to drive out the devil," said Luther, "if he will not yield to texts of Scripture, is to jeer and flout him, for he cannot bear scorn."[21]

The successive flashbacks that uncover the circumstances of Asbury's illness have this same comic effect. Rather than mercilessly obliterating his pretense, they comically expose it. In the first of these narrative returns to the past, we discover that Asbury had affected a cool indifference toward the prospect of his anticipated death. He could even make his supposed dying the topic of cocktail conversations. The (unintentionally) funniest of these encounters occurred after Asbury and his New York friends had attended an expensive lecture on Vedanta Hinduism. Asbury would have sneered, of course, at the idea of attending a free worship service or Sunday School in his own Methodist tradition. Having heard the highfalutin discourse, Asbury and his fellow sophisticates gather to discuss—as if it were a matter of intellectual debate—the youth's prospective death. Their leader is a complacent nihilist named Goetz, a youth whose face is "purple-splotched with a thousand indignations."[22] His aim, like Hulga Hopewell's in "Good Country People," is to convince his audience that the universe is a cosmic void. Always citing someone else rather than speaking his own word, Goetz declares to the "dying" Asbury that "salvation . . . is the destruction of a simple prejudice and no one is saved."[23]

At the same lofty lecture on Vedanta, Asbury had met Father Ig-

natius Vogle, S.J. The Timberboro youth is drawn to the Jesuit priest because he seems to share Asbury's own unillusioned attitude toward life.
He asks the priest, therefore, to answer Goetz's Sartrean-cum-Hindu
nihilism. Wanting not to offend but to ingratiate, the priest avoids an
overt and plain-spoken witness to this crowd of culture vultures. He
chooses, instead, to state his faith in abstractions that he hopes will appeal to his urbane listeners. But Goetz and his harem of girls dressed in
saris are not moved to Christian faith. For Father Vogle's credo is hilariously affected: "There is," the priest said, "a real probability of the New
Man, assisted, of course," he added brittlely, "by the Third Person of the
Trinity."[24]

This is, of course, exactly what Asbury wants to hear—not the radically Good News of sure salvation in Christ Jesus, but the mere
humanistic possibility of a "New Man." Such putative religious renewal, being vague and unspecific, appeals to Asbury precisely because
it impinges so little on the actual circumstances of his life. Nor is it the
gift of the Holy Ghost that the sickly Asbury desires; he prefers the
barest "assistance" of a God who is at best a numerical abstraction.
Hence Asbury's later insistence that his mother not bring the local
Methodist minister to his bedside. It goes without saying that Asbury
has no final confessions to make. He wants a suave Jesuit like Ignatius
Vogle to join him for a literary tête-à-tête. Accommodating as always,
Mrs. Fox finds the only priest available, the uncultured and hard-of-hear-
ing Father Finn. Asbury is extremely disappointed at having been sent a
mere diocesan priest, and so he decides to challenge the man's cultural
knowledge. He wants to learn whether the old priest knows about those
writers who (presumably like Asbury himself) have left behind their
childhood faith for the higher summons of art. Thus does Asbury ask the
elderly cleric what he thinks of Joyce. "Joyce who?" replies Father Finn
with splendid literary obliviousness.[25] When told the Irish writer's full
name, Father Finn admits that he has never met him, and gets down to
the real business at hand: Asbury's eternal salvation.

There follows a side-splitting exchange in which Father Finn rudely
catechizes the stunned Asbury, who tries vainly to parry his questions
with sophisticated answers that the half-deaf priest ignores. Pressing
right to the heart of the matter, Finn asks whether Asbury has difficulty
with moral purity and whether he ever prays:

> "The artist prays by creating," Asbury ventured.
> "Not enough!" snapped the priest. "If you do not pray daily,
> you are neglecting your immortal soul. Do you know your cate-
> chism?"
> "Certainly not," Asbury muttered.
> "Who made you?" the priest asked in a martial tone.

"Different people believe different things about that," Asbury said.

"God made you," the priest said shortly. "Who is God?"

"God is an idea created by man," Asbury said, feeling that he was getting into stride, that two could play at this.

"God is a spirit infinitely perfect," the priest said. "You are a very ignorant boy."[26]

Asbury's ignorance is not only spiritual but also racial. In his desire to transcend the moral confines of his Southern upbringing, Asbury had tried to write a play about Negroes. That his interest in Negroes is more theoretical than real is revealed by his means of gathering material for the play. Asbury spent a week working at the family dairy in order to fathom, firsthand, the plight of black people. He has a social scientific approach to "the Negro," as he abstractly describes the problem.

An artist used to an effete existence, Asbury finds the demands of farm life far from his liking. He is kicked by a cow and does not venture back into the barn. Yet Asbury's moral posturing is not in the least crippled. His mother's regulations for operating the dairy are, in his eyes, mere bigoted attempts to oppress the Negro workers. Asbury especially resents her refusal to let the hired hands drink the nutritious milk that is so abundantly available. He sets out, therefore, to free two Negro workers named Randall and Morgan from bondage to his mother's racist rules. He seeks, in fact, to turn the fresh warm milk into the means for a secular communion with the deprived blacks.

The uneducated Randall and Morgan prove far smarter than the cultivated Asbury. They know that unpasteurized milk can cause serious illness. Yet not wanting to presume upon the prerogatives of their white "master," they freely let him drink the milk. But they themselves politely refuse to join in. The reader thus understands, as Asbury does not, the incisive moral wit of the Negroes' exchange:

"Howcome you let him drink that milk every day?" [asked Morgan].

"What he do is him," Randall said. "What I do is me."

"Howcome he talks so ugly about his ma?"

"She ain't whup him enough when he was little," Randall said.[27]

Asbury's moral arrogance is most funnily exposed when, thinking himself to be nearing the end, he insists that his mother invite the black helpers to his room for a final farewell. Randall and Morgan are put at an utter loss by this violation of the accepted racial zones. They have never been at a white man's bedside before, and they do not know how to act there. Because Mrs. Fox's sense of propriety had put them somewhat at ease, they are socially bereft once Asbury orders her out of the room: "The two Negroes looked as if their last protection had dropped away." In a gesture of forced friendship, Asbury offers them a cigarette, only to have Randall pocket the whole pack. Nor will they bid Asbury the desired valediction; instead, they mockingly assure him of his health. "You sho do look well," Randall says to the Asbury who insists he is dying. "Yessuh," he concludes, "I speck you ain't even sick."[28]

In depicting Asbury as a foolish and presumptuous son, Flannery O'Connor does not sentimentalize Mrs. Fox by making her the embodiment of maternal wisdom. Like nearly all the other mothers who appear in O'Connor's fiction, she is a woman who shares the prejudices of her place and the attitudes of her time. Why anyone would write a play about Negroes escapes her understanding. Regarding Asbury's desire to discover the concerns of black people, she declares acidly that "their interests were in doing as little as they could get by with."[29] Yet there is nothing vicious about this typical Southern mother. On the contrary, her miscomprehension of the literary life is so hilariously total that the reader finds it amusing rather than offensive. She believes, for example, that if her son would do real work—rather than mere writing—he would not be so emotionally overwrought. Yet if he remains bent on a literary career, she wishes that he would write "a book about down here. We need another *Gone With the Wind*." He can always put the Civil War in his works, she assures Asbury, if he wants to make them long. Failing that, he can take the easier tack of writing poetry: "If you don't feel like writing a book," Mrs. Fox consoles her son, "you could just write poems. They're nice."[30]

Flannery O'Connor herself must have often received such gratuitous and uncomprehending advice. That she makes it an occasion for humor rather than rage demonstrates, once again, the unity of her life and her art. She is also willing to depict Mrs. Fox as more than a meddling mother. Within her limits, she is shown to be a deeply honorable and admirable woman. Whereas Asbury's callous sister mercilessly mocks her brother's literary pretensions, Mrs. Fox is stricken with concern for her ailing son. She rightly fears that his trouble may be more mental than physical, and yet she does not stint his medical care. On the contrary, she obtains the help of Dr. Block, a local physician for whom Asbury has total contempt. He regards Block as a rube who could not possibly fathom his trouble. Yet it is the small-town doctor who finally diagnoses Asbury's illness: undulant fever, a painful alternation of chills and fevers, but not a fatal disease. It is caused by drinking unpasteurized milk.

This surprising sentence to life rather than death totally appalls Asbury. Had he been able to die as a martyr suffocated by his mother's smothering love, he would have persisted in his complacency and presumption. He must face, instead, the startling news that he will live rather than die. These unwelcome tidings force him to acknowledge the ugly truth about himself. It is a withering judgment, he sees, that must fall upon him for his many sins. He is compelled at last to identify the strange shape of the ceiling stain that has looked down upon him since his childhood. It is not the vague and anonymous Third Person whom Father Vogle had mentioned. It is the very concrete dove of the Spirit who descends upon Asbury, bearing not an olive branch of peace but an icicle of wrath in its beak:

> Asbury blanched and the last film of illusion was torn away as if by a whirlwind from his eyes. He saw that for the rest of his days, frail, racked, but enduring, he would live in the face of a purifying terror. A feeble cry, a last impossible protest escaped him. But the Holy Ghost, emblazoned in ice instead of fire, continued, implacable, to descend.[31]

This horrific ending is all too typical of Flannery O'Connor's stories. It reveals once again her dubious conviction that the iron fist of negation must smash all human pretense before the glad hand of grace can lift up. Such a fearful negativity threatens, I have argued, to convert the joyful tidings of the Gospel into a baleful word that is spat upon the world in nearly misanthropic contempt. In this case, the offense is literary as well as theological. The fury that falls upon Asbury is out of character with the rest of the story. It breaks the jaunty tone that O'Connor has maintained up to the very end. Asbury has been depicted at a sinner whose offenses are vain and silly rather than monstrously wicked. Until this last scene, his moral pretense is deflated with an appropriately comic touch. This final devastation seems, therefore, both literarily and theologically out of place. The reader is made to ask whether Asbury's false righteousness might not be hardened rathered than mollified by the dread descent of this vengeful Bird.

It would have been better, in this interpreter's opinion, for O'Connor to have given Mrs. Fox the final word. She knows the truth about her son most discerningly of all: Asbury's intelligence and learning, far from being aids to his enlightenment, have skewed his vision. Mrs. Fox voices this insight to herself early in the story: "When people think they are smart—even when they are smart—there is nothing anybody else can say to make them see things straight."[32] This is a wickedly accurate deflation of Asbury's distended self-estimate, and yet it falls like a pinprick rather than a hammer blow. Such is the stuff of truly redemptive comedy, the kind that cheers rather than chills. Such also is the humor that characterizes, if not the whole of Flannery O'Connor's work, then surely the best of her stories, and especially "Revelation."

IV. The Hope of Being Least and Last of All God's Children: "Revelation"

In a letter written a little more than a year before her death, Flannery O'Connor petitioned Sister Marietta Gable for prayer about a matter other than her illness: "I've been writing for eighteen years and I've reached a point where I can't do again what I know I can do well, and the larger things I need to do now, I doubt my capacity for doing."[33] In an earlier but similar letter to Father James McCown, O'Connor confessed her "sense of having exhausted my original potentiality and being now in need of the kind of grace that deepens perception, a new shot of life. . . ."[34] Such poignant admissions reveal, in my opinion, that O'Connor had grown weary of satirizing the vagaries of human sinfulness. She had demonstrated, unforgettably, how overrighteous unbelievers and smug half-believers must be blasted by the withering winds of God's grace. Yet up to this point her accomplishment had remained largely negative. O'Connor's desire to puncture the pretensions of our complacent age had threatened to turn her satiric vision admonitory and bilious. Her work had come dangerously near to making evil the creative counterpart of good, and thus of conceiving the Gospel as ill tidings rather than glad news.

O'Connor's very last stories overcome this unhappy tendency. There she proves that her vision is comic in the Dantesque sense of the word—indeed, in the *evangelical* meaning of the term. These final works are concerned with the positive impact of revelation as her early pieces are not. In "The Displaced Person" and "Greenleaf," O'Connor recounts the lives of two whining farm women who are virtually eviscerated by their encounter with divine truth. In "Revelation," by contrast, she shows us a country woman who is not so much obliterated as reborn by her experience of grace. In this story as well as in "Judgement Day," the unfinished work found on her desk after her death, O'Connor demonstrates that her art is not animated chiefly by the animus to name all the species of sin, but by the desire to echo the hope of the Gospel.[35]

"Revelation" is O'Connor's quintessentially comic story. It concerns a farm woman named Ruby Turpin who has brought her husband Claud to the doctor's office to be treated for a leg ailment. Mrs. Turpin presides over the waiting room with a self-certainty that is wonderfully funny. Unlike the self-pitying Mrs. May, Ruby is outgoing and ingratiating. Her disposition is as sparkling and ruddy as her name. Her few facial wrinkles come, in fact, "from laughing too much."[36] Mrs. Turpin can indeed joke about everything, including her own fatness. Her prejudices are, at least initially, far more humorous than monstrous. Even her classification of the other patients according to the shoes they wear is more laughable than contemptible. Her pretensions to gentility cannot be taken seriously, if only because they are so marvellously undermined by her blundering grammar. "Above she and Claud" and "below she and Claud"[37] are the constructions of a mind striving vainly for correctness.

Surely the funniest of Mrs. Turpin's complacencies is her method for dozing off at night. She tries to imagine what kind of woman she might have been had God not made her the splendid person that she is. Ruby envisions Jesus as offering her the bitter choice of being enfleshed as either a "nigger" or "white-trash." Though she would have protested against such equally unpalatable alternatives, Mrs. Turpin confesses that she would finally have chosen to be a dignified black rather than a shameless white: "'All right,' [she would have said to Jesus], 'make me a nigger then—but that don't mean a trashy one.' And he would have made her a neat clean respectable Negro woman, herself but black."[38]

Ruby Turpin is not an ogre of evil. Unlike the self-seeking Grandmother in "A Good Man Is Hard to Find," she does not need someone to shoot her every minute of her life in order to become a good woman. She is much more akin to Julian's mother in "Everything That Rises Must Converge"—a woman who naively accepts the prejudices of her own time and place, who means well rather than ill, and who views the world according to her own best lights. The problem is, of course, that Mrs. Turpin's best lights—like those of fallen humanity in general— are far from adequate. They do not enable her to see herself as God sees her, and thus as she really is. Ruby needs to learn, therefore, not only the horror of her sin but also—and far more importantly—the wonder of her salvation.

Mrs. Turpin's amusing self-satisfaction turns out not to be so innocent as it first may seem. O'Connor uncovers the real terror of evil by showing how it begins guilelessly enough but how, by a strange mutation, it is transformed into something heinously destructive. In her nighttime imaginings, for example, Ruby constructs hierarchies of race and class that are based upon blood and money and property. But then she remembers that there are genteel whites who have lost their possessions, and that there are black doctors who own expensive homes and cars and cattle. The world's refusal to conform to Mrs. Turpin's idea of it poisons her imagination. "Usually by the time she had fallen asleep all the classes of people were moiling and roiling around in her head, and she would dream they were all crammed in together in a box car, being ridden off to be put in a gas oven."[39] This is the working of an incipiently totalitarian mind. As in "The Displaced Person," O'Connor proves that the death camps could have been erected in rural Georgia as surely as in Germany and Poland. Like Mrs. Shortley of the earlier story, Ruby wants the world to be ordered according to her own norms. And if she cannot have her way, she wills to have everything dissolved into the chaos of nihilistic destruction.

Although "Revelation" is a story with a comic beginning and end, it turns very dark and menacing in the middle. What begins as one woman's innocent prejudice and ingenuous self-contentment ends in an arrogance so overweening that it stinks in God's nostrils and thus courts its painful undoing. No longer content inwardly to classify people according to class and dress, Ruby Turpin begins to fling outward insults at the other patients, comparing the cleanliness of her swine to the dirty children in the waiting room. She also reveals how little love there is in her supposed preference for self-respecting blacks over no-count whites: "I sure am tired of buttering up niggers, but you got to love em if you want em to work for you."[39]

Mrs. Turpin's religious sense of service is also revealed to be massively complacent: "To help anybody out that needed it was her philosophy of life. She never spared herself when she found somebody in need, whether they were white or black, trash or decent. And of all that she had to be thankful for, she was most thankful that this was so." Ruby concludes her Pharisaic litany of self-congratulation by praising Christ himself for having created and maintained everything as it is: "Her heart rose. He had not made her a nigger or white-trash or ugly! He had made her herself and given her a little of everything. Jesus, thank you, she said. Thank you thank you thank you!"[40]

Ruby Turpin meets her nemesis in the form of a Wellesley student who, home from college, is also waiting for the doctor. Her name, not unlike Mary Flannery O'Connor, is Mary Grace. She proves to be a most uninviting handmaiden of the Lord: eaten up with acne, wearing Girl Scout shoes, and brimming with contempt for everything, especially for the falsely grateful Mrs. Turpin. Mary Grace is another of those curdled intellectuals who populate O'Connor's fiction, waiting to spew their soured milk on anything that strikes them as saccharine. She rises to angry action when Ruby crows her final chorus of thankfulness to Jesus for making her life so good. Striking Mrs. Turpin over the eye with a huge psychology text, this demon of wrath flings her roughly to the floor and screams at her: "Go back to hell where you came from, you old warthog."[41]

This is indeed a skewering judgment. The horns of condemnation impale Mrs. May no less severely in "Greenleaf," nor do the eyes of accusation rake Julian any more fiercely in "Everything That Rises Must Converge." And yet the effect of this literal blow to Ruby's head is—for once in O'Connor's fiction—more amusing than horrifying. Mrs. Turpin has indeed received her due, but it is delivered so comically that there is no fear it will have an obliterating effect. Nor is the reader tempted to believe that Mary Grace, as an avenging demon of secular righteousness, stands in better spiritual stead than Ruby. The title of her psychology text (Human Development) suggests that she would probably make a reductionist reading of Ruby as a woman "arrested" at one of the early "stages" along the evolutionary path to "maturity." Having no transcendent source for her wrath, Mary Grace has no transcendent hope for her own recovery. We see her for the last time when, having been injected with a tranquilizer, she is taken away to a mental hospital. The ungracious Mary Grace will meet, no doubt, the fate prophesied so crudely by the white-trash woman: "That ther girl is going to be a lunatic, ain't she?"[42]

Ruby Turpin, by contrast, has supernal hope if only because she knows that she has met with supernal judgment. She does not view the attack as the mere insult of a rude and mean-spirited student. Not for a moment does Ruby doubt that this ugly girl is the avenging angel of God. So overwhelming is Ruby's guilt that she expects God's rage to have been visited even upon her farm house: "She would not have been startled to see a burnt wound between two blackened chimneys."[43] Yet Mrs. Turpin's contrition is only momentary. Her tears of meek denial that she is a warthog sent from hell are soon dried into the white-hot fury of metaphysical rebellion. Whether to her husband, to the black farm workers, or to the circumambient air itself, Ruby makes an embittered protest against the God who has ceased to uphold the established order, and who has unleashed his judgment upon her and all the things she stands for: "Occasionally she raised her fist and made a small stabbing motion over her chest as if she was defending her innocence to invisible guests who were like the comforters of Job, reasonable-seeming but wrong."[44]

Mrs. Turpin is unable, alas, to convince anyone of her innocence, and herself least of all. Claud's kisses mean nothing. The false flattery of the Negro tenants is more maddening still. When Ruby tells the black laborers about the indignity she has suffered in the waiting room, they enrage her with their feigned compliments. Like the black laborers in "The Enduring Chill," these Negroes are adept at the art of "signifying"—of saying polite words that are loaded with venom. Not only is she "pretty," the blacks assure her, but also "stout," as if one's weight were a measure of one's beauty. Nor, in their view, should Mrs. Turpin regard the ugly girl's attack as a sign of God's judgment: "Jesus satisfied with her," they declare with wicked irony. Using a splendidly condescending qualifier that limits Ruby's supposed virtues to her own race, one of the Negro women declares that "I never knowed no sweeter white lady."[45]

Mrs. Turpin is driven at last to her final refuge—to the pig "parlor" with its sanitation system so advanced that it makes her hogs cleaner than certain unkempt children. There she spies a huge pregnant sow lying on her side, grunting softly and panting with the new life teeming inside her. This image of animal innocence and contentment, because it contrasts so irksomely with her own guilt and turmoil, infuriates Ruby. She asks anyone who might be listening—chiefly God, of course—how she could be compared to such an ugly creature? "Why me?" she protests in splenetic self-defense. "It's no trash around here, black or white, that

I haven't given to. And break my back to the bone every day working. And do for the church." Yet Ruby cannot forget the irksome fact that the ire of God broke not upon "niggers" or "trash" but upon this self-respecting woman who does not lie down in the middle of the street or "dip snuff and spit in every puddle and have it all over my chin."[46] She is angry, above all, that God has not shown himself to be the Protector of white middle-class virtues that she had thought him to be.

None of her desperate self-justifications can calm Ruby Turpin's wrath. With the sky darkening into a deep bruised purple, she flings out her final taunt. Though God may overturn her idea of the social and moral hierarchy, putting the last first and making foolish the world's social wisdom, Ruby vows to keep clear the distinction between the bottom rail and the top. Again it is the humor of these scenes—unlike many of O'Connor's other judgment episodes—that is most notable. Ruby is indeed being painfully stripped of her confidence that the Lord helps those who help themselves and that cleanliness indicates godliness. Yet there is no fear that she will be overwhelmed by the loss. She is being forced, after all, to surrender what is not merely inessential but false.

Though her protests grow ever more profane—until finally she screams out, like an uninnocent Job, "Who do you think you are?"— they are also increasingly childish and futile. For the merest mortal sinner to demand that God account for his action is more silly than it is egregious. Sin is less cunning, O'Connor understands, than it is foolish. Thus is Ruby's arrogant query answered with an echo that turns the question back upon the questioner—as if God were asking *her*, "Who do you think you are?" This talky woman is left speechless at last. Like Nelson and Mr. Head, she is made to stand silent before a vision of purgatorial judgment that is also redeeming grace. It is imaged in the elongated purple cloud that arches above the lowering sun:

> She saw the streak as a vast swinging bridge extending upward from the earth through a field of living fire. Upon it was a vast horde of souls rumbling toward heaven. There were whole companies of white-trash, clean for the first time in their lives, and bands of black niggers in white robes, and battalions of freaks and lunatics [perhaps even Mary Grace] shouting and clapping and leaping like frogs. And bringing up the end of the procession was a tribe of people whom she recognized at once as those who, like herself and Claud, had always had a little of everything and the God-given wit to use it right. She leaned forward to observe them closer. They were marching behind the others with great dignity, accountable as they had always been for good order and common sense and respectable behavior. They alone were on key. Yet she

could see by their shocked and altered faces that even their virtues were being burned away.[47]

This passage is more powerful and convincing than the similar scene at the end of "The Artificial Nigger." Not only is it an affirmation visually rendered rather than discursively explained—"shown" rather than "told"—it is also a consummation that unites the entire story into a theological no less than a literary whole. Here, perhaps for the first time in O'Connor's fiction, divine wrath is couched wholly within the terms of divine mercy. It is a mercy that is like a refiner's fire—cleansing rather than consuming. Ruby Turpin's pride is purged by the flaming vision of all those "inferior" folk who are entering the Kingdom of God before her. O'Connor does not romantically exalt the poor and the outcast as intrinsically righteous. The down and out are God's favorites, compared to the clean and dignified Turpins of this world, simply because they are less bent on their own justification. Nor does O'Connor deny the importance of "good order and common sense and respectable behavior." Society could not exist without them. But because they often lead to spiritual arrogance, these very virtues become more pernicious than the common vices. Such spurious goodness must be burned away by the fires of God's grace.

The first and the last words of the Gospel are hopeful rather than baleful, and so are the beginning and the ending of this story. No one admitted entrance to purgatory can regress out of it. One's cleansing there may be greatly prolonged by one's own recalcitrant will, but there is no changing of direction, no going back on grace, no descent into hell from the precincts of mercy. However much they may differ about the doctrine of purgatory itself, classic Catholicism and classic Protestantism are here profoundly agreed: true faith is indelible and irreversible. Hence O'Connor's determination to embody, in this final scene of her finest story, the vision of an eschatological community that includes all of the redeemed.

Ruby Turpin has no *rightful* place there. Yet, for all the horror of her sin, she is not driven out of the New Jerusalem and consigned to the realm of weeping and wailing and gnashing of teeth. She is given a glimpse, instead, of her own humble place in the economy of grace. This is cause not for lament but for rejoicing. So, as Ruby trudges home after the darkness has fallen and her vision has faded, she hears the sounds of jubilation rather than condemnation: "In the woods around her the invisible cricket choruses had struck up, but what she heard were the voices of the souls climbing into the starry field and shouting hallelujah."[48] Ruby can hear this joyful noise not chiefly because she has met her own dreadful judgment, but because she has the prospect of being numbered among those singing souls. By God's grace alone, and not at all by her own good works, is her name written in the Lamb's Book of Life. Although she will surely not lead the roll, she has the comic and life-engendering hope of being least and last among all of God's children.

This, I submit, is the real comedy of our redemption. Flannery O'Connor is its superb artist and advocate because, in the best of her stories, she seeks not to wound but to heal, not to divide but to unite, not to shout but to jest, not to draw caricatures of damnation and salvation but to limn the subtleties and ironies of grace. This final concern with divine mercy explains her refusal to give the standard moralistic account of black-white relations. Only because God's justice is not primarily wrath but forgiveness can human injustice also be made redemptive rather than destructive. Like Mr. Head and Asbury Fox, Ruby Turpin is prepared to enter Paradise—and thus to live graciously in the quotidian world—because she has seen the gracious hierarchy of heaven.

7

WALKER PERCY AS A CATHOLIC EXISTENTIALIST

The political commentator William Buckley maintains that all future presidents of the United States should be made to take a *double* oath of office. They should swear not only to uphold the Constitution, says Buckley, but also to have read, marked, learned, and inwardly digested Walker Percy's novel *Love in the Ruins.* "It's all there in that one book," Buckley declares, "what's happening to us and why." Such willfully extravagant praise may put off those who dislike Buckley's conservative politics. Yet it jauntily points up both the comic and the prophetic character of Percy's work. Percy is a writer with a message, a novelist concerned to convey a vision. His fiction makes a withering critique of what is spiritually inane about contemporary American life, even as it also hints at a way beyond our current malaise. Yet Percy remains an artist rather than a preacher. His Catholic existentialism is couched in literary terms that appeal to the imagination more than the will. Though Percy may seek to revolutionize our way of seeing, he leaves to the church the task of proclaiming and enacting the Gospel of the world's salvation.

The satiric character of Percy's work is unmistakable. Unless he can generate a good deal of polemical steam, Percy admits, he has difficulty writing. "There has to be something under attack," he confesses.[1] No wonder that Percy has been so productive a satirist in the quarter century since *The Moviegoer* was first published in 1961. He refuses to tolerate the malodorous character of our common life. His fiction names the public and private stench for the foul thing that it is. The aim of this chapter is to trace the biographical origins of Percy's satire, to show how Southern Stoicism has been at once his model and nemesis, and then to describe the Catholic existentialism that Percy came to embrace as an answer to the pseudoscientism of our age. Percy developed his unique satiric vision, I will argue, in response to the two chief influences on his life: his adoptive father, William Alexander Percy; and his adopted philosopher, Søren Kierkegaard.

I. Will Percy as Model and Nemesis

The curse of either actual or threatened suicide haunts nearly all of Walker Percy's work. There are biographical no less than religious reasons for this near obsession with self-destruction. The first American Percy, as if to foreshadow the fate of his descendants, killed himself. Charles Percy was sometimes called Don Carlos because he migrated from England to the West Indies before coming to this country bearing a Spanish land grant. This exceedingly progenitive Percy left behind wives and children in both England and the Bahamas. The English bride pursued him to Mississippi, demanding her son's right of inheritance, despite the fact that Don Carlos had married yet again and fathered six children by his new American wife. Though Charles Percy became a wealthy and powerful indigo merchant, he finally wearied of his peculiar burden. Tying a sugar kettle around his neck one winter night in 1794, he waded into Percy Creek and drowned himself.[2]

As if to take up the legacy left him by his ancestor, Walker Percy's own father also elected not to go forward with life and, in 1927, killed himself. Young Percy was only eleven. Three years later, Percy's mother died in an automobile crash, orphaning fourteen-year-old Walker and his two younger brothers. The three boys were adopted by their father's first cousin, William Alexander Percy, who raised them as if they were his own sons. Though an enormously generous man, there was something essentially melancholy about "Uncle Will," as Percy came to call his foster father. He was given to a deep personal pessimism. Neighbors remarked how in the evenings he would walk up and down the sidewalk in front of his house, pondering the tears of things. His friend David Cohn described Will Percy as "the loneliest man I have ever known." Though often charming and winsome, he was convinced that all of life's glory lay in the irrecoverable past, all of its evil in the looming future. It is no wonder that there are so many melancholiacs in Walker Percy's fiction, so many protagonists who consider killing themselves rather than tolerating this intolerable age.

Yet it is not Hemingway's sense of an inherited familial curse that causes Percy's fiction to be shadowed by suicide. The fact that more than one ancestor commited suicide provides Percy a cultural even more than a personal sign. It serves to convince him that something has gone profoundly awry with the whole modern experiment. Like Albert Camus, Walker Percy is convinced that suicide is the single inescapable question for our age. Why, given the cultural and spiritual wasteland which we inhabit, should one *not* refuse to live in it? Though often a merely selfish act, the taking of one's own life can also serve as a way of asking whether human existence is ultimately worth affirming. It raises the metaphysical quandary that ethics alone cannot answer. Ethics determines why we should do one thing rather than another: why to act with noble rather than base motives, why to live cowardly or courageous lives, why to speak truthfully rather than deceptively. For Percy the real question is not ethical but metaphysical and theological: why should one do *anything* at all? What is there, either within human life or beyond it, that justifies all of its trouble? This most fundamental of problems Percy's fiction relentlessly seeks to analyze and also to answer.

Percy raises the life-and-death question within the framework set for him by William Alexander Percy. The younger Percy has often seemed scornful of his foster father's moral and metaphysical vision. Aunt Emily, Binx Bolling's mentor and antagonist in *The Moviegoer*, is indeed a parody of Will Percy. Yet Percy is critical of Uncle Will's world view precisely because he is so indebted to it. Not frivolously but with genuine gratitude is *The Moviegoer* dedicated to "W.A.P." That William Alexander Percy was indeed a great man is evident from even a cursory reading of his celebrated memoir of 1941, *Lanterns on the Levee*. It is at once a charming and angry book. The elder Percy describes, with splendid poetic grace, the tenor and character of life as it was lived in the Mississippi Delta prior to the Second War. He memorably recalls the virtues that abounded in the old aristrocratic South. At least for its beneficiaries if not also for its victims, it was a culture at once genteel, tolerant, mannered, and hospitable. Even a latter-day reader can sympathize with Will Percy's bitter lament at the decline and fall of a world so elegantly accomplished.

About Will Percy, it must be admitted, there was something veritably Olympian. What other word can describe a man who, at various times in his life, operated a 3000-acre cotton plantation, wrote both English and Latin verse, taught literature for a semester at Sewanee, received a Harvard law degree and presided over his family's Greenville law firm, served with distinction as a volunteer in World War I, cared for impoverished blacks rendered homeless by the flooding Mississippi, stood up to the Ku Klux Klan with solitary courage, and reared three orphaned boys who were only distantly kin to him? No wonder that Walker Percy calls his Uncle Will "the most extraordinary man I have ever known," and speaks of owing him "a debt that cannot be repaid."[3]

It is not Will Percy's personal virtue alone that Walker Percy salutes. He also pays tribute to the social charity and restraint that characterized the South his adoptive father helped to build. Great though its evils may have been, Southern paternalism was also capable of producing much good. Percy praises, in particular, the bond of fellow feeling and mutual regard that linked the white patricians and free blacks who accepted their leadership. It was honor and duty, Percy admits, more than charity and justice, that promoted the white gentry's care for their Negro "inferiors." The white masters befriended their black neighbors " . . . not because they were made in the image of God and were therefore lovable in themselves, but because to do them harm would be to defile the inner fortress which was oneself." Even so, Uncle Will's world deserves a qualified commendation: "Whatever its abuses, whatever its final sentimental decay, there was such a thing as *noblesse oblige* on the one side and an extraordinary native courtesy and dignity on the other, by which there occurred, under almost impossible conditions, a flowering of human individuality such as this hemisphere has rarely seen."[4]

This explains why Binx Bolling is not at all ironic when he assures his Aunt Emily Cutrer than he does not despise her aristocratic standards and commitments. On the contrary, he admires her confident ability to fight the good fight without regard for victory. He listens with patience, moreover, to her repeated demand that he resume his career in medical research, that he cease being a playboy, and that he honor his patrician heritage by living a long and useful life in the service of his fellows. Binx freely confesses that there is nothing wrong with his aunt's ethical ideals. Yet something positive is missing from her exhortations. There is neither grace nor mercy in her Stoic humanism. "A man must live by his lights and do what little good he can and do it as best he can," Aunt Emily harangues her nephew. "To do anything less is to be less than a man." Yet Binx responds to his aunt's high summons with bemused puzzlement rather than eager endorsement: "She is right. I will say yes," he concedes. "I will say yes even though I do not really know what she is talking about."[5]

The key to Bolling's sardonic incomprehension of his aunt's wintry philosophy lies in a scene at the very beginning of the novel. It also provides a clue to Walker Percy's own misgivings about Will Percy's moral vision. Binx recalls that he was a boy of only eight when his brother Scotty died of pneumonia. He remembers how Aunt Emily broke the news to him during a walk behind the hospital. She did not commiserate with the child or offer him religious faith and hope. She enjoined Binx, instead, to buck up and be strong, to behave like a little trooper. Already as a mere youth Binx was befuddled by such advice: "I could easily act like a soldier," he had told himself. "Was that all I had to do?"[6] Does one greet the news of a brother's death with the grim determination to grit one's teeth and bear up? Any ordinary eight-year-old would have wanted to know what had become of his brother. Was his life as pitilessly extinguished as if a pet animal had been run over by a car? If so, does one go on living with nothing more bracing than a tight-lipped endurance?

It is not chiefly Will Percy's racial paternalism, I maintain, that troubles Walker Percy, nor is it his adoptive father's reactionary politics

that gives him final pause. Indeed, Percy is himself capable of a curmud-
geon's impatience with the follies of the present age. What palsies
Walker Percy's confidence in Uncle Will's faith is its cheerlessness.
Though himself not a professed Christian, one of W. A. Percy's poems,
"They Cast Their Nets in Galilee," has been set to music by D. McK.
Williams and is often included in Protestant hymnals. This despite the
fact that Will Percy's poetic praise for the restless peace of God has an undeniably pagan ring. It tells how the first disciples were simple and contented "fisherfolk" until they were called to a nobler, if also colder, kind
of peace: John died in exile on Patmos, and Peter was crucified head
down. The hymn's final stanza is a veritable paean to Stoic heroism:

> The peace of God, it is no peace,
>   But strife closed in the sod.
> Yet, brothers, pray but for one thing—
>   The marvelous peace of God.

Not salvation and the forgiveness of sins, not the joy and hope of life
everlasting, but a bootless "strife closed in the sod" is what Will Percy
understands the spiritual life to entail. It is also the duty Aunt Emily enjoins her nephew to embrace. No wonder that Walker Percy shares Binx
Bolling's addled consternation at such a command.

Will Percy's bleak skepticism is made especially evident in a poem
entitled "An Epistle from Corinth." There, in a Browningesque mono-
logue, he undertakes to correct the Apostle Paul for the naivety of his
faith, particularly for his "distortion" of Jesus' this-worldly ethic into a
gospel of eschatological redemption. Like a latter-day Nietzsche, the
poet complains that Paul has turned the high human struggle for perfection into an other worldly anodyne valued chiefly by "the slave and sick
and poor." It is the valorous Greek in him, the narrator confesses, that
trusts in earthly glory, and not in the heavenly hope proffered by the
Apostle:

> Gods, gods! this fool would have the harlot's mouth
> Immortal as the soul of Socrates!
> Forgive me, follower of Jesus. I
> Am Greek, all Greek; I know the loveliness
> Of flesh and its sweet snare, and I am hurt
> At finding nothing where I sought for much.
> O Paul, had you been more as other men
> Your wisdom had been wiser![7]

Will Percy's melancholy rejection of Christian faith and hope is
made even more poignant when one learns that he started out to be a
priest. He was an unusually religious child, having been dissuaded from
the priesthood largely because his Catholic mother thought it an unfit-

ting vocation for a Southern gentleman.[8] Soon after becoming a student at Sewanee, Will Percy threw over his ardent Catholicism for an equally ardent atheism. This conversion was tied to Percy's lifelong melancholia. Pessimism was the prevailing mood of his life, and it permeates the whole of *Lanterns on the Levee*. The title itself recalls Will Percy's late evenings spent walking the Mississippi's high embankment above his native Greenville, communing solitarily with the murmuring waters below.

The Mississippi River becomes an emblem of Uncle Will's Stoic conviction that the world undergoes an endless cycle of beginnings and endings. The elder Percy notes how the river constantly creates and destroys, how it both fertilizes and floods, how it eternally changes and eternally remains the same. Amidst the fearful Heraclitean flux, he says, we are but paltry creatures who throw up frail barriers against time's terrible rolling indifference to human pomp and folly. Nature's massive unconcern for our species is the fundamental fact of life as it is lived alongside the great brown river:

> Man draws near to it, fights it, uses it, curses it, loves it, but it remains remote, unaffected. . . . The gods on their thrones are shaken and changed, but it abides, aloof and unappeasable, with no heart except for its own task, under the broken and immense arch of the lighted sky where the sun, too, goes a lonely journey.[9]

Nothing less than an icy self-sufficiency can inure us, he argues, to nature's utter carelessness.

Had Will Percy been content with such Stoic naturalism, perhaps Walker Percy would not have reacted so vigorously to his foster father's vision of life. Yet Uncle Will's unbelief led him beyond pessimism to an embittered scorn for nearly everything modern. Rare is the Stoic who does not also become, at least in our age, an egomaniacal *furioso*. As T. S. Eliot observes of Nietzsche's inverted Stoicism, "There is not much difference between identifying oneself with the Universe and identifying the Universe with oneself."[10] Though W. A. Percy did not end in Nietzsche's raving madness, Walker Percy had to reckon with Uncle Will's seething contempt for the modern world. While the two are not unconnected, this deep-seated disdain was perhaps a more alluring legacy than the familial bent toward suicide.

II. The Lure and Peril of Catonism

Will Percy believed that a serene resignation is the essence of Stoicism, and that all religious reliance on divine hope and succor is something unworthy of adult humanity. As a matter of fact, the Stoics were far more optimistic than pessimistic, far more religious than atheistic.

For all their cosmic determinism, they were believers in moral freedom—in the power of human will consciously to conform its action to the orderliness of the universe and thus to live "according to nature." The true Stoic ethic is not a passive resignation to the chances and changes of a godless cosmos; it is a vigorous call—often in the name of the divine Logos—to moral liberty and sovereignty. The undisturbed person is not nostalgically despairing, like Will Percy. The real Stoic aims at a life of *apatheia*—a triumph over the momentary passions by means of an active philanthropy. "Nature bids me," writes Seneca, "to be of use to men whether they are slave or free, freedmen or free born. Wherever there is a human being there is room for benevolence."[11]

Given such severe differences between classical Stoicism and Will Percy's modern pessimism, Walker Percy is only partially right to call his foster father a Southern Stoic. Richard King, borrowing a term from the historian Barrington Moore, is much more accurate in describing W. A. Percy as a "Catonist." Like Cato the Younger lamenting the fallen glory of Rome, Will Percy exalts the austere aristocratic virtues and decries modern innovations and extravagances. Whether it occurs in antique Rome, modern Germany, or the post–Civil War South, Catonism appeals to traditional order and hierarchical unity against the threat of modernization. King describes Catonism as "the ideological response of a landed upper class . . . which is economically, socially, and politically on the defensive. The Catonist fears the encroachment of alien values and impersonal commercial forces which disrupt an aristocratic and organic order cemented by ties of family, status, tradition, and, sometimes, race or nationality."[12]

Catonism is the perpetual enticement of a displaced aristocracy. It tempts those who regard themselves as a social and spiritual elite to have a reactionary scorn for democracy. The Catonist fears and hates the *demos* as the enemy of all excellence. Beginning with a high call to morality and order, the Catonist often ends in repressive disdain for the masses. Walker Percy discerns the political danger of Will Percy's aristocratic chauvinism. But he criticizes it for theological rather than political reasons. In his elegiac nostalgia for the lost heroic world of the plantation South, Will Percy can envision neither racial reconciliation nor social renewal. Like Catonists of all ages, he equates the collapse of his own aristocratic tradition with the loss of virtue and order as such.

There is no room, in W. A. Percy's Catonist theology, for the Lord who judges peckerwood and patrician alike, who finds squire and slave equally wanting, but whose grace can redeem and reform them both. His rage is most hotly kindled against the greedy rednecks who, in his view, have destroyed the civility and gentility that characterized the premodern South. Percy's friend William Faulkner often shared his scorn for the poor whites who, in becoming prosperous, were able to impose their

ugly will and way on Southern society. Faulkner called them the
Snopeses. Will Percy describes these white trash despoilers of antebel-
lum Dixie as "probably the most unprepossessing [breed] on the broad
face of the ill-populated earth." Though he claims boastfully to "forgive
them as the Lord God forgives," he adds this bitter qualifier: "admire
them, trust them, love them—never."[13]

Will Percy's Catonist contempt for rednecks also extends to Negroes who refuse childishly to entrust their lives into the gentry's care.
Though the elder Percy was a dauntless foe of the Klan and a friend of the
flood-ravaged blacks, he would have perhaps joined William Faulkner in
opposition to the civil rights movement of the 1960s. Many Southern
patricians became leaders, in fact, of the infamous White Citizens Councils. The reason, in Walker Percy's view, is not obscure. Will Percy and his
kind were opaque to the transcendent mercy and judgment of God, and
thus blinded to our total equality in sin and grace. Southern white
leadership was robbed, therefore, of the ethical imperative that might
have saved the South from the wrath that fell upon it. Addressing his
own region's racism on the eve of this crisis, Walker Percy strikes straight
at the theological heart of the matter. "What we are faced with now,"
Percy writes, "are not 'democratic ideals' but religious ultimates: is
there any real reason, beyond democratic values, why a man should not
be cruel to another man?"[14] In Percy's view, there is indeed such a
reason, and it is contained in the Gospel. Negro-hating Southerners have
not failed their own noble traditions, he argues, so much as they have
transgressed the grace of God:

> The Christian is optimistic precisely where the Stoic is pessimis-
> tic. What the Stoic sees as the insolence of his former charge—and
> this is what he can't tolerate, the Negro's demanding his rights in-
> stead of being thankful for the squire's generosity—is in the Chris-
> tian scheme the sacred right which must be accorded to the indi-
> vidual, whether deemed insolent or not. . . . The Stoic has no use for
> the clamoring minority; the Christian must have every use for it.[15]

If one reads the word *Stoic* to mean Catonist, one will discern the
truth of Walker Percy's claim. Will Percy, writing fifteen years earlier, pro-
leptically confessed the rightness of his adopted son's charges. Forgiveness and redemption mean little to him. Original sin, virgin birth, salvation by faith, blood atonement, descent into hell, resurrection of the
dead—these are but moribund abstractions for Uncle Will. "They speak
a beautiful dead language," he insists, "when what we need is live words,
tender with meaning and assurance."[16] Given the demise of the old
theological verities, his one remaining fortress is the inner bulwark of
his own solitude.

Will Percy came to feel himself more at home in the cemetery than any other place; for in death, he believed, one achieves the final alone-ness—the ultimate marriage, as it were, to oneself. "Of all the people I have loved, wisely and unwisely, deeply and passingly, I have loved no one so much as myself. Of all the hours of happiness granted me, none has been so keen and holy as a few unpredictable moments alone."[17] A solitary inwardness is the only solace before the ultimate silence of the cosmos. "There is left to each of us," Will Percy icily affirms, "no matter how far defeat pierces, the unassailable wintry kingdom of Marcus Aurelius, which some more gently call the Kingdom of Heaven. However it be called, it is not outside but within, and when all is lost, it stands fast."[18]

Richard King has demonstrated how fully Will Percy's retreat into Catonist pessimism was also a deep psychological recoil from the intolerable burden of his paternal past. For all his exaltation of the planter tradition, Uncle Will found the heroic example of his forebears to be far more shackling than liberating. His grandfather had been a gallant Civil War hero, and his own father was a courageous United States senator who had stood down such race baiters as Theodore Bilbo and James Vardaman. Unlike his valorous and procreative ancestors—men of action all—Will Percy was a poet and a bachelor, a man of words more than deeds, a dreamer and "jackdaw in the garden" despite his impressive worldly accomplishments. Hence the haunting need to prove himself worthy of the manly tradition he had inherited.

Not only did Will Percy volunteer for the Belgian Relief commission at the outbreak of the First War; he was also far more jingoistic about the American entry into that war than was his fearless father. Will Percy put on twenty-three pounds in thirty days in order to make himself eligible for the American army, and he fought valiantly in the Meuse-Argonne operation. Impatient again at the American delay in entering the Second War, the fifty-four-year-old Percy volunteered unsuccessfully for service in the French and Canadian armies.[19] Yet none of these heroic efforts could convince Will Percy that he was the worthy heir of those who had sired him. His theological skepticism may be read, in fact, as the expression of a deep uncertainty about his own sexual identity. Will Percy's onerous patrimony fundamentally "unmanned" him, as King rightly observes.[20]

This psychological byway into Will Percy's past is significant, for our purposes, only because it reveals Walker Percy's own difficulty in assuming the burden of the Percy legacy. Just as Will Percy had become an attorney because most of his forbears had been lawyers, so did Walker Percy become a physician because it was the thing expected of him more than the vocation he was summoned to pursue. Like Uncle Will, he cast about for something right and good to do with his life. Will Percy had faced the same vocational quandary upon receiving his Harvard law degree in 1908: "What does one do with a life, or at any rate intend to do?" Not long before his death, the elder Percy was still asking the question: "For months (maybe for years, maybe until now) I hunted about for a good ambition."[21]

It is a well-known fact that Walker Percy contracted tuberculosis while completing his residency in pathology at New York's Bellevue Hospital, and that he underwent two lengthy periods of isolated convalescence. What seems equally clear is that a certain perplexity of soul had infected Percy long before he was physically diseased. One can speculate upon the sources of Percy's inward turmoil: the world that was then rending itself in a horrible war, the embittered conclusion to *Lanterns on the Levee* and Uncle Will's death soon thereafter, the remembrance of his father's decision not to carry on with life, and Percy's own vocational uncertainty about pursuing a career in medicine. Whatever its causes, the ache in Walker Percy's soul was something that medical science could not cure. Percy had learned the craft of healing but not the answer to the question whether human beings are *worth* healing. He was a physician, alas, who could not heal himself and thus a man in search of "a good ambition."

There is an undeniable link between Walker Percy's inward and outward peregrinations. After completing his medical degree at Columbia in 1941, Percy lived for a while in Santa Fe with the writer Shelby Foote, then came back to Mississippi to marry a Greenville nurse, then moved with her to the hills of Tennessee near Sewanee, then returned to dwell in the Garden District of New Orleans, before finally settling with his family across Lake Ponchartrain in Covington, Louisiana.[22] Percy has never practiced the profession for which he was trained. He has devoted himself less to medical research than to reading and thinking and writing. The heaviness of the Percy patrimony is implicit in a passage near the beginning of *The Last Gentleman*, where Percy's narrator examines the problem of paternal lineage as it plagues Will Barrett:

> The great-grandfather knew what was what and said so and acted accordingly and did not care what anyone thought. He even wore a pistol and holster like a Western hero and once met the Grand Wizard of the Ku Klux Klan in a barbershop and invited him then and there to shoot it out in the street. The next generation, the grandfather, seemed to know what was what but he was not really so sure. He was brave but he gave much thought to the business of being brave. He too would have shot it out with the Grand Wizard if he could have made certain it was the thing to do. The father was a brave man too and said he didn't care what others thought but he did care. More than anything else, he wished to act with honor and to be thought well of by other men. And so living for him was a strain. . . .

As for the present young man, the last of the line, he did not
know what to think. So he became a watcher and listener and a
wanderer.[23]

This passage is significant not only because it describes Walker
Percy's own paternal history; it also helps explain why nearly all of his
protagonists are watchers and listeners and wanderers. They do not
know quite what to do with themselves. Their passivity and indecision
can be attributed, at least in part, to the crippling effects of a noble patrimony. It is a fundamental paradox that a powerful moral inheritance
can be as much binding as loosing. It can be graceless toward those who
do not measure up to its high ideals, merciless toward those who fail to
achieve its moral mission. Much of Walker Percy's concern with Christian faith springs from his desire, I believe, for a more liberating vision of
life than a venerable past can itself supply. The comic freedom implicit
in the Gospel will provide Walker Percy an alternative not only to Will
Percy's tragic outlook, but also to the spiritual and sexual malaise that a
heroic legacy often begets.

Yet the chief problem remains religious rather than moral. What
would Walker Percy make of Uncle Will's Catonist pessimism? Within
the eyrie of his lonely inwardness, the elder Percy came to value more
than to lament the fall of his own aristocratic way of life. "Nothing is so
sad as defeat," he writes, "except victory."[24] Triumphant success is
never so sweet as courageous failure. To lose against insuperable odds is
to be strangely justified in one's own valor. Virtue, he declares in good
Stoic fashion, guarantees no "reward except itself." But in bitter anti-
Stoic denial of the world's ultimate justice and goodness, he adds that
"the good die when they should live, the evil live when they should die;
heroes perish and cowards escape; noble efforts do not succeed because
they are noble, and wickedness is not consumed in its own nature."[25]

The only real hope lies in the annihilation provided by the grave. If
beyond death's bourne he is questioned by the high gods, W. A. Percy
vows not to bow down in humility and supplication before them. He
pledges, instead, to straighten his shoulders and answer defiantly, "I am
your son."[26] He expects, in fact, no such encounter. It is oblivion that he
honestly awaits, a welcome return of the transient part to the everlasting
whole.

Our dread and torment in this life we lead are its apartness, its eternal isolation. We try to rid us of ourselves by love, by prayers, by
vice, by the Lethe of activity, and we never wholly succeed. Above
all things we desire to be united and absorbed. Must we insist that
our besetting anguish go with us past the grave? To become part of
the creating essence of all things created by it, in this alone might

be found fulfillment, peace, ecstasy. At the intensest peak of our emotions—lying on the bosom we love, or lost in a sunset, or bereft by music—being then most ourselves, we dissolve and become part of the strength and radiance and pathos of creation. When most ourselves, we are most not ourselves and lose our tragic isolation in the whole. To be a drop of water, trembling alone forever, lacks something of the peace and grandeur of being one lost drop in the immortal undivided ocean.[27]

Such genteel Dover Beachism cannot answer, at least for the younger Percy, the modern problem of anxiety and despair. The prospect of reabsorption into the cosmic sea may have sufficed for Uncle Will, but it will not satisfy his foster son. Nor is Will Percy's pessimism the Senecan virtue he thinks it is. "It is a great man," wrote the great Roman philosopher, "who not only orders his death but contrives it." Yet Seneca could open his veins and die nobly in the act of self-slaughter because, at least in part, he lived in a pre-Christian age and was thus oblivious to the Gospel's hope. For Walker Percy, by contrast, there is no pagan immunity from transcendent judgment and joy. Now that the Jewish-Christian dispensation of eschatological life has been decisively given, the whole business of dying—and self-imposed death most of all—has been rendered radically problematic. Even the unbeliever must ask whether the suicidal act puts off one world only to confront another. Percy's problem, therefore, is to find a way for preserving the genuine virtues embodied in his foster father's despairing Catonism, while avoiding its final gracelessness. The answer, Percy came to believe, lies in what Jacques Maritain called the "true humanism" of Roman Catholic faith.

III. Scientific Humanism and Its Existentialist Critique

It is clear that Walker Percy underwent a personal crisis of faith not unlike the struggle Will Percy experienced while he was a student at Sewanee. Yet the outcome of the two battles could hardly be more opposed. W. A. Percy abandoned his inherited Catholicism for a nominal Episcopalianism that was more Catonist than Christian. He vividly recalls the Sunday when, as an undergraduate at the University of the South, he discovered the uselessness of attending confession any more: "No priest could absolve me, no church could direct my life or my judgment, what most believed I could not believe." He knew that thenceforth he would live an unaided life, that he would "breathe a starker and a colder air, with no place to go when I was tired." "From now on," he concluded, "I would be living with my own self."[28]

For Walker Percy, the quandary of faith and doubt led in an exact counterdirection: from secular self-sufficiency to the same Catholicism

Will Percy had surrendered. It was as if the younger kinsman were knotting a severed cord, reforging the link his foster father had broken. If Uncle Will's profoundest sympathies had lain with Marcus Aurelius, Walker's allegiance would be given to Søren Kierkegaard. And yet it was hardly a smart aleck's desire to turn the tables that prompted Walker Percy's conversion to Christian faith. He was less disaffected, at least originally, with Will Percy's aristocratic Stoicism than with the behaviorist scientism of the modern age.

What the two have oddly in common is a closed view of the universe. For the Stoic, nature is an embodied spiritual force, a living reality governed by an all-pervading Logos that is synonymous with God. This nameless and impersonal Deity neither creates nor redeems the world. The Stoic cosmos is, on the contrary, a self-contained pantheistic system that originates nowhere and proceeds nowhere. The universe is born and destroyed and reborn by fire. These repeated conflagrations constitute an eternal series of world constructions and destructions.

The modern scientific perspective, at least as it is commonly understood, is a vulgarized and secularized parallel to this self-enclosed process. Like ancient Stoicism, it leaves no room for the self-revealing God transcendently to create, redeem, or judge. The central reductionist premise is that the human and physical worlds are alike in being utterly self-contained: they are both finely tuned organic mechanisms which can be mastered by means of scientific technique. Indeed, the grand hope of modern scientism is to overcome the "cultural lag" whereby the humanities have supposedly fallen behind the sciences. To the human and spiritual realm it hopes to apply the same instruments of analysis and control that have so successfully subdued the natural order. The desired result is a conquest of humanity's inner sphere that will be commensurate with its mastery of outer space.

It must not be thought that Walker Percy has contempt for modern science. On the contrary, he admires the symmetry and beauty and elegance of scientific study. Disease itself, as the disruption of nature's orderly process, can be logically comprehended. Even as a novelist, Percy remains something of a physician. He cannot resist the urge, he says, to thump the patient and to discover the trouble. It is the body politic, of course, and the human soul itself that are the objects of Percy's diagnosis. Yet Percy seems determined to keep the worlds of medicine and literature healthily separate. They are fundamentally distinct enterprises whose differences must not be collapsed. If the humanities ignore the body's brute reality, they render themselves angelically irrelevant. And if science attempts to mend the broken human soul, it will wreak nothing but havoc. Medical science can treat symptoms insofar as they are instances of a generally describable complex. But about our unique condition—what we are as singular individuals—it cannot utter a solitary word.

This is the drastic limit, Percy discovered, set upon all scientific knowledge. Science can comprehend the meaning of life within its own horizon, but it is powerless to deal with the transcendent Reality—if there be any such—that impinges upon us. Percy's melancholy recognition of this fact left him feeling strangely empty. Three years of psychoanalysis alongside more than a decade of scientific education had not provided the answers Percy needed. He wryly describes his alma mater "as almost the quintessential institution of scientific humanism" and thus as a place woefully oblivious of its limits: "After you learn everything that you can at Columbia about what it is to be a human being, there is something awfully important left over." He compares what was unsatisfactory in his scientific training to the frustration Kierkegaard experienced upon reading Hegel. Percy says it struck him like a bombshell to find Kierkegaard's jibe that "Hegel knew everything and explained everything, except what it is to be born and to live and to die."[29] Thus had medical science taught Walker Percy nearly all that he needed to know about pathology, but very little about how he could find the courage to draw the next breath, how to put one foot in front of the other, and thus how to stick himself into what William James called the blooming, buzzing confusion of the world.

In his reaction against the pretense of modern science, Percy had turned away from the American pragmatic tradition to the European existentialists. Though John Dewey was then reigning American philosopher, Percy found Dewey's brittle kind of scientific humanism to be of no avail.[30] He immersed himself during these post-Columbia years in the work of Camus and Sartre, Kafka and Heidegger, Marcel and Jaspers, Dostoevski and Tolstoy. In differing ways, they provided him a vision of the human realm as unique and distinct, if also deeply vexed and miserable. Whatever else we may be, these writers taught Percy that our *humanity* cannot be fully understood through the categories of the sciences.

Yet Percy's real breakthrough came by way of the eccentric Danish poet-theologian-philosopher, Søren Kierkegaard. Percy discovered that Kierkegaard's critique of Hegel helped clarify his own misgivings about secularist science. "The same thing he said about the Hegelian system," Percy notes, "might be said about a purely scientific view of the world that leaves out the individual."[31] Percy takes delight in Kierkegaard's description of Hegel as the philosopher who, upon completing the magnificent crystal palace of his philosophical system, had to build a shanty wherein he could actually live. Like Hegelianism, the scientific humanism of our time has also created an uninhabitable system of existence. It threatens to obliterate the unique individual and to exile the redemptive God. Kierkegaard enabled Percy to rediscover both.

Although Percy would later make extensive artistic use of *The Sickness Unto Death*, it was Kierkegaard's revolutionary little essay entitled "Of the Difference Between a Genius and an Apostle" that turned his life around. Kierkegaard argues, in this sprightly piece, that geniuses outstrip their peers by dint of superior intelligence—by unexampled brilliance of mind and acuity of insight into all things human. Though Kierkegaard cites only Plato and Shakespeare as examples of genius, one could just as easily name Michelangelo or Beethoven, Einstein or Joyce. They have all created works of art or science or philosophy that go uncomprehended during their own time. So far are geniuses ahead of their age that we doltish souls are still seeking to fathom their meaning. Yet fathom them we finally will.

Indeed, the pathos of genius is that its achievements are eventually comprehended, assimilated, and even surpassed. Every great discovery in thought or imagination is succeeded by another that builds upon it. The work of genius can be penetrated and mastered, says Kierkegaard, because it moves within the sphere of immanence and homogeneity. For all its extraordinary keenness, the work of genius discloses nothing that is not already latent within the world. Though it awakens us powerfully to what lies dormant and unexpressed within ourselves, it tells us nothing essentially heterogeneous or new. Indeed, the genius operates within the horizon of the humanly known and the humanly knowable. About the world that lies supernally beyond us, the genius announces nothing whatever.

It is the unique office of the apostle, Kierkegaard contends, to bring tidings from the sphere of transcendence and heterogeneity. The apostle is distinguished neither by keenness of mind, eloquence of speech, nor depth of learning. Indeed, the apostle may be an illiterate fisherman, an indifferent tax collector, even a humble tentmaker. Kierkegaard waxes ironic in emphasizing the apostle's ordinariness: "As a genius St. Paul cannot be compared with either Plato or Shakespeare, as a coiner of beautiful similes he comes pretty low down on the scale, as a stylist his name is quite obscure—and as an upholsterer: well, I frankly admit I have no idea how to place him."[32] This is a witty way of saying that the apostle is set apart from the run of human beings not by an extraordinary talent but by an extraordinary calling. The apostle is appointed by God to bring what neither eye has seen nor ear heard—namely, deliverance to the captives, hearing to the deaf, sight to the blind, and the good news of salvation to all. Percy likens the apostolic tidings to a message found in a bottle by castaways dwelling on an island. It is not tidings which they bring to themselves—not island news—but "news from across the seas."[33]

There is no way the work of the apostle can be humanly assimilated and historically outstripped. What the apostle announces is utterly and perennially new. So incomparable and heterogeneous is the apostolic message that it cannot be received by ordinary means. The work of genius, by contrast, can be judged by aesthetic and moral criteria: how well it coheres, whether it possesses balance and unity, what new truths it opens up, what old falsehoods it closes off. The apostle's revelation is immune to such judgments. The news of God's justifying and redeeming grace is too paradoxical and surprising thus to be evaluated. It stands or falls solely on the authority of the God who has commissioned it. The Gospel demands, therefore, either radical assent or radical rejection, total obedience or total defiance, absolute trust or absolute suspicion. "I cannot and dare not compel you to obey," Kierkegaard reports the apostle as saying to his audience, "but through your relation to God and in your conscience I make you eternally responsible to God. . . ."[34] Kierkegaard helped make Walker Percy responsible to God not in a vaguely religious way, but in specific conversion to the Roman Catholic faith.

IV. Human Speech and the Human Longing for God

"Here I am a Catholic writer living in Louisiana," Percy confesses, "and the man to whom I owe the greatest debt is this great Protestant thinker."[35] There was no dramatic Damascus road revelation, Percy says, but a gradual clarification of mind and spirit that led him and his wife to take instruction in the Catholic faith.[36] Perhaps it is not too farfetched to say that Kierkegaard helped generate Percy's 1947 conversion to Christianity. It was nothing less than liberating, Percy acknowledges, to read Kierkegaard's declaration that "the only way to be yourself is to be yourself transparently before God."[37]

It is ironic in the extreme that Kierkegaard prompted Percy's conversion not to a lonely Protestant inwardness but to Roman Catholicism. The Percy family had a long Catholic heritage which, as we have seen, Will Percy abandoned while he was a student at Sewanee. Yet Percy's adherence to Rome was far more than an act of filial piety. It was also his means of acquiring a faith that would be scientific and humanist as well as Christian, that would reclaim the strong moral emphasis of W. A. Percy's aristocratic Catonism but without its reactionary bitterness, and that would thus constitute a modern existentialist expression of the venerable Catholic tradition.

The chief debt that Percy owes to Kierkegaard is his radical insistence that God's self-disclosure in Jesus Christ is incomparably authoritative. As Percy himself puts it, Christianity "is not a member in good standing of the World's Great Religions but a unique Person-Event-Thing in time."[38] Yet Kierkegaard was of little use in reconstructing a faith wherein reason and revelation would be held in harmony rather than tension. For Percy as not for Kierkegaard, there is a natural bridge from humanity to divinity, from the human heart to the grace of God. We are filled, Percy believes, with a deep and irrepressible yearning, a nostalgic longing for a home other than the earth. By virtue not only of our sin but also of our birth, we are castaways from the ship whereupon our true destiny rides:

> In his heart of hearts there is not a moment of his life when the castaway does not know that life on the island, being "at home" on the island, is something of a charade. At that very moment when he should feel most at home on the island, when needs are satisfied, knowledge arrived at, family raised, business attended to, at that very moment when by every criterion of island at-homeness he should feel most at home, he feels most homeless. Not one moment of his life passes but that he is aware, however faintly, of his own predicament: that he is a castaway.[39]

Percy's emphasis on humanity's eternal homesickness would seem to be Augustinian. Percy insists, however, on calling it Thomistic. He does so in order to retain Aquinas's emphasis on faith as a form of knowledge—neither a pure Kierkegaardian leap into the absurd, nor an Augustinian deliverance of the will. For while Saint Thomas denies that faith is a purely rational assent achieved through objective knowledge, he maintains that it is an assent which includes cognition. There is no final antinomy between reason and revelation, in Percy's view, because the Gospel is the knowledge that humanity truly longs and needs to have. He does not share Luther and Calvin's conviction that sin so totally penetrates our lives that we do not rightly perceive even our misery. Quite to the contrary for Percy: we know ourselves to be castaways because we still dimly remember the ship whence we were thrown overboard. The stranded exile combs the beaches daily, therefore, in search for "the message in the bottle"—for news from beyond the seas, not island news: "news of where he came from and who he is and what he must do."[40]

Percy agrees with Kierkegaard that the apostolic tidings cannot be aesthetically and morally evaluated like any other piece of news. Yet it can—by the miracle of grace—be heard and received in knowing response to the divine beneficence. This is the irony that, in Percy's view, Kierkegaard missed. In his rightful concern with the transcendent authority of both the Gospel and its bearers, the Danish existentialist underestimated its hearers. It is true that the objective-minded rationalist and the person utterly at home in the world remain deaf to the Gospel. But it is truer still that the glad news of deliverance can speak "to a castaway who knows he is a castaway."[41]

Percy's fiction rivets its attention precisely upon this stranger and wayfarer and castaway. Like the Prodigal Son, the Percy protagonist usu-

ally "comes to himself." His Copernican revolution often happens by
means of the shattering discovery that he can no longer live as a well-adjusted anthropoid. In a crucial essay of 1956, "The Man on the Train,"
Percy recounts the awakening of such a man to existential despair:

> It is just when the alienated [suburban] commuter reads books on
> mental hygiene that he comes closest to despair. One has only to
> let the mental-health savants set forth their own ideal of sane liv-
> ing, [and then to behold] the composite reader who reads their
> books seriously and devotes every ounce of his strength to the pur-
> suit of the goals erected: emotional maturity, inclusiveness, pro-
> ductivity, creativity, belongingness—there will emerge, far more
> faithfully than I could portray him, the candidate for suicide.[42]

Though Percy makes a brilliant existentialist analysis of the castaway created by the modern sciences, he wants also to make a scientific
critique of these same sciences. He is concerned, therefore, to demonstrate anthropologically that we are not anthropoids. We are "hearers
of the Word," Walker Percy believes in accord with his fellow Catholic
Karl Rahner. We cup our ears in the hope of hearing God's voice chiefly
because we are creatures who speak. Language enables us to have commerce not only with ourselves and our fellow creatures; it is also our vehicle for the knowledge of God.

The mysterious phenomenon of speech is the real basis of Percy's
natural theology. It receives most careful analysis in Percy's main nonfiction work, *The Message in the Bottle*. There he seeks to show how the
gift of articulate breath is the single characteristic distinguishing our
species from all others. Confronting the behaviorists and linguists on
their own ground, Percy argues that the acquistion of language entails a
quantum leap out of animality and into humanity. In the act of speaking,
we cease merely to respond to our environment like predictable Pavlo-
vian beasts. Instead, we become individuals capable of sadness and joy,
remembrance and anticipation, damnation and beatitude. We reveal ourselves, in fact, to be formed in the image of God.

It is for this reason that Percy keeps reverting to the summer day of
1887 when, in Tuscumbia, Alabama, Helen Keller made her discovery of
language. Suddenly it broke upon the deaf and mute girl that the marvelous something flowing over her hand was more than a means of slaking
her thirst, that it was an object called *water*, that all things have names,
and that they can be summoned into being with the gift of language. To
acquire the appelative faculty is, Percy argues, to surrender an anthropoid existence. In that transforming moment, Miss Keller ceased
being a higher animal gratifying her needs and satisfying her desires like
any other organism habituated to an environment. She became, on the
contrary, a creature akin to Adam and Eve in Eden: a human being able

to give names to things, to hold an entire universe in her head, to commit sin and to confess faith, and thus to live and die before God no less than her fellow humans. "For the first time," Miss Keller later wrote, "I felt repentance and sorrow." For Percy it was nothing less than a transcendent event:

> Eight-year-old Helen made her breakthrough from the good responding animal which behaviorists study so successfully to the strange name-giving and sentence-uttering creature who begins by naming shoes and ships and sealing-wax, and later tells jokes, curses, reads the paper, writes *La sua volontade é nostra pace*, or becomes a Hegel and composes an entire system of philosophy.[43]

Percy attempts to construct a theory of language that will take full account of both the physical and mental worlds, and yet not imprison us in either of them. Drawing heavily on the work of both Susanne Langer and Charles Peirce, he contends that the symbol is what differentiates human from animal life. Animal behavior is controlled by what Peirce called dyadic events: one thing directly causes another, a stimulus leading to a response, as in Newtonian mechanics. Very little human action, in Percy's estimate, occurs in this fashion. The phenomenon of talking and listening, Percy argues via Peirce, is not dyadic but triadic. The causal circuitry is indeed present as it is in the dyadic events of animal life. But in human exchanges, there is a third reality standing between the creature and the world—namely, the symbol whereby the two are joined. Nor is it a bare sign pointing to an object and describing its physical characteristics. The symbol is also a means of grasping and asserting the significance of the thing symbolized.

"When Helen Keller learned that water was *water*, she then wished to know what other things 'were'—until the world she knew was named."[44] The relation between a symbol and its referent is not causal, therefore, but intentional. Naming is the unique and mysterious act whereby we project into existence a world of spiritual meaning. Sign-using animals inhabit, by contrast, a merely external environment. There is thus a mysterious union between the knower and the known that keeps us from being locked in either the mental productions of our heads or the energy exchanges of animal behavior. "Knowing is not a causal sequence but an immaterial union. It is a union, however, which is mediated through material entities, the symbol and its object."[45]

Yet a very real question remains: Is Percy's *description* of symbolic behavior also an *explanation* of how it actually works? In his early essays Percy denies that any scientific method could ever span the gap between physical events and animal responses on the one hand, and human intentions and spiritual propositions on the other: "Thomas Aquinas called attention to the qualitative difference between the events which take place in the world and the act by which the intellect grasps these events."[46] Yet in more recent articles and interviews, Percy seems determined to find a scientific explanation for the mystery of speech and symbol. He praises semiotics—the systematic study of semantic signs and linguistic structures—as the *Novum Organum* for our age. It will accomplish what theology and psychology and sociology have failed to do—namely, to define scientifically the phenomenon of human uniqueness. Whereas the old behaviorist science ignored the importance of consciousness, the radical new science of semiotics will restore the self to its proper place as the central human reality.[47]

This scientific confidence seems naive at best. Semiotics overcomes the old reductionistic theories of language only at a terrible price: it turns *everything* into a potentially meaning-laden sign. Percy ignores the nihilistic conclusions to which such open-endedness can lead: if everything signifies, perhaps nothing does. Weldon Thornton has also pointed out the reductionism latent in Percy's own argument for a "neurophysiological correlate" to the triadic establishment of meaning. Like an unironic Dr. Thomas More, Percy even attempts to locate the portion of the brain where this symbolic activity originates: the "massive interconnections between the auditory and visual cortexes."[48] Percy's search for a physical substratum to the act of naming is, as Thornton observes, a fundamental denial of his original insight. The birth of language thrusts us out of an animal at-homeness in the world, Percy once saw, and into a perpetual castaway condition. Our divided state of being will persist, Thornton contends, no matter what theories of language we develop to explain it.[49]

Whatever the limits of Percy's scientific theorizing, one salient fact holds true: his intention is to create a Catholic existentialism with a firm anthropological base. He begins with the mystery of the human, and then seeks to find its suprahuman Source. Not for Percy the radical Protestant insistence that all true knowledge of God issues from God's own self-disclosure in Israel and Christ. The perennial relevance of Christian faith lies, for Percy, in its power to answer our divinely ingrained longing. He attempts to develop a theory of language that will account for this irrepressible human desire for God.

Only through an anthropologially up-to-date faith, Percy believes, can any appeal be made to the cultured—and the often uncultured—despisers of religion. Nothing do secularists wish for more fondly than an easy means of dismissing the Jewish-Christian scandal as a mere absurdity. It will not suffice, in Percy's view, for believers to maintain the integrity of the Gospel within the walls of the church. Believers must also demonstrate, in worldly terms, how this transcendent message impinges on secular culture. Percy is thus the advocate of a Catholic existentialism which will not abandon humanity to its scientifically humanist friends, who are in fact its real enemies.

The heart of Percy's Catholic existentialism lies in the Pascalian belief that paradox and incommensurability are our essential inheritance. This means, above all, that the human condition is not a problem to be solved so much as a mystery to be lived. Yet Percy is convinced that for the past three hundred years—at least since the time of Descartes—powerful cultural forces have been at work to deny the mystery of the human. The Western world has been bent on a repudiation of our divinely ingrained and irrepressible longing for God. The galling contradiction, for Percy, is that our secular and scientific humanism has virtually destroyed humanity.

Whatever political or economic sources one may assign to them, the totalitarian horrors of our age have their real root, Percy believes, in the legacy of the Enlightenment. "The triumphant secular society of the Western world, the nicest of all worlds, killed more people in the first half of this century than have been killed in all history."[50] Yet our calamity is writ large not only in Hiroshima, the Gulag, and the Holocaust. The inward spiritual collapse of the West is altogether as appalling. Percy finds it especially devasting in his own native land.

The American experiment, like the modern epoch itself, was born amidst high-sounding declarations about humanity's inalienable rights, the sacredness of life, the value of freedom, and the dignity of the individual. These exalted humanist phrases were once held in place, Percy believes, by their theological anchorage. Gradually, however, they have slipped their moorings. Now they are totally at sea, pitching and listing and floundering. The grand theological humanism of the past has been replaced by a scientific humanism that is an absurd caricature of the original. Ours is a humanism unable, ironically, to accord unique value to humanity. Here, in Percy's words, is what we have come to believe about ourselves and our kind:

> Man can be understood as an organism in an environment, a sociological unit, an encultured creature, a psychological dynamism endowed genetically like other organisms with needs and drives, who through evolution has developed strategies for learning and surviving by means of certain adaptive transactions with the environment.[51]

Yet it will not suffice simply to reassert, intact and unmodified, the venerable humanism of the Catholic Middle Ages. Though himself a convert to pre-Vatican II Catholicism—the narrator of *Lancelot* remarks, acerbically, that the new "guitar-strumming, ass-wiggling nuns" looked much better in their habits than in J.C. Penney pantsuits!—Percy is convinced that the traditional theological categories are dead for most modern secular people. Sin and salvation, grace and redemption, eternal perdition and the life to come—these terms have been virtually bankrupted of their rich originality. "The old words of grace are worn smooth as poker chips and a certain devaluation has occurred, like a poker chip after it has been cashed in."[52] As Binx Bolling will say in *The Moviegoer*, a curtain lowers in his head whenever the word *God* is mentioned.

How, then, can we recover the perduring—far more, the indispensable—Reality to which the theological categories point? Percy in his later essays may hold out hope for a theory of language that would physiologically explain the divine Presence at work in our human midst. But in his fiction he knows better. By means of a reconstructed Catholic existentialism, Percy shows nearly all of his protagonists backing their way into the household of faith. They are made to discern that it is not a new science that we need so much as a renewed faith. Even if Percy cannot announce the glad tidings of salvation, his novels can alert us to our unacknowledged despair. If they cannot reestablish the Catholic humanism upon which the Western tradition was built, they can alert us to the inanity and inhumanity of the scientific humanism that has taken its place. And for Percy the doctor, diagnosis is at least half the cure. Indeed, his prophetic satire is premised on the conviction that to detect one's disease is to begin one's recovery.

8

PERCY AS THE SATIRIST SATIRIZED: THE MOVIEGOER

Readers have sometimes complained that Walker Percy keeps writing the same book over and again: a book about a man who, like the Prodigal Son, "comes to himself" by awakening to his unacknowledged despair. If such a charge be true, then *The Moviegoer* (1961) is Percy's quintessential work. It is his most convincing portrayal of the prototypical Percy hero: a choleric man who is weary of modern life, who can smell its stench in his very nostrils, who ridicules its idiocies with brilliant mockery, yet who himself is caught in a malaise worse than the deadness he derides, who is delivered from his own gelidity of soul by an uncanny transformation of grace, and who, almost inadvertently, takes up a *vita nuova* of marriage and work and worship. For all its indebtedness to Camus's *The Stranger*, therefore, Percy's novel is not only an American account of personal and metaphysical alienation; it is also a depiction of comic victory over religious despair.

This triumph is the implicit concern of Percy's entire work, yet nowhere is it achieved so convincingly as in this first novel. In *The Last Gentleman* (1967), Will Barrett is an American and amnesiac version of Dostoevski's Prince Myshkin. He is an addled spiritual naif possessed of a scandalous immunity to the allurements of sex and money and tradition. He seeks God. Yet—and this is the novel's chief irony—Barrett's passionate pilgrimage leads nowhere. The novel's funniest passages show him attempting to extract religious wisdom and guidance form Dr. Sutter Vaught, a profane and very unwilling Vergil. Vaught's own medical casebook brilliantly catalogues the spiritual and sexual ills that plague our culture, while proposing no other solution to the modern ailment than suicidal drinking and whoring. At the novel's end, as in no other Percy work, Barrett still has not found his way to transcendent faith. Yet the reader remains convinced that Will has learned from his wanderings what moral and metaphysical dead ends he must now avoid. Even so, the novel is so outrageously picaresque—especially the travel scenes in the middle—that it often reads like a cartoon rather than an accomplished piece of fiction.

Love in the Ruins (1971) is Walker Percy's most hilarious analysis of the spiritual disaster that has befallen late-modern America. It recounts, futuristically, the life and times of a lapsed Catholic named Dr. Thomas More, a lineal descendant of the Renaissance humanist-saint. The novel is set during the week of July 4, 1983—at the apocalyptic eve of Orwell's predicted end of the modern experiment. Though it may have seemed like zany hyperbole when it was first published, Love in the Ruins reads now like a palpable prophecy. More is a man who cannot thrive in our consumer's paradise. Like all the other Percy protagonists, he is an American lost in America. It is a country which has spiritually fallen apart. Its religious and political center has not held. It has unleashed, in fact, a terrible monstrousness upon itself and the world.

Wolves howl in the streets of Cleveland. Buzzards circle New Orleans seeking carrion. Vines sprout through cracks in the interstate highways. Parking lots lie full of moldering cars. Ours is a nation, More laments, where one can buy anything but get nothing fixed. It is neither the communists nor the atheists who have done us in. America is dying for want of repairpersons! Unlike his canonized ancestor, Dr. More's condition is worsened because he is both a Christian and a humanist. His science triumphs over his faith—until, at the very end, he undergoes an unbidden redemption. The dread apocalypse More has feared does not occur. Almost against his will, he is catapulted into a responsible and faithful life. Yet More's mock-epic damnation and deliverance are so satirically portrayed that the reader's credulity is frequently strained.

Lancelot (1977) is a far more successful work of fiction. It is the gripping confession of a Nietzschean madman named Lancelot Andrewes Lamar. He is enraged by the decadence of our time. Lamar prefers war, he says, to "what this age calls love," and he had rather "die with T. J. Jackson at Chancellorsville [than] live with Johnny Carson in Burbank." There is no mistaking Percy's deep sympathy for this man's moral fury. He is rightly angered at what he calls the American baboon colony, where men and women cohabit as indiscriminately as characters in a soap opera. In opposition to our sodden sexuality, Lamar proposes a stern new morality of courtly righteousness. Percy's implied critique of such nostalgic Catonism is largely lost amidst the ethical rage that Lamar so powerfully ventilates. Lancelot is thus, as Percy says, "a cautionary tale." The tone of the novel is so indignant that it overwhelms whatever hope may be implicit in the psychiatrist-priest who patiently listens to Lancelot's ravings.

If misanthropic scorn is Percy's temptation on the one side, sentimental romanticism is his tendency on the other. The Second Coming

(1980) purports to be a sequel to *The Last Gentleman*, and yet the Will Barrett whom we meet there has turned strangely saccharine. When a retired stockbroker finds salvation between the thighs of a girl young enough to be his granddaughter, there is indeed cause for alarm. Nor does Barrett's newfound happiness have much to do with the ordinary world—work and worship, politics and the family—where real faith is tested and confirmed. He makes brave *übermenschliche* claims about finding the absent God and thus transcending both species of contemporary nonsense: the "Christian assholes" who blandly believe everything, and the "atheist assholes" who fatuously believe nothing. Yet for all his hard talk, there is something spiritually soft about Barrett. He cares more about his own religious journey than the shrine toward which he presumably travels. His own going seems to matter more than the Goal.

The Moviegoer, by contrast, is a theological no less than a literary triumph. It is not only Walker Percy's most successful but also his most autobiographical novel. Though artfully transmuted into fiction, there is more of Percy's own story in this novel than in any of his other works. He gives to Binx Bolling his own vagrant delay in deciding upon a vocation, to Kate Cutrer his unsuccessful venture into psychoanalysis, to Aunt Emily the Southern Catonism of his Uncle Will, and to Binx's paraplegic half-brother Lonnie Smith his unapologetic Catholic faith. These deep strands of Percy's own life are woven into a work of convincing artistic unity and power. Percy's bilious disdain for our American torpidity of spirit is here checked by the gracious recognition that anger is not enough. The novel's final irony is that Bolling can cast out the mote in everyone else's eye but is powerless to remove the beam in his own. The physician himself needs healing.

The novel's success does not derive from a well-made plot. Very little in the way of external action occurs during the eight days of his life that Binx Bolling recounts. There is indeed no mystery to be solved except the quandary of what this twenty-nine-year-old New Orleans stockbroker and skirtchaser will do with his life. Aunt Emily repeatedly reminds him that he is a shirker for not using his scientific skills to do medical research. Yet neither his own hedonism nor his aunt's moralism is a sufficient answer for Binx Bolling's condition. The inadequacy of these conventional alternatives is suggested by the fact that the novel's action unfolds during Mardi Gras, the week of carnival preceding the season of Lent. Binx may have lived a wastrel life, as Aunt Emily insists, but her stern summons to duty will not deliver him from his self-absorption. Nothing less than the miraculous grace of Ash Wednesday can serve, in the arresting phrase of Kafka, as an axe to break the frozen sea within him.

The real target of Percy's satirical spleen is made evident in the novel's epigraph from Kierkegaard in *The Sickness unto Death*: "The specific character of despair is precisely this: it is unaware of being despair." *The Moviegoer* aims at satirically awakening the reader, and finally the narrator himself, to our shared but unacknowledged despair. The failure to recognize one's hopelessness—usually in the midst of thriving prosperity, and while thinking all to be well—is the real "sickness unto death." Like Kierkegaard, Percy does not attempt a frontal assault on our spiritual inertia. Not for him "the old military science," as Kierkegaard calls it, that seeks to assail untruth head-on. Such overt confrontation assumes our unimpaired capacity to recognize the truth when it is demonstrated. If, however, our fundamental problem is that we labor under a massive cultural and theological illusion, then an open strike is the worst possible strategy. "A direct attack," says Kierkegaard, "only strengthens a person in his illusion, and at the same time embitters him. There is nothing that requires such gentle handling as an illusion, if one wishes to dispel it. If anything prompts the prospective captive to set his will in opposition, all is lost."[1]

Neither condemnation nor denunciation, says Kierkegaard, can stir one from the deadness of despair. The best offensive is indirect, an assault from the rear. To be prodded from behind by some unknown force, to be turned around in surprise and astonishment, and thus to be puzzled into the truth: this is the deliverance that neither prematurely antagonizes nor falsely compels the will. On the contrary, it enables the free confession that one must make "to himself alone before God—that he has lived hitherto in an illusion."[2] For Percy, therefore, as for Kierkegaard, satiric comedy is a means for deceiving an audience into honesty before oneself and before God. To laugh at one's own false ease within an uneasy world is to be liberated from spiritual complacency. Yet it is not finally the folly of others that Percy invites to self-scorn. The comedy of *The Moviegoer* is gracious rather than bilious because Percy also turns his mockery upon himself, satirizing the satirist.

I. Binx Bolling as a Man in Conscious Despair

When we first encounter Binx Bolling, he is living the gently amoral life of a moviegoer and womanizer who has surrendered all religious aspirations. His "old longings" and "grand ambitions" led nowhere but to a detached sense of himself as a creature existing *sub specie aeternitatis*. His "vertical search," as he calls it, had rendered him angelically unreal. It tempted him to view life abstractly from above, as if by reading "key books on key subjects" he could solve the riddle of the universe. His philosophic quest afforded him a high and airy perch whence he could obtain the kind of "knowledge which can be arrived at anywhere by anyone at any time."[3] Such knowledge also enabled him to ignore the concrete conditions and problems of his own particular life. He recalls with special vividness the night he finished a book entitled *The Chemistry of Life*. There was something strangely unsatisfying, he discovered, about having a final explanation of reality: "The only difficulty was that though the universe had been disposed of, I myself was left over. There I lay in my hotel room with my search over yet still obliged to draw one breath and then the next."[4]

This is a direct echo, even a plagiarizing, of Kierkegaard's witticism about Hegel: that he was the philosopher who had to live in a shanty outside the palace of his all-encompassing but uninhabitable system of ideas. Yet Binx is not really sorry that his religious and philosophical quest has ended. It has left him happily aloof from everything. He is not at all eager to saddle himself permanently with any earthly attachments. Binx Bolling is in fact an aesthete, and precisely in Kierkegaard's sense of the word. Kierkegaard defines an aesthete not, in conventional fashion, as one who lives for fine things, but as one whose love of wit and sex is a means of holding oneself apart from life. Aesthetes keep the world at arm's length, committing themselves to nothing and distancing themselves from everything that would ensnare their triumphant self-awareness:

> The essence of pleasure does not lie in the thing enjoyed, but in the accompanying consciousness. If I had a humble spirit in my service who, when I asked for a glass of water, brought me the world's costliest wines blended in a chalice, I should dismiss him, in order to teach him that pleasure consists not in what I enjoy, but in having my own way.[5]

So speaks Kierkegaard's pseudonymous aesthete, and so reasons Binx Bolling. He does not want pleasure so much as he desires to have his own way. The means for such mastery is an exquisite self-consciousness. In sardonic mockery of Saint Thérèse of Lisieux, Binx has adopted what he calls "the Little Way." Instead of following the girl saint's example of self-renunciation in even the smallest of matters, he is determined to indulge himself in the benignly hedonist life of "drinks and kisses, a good little car and a warm deep thigh."[6]

Bolling has embarked, in fact, on what he calls "a horizontal search." Having despaired of transcendent truth, he has become a connoisseur of the earthly and the ordinary. Rather than ascending the heights, he will descend to the *terra firma* of specific and unpretentious pleasures: the sight of fine aluminum finishing on the local Catholic school, the sound of squeaking cartilage in the wings of low-flying birds, the very taste of the Gulf air. Above all, he will cultivate his own omnipotent self-awareness. It alone can make him the master of every situation, and thus free him from enslavement to anyone or anything other than his own unconquerable soul. Rather than die an ignominious death by living according to conventional expectations, Bolling determines to stay spiritually alert by living on his own terms and having his own way.

Just as Kierkegaard's aesthete attends the middle portion of plays and reads the third part of books, so does Binx live with a willful arbitrariness. He has chosen to reside, for example, in an undistinguished middle-class New Orleans suburb called Gentilly. Not for him the decadent artiness of the French Quarter nor the elegant luxury of the Garden District. The residents of both these fashionable neighborhoods, though seeming to have nothing in common, are alike in their belief than an ideal environment can make them spiritually alive.

In revolt against such emptiness of soul, Binx decides to live in an utterly nondescript place. Instead of chafing at bourgeois stupidities, he mockingly embraces them. Determined to hug rather than to orbit the earth, Bolling occupies a basement apartment owned by a fireman's widow with an ironic name: Schexnaydre (pronounced "She's nadir"). There he leads a pseudoconformist life:

> I am a model tenant and a model citizen and take pleasure in doing all that is expected of me. My wallet is full of identity cards, library cards, credit cards. . . . It is a pleasure to carry out the duties of a citizen and to receive in return a neat styrene card with one's name on it certifying, so to speak, one's right to exist. What satisfaction I take in appearing the first day to get my auto tag and brake sticker! I subscribe to *Consumer Reports* and as a consequence I own a first-class television set, an all but silent air conditioner and a very long lasting deodorant. My armpits never stink. I pay attention to all spot announcements on the radio about mental health, the seven signs of cancer and safe driving. . . . Yesterday, a favorite of mine, William Holden, delivered a radio announcement on litterbugs. "Let's face it," said Holden. "Nobody can do anything about it—but you and me." This is true. I have been careful ever since.[7]

There are limits to Binx's antic acceptance of our cultural inanity and spiritual triteness. He seeks to make gentle fun of it, but there are times when the bile comes boiling out of him. He is especially impatient with people who eagerly embrace life without ever asking where it comes from, where it ends, why it is so miserable, or what it ultimately signifies. Bolling's cousin Nell Lovell and her husband Eddie are two such dead souls who have all the appearance of life. They claim, in fact, to have begun their marriage anew, now that their children have grown up and left home. The Lovells are taking philosophy courses and working at the Little Theater. At night they sit by the fireside, read Kahlil Gibran, and refuse to regard life as gloomy at all. "Eddie and I have re-examined our values," Nell assures Binx, "and found them pretty darn enduring."

"Books and people and things," she gushes, "are endlessly fascinating." To such unconscious spiritual vapidity, Binx cannot make a reply; but he does feel a rumble commencing in his "descending bowel, heralding a tremendous defecation."[8]

Scatological images run throughout *The Moviegoer*. Like Nietzsche, Binx is a man whose genius lies in his nostrils. He can *smell* the lie that passes as the truth, the excrement that our age has confused with wild honey. In one of his fiercest diatribes, Bolling calls this "the very century of *merde*, the great shithouse of scientific humanism where needs are satisfied, everyone becomes an anyone, a warm and creative person, and prospers like a dung beetle, and one hundred percent of people are humanists and ninety-eight percent believe in God, and men are dead, dead, dead; and the malaise has settled like a fall-out and what people really fear is not that the bomb will fall but that the bomb will not fall."[9] Though himself an unbeliever, Binx knows how foul is the stench of a humanism without God. It claims to believe only in this present life, and yet it yearns for death. Nuclear annihilation—supposedly our worst dread—is, in fact, our deepest wish. So little do we have to live for that our secret fear is not that we will be incinerated, says Binx, but that we will have to go on endlessly with this charade of lifeless life.

Nowhere is Bolling's impatience with spiritual deadness more amusingly revealed than in his response to Edward R. Murrow's radio program called "This I Believe." He listens to it in secular penance for the inane sins of the world. "Monks have their compline," says Binx; "I have This I Believe."[10] All manner of well-meaning folk call Mr. Murrow to affirm their belief in the sacredness of the individual and the brotherhood of man, in understanding and tolerance, in music and love and a child's smile. None of these things is intrinsically objectionable. But when the gods go, as Emerson noted, the half-gods arrive. What were once exalted ideas and beliefs, able to inspire heroic acts of civic virtue and religious sacrifice, have now become empty and self-serving catch phrases. Hence Bolling's own vitriolic testimonial: "Here are the beliefs of John Bickerson Bolling, a moviegoer living in New Orleans. . . . I believe in a good kick in the ass. This—I believe."[11]

Bolling believes that our banal brand of humanism dehumanizes us by destroying our particular identity and character. In the name of such universal values as tolerance and openness, we are becoming ever more bland and mediocre. G. K. Chesterton once declared tolerance to be "a virtue only to those who believe nothing." He also said that "the object of opening the mind, as of opening the mouth, is to shut it again on something solid." Like Chesterson, Binx is healthily intolerant. His mind is unapologetically clamped on the conviction that human existence thrives amidst the rooted particulars of history and place. This is why travel threatens to turn him diaphanous and unreal. Nothing does

Bolling dread more than a stockbroker's convention in San Francisco or Chicago. As a man of Southern soil and air and speech, he cannot take lightly the prospect of closing his eyes in New Orleans and waking up in a place whose concrete life is unknown to him:

> It is my fortune and misfortune to know how the spirit-presence of a strange place can enrich a man or rob a man but never leave him alone, how, if a man travels lightly to a hundred strange cities and cares nothing for the risk he takes, he may find himself No one and Nowhere. Great day in the morning. What will it mean to go mosying down Michigan Avenue in the neighborhood of five million strangers, each shooting out his own personal ray? How can I deal with five million personal rays?[12]

Binx is convinced that our pseudoscientific humanism renders us most ethereal and falsely angelic in what it teaches us about sex. Our obsession with the erotic is the sign not of a gross materialism but of a spiritual unworldliness. It does not take us deeper into ourselves but abstracts us into the realm of idealized possibility. Kierkegaard's Don Juan has "a thousand and three in Spain alone," but not one lasting love. Our abstracted eroticism, like his, makes us fall in love with a sexual ideal that no living, suffering human being could ever embody. This, if nothing else, Binx Bolling understands.

On the train to Chicago, Binx finds himself sitting next to a man reading an advice column on marital relations. That so deep a mystery as marriage and sex should be treated as a matter of journalistic counsel reminds Bolling of his own encounter with a couple of sex evangelists named Dr. and Mrs. Bob Dean. They were hawking their manual entitled *Technique in Marriage* at a department store. These apostles of the orgasm, convinced that intimate love depends on simultaneously achieved climacterics, reveal how dreadfully impersonal and mechanical our idea of sex has become. For the Deans, as for popular psychology in general, successful copulation is one of the primary human "needs," and thus an act not essentially different from excretion or ingestion. It is a skill to be mastered with scientific proficiency. Binx recalls a passage from the Deans' love manual, and then offers his own acerbic vision of these "sexperts" at work:

> "Now with a tender regard for your partner [Binx had read] remove your hand from the nipple and gently manipulate." It is impossible not to imagine them at their researches, as solemn as a pair of brontosauruses, their heavy old freckled limbs twined about each other, hands probing skillfully for sensitive zones, pigmented areolas, out-of-the-way mucous glands, dormant vascular nexuses. A wave of prickling passes over me such as I have never experienced before.[13]

II. The Hierarchy of Unconscious Despair

It is not easy for Binx to retain his sanity amidst such an insane world. When the hair on his neck is not rising up like a dog's in shuddering disbelief, he is acutely dissecting the spiritual corpses around him. His awareness of their moribund condition serves as a bleak reminder that, at the least, he is alive as they are not. In fact, Bolling ranks his acquaintances on an ascending hierarchy of self-consciousness: from those who are inwardly so inert as to be near animals; to those who, like himself, have such overwrought spirits as to be virtual angels. Yet Binx's acute perception of our spiritual malaise has the paradoxical effect of making him its worst victim. He is in danger of becoming a diagnostician without a cure—indeed, a physician who is blind to his own disease.

Bolling's Uncle Jules Cutrer occupies the lowest rung on the ladder of oblivious despair. So genial and generous a soul is he, so utterly untroubled a businessman and citizen and husband, that his brow is never creased with woe except when someone mentions the annual football trouncing that Louisiana State University visits upon Tulane, his hometown alma mater. Jules Cutrer is a man, says Binx, "whose victory in the world is total and unqualified." Not for a moment does Bolling want to shatter the comfortable illusion wherein his uncle happily resides; on the contrary, Binx envies this genial man's contented state. What puzzles Binx, however, is Jules's faithfulness as a Catholic. He wonders why his uncle would bother with sacramental communion and eschatological expectation when he finds secular life so completely satisfying: "The world he lives in, the City of Man, is so pleasant that the City of God must hold little in store for him."[14]

Somewhat higher up the scale of self-consciousness is the Cutrer's Negro retainer named Mercer. Rightly discontent at being a docile Uncle Tom, Mercer has become a man with "aspirations." He wants to enter the white world of culture and education, and so he reads news magazines and speaks knowledgeably about current events. The awful irony is that, in transcending the servant role white society thrust upon him, Mercer has also abandoned his distinct character as a black man. Binx is especially troubled when he finds that Mercer has taken up with the Rosicrucians and is reading a book entitled *How to Harness Your Secret Powers*. If this be freedom from the stereotypical behavior that whites expect of blacks, then Binx prefers the stereotype. Mercer is lost in the no man's land between the "Tomming" lackey and the aspirant to higher things. This neither-nor status explains why Mercer's "eyes get muddy and his face runs together behind his mustache," and why Binx calls him a "poor bastard."[15]

Further still up the ladder of reflective consciousness is Binx's father. Though he was killed in the First War, Binx remembers him vividly, especially his sharp sense of irony. Binx keeps looking at a photograph that shows him on the European grand tour, his arms planted around an alpenstock, his hat pushed back on his forehead, his eyes afire with an impish delight. Everyone else in this group picture "coincides with himself," Binx notes, "just as the larch trees in the photograph coincide with themselves."[16] The other youths are the sum total of their parts, just as a plant or animal is. But young Dr. Bolling is no such well-adjusted creature with an inward self totally commensurate with his public person. There is something unique and unaccountable about him, something that would not register on the Rorschach or the Minnesota Multiphasic.

The sad fact is that Dr. Bolling never found a way of realizing his special selfhood. Like W. A. Percy, he was at once a rationalist and a romantic. Because he could not reconcile these contradictory inclinations, his life oscillated between the fact-world of science and the feeling-world of poetry. He also experienced mood swings of both ecstasy and dismay. There were times when Dr. Bolling was so sickened with himself and the world that he could not swallow a single bite of food, not even grits. But at the outbreak of the First War, he put on thirty pounds (again like Uncle Will) in order to make himself eligible for military service. As a member of the Canadian Air Force, he was killed in Crete making a heroic Byronic defense of freedom. Yet Binx fears that his father became a romantic about war because he was "a left-over from his own science."[17] Those who live strictly by analytic reason, Binx suggests, are so emotionally starved that they must perform extraordinary acts of passion or will to keep their souls alive. It is evident that neither his science nor his poetry afforded Dr. Bolling any ultimate basis for living. His may have been an exalted form of despair but, for Binx as also for Percy, it was despair nonetheless.

At the apex of self-conscious hopelessness stands Binx's aunt, Emily Cutrer. She is one of those fierce, high-minded Southern women who not only do right themselves but who make sure everyone else does right as well. Though she is now sixty-five, she retains the same soldierly outlook that made her a Red Cross volunteer in the Spanish Civil War and that makes her still regard twenty-nine-year-old Binx as her own special charge. Aunt Emily is to Binx Bolling very much as Uncle Will was to Walker Percy. She has taught Binx to honor truth and beauty, to reverence Plato and the Stoics, and above all to live by the venerable ideal of *noblesse oblige*. Aunt Emily has a religious obligation, she believes, to transcend the limits of particular confessions, even of particular religions. She describes herself—in a declaration not meant to be funny—as "an Episcopalian by emotion, a Greek by nature and a Buddhist by choice."[18] Though Binx finds Aunt Emily's arrogant claim amusing, he cannot laugh at her stern Stoic heroism:

> "I don't quite know what we're doing on this insignificant cinder spinning away in a dark corner of the universe" [she confesses to Binx]. "That is a secret which the high gods have not confided in me. Yet one thing I believe and I believe it with every fibre of my being. A man must live by his lights and do whatever he can and do it as best he can. In this world goodness is destined to be defeated. But a man must go down fighting. That is the victory. To do anything less is to be less than a man."[19]

Binx Bolling is unwilling to dismiss Emily Cutrer's dutiful pessimism. Far from scorning her bleak humanism, he wished he could subscribe to it. When on the novel's first page Binx prepares for one of his periodic meetings with Aunt Emily to talk about his future, he knows that he faces still another stern lecture. Yet Binx does "not find the prospect altogether unpleasant."[20] Her fierce moral probity assures him that the world has an ethical character, that he is not free to shape his life in whatever way proves expedient, and that there are standards which he contravenes only at his peril. Yet Binx discerns something existentially, indeed theologically, empty about his aunt's ethical call to arms. She can tell Binx *what* he should do but not *why* he should do it. Her secular summons to courage and bravery in face of the lowering gloom cannot truly register upon a man whose questions are more religious than ethical. When, therefore, she asks an obvious question that seems to demand an obvious answer—"Don't you feel obliged to use your brain and to make a contribution?"—Binx replies with wry and unobvious honesty, "No'm."[21]

Bolling's conflict with Aunt Emily comes to its sharpest focus near the end of the novel. Her moral vision is there revealed as indeed Catonist rather than Stoic. She does not have the Stoic's conviction of the world's ultimate order and significance. She envisions, instead, the decay and loss of everything. Her diatribe against American mediocrity is perhaps the fiercest to be found in our fiction. Like the Younger Cato, Aunt Emily decries the death of classic piety and grace, of noble duty and morality. In their place, she says, we have enthroned the common man as our final standard. Playing upon the old usage of the term *common* to mean something vulgar and unworthy, she unloads her invective against Binx's sorry character and the many others who share it:

> "Our civilization has achieved a distinction of sorts. It will be remembered not for its technology nor even its wars but for its novel ethos. Ours is the only civilization in history which has enshrined

mediocrity as its national ideal. Others have been corrupt, but leave it to us to invent the most undistinguished of corruptions. No orgies, no blood running in the street, no babies thrown off cliffs. No, we're a sentimental people and we horrify easily. True, our moral fiber is rotten. Our national character stinks to high heaven. But we are kinder than ever. No prostitute ever responded with a quicker spasm of sentiment [than] when our hearts are touched. Nor is there anything new about thievery, lewdness, lying, adultery. What is new is that in our time liars and thieves and whores and adulterers wish also to be congratulated and are congratulated by the great public, if their confession is sufficiently psychological or strikes a sufficiently heartfelt and authentic note of sincerity. Oh, we are sincere, I do not deny it. I don't know anybody nowadays who is not sincere. . . . We are the most sincere Laodiceans who ever got flushed down the sinkhole of history."[22]

Walker Percy's fan mail may have congratulated him for having Aunt Emily tell the unvarnished truth, but there is something almost pathetic about her final fury. Like the dying Kierkegaard inveighing against decadent Christendom, Emily Cutrer knows that her world is dead beyond all reviving. Riven with grief that Binx will not carry on her heroic tradition, she has become bitterly desperate in upholding her vanishing ideal: ". . . all I can say is that I am content to be fading out of the picture. Perhaps we are a biological sport. I am not sure. But one thing I am sure of: we live by our lights, we die by our lights, and whoever the high gods may be, we'll look them in the eye without apology."[23] This scene recalls the ending of *Lanterns on the Levee*, where Will Percy also vows not to genuflect before the gods but to straighten his shoulders and to announce that he is their son. Yet for all their seeming confidence, both speeches breathe an air of unrecognized futility.

Binx is more bored than stricken by Aunt Emily's denunciation. All the while she is pummeling the delinquencies of our age, Bolling stares at a letter opener whose point he bent, many years ago, when prying open a drawer. Emily Cutrer's stern moralism is, for Binx, as pointless as this blunted instrument. Her fierce righteousness is not so much untruthful as it is ungracious. It fails to register upon Binx because it is void of ultimate hope. Why live and die by one's lights if life is but a tale told by an idiot, if we are to the gods as flies to wanton boys, a cruel sport for monstrous deities? Percy hints, in fact, that Aunt Emily's moral rigor must itself be purged. During her fulminations against modern mediocrity, a black chimney sweep passes outside the window advertising his services: "*R-r-r-ramonez la cheminée du haut en bas*," he cries.[24] Emily Cutrer's graceless call to duty is a sooty flue, Percy suggests, in need of its own top-to-bottom cleansing.

III. The Emptiness of a Purely Self-Conscious Life

Despite his ability to discern the emptiness of the world around him—and especially of his Aunt Emily's Catonist humanism—Binx Bolling remains an imperfect judge of his own condition. He is far clearer about what he despises than what he loves. He can name all the species of hopelessness but cannot point to the way of hope. However admirable his refusal to drink the swill that our culture regards as wine, Binx is in danger of becoming what Kierkegaard calls a figure of defiant despair—a man who relishes his own melancholy, who desperately wills to be himself even if his life becomes a hellish torture:

> Even if at this point God in heaven and all his angels were to offer to help him out of it—no, now he doesn't want it, now it is too late, he once would have given everything to be rid of this torment but was made to wait, now that's all past, now he would rather rage against everything, he, the one man in the whole of existence who is the most unjustly treated, to whom it is especially important to have his torment at hand, important that no one should take it from him—for thus he can convince himself that he is in the right.[25]

Like Kierkegaard's defiant man of despair, Binx professes an invincible unbelief. Whenever the word *God* is mentioned, he says, a curtain lowers in his head.[26] Yet Bolling is unlike the Kierkegaardian demoniac in being unable to believe himself always in the right. Binx has longings that he cannot suppress. There are moments when he cannot deny his own entrapment in what he calls "everydayness." Percy borrows this term from Martin Heidegger, whose idea of *Alltäglichkeit* he interprets as a thoughtless conformity to the world, a massive boredom and indifference toward life. Yet it infects Binx no less than the moribund creatures he indicts. As the acerbic critic of our cultural deadness, Bolling is not himself positively alive. Indeed, he is in danger of the worst death of all: the living death of conscious but immobilized despair.

Binx's one hope for deliverance from this spiritual torpor lies in what he calls his "search." "The search," Binx declares early in the novel, "is what anyone would undertake if he were not sunk in the everydayness of his own life."[27] He knows, at least secretly, that his aesthete absorption in the viscous reality of the horizontal is no more authentic than his old angelic quest for vertical significance. Both endeavors have left him immured in an "invincible apathy,"[28] unable to escape his own disordered and purposeless life.

Yet Binx cannot forget his first awakening to transcendent self-awareness. It occurred when he was wounded in the Korean War. Like Tolstoy's Prince Andrew lying injured at the battle of Borodino and being suddenly struck by the immensity of the sky, so did the prostrate Binx undergo a fundamental shock of recognition. It was neither pain nor the threat of death that stirred young Bolling; what moved him was the sight of a dung beetle scratching in the dirt right beneath his face. This experience made Binx ask the unavoidable question of life's final worth: whether it is created and redeemed by God, or whether it is a mound of refuse where dung beetles matter altogether as much as human beings. For Percy, the unavoidability of this question is what proves our species to be *homo religiosus*. However unbelieving Binx thinks himself to be, he has had an irreducibly religious encounter. His Augustinian confession that "there awoke in me an immense curiosity. I was onto something,"[29] proves him more than a blithe pagan.

Only intermittently has Binx lived the life of wonder that his mystical encounter summoned him to pursue. Like the great generality of our human kind, he has been consumed by the metaphysical malaise that knots our stomachs and makes our heads roar like conchs. Yet there are times when he cannot evade the mystery of his own existence, when he must probe the clues implicit in the accoutrements of his daily commerce with the world. He finds himself stirred to amazement, for example, at the mere contents of his pockets. Instead of feeling a Sartrean nausea at the sheer facticity of his life, Binx gazes at these objects through a "spyhole" made of joined thumb and forefinger. He sees that they could just as easily belong to someone else, but that they are somehow uniquely his—indeed, uniquely *him*. "A man can look at this little pile on his bureau for thirty years," Binx observes, "and never once see it. It is as invisible as his own hand."[30]

Bolling has stopped going to movies because they miss this most fundamental mystery of human strangeness and astonishment. Popular cinema begins in the right place, says Binx, by asking the question of life's meaning and significance. It shows people caught in terrible distress or suffering grievous loss. Almost invariably, however, the movies provide easy answers to difficult problems. In the Ray Milland film called *Amnesia*, a man loses all recollection of his family and friends and home, and then "comes to himself" in a strange place. Far from being bereft at such fearful deprivations, he "takes up with the local librarian, sets about proving to the local children what a nice fellow he is, and settles down with a vengeance. In two weeks he is so sunk in everydayness that he might just as well be dead."[31] The slogan posted on the movie marquee near Binx's home in Gentilly is ironically appropriate: "Where Happiness Costs So Little."[32] That Binx is now an ex-moviegoer is thus a sign of hope. He is on his way toward becoming more than a mere *voyeur* who looks at everything but commits himself to nothing.

Bolling is opaque to authentic Christian hope because he associates it with the vulgar faith of the masses. Popular Christianity is to religion as the movies are to culture: neither can provide a solution to

Binx's quandary. He refuses, in fact, to identify his search with the pro-verbial quest for God. So to phrase the matter would amount, as he grimly notes, "to setting myself a goal which everyone else has reached.... Who wants to be dead last among one hundred eighty million Americans? For, as everyone knows, the polls report that 98 percent of Americans believe in God and the remaining 2 percent are atheists and agnostics—which leaves not a single percentage point for a seeker."[33] This declaration makes Binx sound all too much like Will Barrett in *The Second Coming*. They both want a faith that will keep them pure and untainted by the paltry run of Christians. Only in the figure of Dr. Thomas More do we find a Percy protagonist who recovers his faith by way of the church's wit-ness, and he does so through a bare double negative confession that he is sorry about not being sorry for his sinful condition.

Binx boasts of being "onto" God even if he cannot believe what con-ventional Christians believe. He subscribes, implicitly at least, to Kier-kegaard's thesis that "Christianity may be taken away from Europe as the one way of convincing people of its truth." Bolling insists that the contemporary absence of God may be the surest sign of his undiscerned presence: "Abraham saw signs of God and believed. Now the only sign is that all the signs in the world would make no difference. Is this God's ironic revenge? But I am onto him."[34] Were Christ to return in our own time, Percy has said, we would make his coming the subject of a late-night television special, thus ignoring its world shattering significance. Yet God will not be evaded by our evasions. His ultimate trick, Binx be-lieves, is to let us vacate our souls of all substance in order that he might fill them with real meaning. The irony is that Binx himself is as empty as the folks he derides. His life of genteel despair and antic mockery will not finally suffice. Sooner or later he will have to confront the fact of his own spiritual inertia. What is far more important, he must comprehend the paradoxical trickery of grace—that it is less a matter of our seeking than of God's finding.

IV. The Human Summons to Transcendent Grace

Binx Bolling gradually discovers that the ego is a vortex. A life of pure consciousness leads to the solipsistic conclusion that nothing but one's supreme selfhood is real. If there be resurrection from this solitary grave, it is found in a transcendent summons out of self-absorption and into community. With Martin Buber, Percy believes that the otherness of the "Thou" has the power to challenge the "I" to recognize its ultimate source and limit. Yet Binx lacks any such human impingement on his omnivorous ego. For all his acute discernment of his fellows, he has re-duced nearly everyone he knows to an "it"—to an object which he can coldly observe and impersonally categorize. Yet there are two people who will not submit to Binx's objectivizing satire: his half-brother, Lonnie Smith, and his first cousin by marriage, Kate Cutrer. Each of them becomes a "Thou" to Binx. They compel him to encounter and address them in the full freedom of their otherness—not as an "it" whom Binx can classify according to the gradations of consciousness.

Lonnie is one of several children born to Binx's mother after his father's death and her remarriage. He is a cripple, indeed a paraplegic; and in the end he dies of hepatitis. He is also a fourteen-year-old possessed of a convinced Catholic faith. Like Dostoevski's Alyosha in *The Brothers Karamazov*, Lonnie is a boy whose purity of devotion may tempt readers to a psychological reduction. Percy dares the audience, one might say, to dismiss Lonnie's faith as a spiritual crutch for his physical weakness. Yet, Lonnie's orthodox Catholic belief does not constitute a flight from reality so much as a firm grip upon it. Lonnie is, in fact, the one person in the novel whom Binx does not mock. He sees that the boy, unlike nearly everyone else, has broken the shackles of conformity that chain us to the imprisoning self. Lonnie can laugh at himself and live redemptively in the world because he knows that he is bound for a better country, the city which has foundations, the kingdom whose maker and builder is God.

Binx sees that Lonnie's eschatological faith issues in a transformed life. Though seemingly a victim of an absurd suffering, Lonnie regards himself as far more sinning than sinned against. He confesses, in traditional Catholic terms, to having "an habitual disposition" to envy.[35] Not natural evil, Lonnie knows, but unnatural sin is the essential human calamity. So deeply did Lonnie resent his brother Duval's academic and athletic prowess that he was secretly glad when Duval drowned. Now Lonnie has undertaken penance for his "capital" sin. He believes—as Binx observes in unabashedly pious language of his own—"that he can offer his suffering in reparation for men's indifference to the pierced heart of Jesus Christ."[36] Binx's deep attraction for Lonnie proves again how profound are Bolling's own religious longings, how ineluctably he possesses a naturally Catholic soul. He confesses, in fact, that he would gladly exchange his own miserable existence for Lonnie's serenely happy life.

Yet while the dying Lonnie remains a real "Thou" for Binx, he is not a figure whose life impinges permanently upon Bolling's. Kate Cutrer's does. She is his troubled twenty-five-year-old cousin by marriage, and finally she becomes his wife. Though Binx can exalt Lonnie's vigorous faith as his ideal goal, he cannot romanticize Kate's pathetic neediness. She is a woman in such dire personal straits that Binx ought not be attracted to her at all. His successive Lindas and Marcias and Sharons provide him, as Kate cannot, the "drinks and kisses and warm deep thighs" that are the staples of his hedonist life. Yet Binx wearies of his concubinous secretaries as he does not tire of the importunate Kate.

They are splendid athletes with whom he can perform sexual calisthenics, but there is something humanly insubstantial and unreal about them. Kate, by contrast, is an utterly authentic woman in all of her hapless anxiety.

Though she is the daughter of Jules Cutrer, Kate has sought to live according to the high-toned civic duty espoused by her adoptive mother, Binx's Aunt Emily. She began as a social worker concerned especially about the plight of her women clients. Their worst deprivation, she believed, was their failure to achieve orgasm during intercourse. After the collapse of this uninspired do-gooding, Kate has become fearfully dependent upon her parents, casting her loyalty first with the one and then the other. She has also become addicted to barbituates, and on one occasion makes a half-attempt at suicide. Yet for all her troubles, Kate has the acuity to see that she and Binx are fundamentally akin. "You're like me," she tells him, "but worse. Much worse."[37] Because she is in dread difficulty and knows it, she can confront Binx with the unwelcome news that he is in an evil way himself.

What they share most in common is a love of bad times. They both feel more fully alive amidst turbulence and crisis than within the calm waters of ordinary existence. In outward trouble their own inner misery finds its public parallel. Like Dr. Bolling going excitedly off to war, Kate confesses paradoxically that "suicide is the only thing that keeps me alive."[38] The possibility of self-murder represents a freedom of action, albeit negative and destructive, that her psychiatrist cannot fathom. He is convinced that Kate needs to be more healthily conformed to her environment. For her, as also for Percy, such animal adjustment is the way of death. Like Dostoevski's Underground Man, Kate knows that willful suffering is more pleasurable than mindless health. However dimly, she perceives that we are creatures with a transcendent origin and destiny, and that no anthropoid at-homeness in the world will satisfy us.

This intuitive knowledge of her own condition is what makes Kate such an incisive judge of Binx. She sees that his satiric scorn for the world's spiritual inertia tempts him to an Olympian self-sufficiency. He is prone to a cold disdain for weak souls like herself. "You are the unmoved mover," she accuses Binx. "You don't need God or anyone else— no credit to you, unless it is a credit to be the most self-centered person alive."[39] Perhaps because she penetrates Binx's antic guise so sharply, Kate can also put herself into his keeping, demanding that he care for her. She has an almost apostolic certainty about Binx's obligation to her. Like a peremptory bearer of grace, she lays on him an offer he cannot refuse. Among the novel's funniest scenes are those where Kate interprets Binx's offers of help as proposals of marriage. He means nothing of the sort, yet neither can he deny his lasting regard for this woman who has put herself at his disposal.

In Aunt Emily's stern moral view, Binx compromises Kate's virtue when he takes her with him to Chicago on a business trip. But far from having spent a debauched weekend together, Kate and Binx were much more "moral" than Aunt Emily can imagine. They are both so vexed by their own respective troubles that they cannot perform as masters of sexual exercise. As Binx says of their Chicago venture, "We did very badly and almost did not do at all. Flesh poor flesh failed us. The burden was too great and flesh poor flesh . . . now at this moment summoned all at once to be all and everything, end all and be all, the last and only hope—quails and fails."[40] Binx's inflated rhetoric points to the pretentious expectations inherent in "post-Christian sex," as he calls it.[41] No longer taken as pagan easement nor forbidden as religious sin, sex has become the American idol. That Kate and Binx are its failed worshippers is all to their credit. They are not aficionados of the orgasm bound together by a finely tuned sexual compatibility. On the contrary, they are a troubled man and woman called, almost against their wills, to care for each other despite their failures in bed.

In the end, they come humorously and graciously to admit that they cannot make their lives alone: they marry and begin a new life together. Through his love for Kate Cutrer, Binx Bolling discovers that his cynical contempt for the world's unconscious despair will not suffice. It may provide him a certain immunity from our culture's peculiar sickness unto death, but it does not offer him true life. Only by yielding his will to a radically needy woman can Binx escape his own egoistic scorn, and enter thereby into that *vita nuova* of which both Dante and the New Testament speak. In obligating himself to Kate, Binx makes the most fundamental discovery about both ethical and religious reality: it begins at the point where self-absorption ends—namely, in true community.

Binx's marriage to Kate Cutrer is evidence enough that *The Moviegoer* is a novel in the classic comic tradition. Nuptial union signals the end of bitterness and isolation, the beginning of joy and new life. Yet the novel's ending may be interpreted another way—namely, as Binx's bemused resignation to bourgeois conformity. He agrees, after all, to Aunt Emily's insistence that he return to medical school and that he thus make his contribution to the world's betterment. Such an uncomic reading of Binx's destiny holds true only if Aunt Emily is right in reaming him out for his moral delinquency. I have sought to show how her fierce Catonist denunciation is not only unavailing but hopeless in the religious sense of the word. The novel itself confirms this view in two important episodes, one at the end of the book's main action and the other in the Epilogue that follows. They both gesture at the grace that fiction cannot overtly announce, and they point up what is deeply, indeed theologically, comic about *The Moviegoer*.

V. The Life of Faith as Comic Hope

The first of these transcendent glimpses of grace occurs, appropriately, on Ash Wednesday. The preceding week of Mardi Gras, far from making Binx fat with joy, has left him lean with desire and empty of life-sustaining hope. He has abandoned his search, he confesses, and resigned himself to an aesthete's career of womanizing and ass-kicking. Like Dante lost in life's dark wood, Binx finds himself living in earthly damnation. Though he is standing in a telephone booth at the edge of a schoolyard watching children whirl themselves merrily on a roundabout, the whole scene takes on the aspect of hell. The New Orleans suburb with the idyllic name of Elysian Fields "glistens like a vat of sulfur; the playground looks as if it had survived the end of the world." Binx's life and environs are burned out, devastated, wasted. Only after reaching the bitter end—again like Dante—can he be made to wonder if there is a way out. "Is it possible," he asks himself, "that—it is not too late?"[42]

Having called up one of his compliant Midwestern secretaries to arrange for a weekend fling, Binx suddenly spies Kate from the telephone booth. Perhaps in order to insult the secretary for being sexually so available, Binx asks whether he might bring along his fiancée on their date. This is a wholly unaccountable act. Never before has Binx spoken of an engagement to Kate, and yet he suddenly tells a prospective playmate that he is betrothed to this miserable woman. No sooner does Binx meet Kate there at the parish schoolyard than they begin to discuss the implications of their future life together. There is hardly any romance at all in their relation. "You'll have to be with me a great deal," Kate reminds Binx while shredding her thumb in finger-gnawing anxiety.[43] A long course of psychiatric treatment awaits her, she warns, and there is no guarantee that she will ever overcome her neurasthenia. Yet Binx has faith in Kate despite her troubled condition. He kisses the blood from her torn flesh and urges her not to be so hard on herself.

How can such a total reversal of attitude be explained? Is Binx giving up his aesthete life out of weariness, and resigning himself to ethical conformity as a bleak consolation? The novel's ending is often read this way. Yet there is a strange spiritual logic to Binx's maladroit marriage to Kate. He backs into life companionship with her by the inadvertence of grace, as the succeeding scene makes clear. For as Binx and Kate sit in her old Plymouth near a suburban Catholic church, they spy a Negro emerging from the Ash Wednesday service. Driving a Mercury no less flashy than his clothes, he would appear to be a black man making his way up into the white world: he is attending what, in 1961, was the only racially integrated church in New Orleans. In every way, the Negro's reception of the penitential ashes is ambiguous. His skin is so dark that it is impossible to see the mark of the cross on his forehead. He stares down at some unknown object in the car seat beside him, perhaps in gratitude for the blessing he has just received, perhaps preparing for his next business call. Yet neither explanation accounts for what Binx has witnessed. He suspects, on the contrary, that God is having sport with his creature—not monstrously as Aunt Emily would suspect, but graciously, as befits the God of the Gospel.

It occurs to Binx that the black man may have indeed come to the church for worldly advancement, only to receive the divine benison by surprise. Binx asks rhetorically whether the Negro may be present at the Ash Wednesday service "for both reasons: through some dim dazzling trick of grace, coming for the one and receiving the other as God's own importunate bonus?"[44] The Hopkinsesque character of Binx's question points to the gracious nature of his own deliverance. Perhaps in agreeing to marry Kate Binx does intend to give up his search and to settle for a dull bourgeois life. Yet even if these are his intentions, the sovereign and sportive God will not honor them. His bonus is too great a gift to be received or rejected like any other. God is as implacable in his giving, Percy hints, as Kate is in her asking. Prevenient grace cannot be resisted and refused as if it were a human offering. It drives from the highways and hedges those who would not attend the king's banquet. It is troublesome, pressing, urgent. Like the importunate widow in the New Testament, it does not countenance negative answers. It persists in soliciting our acknowledgment and acceptance.

That Binx's marriage to Kate is the product of such grace, and not a flaccid resignation to Aunt Emily's demand, is confirmed by the novel's deeply affecting final scene. There Binx is beginning to push Kate away from her enslaving dependence upon him and toward a new freedom of her own. She is so confused and uncertain about both herself and the world that she would like Binx to direct her life, to order her every action. Yet Binx refuses to become a surrogate savior for Kate. He is not the Olympian egoist she once accused him of being. On the contrary, he wants Kate to have her own firm sense of selfhood. Only thereby will their marriage be rooted in real commonality. Binx sends Kate on a simple mission, therefore, to pick up a set of bonds at his downtown office. She is so fearful of undertaking any deed of her own that she expects to fail at even this small act. She agrees to go only if Binx will promise not to stop thinking of her while she is gone. And yet she does go. The novel concludes with this immensely hopeful image of Kate as a still deeply troubled woman who is nevertheless embarking, with Binx's help, on a new life.

Yet if the Epilogue were centered wholly upon this final episode, the novel might be read in purely ethical terms. It would remain a comic work only in the broad secular sense: though once disturbed and imperilled, Binx's world has been restored to order and health. The Epilogue suggests, in fact, that Binx's reordered life is premised on something at once darker and brighter than mere marriage can supply. *The Moviegoer* is anything but a conventionally comic novel. As we have seen, it is a harsh and angry book about a man whose only talent, he claims, is his ability to recognize "merde when I see it, having inherited no more from my father than a good nose for merde, for every species of shit that flies."[45] Even in the Epilogue, where Binx records his state of mind more than a year after the novel's action closes, he still refuses to make a confident declaration that all is well with him or his world. The time is "much too late," he says, "to edify or do much of anything except plant a foot in the right place as the opportunity presents itself—if indeed asskicking is properly distinguished from edification."[46]

Binx's talk about "edification" is still another allusion to Kierkegaard, who distinguishes between a straightforward "edifying" appeal for belief in the Gospel and an indirect "aesthetic" awakening of an audience to its unconscious despair. A sermon is the occasion for the former, a work of art for the latter. Hence Percy's refusal to end *The Moviegoer* with Binx on his knees before the altar of the local Catholic church. He does not want his readers to collapse the distinction between art and faith, between imagination and edification. A work of fiction can serve as a preparation for the Gospel only by disturbing our spiritual slumbers, by waking us from a deadly sleep. This is the one religious function that art can legitimately perform. The church alone has the apostolic vocation of proclaiming and enacting the Good News directly. And yet fiction does have the power, for Percy at least, of gesturing subtly at the grace it cannot overtly announce. For a second and final time, therefore, Percy hints that Binx's renewed life—his marriage to Kate and his return to medical research—is far more than an ethical turnabout. The account of Lonnie's death suggests that it is the result of nothing less than a religious conversion.

Late in his narrative Binx still speaks despairingly of his "dark pilgrimage on this earth."[47] Yet in the Epilogue only a year later, he echoes Dante's *Commedia* by referring to his "thirtieth year toward heaven."[48] This unexplained reversal is evident in Binx's unsentimental response to Lonnie's death. In their last colloquy, Lonnie had retained his endearing combination of devotion and ribaldry. He had serenely announced his victory over envy and yet had also teased Binx about Kate's beauty. Knowing that Lonnie's faith is intact, Binx feels no need to bid the boy a tearful farewell. But for the still unbelieving Kate, the sadness of death is too tantalizing to resist, and so she goes to have her final interview with the dying Lonnie.

Binx stays, instead, with his other half-brothers and half-sisters. They ask about Lonnie the same question that Binx must have wanted Aunt Emily to answer about Scotty at his brother's death many years earlier. "When our Lord raises us up on the last day," one of the children asks unembarrassedly, "will Lonnie still be in a wheelchair or will he be like us?"[49] Binx answers with equal candor that Lonnie will indeed be made whole, and that he will be able to water ski like them. Later, when Kate returns from the hospital to discover that the children are joyful despite Lonnie's death, she commends Binx for being "sweet" to them. She assumes that he has fed them pie-in-the-sky hope in order to stanch their tears. Binx is grievously disappointed by Kate's response. He has not filled the children with empty cheer. Nor has he told them the usual polite lie that Lonnie's spirit would remain alive because they will remember him always. No: Binx has spoken the truth which, however little he may yet believe it, he knows to be the only thing worth believing—namely, that Lonnie has been redeemed by God and lives forever in his presence.

A final literary allusion confirms this theological reading of the novel's penultimate scene. When Binx declares that the resurrected Lonnie will be able to water ski, two of the children cry out, "Hurray!" and a third shouts, "Binx, we love you too!" These affirmations are Percy's deliberate echo of the last episode in Dostoevski's *The Brothers Karamazov*. There at the funeral of a child named Ilyusha, Alyosha Karamazov speaks similar words of eschatological hope to a group of boys who had once tormented but finally come to love the one they are burying. Alyosha tells them that the event has transcendent significance. No matter how wicked they may again become, he reminds them that they must always look back joyously to that brief, shining hour when they were all momentarily good. Such an unaccountable transformation points forward, says Alyosha, to a final transformation. "Certainly we shall rise again," he tells them, "certainly we shall see each other and tell each other with joy and gladness all that has happened!" "Hurrah for Karamazov!" the boys reply. "Karamazov, we love you!"[50]

It is such a "hurrah" that *The Moviegoer* elicits. Walker Percy has written a comic novel in the deepest theological sense. Not only has Binx abandoned his wastrel ways and assumed an ethical life of marriage and medical study; he has also begun to live the faithful life of eschatological hope. Even if Kate's therapy is not successful, all will not be lost. Even if Binx does not finish medical school, the future is not over. And even if he sometimes doubts the resurrection that he so unexpectedly affirmed, his faith will not have been in vain. The "importunate bonus" Binx has received does not depend on his dutiful safekeeping of it. Transcendent grace has laid hold of Binx no matter how fumbling his own hands remain. Just as Binx is a moviegoer who no longer attends movies, so does his narrative hint that God is the Judge who does not behold us according to human justice. God's first and final word is mercy and not wrath, hope and not defeat, grace and not damnation, comedy and not tragedy. The novel is comic because Binx has experienced something far more bracing and cheering than an awakening to his own despair. His life has been made a new creation—not by dint of his own satiric wit, but by the humor of God's grace.

9

JOHN UPDIKE AS AN IRONIST OF THE SPIRITUAL LIFE

That John Updike is one of America's wittiest writers, there is no question. That his work is drenched in overt theological concerns is also self-evident. But what his sprightly comedy has to do with his religious seriousness is far from clear. I contend that Updike is more an ironist than a comedian in the Barthian sense of the term. Updike does not presume to offer his work as an overt proclamation of the world's comic redemption in Christ. Yet neither is Updike chiefly a satirist like Percy and O'Connor. They seek to sting the world—as he does not—into a reforming act of self-recognition. Nor is Updike a humorist who, like De Vries, aims at the belly laugh which confesses our helpless but hilarious plight. Updike differs from the other three in being a writer whose art is neither uproariously funny nor acerbically angry. He is, I shall argue, an ironist of the spiritual life. He envisions human existence as a tragic conflict of opposites that, by faith in God's grace, can nonetheless be affirmed as good.

The comedy of the Gospel lies, as we have seen, in our rightful expectation of judgment and calamity, only to be met with mercy and deliverance instead. Irony can be one of the means to faith, as Reinhold Niebuhr has taught us. Updike the ironist envisions the human condition as containing, within its own tragic dialectic, the surprise of goodness. This inadvertent discovery of natural grace is what repeatedly occurs in Updike's fiction. His characters are startled to find that the same moral realities that constrict their freedom—marriage and children, social convention and religious duty—also enhance it. The same obligations and institutions which threaten to fetter their vaulting consciousness prove liberating as well. Despite their tragic ambiguity, therefore, the social and natural worlds summon Updike's characters to loyalties larger than themselves. The gracious irony evident in Updike's work,

I will argue, is that we are not, as we might seem, the playthings of an unknown and arbitrary Fate, but the products of a beneficent order and the recipients of inestimable gifts.

I. The Dialectic of Human Sexuality

The first thing that nearly everyone remarks about Updike's work is its obsession with sex. It is either the silent undercurrent or the rippling concern of almost every story and scene that Updike has ever written. His fascination with the genital—and hence the spiritual—difference between men and women has put many critics off. They regard Updike as an arrested adolescent, a brilliant stylist who has squandered his talent on the obvious: the fact that we are carnal creatures. Yet so to trivialize Updike is to deny the serious import of his fiction. He is not a highly talented pornographer, but a writer convinced that the vagaries of human sexuality prove us to be more than anthropoids. No beast is engrossed with its erotic life as we humans are. Far from being a sign of our mere animality, the human absorption with sex reveals, in Updike's view, that we are created in the image of God.

This conviction forms the pattern in the carpet of Updike's entire work. His clearest statement of the matter is to be found in an early review of *Love in the Western World*, Denis de Rougemont's book on the medieval origins of romantic love. Updike agrees that romance is largely a chivalric invention, but he is persuaded that its roots are much more ancient. They are at least Adamic and perhaps even Luciferian:

> De Rougemont is dreadfully right in asserting that love in the Western world has by some means acquired a force far out of proportion to its presumed procreative aim. Do we need a heresy [Catharism], or even a myth [Tristan and Isolde], to explain it? Might it not simply be that sex has become involved in the Promethean protest forced upon Man by his paradoxical position in the Universe as a self-conscious animal?[1]

Like de Rougemont, Updike is indebted to Søren Kierkegaard for this reading of human sexuality. It was Kierkegaard who first taught us that sensuousness is not a pagan but a Christian phenomenon. For the Greeks, he argues, sexual love was conceived as a power residing immanently in nature and thus as dwelling largely outside the will. This natural force was to be brought into harmonious accord with civic life by means of reason's restraints. But with the Christian dispensation, a radical negation is set upon the flesh and the world; they are understood as the seat if not the means of the will's corruption. The erotic is no longer an impulse to be put under rational control but an enemy to be subjugated, a rebel to be held in check. The Christian emphasis on God's transcendence over the world, and the accompanying exaltation of spiritual over sexual life, renders sensuousness self-conscious for the first time. Christian denial of the flesh accords it, according to Kierkegaard's pseudonymous author, a certain desperate power:

> The Middle Ages had much to say about a mountain, not found on any map, which is called the mountain of Venus. There the sensuous has its home, there it has its own wild pleasures, for it is a kingdom, a state. In this kingdom language has no place, nor sober-minded thought, nor the toilsome business of reflection. There sound only the voice of elemental passion, the play of appetites, the wild shouts of intoxication; it exists solely for pleasure in eternal tumult. The first born of this kingdom is Don Juan.[2]

The irony is that Don Juan—in Kierkegaard's Mozartian reading of him—is not the sensualist he appears to be. Appearances to the contrary, he is a highly spiritual fellow in search of infinity within the world of sex. His love is faithless and momentary because he lives for the abstract principle of the erotic rather than in desire for any particular woman. The thousand and three conquests he makes in Spain alone do not reveal a promiscuous lover so much as a man living amidst dread and doubt. He is like a stone skimming lightly over the water's surface, declares Kierkegaard's surrogate speaker: "As soon as it ceases to skip, it instantly sinks down into the depths; so Don Juan dances over the abyss, jubilant in his brief respite."[3]

Updike shares Kierkegaard's view of eroticism: it is an attempt to fend off death more than to seek pleasure. Alone among self-conscious creatures, we humans can anticipate our own extinction. This fatal knowledge casts a shadow over the whole of life, calling everything into terrible question. Already in his first novel, *Poorhouse Fair*, Updike demonstrates his obsession with death. There a group of elderly people face their slow doom in a nursing home. Yet their problem is the same that the fairest youth must also confront: how to overcome mortality. Not for Updike the pagan comfort of a David Hume, who said that our previous nonexistence ought to matter no more than our future annihilation. As Updike remarks in his essay on de Rougemont, we cannot live without existential proof that our lives have cosmic consequence:

> Our fundamental anxiety is that we do not exist—or will cease to exist. Only in being loved do we find external corroboration of the supremely high valuation each ego secretly assigns itself. This exalted arena, then, is above all others the one where men will insist upon their freedom to choose—to choose that other being in whose existence their own existence is confirmed and amplified. Against the claims of this mighty self-assertion, the arguments em-

bodied in law and stricture for self-preservation appear trivial and base. The *virtus* of the choice is diminished if others would also have chosen it for us. The heart *prefers* to move against the grain of circumstance; perversity is the soul's very life. Therefore the enforced and approved bonds of marriage, restricting freedom, weaken love.[4]

Humanity is situated so precariously upon the narrow divide between the angels and the animals that calamity is virtually assured. Updike is willing indeed to affirm with Tillich that existence equals fallenness. *The Centaur*, Updike's award-winning novel of 1964, declares our tragic doubleness in its very title. Our human heads endow us with a self-transcending consciousness that no earthly joy can fully satisfy; yet our equine torsos root us in mortal passions that no heavenly hope can assuage. There is no permanent reconciliation of the flesh's downward pull with the spirit's upward yearning.

To be permanently out of phase is, in Updike's lexicon, to be fully human. "Unfallen Adam is an ape," he declares in a typical maxim. It follows that mere contentment and satisfaction are a denial of our humanity. "To be a person," Updike insists, "is to be in a situation of tension, is to be in a dialectical situation. A truly adjusted person is not a person at all—just an animal with clothes or a statistic."[5] He calls popular psychology the peculiar voodoo of our age, a magical attempt to deny the unhappiness inherent in human life.

The narrator of a story entitled "The Music School" voices Updike's own sardonic opinion when he declares that his wife "visits a psychiatrist because I am unfaithful to her. I do not understand the connection," he confesses drily, "but there seems to be one."[6] Psychotherapy cannot relieve the grief of a betrayed spouse whose mate suffers the incurable condition called human nature. Vagrant desire springs not from mere animal urges but from our ambiguous and fallen condition as self-surpassing creatures. And this condition—because it is at once unpredictable and intractable—submits more readily to religious analysis than to behavioral therapy.

That we are inevitable egoists is, for Updike, no metaphysical absurdity; it is the paradoxical necessity of our incarnate spirituality. God himself has rendered our existence double, planting us amidst the contraries of inward and ourward life, and thus insuring the taut oppositions without which our lives would go slack and lose all significance. Every human event, even the most ordinary, has sovereign import because it partakes of an eternal tension. This conviction is what gives Updike's fiction its mythic dimension. The obscure science teacher named Caldwell in *The Centaur* confronts far more than a class of obstreperous students. He also faces "Jason, Achilles, Asclepios, the daughter of Ochyroe, and the dozen other princely children of Olympus abandoned to his care."[7]

In Updike's Christian humanist view, there is no essential discontinuity between Athens and Jerusalem. Peter, the psoriasis-eaten son of the elder Caldwell, is a latter-day version of both Greek and biblical saviors. His physical disfigurement is the price he pays for his spiritual anxiety. In his own adolescent way, Peter Caldwell is both Prometheus and Christ: a figure bound and crucified by life. Updike's Niebuhrian reading of Greek myths and biblical stories thus finds them both sharing a vision of humanity as dwelling on the boundary between heaven and earth. What divides the two traditions is that Christians have greater cause than the Greeks—an incarnate Lord—for accepting and affirming our tragic condition.

From the pagan perspective, the gods are threatened by the ability of our species to span not one realm but two, uniting both the physical and the spiritual worlds within the single compass of the self. "Indeed it was rumored," says Caldwell the father, "that Zeus thought centaurs a dangerous middle ground through which the gods might be transmuted into pure irrelevance."[8] The vitalities of human selfhood, far from undermining confidence in God, are for Updike the surest sign of his reality. We would not be such anxious and troubled creatures, Updike believes, if something ultimate were not disturbing our peace. Human inwardness is the locus of God's activity because there resides the guilt that stirs us to spiritual life. Whether they be animals or humans, the innocent are dead to God. Guilt, in Updike's ironic vision, is the great life-enhancing reality. It is the tragic cost we pay for existing as creatures desperately aware of our own creatureliness. Our guilt-ridden selves force us to seek ultimate justification for our existence. Sin is thus oddly fecundating, as Updike declares in his autobiographical poem called "Midpoint":

> Our Guilt inheres in sheer Existing, so
> Forgive yourself your death, and freely flow.

Guilt is the leavening lump without which the world would remain a flat and tasteless loaf. Sin, death, and the devil—far from being the last enemies to be overcome—are the secret friends of the human spirit. They can become, in fact, the very instruments of our salvation, prompting us to the spiritual and sexual awareness without which we would remain living corpses. The deepest irony of all is that opposites coincide, that the love of death is the way to life, that fleshly indulgence assures spiritual vigor, that excremental reality is the basis for mental ideality, and that the way to hell can be the path to heaven. The narrator of *The Witches of Eastwick*, shifting notably to the personal voice of the author himself, articulates this Goethean conviction:

We all dream, and we all stand aghast at the mouth of the caves of our deaths; and [sex] is our way in. Into the nether world. Before plumbing, in the old outhouses, in winter, the accreted shit of the family would mount up in a spiky frozen stalagmite, and such phenomena help us to believe that there is more to life than the airbrushed ads at the front of magazines, the Platonic form of perfume bottles and nylon nightgowns and Rolls-Royce fenders. Perhaps in the passageways of our dreams we meet, more than we know: one white lamplit face astonished by another.[9]

Hypertrophied human consciousness renders the external world so gossamer that we need corroborations of its unillusory facticity. Sexual adventure provides the universal evidence that we are not phantoms. Yet the egoistic pleasure it produces tempts us to guilty abandonment of duty. This paradox explains why sex, in Updike's fiction, is so nearly all consuming. Human beings are sex-obsessed as beasts are not, Updike believes, because only erotic love can outwardly confirm our inward self-importance. We are not carnally minded creatures out of a mad desire for sensate pleasure. Copulation thrives because nothing else on earth enables human beings so concretely to prove that they are for real and not merely dreaming. Yet as the earthly fulfillment of a supernal need, sex is bound finally to disappoint. It circles upon itself in endless arousal and frustration. Neither the enjoyment nor the denial of sex brings any final satisfaction to the clamant demands of the spirit. The question for Updike is whether, amid such tragic sexual ambiguity, there can be real hope for happiness. Marriage is civilization's answer to this dark question. It is also for Updike the largest secular embodiment of the ancient human urge for lasting joy. Yet only with ironic self-restraint can it be the bearer of divine grace.

II. Marriage as a Blessedly Difficult Estate: *Couples*

Updike has a profoundly ambivalent regard for our culture's emancipation of human sexuality from its ancient restraints. He is at once its champion and its critic. For the most part, of course, Updike is the celebrant of the sexual revolution. Yet he is no naive Dionysiac reveler in the fields of flesh. His candor about sex is, he insists, but an effort to affirm the actual dimension that the erotic occupies in our lives. Its place, he says, is "huge but not all-eclipsing."[10] His aim is at once to remove sex from the closet, where our Victorian forbears hid it, and to take it off the altar, where our own culture is eager to worship it.

Updike is less concerned about contemporary sexual excess than about the deep sexual denial implicit in the unworldliness of the American character. Like the Jansenists of seventeenth-century France, our Puritan ancestors made what Updike calls "a vast gamble" on transmundane happiness. They refused to hedge their bets by acknowledging the glories of carnal life. Updike argues that the waning of Christian faith in both America and France is "peculiarly desolating" because neither nation was willing to take seriously "the pagan gods, whether Hellenic or Teutonic."[11] The heirs of Blaise Pascal and Cotton Mather feel cheated, Updike contends, and they are getting their vengeance by means of a determined wager on bodily bliss. There is indeed a direct correlation, in Updike's view, between the modern obsession with sex and the contemporary eclipse of God.

Ours is a cultural no less than a religious crisis. Updike maintains that most American literature treats carnality as something extrinsic to the moral and spiritual life, something peripheral rather than central to human existence. We have been embarrassed over this most fundamental of facts. "America has always tolerated sex as a joke," Updike declares, "as a night's prank in the burlesque theatre or fairground tent; but not as a solemn item in life's working inventory." In paying homage to Edmund Wilson for having overcome such dishonesty, Updike also describes his own literary program: "to dramatize sexual behavior as a function of, rather than a suspension of, personality."[12]

It is in marriage that the dialectic of sexuality becomes most unavoidably evident. There we confront, as nowhere else, the paradoxical fact that we are creatures both bestial and angelic, both material and spiritual, both mortal and immortal. American middle-class marriages embody this tension, Updike contends, with an especial poignancy. Hence his confession that he is an elegist of middle class Protestant life and its "peculiar domestic fierceness." Unlike the many Europeans who do not look for romantic love in marriage, most Americans—as legatees of the Puritan heritage—have sought to confine their sexual passion to the marriage bed. Mere spouses are thus made to suffice as the Unattainable Knight or the Impossible Lady. The result, Updike maintains, is something at once wondrously good and fiercely difficult.

Updike affirms conjugal commitment as the indispensable means for channeling the vagaries of sexual desire toward productive ends. It is through life partnership that children are brought to moral maturity, households are established for the good of others as well as oneself, and vocations are sustained amidst mutual self-sacrifice. Far from being a mere sensualist or pornographer, Updike is our premier novelist of marriage and its dilemmas. There are virtually no playboys or penthouse girls in Updike's fiction. Their merely athletic and anonymous sex is of little moral or theological consequence. Rabbit Angstrom, Thomas Marshfield, Piet Hanema, Richard Maple and nearly all of Updike's other protagonists are troubled adulterers rather than guiltless fornicators. They are married men who cannot leave their wives as if their wedding vows meant nothing.

Many of them do break the nuptial bonds, but only with a terrible sense of the cost. Among the most rending passages in all of Updike's fiction is the scene where Richard and Joan Maple inform their children that they have decided to separate:

> It was the thought of telling Judith—the image of her, their first baby, walking between [Maple and his wife] arm in arm to the bridge—that broke him. The partition between his face and the tears broke. . . . He blinked, swallowed, croakily joked about hay fever. The tears would not stop leaking through; they came not through a hole that could be plugged but through a permeable spot in a membrane, steadily, purely, endlessly, fruitfully. They became, his tears, a shield for himself against these others—their faces, the fact of their assembly, a last time as innocents, at a table where he sat the last time as head.[13]

The annunciation of these ill tidings, Maple later confesses to his son Dickie, is one of the worst moments of his life. "I hate this," he laments. "*Hate* it. My father would have died before doing it to me."[14]

An earlier generation of Americans—indeed, nearly all our forbears—would have suffered the quiet despair of an unhappy love. We are free, by contrast, to break the shackles of marital misery without unbearable social stigma. Though hardly an unmixed blessing, our new liberty at least acknowledges the difficulty inherent in marriage. Even when it is not riven by the animosity that drives the Maples to divorce, wedded love faces insuperable obstacles. It rests, in fact, upon an unsteady, even a contradictory basis. The spouse who gives sex its ethical significance may also constrict its romantic expression. Conjugal life always threatens, in Updike's fiction, to turn the most exalting of human encounters into a stale and predictable business. Nowhere in Updike's work is there an example of lasting matrimonial bliss. All his spouses have either resigned themselves to the routineness of married sex, or else they have embarked upon extramarital adventure.

The tensions inherent in marriage are fictionalized most powerfully in *Couples*, Updike's notorious novel of 1968. Its action is set in the New England suburb called Tarbox. This hotbed of sexual liberation is also, as its name suggests, something of a hellhole. The evil spirit of Puritan inhibition having once and forever been cast out, the new devil of sexual unrestraint takes its place, making the condition of these latter-day pilgrims both better and worse than the first. Old-fashioned connubial fidelity, sanctioned as it was by church and society alike, no longer suffices for the ten pairs of secular swingers who constitute the *dramatis personae* of this immorality play. God is dead for them. As one of their own members declares, they have made "a church of each other."[15] Theirs is a priapic religion created amidst the *"post-pill paradise,"*[16] and adultery is its only sacrament. Swapping and recombining in nearly every heterosexual permutation possible, these new Bacchanalians abandon themselves to a life of heavenly wantonness and hellish re- crimination.

The novel's protagonist is Piet Hanema. His name suggests the bundle of contradictions that characterize his life: religious piety, the male sex organ, Petrine solidity in both faith and doubt, and yet also the airy soulfulness (*anima*) that makes him ultimately discontent with all worldly satisfaction. He is especially dissatisfied with his wife Angela, whom he regards as angelic in the bad sense: she is an unguilty, unself- conscious, and therefore largely uninteresting creature. As the occupant solely of this world, Angela shares none of Piet's religious anxiety about the next life. Although she is a genial and kind woman, she lacks the vol- atile admixture of spirit and flesh that sets human relations aflame:

> Piet had been raised in a sterner church, the Dutch Reformed, amid varnished oak and dour stained glass where shepherds were paralyzed in webs of lead. He had joined this sister church [Con- gregationalist, no doubt], a milder daughter of Calvin, as a com- promise with Angela, who believed nothing. Piet wondered what barred him from the ranks of those many blessed who believed nothing. Courage, he supposed. His nerve had cracked when his par- ents died. To break with a faith requires a moment of courage, and courage is a kind of margin within us, and after his parents' swift death [in an automobile accident] Piet had no margin. He lived tight against his skin, and his flattened face wore a look of ten- sion.[17]

The irony of Piet's confession is not to be missed. Rarely does Up- dike make unbelief, however courageous, a sign of virtue. It is nearly al- ways the indication of shallowness and false bravery. Only by living tautly and nervously against one's skin, close to the raw edges of faith, does one find real truth and vitality. Atheism is too easy an answer to life's enigma. It renders the world bland and one-dimensional and un- bearably sad. Yet neither can doubt be driven out by mere volition. It is our fate, as Freddy Thorne declares in Heideggerian fashion, to dwell in "one of those dark ages that visit mankind between millenia, between the death and rebirth of gods, when there is nothing to steer by but sex and stoicism and the stars."[18] With the eclipse of God, sex has become the single transcendent reality. It is the last frontier awaiting explora- tion, the spirit's true West, the one opportunity for Updike's adult Huck Finns to "light out for the territory."

Yet Piet lusts for something other than a mere sexual change of scene. He is not, like Mozart's Don Juan, in love with the abstract idea of Woman As Such, but with the gorgeously specific Foxy Whitman. Her name suggests that she possesses exactly what Angela lacks: a duplicitous desire to sing and celebrate herself. Like her namesake, the American bard of the triumphant ego, Mrs. Whitman is no empty-souled sensualist. On the contrary, she shares Piet's desperate faith in God as well as his yearning for companionship in both guilt and glory. Foxy is primed for seduction because her husband Ken, like Piet's Angela, is a prelapsarian creature lacking any sense of life's checkered mystery. His "weatherproof righteousness"[19] makes him a corpse of dull predictability beside whom Foxy does not want to be buried alive.

In Piet, by contrast, she finds a man who is spiritually no less than sexually alive. They are both seeking erotic deliverance from the grind of everydayness. More even than Piet, Angela wants to break the wearying dailiness of life by experiencing something supernal and transcendent, something beyond

> ... this chronic sadness of late Sunday afternoon, when the couples had exhausted their game, basketball or beachgoing or tennis or touch football, and saw an evening weighing upon them, an evening without a game, an evening spent among flickering lamps and cranky children and leftover food and the nagging half-read newspaper with its weary portents and atrocities, an evening when marriages closed in upon themselves like flowers from which the sun is withdrawn, an evening giving like a smeared window on Monday and the long week when they must perform again their impersonations of working men, of stockbrokers and dentists and engineers, of mothers and housekeepers, of adults who are not the world's guests but its hosts.[20]

A Marxist critic would dismiss Angela's worries as narcissistic—as if the ennui at the close of a bourgeois weekend were the world's chief ailment. Yet, for Updike, the problem of the dull daily round is not only real but universal. Repetitiveness is the grief that life imposes on rich and poor alike. Anywhere there is self-consciousness, there is also a critical resentment against enervating routine. It blinds us to what Walt Whitman called the "glows and glories" of the world. As Foxy asks Ken, her uncomprehending husband, "We all live under wraps, don't we? We hardly ever really open ourselves to the loveliness around us. Yet there it is, every day, going on and on, whether we look at it or not. Such a splendid waste, isn't it?"[21] Because her husband Ken cannot indulge himself this irresponsible freedom, egoistically abandoning himself to unrighteous delight, Foxy is ripe for adultery.

Updike agrees with de Rougemont that the forbidden character of illicit love insures its passionate keenness. Without obstacles and frustrations, adultery would lose much of its allurement. Piet is Tristan to Foxy's Isolde—not only because she is another man's wife, but also because she is pregnant with his child, and thus made doubly inaccessible. Her obstructed condition provides Piet the thrill that de Rougemont describes as "an avidity for possession [that is] so much more delightful than possession itself."[22] Foxy finds herself transported by furtive as not by legitimate love: "Adultery lit her from within, like the ashen mantle of a lamp, or as if an entire house of gauzy hangings and partitions were ignited but refused to be consumed, rather billowed and glowed, its structure incandescent."[23]

In Updike's dialectical vision of life, truth lies always within balanced opposites, never in monopolar extremes. To remain either complacently assured or faithlessly contemptuous of marriage is to court death, which is exactly what Piet and Foxy do. The affair which wondrously amplifies their lives also threatens to destroy their marriages. What is worse, it tempts them to think that, if only they could be rid of their spouses and possess each other completely, their ecstasy would be permanent.

This delusion arises in no small part from their loss of transcendent faith. Were Foxy and Piet able to believe in a God who could guide their wobbly passage along the world's dizzying divide, they might not fall so precipitously. Yet the very lack of such belief is what renders their romance both desperate and vital. The affair with Foxy is the only stay against Piet's overwhelming sense of God's absence and of the world's consequent emptiness. Unable to sleep after dreaming of his own death in an airplane crash, Hanema makes this fractured and pathetic confession of doubt:

> Horribly awake, Piet tried to pray. His up-pouring thoughts touched nothing. An onyx dust of gas above his face. Something once solid had been atomized. *Thou shalt not covet. Whosoever lusteth in his heart.* . . . A dour desert tribe: Dead Sea. Pots broken by a shepherd boy. Orange dust. One more dismal sect. Mormons. Salt Lake. Hymnals unopened all week stink of moldy paper; unwrapping a fish. Forgive me. Reach down and touch. He had patronized his faith and lost it. God will not be used. Death stretched endless under him. Life a scum, consciousness its scum. Piet lay as a shimmering upon an unfounded mineral imperviousness. . . . Why tease God longer? Busy old fellow has widows and orphans to interview, grieving Tehranese, still benighted. Bite down on death. Bite down. No screaming within the plane. All still in falling. Stoic grace learned from the movies. Hope of heaven drains the sky. No Hottentot he. Away with the blindfold. Matter mostly nothing, a titter [skimming] a vacuum. . . . Nothing sacred. Triune

like cock and balls. . . . Oh Lord, this steepness of sickness, this sliding.[24]

Piet's despairing faith is premised on the conviction that every-thing—himself most of all—is caught in a terrible self-cancelling con-tradiction. His erotic embrace of life has led him, paradoxically, to have deep contempt for it. Everything is so material that it stinks of sex and decay, or else it is so spiritual as to be gaseous and illusory. Piet is indeed sick unto death, lost in the vortex of consciousness, wandering in the dark wood of adultery, and thus sliding down into the inferno of divorce.

The plight of Piet and Foxy is a condition for which they are to be both pitied and held responsible. The metaphysical blankness of the age robs them of the moral buoyancy that might have enabled them to skate lightly on life's "thin ice," as Updike calls our fragile existence. Yet they turn the surrounding emptiness into an occasion for their own self-in-dulgence. They crack the thin ice of marital order and plunge into the cold waters of spiritual chaos: they leave their respective spouses and marry each other. That Hanema and Whitman have chosen death rather than life Updike makes unambiguously evident. Amidst their self-aban-doned ecstasies, she becomes pregnant with her lover's child and later, on his demand, has it aborted. Piet and Foxy thus find spiritual rebirth in each other only to destroy their respective marriages and also the new life they have engendered.

The death they bring into the world is spiritual no less than physi-cal. As a builder of elegant homes, Piet once took honor from his craft. But in the end he becomes an inspector for the construction of military barracks, and thus a man without a vocation. Nor is there any doubt that, at the novel's close, Piet and Foxy are on their way to becoming still another suburban couple. Empty of the life-giving tension that their original marriages afforded, they are now physically satisfied but spiritu-ally dead. Soon, we must assume, they will grow weary of their sexual familiarity and thus strike out for new erotic territory.

There is a frightful circularity at work in *Couples*, as there is in all of Updike's fiction. Repeatedly he uncovers the fearsome coincidence and equation of opposites: sex equals life equals death. This dread paradox that contraries do not really differ explains Updike's exceedingly mild description of *Couples* as "a book about sex as the emergent relig-ion, as the only thing left." Though unable to sanction "this community founded on physical and psychical interpenetration," neither can Updike condemn it: "What else shall we do, as God destroys our churches?"[25] He refers to the scene, near the novel's end, when lightning strikes the picturesque New England church where Piet once wor-shipped, burning it to ashes. The only thing rescued is the rooster atop the steeple—itself a hint, perhaps, that sex may already have been the Puritans' secret obsession.

This celebrated incident points up the moral passivity of Updike's work: his reluctance to find fault and to assess blame, his conviction that our lives are shaped by forces too vast for mere mortals to master. There is a deep tragic pessimism pervading the entirety of his fiction. For Updike, as for few other contemporary writers, there are problems that admit of no solution, that must be patiently endured, and that have their ultimate source in God as the primordial origin and end of life. The novel's most revealing theological declaration comes near the end. Speaking for the author no less than himself, Updike's narrator avows that "there was, behind the screen of couples and houses and days, a Calvinist God who lifts us up and casts us down without recourse to our prayers or consultation with our wills."[26]

Couples is a book that, as Updike cleverly remarks, earned him solvency and notoriety in a single stroke. Yet it demands theological no less than sociological interpretation. The novel reveals how fully Updike is inclined to an ethical quietism. It derives, I believe, from an overly transcendent sense of God's otherness. Having so little sense of God as incarnate either in Christ or the church, Updike takes refuge in an abstract monotheism that makes him ambivalent about every moral reality, especially marriage. The married life is a blessedly difficult estate because it both kills and brings to life. It threatens, on the one hand, to kill the erotic excitement without which life becomes a tedious round. On the other hand, wedded love alone delivers us from the slavery inherent in the sexual unrestraint of the modern age. This deeply paradoxical conviction makes him unwilling to point an accusing pen at our adulterous generation. Nothing less than transcendent faith, he believes, can enable couples to live within the tension and frustration of married life. Yet this God is rarely present to us, making faith a matter of anxiety more than surety. He is a God who is discernible largely by his absence.

III. God as the Absent Lord of the Cosmos

It comes as no surprise that Updike should find the reality of God to be a paradox not unlike life itself. As a writer much influenced by the existentialists—chiefly Kierkegaard—he is determined to locate the evidence for faith within human experience and existence. What he finds there is a God who is double if not duplicitous in character: a Power making for terror no less than wonder, a Savior who redeems but also a Bungler who must be forgiven. He is at once the God of Calvin's "horrible decree" and of Luther's all-justifying grace.

Updike does not shrink from making God responsible for evil. "I've never really understood theologies," he admits, "which would absolve

God of earthquakes and typhoons, of children starving." Updike has no patience with the merely "nice" Deity worshipped in most of our churches, the friendly Fellow with whom we can "empathize."[27] In his closet drama about President James Buchanan, Updike has the dying statesman make this fearful accusation: "I am not troubled by the sins of men, who are feeble; I am troubled by the sins of God, who is mighty."[28] In *A Month of Sundays*, the Reverend Thomas Marshfield makes even darker allegations by rehearsing a litany of the divine crimes inherent in God's world:

> . . . the pain of infants, the inexorability of disease, the wanton-ness of fortune, the billions of fossilized deaths, the helplessness of the young, the idiocy of the old, the craftsmanship of torturers, the authority of blunderers, the savagery of accident, the un-breathability of water, and all the other repulsive flecks of the face of Creation.[29]

Such an obsession with what Barth calls the "shadow-side" of God's good cosmos makes Updike a virtual dualist. He attributes his rev-erence for the Satanic to his upbringing in the Lutheran church. In a deeply Kierkegaardian confession, Updike speaks of his childhood faith as having branded him with a cross. It planted in him, he asserts, the ob-durate conviction that, "at the core of the core, there is a right-angled clash to which, of all verbal combinations we can invent, the Apostles' Creed offers the most adequate correspondence and response."[30] Chris-tian faith has validity for Updike because it attests so fully to life's own in-herent perplexity—the paradoxical clash of heaven and earth, spirit and flesh, even God and the Devil.

Updike goes so far, in fact, as to interpret "A Mighty Fortress Is Our God" as "an immense dirge of praise for the Devil and the world" that nourished in him a vast respect for the reality of the demonic. It con-vinced him that Satan has more than subjective and symbolic status. He is far more than the evil within us that makes for hatred and destruction, "torture and monstrosity."[31] He is also God's own "malevolent near-equal":

> But can we tolerate a God [Updike asks] who would permit such an opponent to arise, who would arm him with death and pain, who would allow suffering Mankind to become one huge Job, teased and tested in heavenly play? Alas, we have become, in our Protestant-ism, more virtuous than the myths that taught us virtue; we judge them barbaric. We resist the bloody legalities of Redemption; we face Judgment Day, in our hearts, much as young radicals face the mundane courts—convinced that acquittal is the one just verdict. We judge our Judge; and we magnanimously grant our Creator His

existence by a "leap" of our own wills, incidentally reducing his "ancient foe" to the dimensions of a bad comic strip.[32]

Updike laments the loss of a radical sense of evil in the mainstream Protestant churches. He much prefers the Luther who flung ink wells at the devil and who chalked *Baptizatus sum* on his slate in order to rout "the prince of darkness grim." Yet Updike does not share Luther's confident faith that "one little word" shall fell the Father of Lies. This Word is, of course, the incarnate Christ against whose kingdom of forgiveness the gates of graceless hell shall not prevail. Such solid assurance modern skepticism has fatally undermined. At best we can know God negatively, through human misery. For Luther, by contrast, it is not the negative judgment but the positive grace of God that reveals him aright: "If we apprehend him not by his power and wisdom, which terrify us, but by his goodness and love; there our faith and confidence can then stand unmovable and man is truly thus born anew. . . ."[33]

Updike is drawn, instead, to the Luther who spoke darkly of the *Deus absconditus*, the God whose unaccountably left-handed operations make him opaque to our understanding. Updike is haunted, in fact, by God's withdrawal from history. Ours is an age of anxiety not only because unprecedented political and intellectual calamities have befallen us, but also because a certain spiritual vacancy has invaded and hollowed out our lives. It is not God's death, Updike argues, but his absence that creates such inward emptiness. With Matthew Arnold and a great cloud of similar witnesses, Updike agrees that we live in the twilight of Christendom. We dwell at the ebbing edge of the once brimming sea of faith. The cosmos no longer resounds with the supernal music of the spheres; it echoes instead with the "melancholy, long, withdrawing roar" of Dover Beach.

Yet Updike rejects the trite notion that God is dead or nonexistent. For him—as also for Job and Jeremiah—God has hidden himself, absconded, exited the human realm. Early in life, Updike confesses, he learned to compare the absent God to the wealthy people whose mansion he passed on lonely Sunday afternoon walks with his parents:

> The road down into Shillington by the way of the cemetery led past the Dives estate, another ominous place. It was guarded by a wall topped with spiky stones. The wall must have been a half-mile long. It was so high that my father had to hold me up so I could look in. There were so many buildings and greenhouses I couldn't identify the house. All the buildings were locked and boarded up; there was never anybody there. But in the summer the lawns were mowed; it seemed by ghosts. There were tennis courts, and even—can it be?—a few golf flags. In any case there were a great deal of cut

lawn, the gray driveway, and ordered bushes; I got the impression of wealth as a vast brooding absence, like God Himself.[34]

Absence is not a synonym for unreality. It is the mark of a God whose presence is felt more negatively than positively, who hovers over the world like a cloud or shadow, at once sheltering and menacing. As if he were a fugitive animal, this God is detected not by sight so much as by scent and footprint. He is present in his absence. We know that Someone has *been* here, even if his traces are no longer plainly discerned. That this enormous something called the cosmos should have come from nothing is, for Updike, unthinkable. Yet he cannot discern God unambiguously anywhere in the world; on the contrary, he is haunted by God's deep duality. At times God appears to be a cretinous Mangler who causes much of the world's pain. Yet he is also the gracious Creator who has so generously endowed his creation that it sings of his goodness rather than his malevolence.

There is something deeply Augustinian in Updike's denial that the cosmos could be self-generated. The very existence of the world provides him irrefutable evidence that we are not our own makers but the recipients of an unbidden gift. He agrees with Augustine that the earth and everything within it cry aloud a single refrain: I have been created!

> Earth and the heavens are before our eyes. The very fact that they are there proclaims that they were created, for they are subject to change and variation; whereas if anything exists that was not created, there is nothing in it that was not there before; and the meaning of change and variation is that something is there that was not there before. Earth and the heavens also proclaim that they did not create themselves. "We exist," they tell us, "because we were made. And this is proof that we did not make ourselves. For to make ourselves, we should have had to exist before our existence began." And the fact that they plainly do exist is the voice which proclaims this truth.[35]

Updike's reverence for the mercy implicit in the world's utter givenness is reminiscent of Luther's celebrated saying that "if you really examined a kernel of grain thoroughly, you would die of wonder." Updike shares Luther's humbled gratitude before everything created. Whether they be human fabrications like window sashes and telephone poles, or natural creations such as horse chestnut trees and green hedges, all things *made* bespeak their maker. Their bare existence suggests "a teleologic bias in things."[36] They constitute a sign that the universe is not purposeless and absurd but designed for the glory of God and his creatures. Updike the denouncer of God's cruel creation is thus also Updike the praiser of God's wondrous world.

"The instinct that life is good," Updike confesses, "is where natural theology begins."[37] His own theology rests, in fact, upon the natural goodness implicit in the world's gratuitous beauty. Its infinite fineness of detail makes Updike all the more acutely aware that any dissection or description of it is bound to seem murderously coarse. Yet this difficulty exalts rather than debases the artist's fundamental obligation, which is to render homage to the world's splendor. Its mute objectivity does not mock our garrulous subjectivity, no matter what the French nihilists argue to the contrary. Created things serve, in Updike's view, as *larvae Dei*, as "masks for God."[38]

Such an unabashedly theological reading of creation explains Updike's positive regard for Marcel Proust as a religious novelist. Despite the remorseless pessimism he finds in *Remembrance of Things Past*, Updike contends that there is something transcendently heroic in Proust's attempt "to carry sensation to its final little tendril root."[39] "In the interminable rain of his prose," Updike recalls of his first look into *Swann's Way*, "I felt goodness. Proust was one of those men—increasingly rare, as faith further ebbs—who lost the consolations of belief but retained the attitudes and ambitions of a worshipper."[40]

In so describing Proust, Updike reveals more than a little of his own literary intention. He is himself stricken with a sense of Proustian wonder before the world's mysterious givenness. God himself may be absent, but his evidence is everywhere present. An early story called "Pigeon Feathers" discloses Updike's own attempt to trace life's gift character down to its "final little tendril root." Like much of Updike's short fiction, this story is more a vignette and meditation than an embodied action. It deals with a boy named David Kern and his first awakening to the threat of nihilism. A reading of H. G. Wells has shattered his faith in God, Christ, and Scripture. Wells's skepticism has filled him with the fear that religion is built on credulity and that we are all bound for eternal extinction.

The youthful Kern discerns no satisfactory answer to these doubts in either his father's cynicism, his mother's humanism, or his minister's rationalism. "Nowhere in the world of other people," David concludes, "would he find the hint, the nod, he needed to begin to build his fortress against death. They none of them believed. He was alone."[41] Like many adolescents, David seeks an individual rather than a social salvation, and he is obsessed with the problem of mortality rather than sin. His desire is for a faith at once biblical in its intensity and promise, and yet secular in its provenance and implication. He demands, in sum, the transcendent God proclaimed by Christian faith, but without either the historical revelation incarnate in Christ and recorded in Scripture, or the communal allegiance to God found in the church.

Young Kern is granted such an unconfessional faith quite by happenstance. It is something he does not produce but discovers. His father sends him to kill the pesky pigeons roosting in the family barn. Feeling himself a divine avenger, David slays the birds with the same guiltlessness he believes God must possess in order to create a suffering world. If the farm is to thrive—he ruthlessly reasons—these pigeons must die. Yet it is not only God's necessary cruelty that the boy thinks he has understood. He also comes to comprehend the bright upper side of this dark paradox. Like Luther inspecting the solitary kernel of grain, David examines but a single feather from one of the pigeons he has slain. He is overwhelmed by the gratuitous beauty contained in the plumage of these dead birds. It convinces him, as neither creed nor church can, that only a gracious Host could lay so sumptuous a feast for the eyes:

> The feathers were more wonderful than dog's hair, for each filament was shaped within the shape of the feather, and the feathers in turn were trimmed to fit a pattern that followed without error across the bird's body. . . . And across the surface of the infinitely adjusted yet somehow effortless mechanics of the feathers played the idle designs of color, no two alike, designs executed, it seemed, in a controlled rapture, with a joy that hung level in the air behind him. Yet these birds bred in the millions and were exterminated as pests. . . . [The boy was thus] robed in this certainty: that the God who had lavished such craft on these worthless birds would not destroy His whole creation by refusing to let David live forever.[42]

Such an affirmation is far removed from Updike's fear that God is a monstrous Demiurge who creates the world in his own cretinous image. Yet David Kern's adolescent insistence that the cosmos has significance only if he personally survives death cannot be dismissed as an uncharacteristic Updikean emphasis. The risk of faith is always wagered, in Updike's fiction, upon such drastic egoistic stakes. Anything less than everlasting gratification is too small a reward for so great a hazard as belief in God.

The Reverend Thomas Marshfield argues this case with special vehemence in *A Month of Sundays*. He interprets the resurrection of Christ as God's miraculous provision for the intransigent human desire not to be annihilated. Christians are most to be pitied, Marshfield says in echo of the Apostle Paul, if there is no resurrection of the dead. Yet Marshfield is concerned not with Christ's victory over death so much as his own ongoing life. If Jesus' death meant his final destruction, Marshfield reasons, then he shall himself be deprived of the heart's imperious longing for immortality—"a craving not for transformation into a life beyond imagining but for our *ordinary life*, the mundane life we so driftingly and numbly live, to go on forever and forever. The only Paradise we can imagine is this Earth. The only life we desire is this one."[43] In Updike's theology, flesh and blood *must* inherit the kingdom.

Such obsession with our own material resurrection is also the theme of Updike's much-quoted but little-understood poem, "Seven Stanzas at Easter." There he makes the entire marvel of the resurrection turn on the physicality of Jesus' resuscitated corpse. The astonishment of Easter morning is not to be confused with nature's glorious self-renewal: the popping of crocuses and the blossoming of dogwoods. Nor is the empty grave to be understood as a spiritual event in the life of the early Christian community. The risen Christ is, instead, the wondrous guarantee of our own perpetual corporeality. In the Good News that the dead Christ resumed his—and thus our—bodily existence lies the one hope that we shall not remain permanently entombed:

> It was not as the flowers,
> each soft Spring recurrent;
> it was not as His Spirit in the mouths and fuddled
>   eyes of eleven apostles;
> it was as His flesh: ours.
>
> The same hinged thumbs and toes,
> the same valved heart
> that—pierced—died, withered, paused, and then
>   regathered out of enduring Might
> new strength to enclose.
> . . . .
> The stone is rolled back, not papier-maché,
> not a stone in a story,
> but the vast rock of materiality that in the slow
>   grinding of time will eclipse for each of us
> the wide light of day.[44]

There is something scarcely creditable about Updike's reading of both death and resurrection. Few people past the age of thirty want their lives to go on perpetually. However little one may actually desire one's own death, it offers a terminal completion and fulfillment without which life would remain an intolerable burden. "Lord, let me know my end," cries Psalm 39, "and what is the measure of my days; let me know how fleeting my life is!" Even if death meant our total annihilation, it would not be entirely horrible. To cease upon the midnight without pain, to drift into dreamless, endless sleep is a consummation that many devoutly wish. Death possesses a dread "sting" not chiefly because it means our final disappearance, but because it signals our alienation from God, our rebellion against him, and thus his terrible judgment upon us amidst "the wrath to come." What matters for the Christian is neither the desire for life's infinite prolongation nor the fear of its total extinction. Resurrection faith believes that, far from the risen Christ's being like us, we shall become like him: we shall be delivered from the death of eternal condemnation into the life of eternal mercy.

This contesting of Updike's interpretation of Last Things is intended not to correct his heterodoxy but to show how his dialectical faith in the absent Lord of the cosmos vacillates between potentially sentimental conceptions of God as either the harsh Crusher of human hope or the soft Provider of the heart's desire. Updike's theological instincts are right in wanting to descry the masks of God within the natural order. He is to be commended for seeking God's *guise* in creation. The problem is that he seeks God's *face* there as well. What Updike finds in creaturely things is not at all surprising: a God whose duality and ambiguity are altogether as problematic as the world's own doubleness. God's signature is written across the whole cosmos, Updike is reported to have said, but his lettering is illegible. It follows that faith springs neither from the revelation of God in Israel and Christ as attested by Scripture, nor from the community of belief that proclaims the Gospel through the church, but from the transcendent self's own egoistic quest.

IV. Faith as Transcendent Egotheism: "Midpoint"

It is evident that Updike's dialectical vision of God's presence-in-absence derives from the Christian existentialist tradition. Like Kierkegaard, he locates our knowledge of God within human subjectivity—within the suffering and longing that characterize every life not sunk in bestial oblivion. We humans dance our tragicomic jig on the tightwire of self-transcending consciousness because God has so placed us. Against atheists like Sartre, Updike insists that we are not our own project, but that God himself has set us halfway between the angels and the apes. Our unique capacity for both misery and delight has a divine derivation. We would not be such wretched and maladjusted creatures were there not a ultimate happiness standing over us as our true norm. Ours would be a contented animal existence were God not the Disturber of our anthropoid peace.

A secular critique of Updike's theological existentialism would charge him with having created a God of the gaps. The haplessness and fecklessness of humanity count *against* the reality of God, not for it. The absurdity of the human situation proves, for the atheist, how random and mindless the natural process is. Nature goes wildly beyond its own bounds by giving rise, in humanity, to a self-surpassing awareness that finds no echo or response either in other humans, in nature, in history, or in the world beyond. As Sartre never tired of repeating we "exist" in the bare etymological sense of the word: our consciousness forces us out of animality and into a metaphysical void. The very fact of this absurd human freedom means the impossibility of a God who could command our loyalty and obedience. Were there a God, we would be his puppets. Or, as Sartre liked to say even more polemically, God's existence would make no difference—so imperiously does the human self transcend its own circumstances, vaulting beyond everything that already exists.

Updike fully understands the atheist critique of religion. He confesses to having read the existentialists because he shares their experience of feeling "suspended quite pointlessly in an immense void of indifferent stars and mathematically operating atoms."[45] For Updike no less than for Sartre, absurdity is the besetting difficulty of modern existence. We dwell, he admits, in a universe which "science discloses to us [as] farcically unrelated to our primitive senses."[46] Updike can sound even more absurdist than Heidegger or Sartre—and not a little Gnostic—in confessing that "I've touched a kind of bottom, when I've felt that existence was an affront to be forgiven."[47]

Where Updike differs from the atheist existentialists is in his insistence that the awful gap separating us from the world is nothing novel. It is but the modern rediscovery of what Updike calls "the great aboriginal distinction between inner and outer, *anima* and *res*."[48] What Sartre describes as a futile passion—our frustrated desire to live by godlike necessity rather than accidental freedom—Updike regards as an enabling paradox. As the only self-reflexive animals, humans are at least partially liberated from natural routine and social convention. It is God's very invisibility that gives us our freedom. "A concrete and manifest God would be an absolute tyrant," Updike declares, "with no place in His universe for free-willed men."[49] Only when God is not pantheistically equated with the cosmos but theistically discerned as the divine Other do we cease being objective "things" and become subjective "souls."

Hence Updike's ironic praise for the metaphysical emptiness and unease that register in nearly every modern man and woman. They provide, in his view, a potentially fertile ground for faith's renewed life. The emptier the world, the greater the spirit's freedom to fill it. The less God can be outwardly located within history or nature or society, the more completely can he reign within the inward consciousness of the believer. Far from being an uninviting wasteland of moral and spiritual desiccation, the age of ambiguity and anxiety can still flower with true faith. Belief in God does not blow, after all, on the winds of the *Zeitgeist*. The evacuation of meaning from the public and natural sphere may be desolating, but it is also strangely invigorating. It makes possible a new vibrancy of inward and subjective life.

It is not an adolescent self-fixation that makes Updike so subjective and autobiographical a writer. He has, instead, an Augustinian obsession with the insatiable restlessness of the human heart. It provides firsthand evidence that we are not alone, but that our lives are transcendently troubled and perhaps even divinely redeemed. Like his master Proust, Updike finds in worldly wonder the occasion for his own enriched subjectivity. Sartre, by contrast, "has no use for the interior life or its explorations, and in fact believes that there is no such thing as an interior life, everything being external to consciousness."[50]

Yet it is not Proust alone but also Augustine who is Updike's spiritual mentor. They both stand within the mystical tradition of meditative inwardness. Our modern novelist is no less convinced than the ancient saint that belief in God is as near at hand as one's own self-awareness. This assurance gives Updike a satirical scorn for what is naive and self-serving in our age's vaunted unbelief. Doubt, he confesses in Whitmanesque fashion, was not the chief problem of his youth. "That God, at a remote place and time, took upon himself the form of a Syrian carpenter and walked the earth willfully healing and abusing and affirming and grieving, appeared to me quite in the character of the Author of the grass."[51] The world and our conscious place in it are so gratuitously unnecessary as to make atheism seem shallow and insipid. The Reverend Thomas Marshfield, Updike's protagonist in *A Month of Sundays*, ridicules the literal-mindedness implicit in all scientific skepticism:

> There once thrived, in that pained and systematic land of Germany, a school of Biblical scholarship that sought to reduce all of the Biblical miracles to natural happenings. The Red Sea's parting was an opportune low tide, and the feeding of the five thousand— the only miracle attested to in each of the four Gospels—was Jesus shaming the multitude into bringing out from under its multitude of cloaks a multitude of box lunches hitherto jealously hoarded. This school of exegetical thought observes that our Lord, before healing the blind man of Bethsaida, spit upon his hands—as if saliva is an attested medication for glaucoma. It notes, with a collusive wink, that the saline density of the Dead Sea is so high that one can virtually "walk" upon it—without noting that Peter, attempting the same maneuver, sank. It whispers the magic word "psycho-somatic"—as if Lazarus merely fancied he was dead, the swine spontaneously decided to go for a swim, and the fig tree withered under hypnosis. The absurdities of such naturalism need no belaboring.[52]

What modern spiritual inertia has forced upon us, Updike believes, is the necessity of saturating the dull stuff of bestial existence with acute self-awareness. Only in so doing can we become living creatures rather than dead souls. We ought to take courage, says Thomas Marshfield, from the strange desert animal called the chuckwalla. His smallness, like the tight-fitting human self, is to his advantage. Instead of heading for open spaces when attacked, he "... *runs* to a tight place, to a crevice in the burning rock of the desert. Once there, does he shrink in shame? No! He puffs himself up, inflates his self to more than half its normal size, and fills that crevice as the living soul fills the living body, and cannot be dislodged by the talon or fang of any enemy."[53]

Updike recognizes, of course, that such wholesale subjectivity can lead to conclusions as nihilistic as Sartre's objective phenomenalism. The self-inflating spirit, knowing no limits to its inward fabrications, is tempted to turn existence inside out like a sock, to make the whole phenomenal world grist for the mind's workings, to sink into the vortex of self-reflection, and thus to consume all matter in the volatility of pure consciousness. The downward plunge of the totally self-reflexive mind may find no final floor whereon to stand. There are fathomless depths, said Augustine, to the inward-turning spirit. "I can probe deep into them and never find the end of them."[54]

It is not only the bishop of Hippo to whom Updike finally looks for guidance in matters of the spirit, but also the Christian existentialists of the last two centuries. In them the joys and woes of modern self-reflexivity come to burning clarity of focus. "Though many theologies of false reasonableness have been offered down through the ages," Updike declares, "Kierkegaard and Barth and Berdyaev and Unamuno in modern times have rooted faith more securely than ever in the native soil of desperation." They all serve as thorns in the flesh of modern self-confidence. The effect of their work is to prove that Christian faith is something more than a useless vestige left over from the evolutionary development of culture. They remind us of our inescapable "sickness unto death." "Like the vermiform appendix," Updike declares in a less than cheering analogy, "Christianity will be with Western man a while longer."[55]

Updike is drawn especially to Kierkegaard because his negative and anthropocentric theology is in such total accord with the modern experience of God's eclipse. It was Kierkegaard who, more than any other nineteenth-century thinker, provided an intellectual basis for twentieth-century faith:

> By giving metaphysical dignity to "the subjective," by showing faith to be not an intellectual development but a movement of the will, by holding out for existential duality against the tide of all monisms, materialist or mystical or political, that would absorb the individual consciousness, Kierkegaard has given Christianity new life, a handhold, the "Archimedean point."[56]

Like Updike, Kierkegaard has a dialectical view of God as both monstrous and merciful. The great Dane is not only the advocate of Christianity, says Updike, but also its accuser. "Christianity is torture," in Updike's reading of Kierkegaard's theology, "and God is a torturer."[57] The deity who is himself pure Spirit can bring humanity out of animal complacency and into spiritual life only through drastic suffering. It is not physical pain that elevates us to the divine condition. We are transformed from animals into spiritual beings through the psychic torment of knowing that we stand at the crucifying juncture of time and eternity.

The forsaken Christ upon the cross represents, in Updike's view, the true situation of every Kierkegaardian Christian. The real believer is called to become an inward if not an outward martyr. The central summons of faith is to imitate the Savior who refused to live merely for the finite, but who surrendered himself to the Infinite. Yet because faith exacts so terrible a price, Kierkegaard bitterly acknowledges its cruelty. He sings alleluias only after shouting execrations at the God who saddled him with the burden of existence. Hence Kierkegaard's final conviction that life itself is a crime, and that to perpetuate it is an act of sexual egoism. Speaking of his own existence as a "mistake," Kierkegaard ends by recommending celibacy to all Christians, and thanking God "that no living being owes its existence to me."[58]

Though he admits that such misanthropy is heretical, Updike honors Kierkegaard for having first discerned faith's inescapable anguish and irony. More powerfully than anyone else, he saw that all of life, whether historical or natural, proceeds more by fits and starts than by the smooth Hegelian synthesis of antecedent conditions. For Kierkegaard, therefore, the act of faith is already implicit in ordinary experience. Any free decision entails an unaccountable leap from a myriad of possibilities to the single actuality chosen. Faith is no more irrational, Updike claims in Kierkegaard's behalf, than the world itself. "The 'leap' does seem to be the way, both in particle physics and human affairs, that things move, rather than [by means of] Hegel's deterministic 'mediation.'"[59]

Updike takes the logic of Kierkegaard's subjectivism to its ultimate extreme in his long autobiographical poem called "Midpoint." There he interprets Christian faith not as a radical transformation of the world, but as a patient acceptance, even a willful maintenance, of life's paradoxical self-contradiction. Like his Danish master, Updike attempts to read divinity off life's irreducible contrariety of opposites. Yet the real gravamen of this poem is not only Kierkegaardian subjectivism but also Whitmanesque "egotheism"—the faith that one's own unique self is the mysterious gift of God.

Updike distinguishes Whitman's "exultant egoism" from ordinary vanity and self-inflation. The latter is mere self-addiction; the former is "the majestic and multitudinous yet unified miracle of being oneself."

True selfishness derives from "a recognition of each man's immersion in a unique and unexchangeable ego which is, in a sense, all he's got, but something he indeed does, short of madness and the grave, have."[60] That countless human personalities, each irreducibly specific, constitute the grand spectacle of history is, for Updike, the unaccountable miracle. Like Pascal, he confesses to having been struck, early in life, at the wonder of his own unduplicated consciousness:

> The mystery that . . . puzzled me as a child was the incarnation of my ego—that omnivorous and somehow preexistent "I"— in a speck so specifically situated amid the billions of history. Why was I I? The arbitrariness of it astounded me; in comparison, nothing was too marvelous."[61]

This solid sense of personal identity—confirmed and enhanced by Updike's rural and religious upbringing—is what the modern world lacks. Transcendent selfhood is dying, Updike fears, from the plague of a trite humanism. In church and culture alike, a vapid hopefulness reigns. It ignores the violent strains inherent in all personal and social life. Updike hails Whitman, therefore, as a man who understood the world's pandemic anguish and yet embraced it all the more vigorously for its pain. He overcame our American enmity for the tragic, Updike insists, by recklessly proclaiming "the mystery of Me."[62] It is Updike's evident aim to undertake his own Whitmanesque program, using the fulcrum of an invigorating egocentrism to dislodge the spiritual inertia of our time:

> An easy Humanism plagues the land;
> I choose to take an otherworldly stand.
> The Archimedean point, however small,
> Will serve to lift th' entire terrestial Ball.
>   Reality transcends itself within;
> Atomically, all writers must begin.
> The truth arrives as if by telegraph:
> One dot; two dots; a silence; then a laugh.
> The rules inhere, and will not be imposed,
> *Ab alto*, as most Liberals have supposed.[63]

Updike's title is meant to evoke a biblical and Dantesque sense of having been written at age thirty-five and thus *"nel mezzo cammin' della nostra vita."* Yet it is a spatial as well as a temporal metaphor that Updike has in mind: he is *himself* the "midpoint," the center around which his universe revolves. In this conviction, Updike is indeed more Freudian than Freud. The master's doctrine of primary narcissism, the idea that the original object of love is one's own self, serves as Updike's call to arms. The ego provides the world its real animus, he argues, the driving power without which it would soon shrivel and die. And genital sex, as we have seen, is the self's main motive force. Nothing other than the clamant eroticism of the self can silence our fear that "Creation is a stutter of the Void."[64] The only sure universe is the cosmos of one's own incarnate condition, and the only certain source of life is the omnivorous self:

> . . . if my body is history
> > then my ego is Christ
> and no inversion is too great for me
> > no fate too special. . . .[65]

Egoism is the spring of social no less than of personal life. God is on the side of all things vital and changing, the enemy of all things static and complacent. He "screws the lukewarm, slays the heart that faints,/ And saves his deepest silence for his saints."[66] Lest his holy ones mistakenly believe they hear and know his voice, God remains mute. He plunges us into the waters of ambiguity that we might swim by faith. It is evil to trust in the morality of certain rewards, Updike argues, and good to risk the life of glorious but uncertain adventure:

> Transcendent Goodness makes elastic claims;
> The merciful Creator hid His Aims.
> Beware false Gods: the Infallible Man,
> The flawless formula, the Five-Year Plan.
> Abjure bandwagons; be shy of machines,
> Charisma, ends that justify the means,
> And oaths that bind the postulant to kill
> His own self-love and independent Will.[67]

Such Dionysian egoism is reminiscent more of Nietzsche than of Kierkegaard. Yet Updike believes that nothing less than deified self-will and self-love can restore the vitality that the modern world has lost. They bring the dull and indifferent stuff of finitude spiritually alive. Pointillism is the ultimate artistic expression of the ego's inward self-transcendence. Like the computer, it turns everything into a collocation of atomistic dots that enable us to generate limitless possibility within the smallest place: "The midget of the alphabet is I;/The Infinite is littleness heaped high."[68]

The task of the energizing ego is inwardly to duplicate nature's vital flux, the heedless onward flow of time that drowns all attempts to stanch it. So to live requires an unsentimental vision of the world's ferocity, a dauntless celebration of what Bergson called the *élan vital*. That the Egyptian pyramids were built at the cost of countless lives is of no great moral moment in a Heraclitean world. Among the billions of deaths wrought by time's perpetual change, says Updike, the Holocaust is but another instance of life's ruthlessness:

> In bins of textbooks, holocausts lie stacked:
> "No life was spared when Ghengis Khan attacked."
> It little counts in History's level eye
> Just how we copulate, or how we die.
> ·
>
> The Judgment Day seems nigh to every age;
> But History blinks and turns another page.
> Our lovely green-clad mother spreads her legs—
> Corrosive, hairy, rank—and, shameless, begs
> For Pestilence to fuck her if it can,
> For War to come, and come again.[69]

Life's only surety is that the cosmos will absorb all extremes back into its capacious and indifferent center. Amidst so perilous a world, there is no staying out of harm's way. We cannot live without threatening other life, without killing. To craft one's project with all the excellence one can muster is inevitably to impinge upon others also creating their own little universe of meaning. There is no ameliorating "advice" that can correct this tragic truth. The only cure for the pain of existing is to discern the sheer gratuity of creation: "Nothing has had to be, but is by Grace."[70] This elevated last word is the reality that enables us to affirm rather than to resent the fact that life is both destructive and creative, a splendid union and coincidence of opposites. Such a recognition alone can enable us to accept both our crime and our pardon: "Our guilt inheres in sheer Existing, so/Forgive yourself your death, and freely flow."[71]

This recognition that we are not ourselves the world's center, but that we have been privileged to live at the juncture of the heavenly and animal realms, saves Updike's egotheistic faith from nihilism. Unlike Nietzsche, Updike does not envision humanity as the inventor of life's meaning and value. He shares the Greek tragic conviction that the world's vitality is at war with its order, destroying itself even as it creates and renews. Yet Updike is not finally a tragedian but an ironist. The world is more creative than destructive, and thus more worthy of gratitude than accusation. Like Joyce Cary's Gulley Jimson, he describes himself as "born laughing." Far from cheering himself up and jauntily whistling through the gloom, his work serves to affirm the utter gift character of life. Hence Updike's overtly religious conclusion to his long poetic self-description:

> The marsh gives way to Pond, to dunes, to Sea;
> Cicadas call it good, and I agree.
> At midpoint, center of a Hemisphere
> Too blue for words, I've grown to love it here.

> Earth wants me, it shall have me, yet not yet;
> Some task remains, whose weight I can't forget,
> Some package, anciently addressed, of praise,
> That keeps me knocking on the doors of days.[72]

Such an insouciant embrace of life is not built on an escapist vision of the world as a cheery place. It is Updike's hard-won conclusion in the face of life's insoluble contradictions. Updike's critics are off the mark, therefore, when they accuse him of having been too narrow and self-centered to confront the great civic questions of our time: poverty and hunger, political oppression and racial strife. The irony is that Updike regards these issues not as too large for his fiction but as too small. Such political evils are at least minimally tractable as life itself is not. The Armageddon being waged in the public sphere has less interest to Updike, therefore, than the universal struggle which perplexes the human heart regardless of time and circumstance. It is for this reason that Updike confesses to having a perduring interest in "surburban, or rural, unpolitical man." He is the chronicler not simply of middle-class complacency but of the ironic bind wherein we are all comi-tragically caught:

> My books feed, I suppose, on some kind of perverse relish in the fact that there are unsolvable problems. There is no reconciliation between the inner, intimate appetites and the external consolations of life. You want to live forever, you want to have endless wealth, you have endless avarice for conquests, crave endless freedom. . . . And yet, despite the aggressive desires, something in us expects no menace. But there is no way to reconcile these individual wants to the very real need of any society to set strict limits and to confine its members.[73]

Updike the ironist serves, then, as both the critic and the apologist of Christian faith. God is not for him Charles Wesley's "pure unbounded love." As the alternately harsh and beneficent God of the cosmic order, he is to be understood in dialetical terms which unite absence with presence. Nor is Updike willing, like Barth, to read the Gospel as God's unilateral act of gladness which redeems and transforms life's endless oscillation between Yes and No. For Updike, on the contrary, the two faces of the divine reality are at once immitigably opposed and yet paradoxically close. So dialectical a vision of ultimate reality can lead to ethical quietism—to an antinomian disregard for the necessary social restraints. Yet there is a moral vision at work in Updike's fiction which serves, at least in part, to vindicate the God whom he so honestly doubts. Especially in the first three volumes of his Rabbit Angstrom saga, Updike's fiction approaches the condition of true comedy. Unlike *Couples*, these novels affirm the possibility that marriage can be graciously sustained rather than bitterly broken. Not in the terror and beauty of the natural order, Updike discovers, but in the irony of perduring human regard is God's mercy most fully mirrored.

10

THE STRANGE MORAL
PROGRESS OF
HARRY ("RABBIT") ANGSTROM

The human condition in all of its immitigable ambiguity is the true subject of John Updike's fiction. His artistic hopes are accordingly modest. His fiction does not envision a grand scheme for our ultimate redemption. Such religious purposes lie, for a Protestant like Updike, outside the scope of art. He agrees with Karl Barth that the aim of fiction is to present the universal in the particular, to "show me man as he always is in the man of today, my contemporary—and vice versa, to show me my contemporary in man as he always is." The novel, Barth concludes, "should have no plans for educating me, but should leave me to reflect (or not) on the portrait with which I am presented."[1] Such, it seems clear, is the intent of Updike's most celebrated work, his novels devoted to the life and times of Harry ("Rabbit") Angstrom. He is a protagonist who poses a problem rather than a solution, who queries us more than he teaches us a lesson. "Rabbit is the hero of [*Rabbit, Run*]," Updike affirms, "but is he a good man? The question is meant to lead to another—What is goodness?"[2]

In depicting the ongoing life of this one character through a series of novels—examining thereby the spiritual state of the nation through each of the last three decades—Updike has created a virtual American saga. He has promised, moreover, to provide continuing reports on Rabbit so long as he and his protagonist shall live. Harry Angstrom has become, in fact, a prototypical American character, an almost epical embodiment of our common hopes and fears. This unlikely figure is no less definitive for our cultural consciousness than Twain's Huckleberry Finn, Hemingway's Nick Adams, or Faulkner's Ike McCaslin. Yet while these earlier heroes inhabit a world now largely irrecoverable, Rabbit dwells in our time and place. He is, in the deepest sense, "one of us."

207

Rabbit, Run began as a counterpart, Updike says, to *The Centaur.* Together, the two novels were intended to "illustrate the polarity between running and plodding, between the rabbit and the horse, between the life of instinctual gratification and that of dutiful self-sacrifice."[3] Yet the familiar Updikean opposites form no easy polarity: one term nearly always dominates the other, as life remains perpetually out of kilter. Romantic flight from responsibility, in heedless obedience to the soul's "urgent inner whispers," has been Updike's chief theme. Transcendent egotheism is, as we have seen, the creed upon which his house of fiction is built. Discontentment is, for him, the quintessence of spiritual vitality. Updike has been drawn, from the beginning, to characters who have an irrepressible urge to vagabondage. He cites the following description of a foolish Irish king to illustrate his high regard for sheer insouciance of spirit: "Unsteadiness, restlessness, and unquiet filled him, likewise disgust with every place in which he used to be and desire for every place which he had not reached."[4]

Et inquietum est cor nostrum, declares Augustine on the very first page of the *Confessions.* Updike is the distant heir of Augustine in his concern for the incurable inquietude of the human heart. There is, however, an immense difference. For Augustine, the human spirit is restless because it has abandoned its peace in God. For Updike, our souls are agitated because God has precariously situated us between the angels and the apes. Yet they are both agreed that human unease is perpetual. Updike insists, in fact, that the heart cannot be kept alive except in revolt against the world's deadening conformity. "The spirit needs folly," one of his recent characters boasts, "as the body needs food."[5] This sentiment echoes a declaration that we heard Updike making at the beginning of his career: "The heart *prefers* to move against the grain of circumstance; perversity is the soul's very life."[6]

Updike has great tolerance for Rabbit Angstrom because he possesses this enabling perversity. For others, such ruthless self-will is the sign of Angstrom's decadence and perhaps even his perdition. Flannery O'Connor, for example, described *Rabbit, Run* as "the best book illustrating damnation that has come along in a great while."[7] Understandable though this judgment is, it is not Updike's. He does not intend to portray the wanton Rabbit as a totally reprehensible character. "I feel a tenderness toward my characters that forbids making violent use of them," Updike confesses. None of his fiction is tainted, he insists, with the jaundice of satirical intent. "You can't be satirical at the expense of your fictional characters," Updike explains, "because they're your creatures. You must only love them."[8] Updike rarely makes his protagonists the butt of satirical scorn, as O'Connor and Percy often do; nor the occasion for creating comic situations, as De Vries frequently does.

Far more than any of our other authors, Updike stands in the realistic tradition of the great nineteenth-century writers. A novelist like Tolstoy, the critic John Bayley has shown, is not chiefly concerned to argue a thesis but to disclose the individuality and lifelikeness of fictional characters. Having intrinsic worth themselves, they do not serve as mere vehicles for revealing the author's own opinions. Rather than seeking to draw the world through the sieve of his own consciousness, Bayley argues, Tolstoy wants to enter the lives of other people and to reveal what is uniquely interesting about them.[9] Updike has this same affectionate regard for his own characters. It is a tenderness that does not prevent his passing judgment on their faults. Yet Updike succeeds best when he is writing not in admonition but in what he calls a "rapt witness to the world that surrounds and transcends us."[10] He is a master of the encomiast mode, and Rabbit Angstrom is his most enduring "character of love."

Like most of Updike's protagonists, Angstrom is a version of his creator. That he begins as a blue-collar worker and never acquires any formal education beyond high school does not negate their deep likeness. Rabbit is roughly Updike's own age, shares his eastern Pennsylvania milieu, and withholds no confession for the sake of decorum. What Updike says of the writer in general is especially true of his own third-person narrator in the Rabbit novels: "Since his words enter into another's brain in silence and intimacy, [the author] should be as honest and explicit as we are with ourselves."[11] Angstrom indeed tells all, and much of his unburdening makes for less than pleasant reading.

This unpleasantness is an essential part of Updike's purpose. Artistically no less than theologically, he wants to show that goodness is not necessarily tied to conventional morality, but that sin and grace are bound ambiguously together. Updike's task is to make Rabbit a character who is at once unattractive and yet sympathetic, angering and yet endearing. He depicts him, therefore, as a sincere but often misguided exemplar of the religious life: a man who commits perverse acts for the sake of his invincible soul. Angstrom is an outrageous sinner and yet not a monster. Present-tense narration—still a revolutionary technique in 1960—helps Updike to accomplish his aim. It gives Angstrom's megalomaniac obsessions and adventures a rushing inevitability. With his youth fleeting past so irretrievably, we are made to ask, what else can Rabbit do than . . . run? Damnable as his deeds are, Angstrom must be honored for his willingness to enact the desire that most people suppress—the egoistic urge, namely, to preserve one's youthful freedom at all costs.

During the course of the three novels thus far issued, Rabbit Angstrom gradually mellows into a wisdom that can accept time as the essential human element. Responsibility, he discovers, can become the very means of freedom. Ever so reluctantly, Rabbit learns what we

Americans are often loath to admit: that most human problems have to be endured rather than solved. Easy answers are unavailing against the fierce strife that rends our personal and social life. The outward and inward apocalypse that convulses our age is thus writ small in the figure of Harry Angstrom. His problem is not local but universal. He is caught, as we all are, in an intractable ambiguity. The least he can do is to suffer his plight without panic. Such a somber prospect is hardly comic. It becomes comic only as Rabbit learns to celebrate rather than to flee the essential ambivalence of life. Even at the end of the third novel, he still dreams of breaking the fetters that morally bind him. Yet to our great surprise, Harry Angstrom cannot escape the redeeming paradox that moral obligation leads to life rather than death.

I. Sinning That Grace May Abound: *Rabbit, Run*

Rabbit, Run is Updike's most persuasive fictional demonstration of his Kierkegaardian conviction that faith cannot be reduced to morality but may have, on the contrary, a strange kinship with immorality. The novel's epigraph from Pascal points up the odd connection between human recalcitrance and divine benevolence: "The motions of Grace, the hardness of heart; external circumstances." Though Rabbit will stand judged for his own flinty heart, Updike will also vindicate him as a man who, in destructive revolt against his confining circumstances, will be moved by grace. Almost alone among all the characters in the novel, Rabbit is depicted as an unshakable believer. Like Kierkegaard's Abraham, he is willing to make a "teleological suspension of the ethical" for the sake of the religious. He remains true to his own sense of divine freedom, even if it means the betrayal of others.

When we first meet him, Harry Angstrom is—as his name suggests—a harried and anxious twenty-six-year-old yearning to be free from the binding commitments and responsibilities that life has thrust upon him all too soon. He is a former high school basketball hero whose dreams of glory are withering amidst the dull routine of adult life. The sexual and social restraints of the Eisenhower decade have set intolerable limits on his fantasies of greatness. Angstrom finds his job as vegetable-peeler salesman especially degrading, premised as it is upon the proposition that "fraud makes the world go around."[12] His wife Janice, pregnant with their second child, is turning into a sloven with her endless drinking and television watching. Once the baby girl is born, she seems always to be crying. Worse still is the deadened sexual life that Rabbit and Janice now experience. Their former sense of exaltation in sex has been replaced by something all too predictable and stale. Rabbit thus has cause for considerable complaint. He wants to get out, to let go, to run.

Rabbit first absconds from moral obligation by leaving his wife and going to live with a semiprostitute named Ruth. Yet this liaison proves Angstrom to be less a lecher than a stymied mystic. Rabbit desires spiritual far more than sexual deliverance. He wants to preserve his early awareness that life is not meant to be all grimness and effort, but that it is graced with limitless possibility and freedom.

> He used to love to climb [telephone] poles. To shinny up from a friend's shoulders until the ladder of spikes came to your hands, to get up to where you could hear the wires sing. Terrifying motion-less whisper. It always tempted you to fall, to let the hard spikes in your hands go and feel the space on your back, feel it take your feet and ride up your spine as you fell.[13]

This dream of unhindered freedom is also a covert death wish, and it is linked therefore with sex. It was not Freud alone who taught Updike the connection between death and sex. Our medieval ancestors knew this truth well when they spoke of the exhausted sadness that follows upon orgasm's "little death." Ruth uses Rabbit's own metaphor to de-scribe the ecstasy that ends bodily concourse: "It's like falling through," she says.[14] It is a plunge into nowhere, a descent into nothingness. Such a paradox—the most transcendent human moment being akin to extinc-tion—explains why sex is both sad and funny in Updike's work. There is truth, of course, in Updike's own twinkly-eyed aphorism: "Not to be in love, the capital N Novel whispers to capital W Western Man, is to be dying."[15] Yet to finish the act of love itself is to be not merely dying but virtually dead. That Updike can find such an irony amusing is one of the redemptive qualities of his books.

Rabbit misses, of course, the tangled ambiguity inherent in sexual love. His first rendezvous with Ruth is, appropriately, more comic than erotic. He attempts to transform this poor slattern into a sex goddess who is also a faithful spouse. Kneeling before his naked lover and kissing her empty ring finger, he insists on calling their first encounter in bed "our wedding night." Rabbit seeks in sex no mere spasm of pleasure but an angelic union of souls, not sweaty coition but unearthly bliss: "It is not her crotch that he wants, not the machine; but her, her."[16] He de-mands, impossibly, that his lover embody both ecstasy and fidelity, both transporting passion and lasting obligation.

Even before he can get in bed with Ruth, Rabbit notices the lighted rose window in the church across the street. It is a sign, to him, of the luminous transcendence everyone else is determined to ignore: "This circle of red and purple and gold seems in the city night a hole punched in reality to show the abstract brilliance burning beneath."[17] Rabbit's mystical longings are lost on Ruth, who unromantically attends to the body's imperious necessity. "I got to take a leak," she irreverently an-nounces to the worshipful Angstrom.[18]

Though Updike makes kindly sport of Rabbit's impossible desire to unite the ideal and the real, he does not mock his sense of sacramental wonder before the world's beauty and mystery. After climbing Mt. Judge with Ruth, Angstrom ponders the meaning of such immense height: "It seems plain, standing here, that if there is a floor there is a ceiling, that the true space in which we live is upward space."[19] This sense of the *mysterium tremendum* also accounts for Rabbit's love of Sundays. Appalled to think that the cosmos is godlessly suspended "in the middle of nowhere," he is comforted at the sight of Sunday worshippers heading for church. They seem to him "a visual proof of the unseen world."[20] Sundays and church windows, like sex and high places, provide Angstrom evidence of a Reality which, though transparent and invisible, is as life-giving as the air we breathe. This seems clearly to be Updike's own view. He likens our thankless dependence upon God to our heedless reliance upon things that, though taken for granted, we could not do without. A writer relies unconsciously on the sheet beneath the pen. An ice skater performs fantastic feats of balance and movement, oblivious to the gravity that makes them possible:

> Just as the paper is the basis for the marks upon it, might not events be contingent upon a never-expressed (because featureless) ground? Is the true marvel of Sunday skaters the pattern of their pirouettes or the fact that they are silently upheld? Blankness is not emptiness; we may skate upon an intense radiance we do not see because we see nothing else. And in fact there is a color, a quiet but tireless goodness that things at rest, like a brick wall or a small stone, seem to affirm. A wordless reassurance these things are pressing to give.[21]

Rabbit Angstrom is the advocate, like Updike himself, of a deeply natural religion. He believes that he would not have insatiable longings were there not a God seeking communion with him. "There's something that wants me to find it," he confesses.[22] "His eyes turn toward the light," the narrator observes of Rabbit's instinct for the luminous, "however it glances into his retina."[23] Angstrom is a virtual evangelist for this unseen but all-invigorating Presence. "I'm a mystic," he announces. "I give people faith."[24] Mrs. Smith, the elderly lady for whom Rabbit works as a gardener after he abandons Janice, confirms this estimate. She praises him for his religious energy and vitality: "You kept me alive, Harry; it's the truth; you did. . . . That's what you have, Harry: life. It's a strange gift and I don't know how we're supposed to use it but I know it's the only gift we get and it's a good one."[25]

The problem with Rabbit's mysticism is that it knows no limits. It makes him a virtual god unto himself. With only his inward deity to worship, Angstrom becomes merciless toward all his rivals, especially those who would make moral claims upon him. He forces Ruth, for example, to ever more abject sexual submission, and finally to fellatio. He demands that she grant him the same sexual surrender she has given her other lovers. Yet Rabbit yields her little in return. Like Piet Hanema, he orders his pregnant lover to have an abortion. Rabbit treats his own wife with similar contempt. His unfaithfulness to Janice sinks her ever deeper into a semialcoholic state.

Angstrom's creative urge to break free from the deadening grind ends in destructive egomania. He comes to have contempt for all outward obligations. "Goodness lies inside," he proclaims, "there is nothing outside."[26] "All I know is what's inside *me*," he confesses. "That's all I have."[27] Rabbit indeed fashions himself as a prophet of inward self-indulgence. He would release others from their bondage to enervating self-sacrifice, teaching them that there is no penalty for a life of self-abandonment. "If you have the guts to be yourself," Angstrom preaches, "other people'll pay your price."[28] Yet this is no mere pagan boast. Updike's narrator makes clear the religious roots of Rabbit's egoism. Seeing himself at the self-conscious juncture of time and eternity, Rabbit believes that he has absolute license to strike the shackles of ethical restraint: "He obscurely feels lit by a great spark, the spark whereby the blind tumble of matter recognized itself, a spark struck in the collision of two opposed realms, an encounter a terrible God willed."[29]

Updike's narrator attributes Rabbit's ambivalent condition to the will of a fierce God who sets humanity on the razor's edge between finitude and infinity. The problem Updike poses for his characters is the same, he believes, that life thrusts upon every human being: how to walk this narrow divide without plunging into animal finitude or else orbiting into angelic infinity. The function of religion in general, and the church in particular, is to teach us how to negotiate this hazardous path between opposites. That Angstrom is not thus instructed gives Updike the occasion for a stinging critique of contemporary American religion.

Its triviality and inanity are embodied in the Reverend Jack Eccles, an Episcopal vicar who, as his name perhaps suggests, is a mere ecclesiastic, a church hack. Eccles has entered Christian ministry by way of family tradition rather than divine summons and conviction. He remains, therefore, a golfing priest who feels more at home on the greens than in the pulpit, a preacher who does not believe the scandalous faith he is commissioned to proclaim, a client-centered therapist who had rather listen to the world's woes than declare its deliverance.

Eccles sees Rabbit's moral vagrancy as a sign of mere immaturity rather than egregious sinfulness. This all-indulgent rector refuses to rectify Angstrom's self-indulgence hardly at all. When at last he does castigate Rabbit, he urges him to do the moral and right thing. What

Angstrom really needs is to worship and fear God, but Eccles tells him that he should keep faith with social expectation and obligation. "With my church," he declares to Rabbit, "I believe that we are all responsible beings, responsible for ourselves and for each other."[30] Far from putting a check on Angstrom's miserable offenses, Eccles's moralizing leaves Rabbit untouched. Even the unbelieving Ruth can discern the truth about this ungodly man of God:

> The damnedest thing about that minister was that, before, Rabbit at least had the idea he was acting wrong but with [Eccles] he's got the idea he's Jesus Christ out to save the world just by doing whatever comes into his head. I'd like to get hold of the bishop or whoever and tell him that minister of his is a menace. Filling poor Rabbit with something nobody can get at. . . .[31]

Posed over against Eccles is his theological opposite, the hardboiled Lutheran minister named Kruppenbach. He is Updike's comical impersonation of Karl Barth. Unlike the suave Eccles, Kruppenbach is—as his name indicates—something of a horse's ass: a preacher who speaks at pulpit volume in casual conversation, a man of faith who looks ordained of God even with his square crew-cut head and undershirt sweaty from mowing the lawn, an unaccommodating and unecumenical prophet whom Eccles regards as "rigid in his creed and a bully in his manner."[32] Not for Kruppenbach, therefore, Eccles's sentimental notion of Rabbit as pilgrim and mystic. Kruppenbach calls Rabbit a *Schussel*: a careless adolescent who is too silly to take the Gospel seriously. It is not the errant Rabbit, therefore, that Kruppenback attacks. He pours out his wrath upon the accommodating Eccles.

"There is no reason or measure in what we must do," Kruppenbach announces to the uncomprehending Eccles. In greater kinship with Kierkegaard than Barth, this incensed preacher holds to the utter absurdity of the Gospel. "If Gott wants to end misery He'll declare the Kingdom now." Kruppenbach is a Lutheran advocate of the two kingdoms, the heavenly and the earthly. He insists that a minister must never confuse, therefore, his holy calling with secular service and comfort. Christians come to church for a single reason, whatever their lesser motives: to hear and receive the Gospel, not to be given psychological and sociological advice. The only solace is faith, Kruppenbach thunders: "faith, not what little finagling a body can do here and there, stirring the bucket." Human existence is a great slop pan of pain. Regardless of one's social or economic condition, suffering is the inevitable concomitant of life. The preacher must call the faithful to bear rather than to shed their suffering. We can shoulder our misery, says Kruppenbach, because Christ has carried it for us: "You must love your pain, because it is *Christ's* pain. . . . There is nothing but Christ for us. All the rest, all this decency and busyness, is nothing. It is the Devil's work."[33]

Kruppenbach believes that a preacher must set his people afire with the scorching intensity of his own faith. He must scald them with the bursting lava of his own deep conviction. Yet the self-absorbed Rabbit has an asbestos resistance to such burning belief. Updike seems to suggest that there is something irrelevant, perhaps even impossible, about Kruppenbach's perfervid religion. He makes belief in God so outrageously absurd and anguishing that only the rare "knight of faith" could affirm it. That Updike poses Kruppenbach and Eccles as Rabbit's only religious alternatives does not mean that there is no position between them. Updike implies merely that, in this late hour of God's absence, no other alternative is available—only the washed out and attenuated religion of Eccles, or else the transcendently alive but ethically irrelevant faith of Kruppenbach.

Yet the fault may not lie wholly with the religious establishment. Blame is also to be laid upon the God who, as Jeremiah says, hides himself from us. Nowhere does Updike depict the *Deus absconditus* more chillingly than in the terrifying scene where the drunken Janice allows the baby Rebecca to drown in her bath. The fury of Updike's prose falls not upon the alcoholic wife or the delinquent husband. The heat of his rhetorical passion is directed at the God who will not lift so much as a finger to pull the stopper from the drowning baby's tub. If God will not save an innocent creature like Rebecca, why should a guilty sinner like Rabbit put any trust in him? We hear little of Janice's responsibility for having drunk herself into a stupor, nor of Rabbit's guilt for having betrayed her. Updike's narrator screams, instead, a Job-like protest in behalf of all whom God has abandoned:

> [Janice] lifts the living thing into air and hugs it against her sopping chest. Water pours off them onto the bathroom tiles. The little weightless body flops against her neck and a quick look of relief at the baby's face gives a fantastic clotted impression. A contorted memory of how they give artificial respiration pumps Janice's cold wet arms in frantic rhythmic hugs; under her clinched lids great scarlet prayers arise, wordless, monotonous, and she seems to be clapsing the knees of a vast third person whose name, Father, Father, beats against her head like physical blows. Though her wild heart bathes the universe in red, no spark kindles in the space between her arms; for all her pouring prayers she doesn't feel the faintest tremor of an answer in the darkness against her. Her sense of the third person with them widens enormously, and she knows, knows, while knocks sound at the door, that the worst thing that has ever happened to any woman in the world has happened to her.[34]

Updike has no patience with Leibniz's tame theodicy—the rationalizing of God's goodness with the world's evil. He seeks, instead, to fathom a God who is as ambiguous as humanity itself. Luther's question—How can I find a merciful God?—is turned upside down. How, instead, can God be forgiven for his spirit-numbing withdrawal from the world, his heinous refusal to intervene at Rebecca's death no less than at the Holocaust? Absent any sense of God's abiding reality, Rabbit lives by the only divinity he knows—his own egoistic energy. By what other polestar can he steer than his own inward flame? The reader is made to notice, toward the end of the novel, that the light shining in the church window across from Ruth's apartment has gone out. No wonder that Rabbit declares *everyone* to be a victim,[35] and that he makes constant confession of his huge but unspecified fault: *"Forgive me, forgive me,"* he cries.[36] In this time of our abandonment, Updike indicates, Rabbit can know only guilt, not salvation. The eclipse of God serves to make our age deeply anxious, but it provides no power to live as the lilies of the field that neither toil nor spin.

What, then, are we to make of Rabbit Angstrom? The fiercest of all judgments passed on Rabbit is declared by his lover Ruth. She calls him "Mr. Death himself. You're not just nothing," she chastizes him, "you're worse than nothing."[37] She is right in ways that she fails perhaps to perceive. Rabbit is indeed the bringer of death. Not only is he a complicit killer in Rebecca's death and Ruth's abortion; he has also given deep grief to both his own family and his wife's. Angstrom is also "worse than nothing" because he, in fact, *thrives* on nothingness. Having discerned the great spiritual vacuum at the heart of a merely moral life, he declines to live it. He will not collapse the distinction between what he calls "the right way and the good way,"[38] the path of self-denying responsibility and the path of self-indulgent adventure.

Rabbit chases down the latter trail because it seems to be the only road toward real life. He will not accept the death of the self which moral conformity entails. In one of the most morally offensive scenes in our entire literature, Angstrom flees the graveside service being held for little Rebecca. Not only does he leave Janice to bear her now compounded grief; he also leaves Ruth to abort the child he has fathered upon her. What is worse, Rabbit does it all in the name of God. Hearing Eccles pronounce the great scriptural promises of everlasting life, he embarks for the regions of unharnessed freedom. He runs. In antinomian justification of his own self-will, he sins that grace might abound.

By all the canons of conventional ethics, Rabbit Angstrom cannot be called good. Yet Updike insists that he is the hero of the novel, and not a man who ought to be put under lock and key. What he means, I think, is that Rabbit would not have become truly good even if he had avoided the sins he so grievously commits. Angstrom is no mere self-pleasuring hedonist; he is a scoundrel of the religious life. Amidst a world that is spiritually dead, Rabbit strives furiously to keep his soul alive. He brings ruin on himself and others not because he is a heartless secularist but because he is an egregious sinner. He is a ruthless destroyer, Updike suggests, because he is a deeply religious soul. His inward spirit is so transcendently important to him that all communal bonds and moral duties seem sad and wearying by comparison. Even if his job had been more challenging and his wife more vital, Rabbit would still have run.

To so disturbing a conclusion does Updike offer any hinted alternative? Does he suggest, even obliquely, a means whereby Rabbit might have preserved his soul's life without destroying everyone who gets in his way? If so, it is in a sermon preached by the otherwise religiously opaque Eccles. His text is the account of Christ's conversation with Satan in the wilderness. Eccles interprets Jesus' encounter with the demonic tempter to mean that "suffering, deprivation, barrenness, hardship, lack are all indispensable parts of the education, the initiation, as it were, of any of those who would follow Jesus Christ."[39] Just as Kruppenbach had insisted that one must regard one's pain as the very suffering of Christ, so does Eccles declare true faith to be a *via crucis*—a pilgrimage through anguish, an endless wrestling with the self-contradiction of being a spiritual animal. Such graciously accepted suffering has no appeal to Rabbit. He believes, as the narrator makes clear, that the only alternatives are grinding routine and ecstatic freedom:

> Harry has no taste for the dark, tangled, visceral aspect of Christianity, the *going through* quality of it, the passage *into* death and suffering that redeems and inverts these things, like an umbrella blowing inside out. He lacks the mindful will to walk the straight line of paradox.[40]

This is the most important theological declaration in the entire novel. It reveals that Rabbit has learned only half of the truth—the truth, namely, that human beings cannot live without a passionate inward life. Sooner or later he must learn the counterpart of ecstatic subjectivity—the truth that the life of pain and sacrifice can be paradoxically good. In defiance of a shallow American moralism, Harry Angstrom has committed outrageous sin. He is an ethical scandal only because he is so intense and perverse a pilgrim of the religious way. In the two novels that follow, Angstrom gradually begins to relinquish the life of heedless self-concern. Reluctantly and to his great astonishment, he ceases running like a rabbit and starts plodding like one of the dutiful horses who shoulder the world's burdens. Yet it is not by means of a dull conformity that Rabbit is thus transformed. It happens through his slow discovery that grace does not abound amidst angelic flight from responsibility, but within the rich confines of temporal obligation.

II. "Time Is Our Element": *Rabbit Redux*

Updike's novel of 1971, *Rabbit Redux*, contains his second portrait of Harry Angstrom. Like the first Rabbit novel, it deals with the quandary over true goodness. As the title suggests, Rabbit has been "led back," restored to responsibility, and thus made well after suffering the malaise of uninhibited youthful desire. Yet Rabbit's rehabilitation is neither facile nor final. He remains ensnared, on the contrary, in the same net of circumstance that proved so constricting in *Rabbit, Run*. Instead of fleeing the webbed reality of the moral life, Rabbit here begins to affirm it. He discovers that the deepest human difficulties must be endured rather than escaped. Yet *Rabbit, Redux* is not a book whose wisdom resides in a tragic resignation to the losing proposition called life. It ends in a genuinely comic affirmation of time: it is not our enemy but our element. Rabbit learns that only in the risk of temporal fidelity do we become genuinely free.

The best of Updike's fiction challenges our American reluctance to acknowledge this bedrock truth. Yet he remains exceedingly patient with our national naivety about the hard paradoxes of social and religious life. In *Rabbit, Run*, as we have seen, Updike makes Angstrom a veritable hero of flight and escape. It is a novel that fondly evokes the Eisenhower epoch as being rich in youthful possibility for all its fabled dullness of spirit. *Rabbit Redux* possesses none of this tender regard for our native moral innocence. It is, quite to the contrary, a vitriolic vision of the late sixties.

What Updike finds objectionable in that revolutionary decade is its consummate moralism, its presumptuous belief that the old order could be overturned without destroying much that was good. As the master of middleness and the singer of "things as they are," Updike stands opposed to the apocalyptic extremism of "the most dissentious American decade since the Civil War."[41] He cannot abide its strident demand for a radical revision—even a wholesale remaking—of the moral and social realm. This is indeed Updike's angriest book, a novel whose venom poisons nearly every scene except the conclusion. Yet even amidst such snappishness Updike reveals what is redemptive about the saga of Harry Angstrom.

The thirty-six-year-old Rabbit we encounter in this novel is a man whose own inherent self-contradiction is exacerbated by the chaos of the age. Though Angstrom finds both dignity and delight in his job as a linotype operator, he is far from happy. His increasing prosperity makes him upwardly but also unhappily mobile. It is not a greater freedom of spirit that middle-class affluence brings, but the mediocrity of life as it is lived in Penn Villas. His wife Janice has been transformed from a homebound dolt into a liberated woman. Yet with liberation also comes experimentation. Janice sexually betrays her husband for the first time by having an affair with Rabbit's friend, Charlie Stavros. Angstrom's old self-abandonment was more alluring to her than his new responsibility. Janice's vision of Rabbit as he prepares for his bath is merciless:

> She sees her flying athlete grounded, cuckolded. She sees a large white man a knife would slice like lard. The angelic cold strength of his leaving her, the anticlimax of his coming back and clinging: something in the combination that she cannot forgive, that justifies her.[42]

Rabbit is enraged not only by his wife's infidelity but also by the faithlessness of the age. He is especially impatient at the antipatriotism of the black revolutionaries and the white protesters against the Vietnam War. He stands too much in debt to his country to allow it to be called racist and imperialist and power-mad. America's motives for being in Vietnam are, he naively claims, to turn it into another free and prosperous country like Japan. Hence his fury at the critics of President Johnson: "Poor old LBJ, Jesus with tears in his eyes on television, you must have heard him, he just about offered to make North Vietnam the fifty-first fucking state of the Goddam Union if they'd just stop throwing bombs."[43] Rabbit's moral rage is not only defensive and excessive; it is also contradicted by his willingness to give bed and board to a black political messiah named Skeeter. The same contradiction is implicit in Angstrom's splenetic denunciations of the new "culture of narcissism," with its endless gabble about looking honestly into ourselves, seeing who we are and where we are going, "searching for a valid identity," and thinking with our "whole person."[44] Yet Harry the hater of the counterculture also takes up with Jill, a hippie who is half his age. And for all of his stern righteousness, Rabbit revels in the soft, sweet "lovingness of pot," as he calls the world of marijuana.[45]

What these contradictions reveal is Updike's perennial conviction that, lacking religious ballast, the ship of culture lists and founders. Men and women desire something other than a mere conformist existence. They cannot live by the bread of political sloganeering and sensate pleasure alone. Updike denies that the radical politics and drug culture of the 1960s were profound criticisms of the age. They were but naive attempts, he implies, to escape a deeper kind of emptiness. The dominating presence of television—especially its coverage of the moon landings—is the real mark of that desolate time. Despite their technological wonder, these scientific feats provide no real sustenance for the soul. Updike's narrator, voicing Rabbit's own thoughts, protests against the popular comparison of modern space exploration with Columbus's discovery of America. There was mystery and wonder in the first adventure, but only empty predictability in the other: "Columbus flew blind and hit something, these guys see exactly what they're aiming at and it's a big round nothing."[46]

Like the vacuous culture which his life mirrors, Rabbit Angstrom is ripe for dissolution. He is a hollow creature, a man awash in ennui because he has no real moorings. The nihilism he detects in the American body politic is also the secret motive of his own spirit. Unable to find outward corroboration of his inward life, he is tempted to think that his self-transcending soul is something monstrous rather than blessed: "He used to try to picture [his soul] when a child. A parasite like a tapeworm inside. A sprig of mistletoe hung from our bones, living on air. A jellyfish swaying between our lungs and our liver."[47]

With so ethereal a notion of the human essence, it is not surprising that Rabbit should himself be virtually vaporized by the sixties. It was a time when, as Updike says in another connection, "the Beatles spiritualized us all."[48] Rabbit is spiritually attracted, therefore, to two seraphic creatures of the time, a flower child and a Negro revolutionary. Skeeter Buchanan is an avenging angel of wrath, a black prophet of destruction, the self-proclaimed messiah of the Chaotic Age. He is an embittered veteran of the Vietnam War who hails it for shattering the American dream of specialness. Our experience in Vietnam demonstrated irrefutably, says Skeeter, that we are a nation like unto every other: a cockroach country which he calls the Benighted States. America is now first in one regard only: we are the place where the world's unacknowledged nothingness has been turned into a cultural and political principle.

The self-taught Skeeter understands both the "big bang" and "steady state" theories of the world's origin, and they both provide him evidence that there is nothing in the cosmos but empty vitality. Whereas the Rabbit of the previous novel had felt a mystical identity with the amoral energy that drives the universe, he is here made to see its demonic consequences in the cynical Skeeter. This apostle of hate argues nihilistically that the hedonism of the ghetto, the self-indulgence of Detroit and Madison Avenue, and the destruction of Vietnam should all be regarded with patriotic pride rather than national shame. They make America the covert envy of the world:

> "I'm not one of those white lib-er-als like that cracker Fulldull or Charlie McCarthy [who] a while back gave all the college queers a hard-on, think Vietnam some sort of mistake, we can fix it up once we get the cave men out of office, it is *no* mistake, right, any President that come along falls in love with it, it is lib-er-al-ism's very wang, dingdong pussy, and fruit. . . . What is lib-er-alism? Bringing joy to the world, right? Puttin' sugar on dog-eat-dog so it tastes good all over, right?. . . We is *the* spot. Few old fools like the late Ho may

not know it, [but] we is what the world is begging *for*. Big beat, smack, black cock, big-assed cars and billboards, we is into it. Jesus come down, He come down here. These other countries, just bullshit places, right? We got the *ape* shit, right? Bring down King-dom Come, we'll swamp the world in red-hot blue-green ape shit, right?"[49]

Rabbit is drawn to Skeeter because the latter's anti-American nihilism is but an inversion of Angstrom's own angelic idealism about his country. "Wherever America is," Rabbit thinks, "there is freedom, and wherever America is not, madness rules with chains, darkness strangles millions. Beneath her patient bombers, paradise is possible."[50] Harry is such a spiritual shell of a man that he is powerless to resist this black anti-Christ who would fill him with the gospel of nothingness. Not only does Rabbit refuse to turn the criminal Skeeter over to the police; he also helps him escape their search. Perhaps Angstrom under-stands that even a demon like Buchanan has his own suffering, and that he is maddened by his experience in Vietnam. Perhaps Rabbit also knows that the United States is not the ideal republic he makes it out to be, and that black terrorism often springs from white injustice.

Rabbit is finally saved from enthrallment to Skeeter by a sudden turn of events that amounts almost to a *deus ex machina* deliverance. It has to do with Skeeter's disciple, a vaporous child of the counterculture named Jill. This rich girl who drives a Porsche and espouses Eastern mys-ticism is also a nymphet who is spookily unpresent when Rabbit has sex with her. She is an innocent not because she is void of guile, but because she is impervious to sin and guilt. When a crowd of angry neighbors burns down Angstrom's house in fury over his sheltering of this hippie and her black revolutionary messiah, Jill dies in the fire. Once more Rab-bit has helped bring death into the world. Yet his sense of complicity in Jill's death jars him to his moral senses. He recognizes, at least dimly, how wrong it is to run, how destructive it is to flee the life of mutality and obligation for the solitary sweetness of one's own will.

The key to Rabbit's recovery lies in his mother's insistence that he leave the unfaithful Janice, skip town, seek his own rebirth, and not miss his life-chance by sitting inert like a lump. Against such a gospel of self-regard, Rabbit sees that his dying mother is summoning him to a free-dom that is the worst form of death. To run from his family and job and situation is, Rabbit now recognizes, not only to slaughter one's own soul but to slay others as well. In one of the most morally discerning passages in the whole novel, the narrator records Rabbit's denial of his mother's call for him to flee:

He feels she is asking him to kill Janice, to kill Nelson. Freedom means murder. Rebirth means death. . . . She is still trying to call him forth from her womb, can't she see he is an old man? An old lump whose only use is to stay in place to keep the lumps on top of him from tumbling?[51]

Rabbit is learning, ever so painfully, the hard lesson that maturity is not measured by the years one has lived. It is marked by one's willingness to accept responsibility both for one's own life and for those other lives one has been entrusted with. Nor is youth merely a matter of physical vitality; it is characterized by the desire to escape time's consequences. Once the selfish *Schussel* that Kruppenbach had called him, Harry Angstrom is gradually becoming an "old man" in the good sense of the phrase. He makes what, for Updike as well as for Rabbit, is the profoundest of discoveries: "Time is our element, not a mistaken invader. How stupid, it has taken him thirty-six years to believe that."[52]

Such a chastened recognition enables Rabbit's reconciliation with Janice. They acknowledge that they are linked inextricably in the knot called life: "ties of blood, of time and guilt, family ties."[53] They both admit that they have taken innocent life—the baby Rebecca and the girl Jill. They are also reunited in confession of their mutual betrayals and infidelities. "I feel so guilty," Rabbit admits. "About everything." When Janice tries to console him, insisting that he must not blame himself for all that has happened, he replies, "I can't accept that."[54] These final words from Rabbit reveal how far he has advanced over his earlier claim that everybody is a victim and that he is thus responsible for nothing.

Updike does not assign his characters the comparatively easy fate of death, but the far more difficult destiny called life. This explains why, for all its apocalyptic atmosphere, *Rabbit Redux* has a comic conclusion that returns us to the quotidian world. Tragedy ends in separation and death, comedy in union and new beginnings. The classic comic ending is marriage, and this is the redemptive state to which Rabbit and Janice are finally restored. Their house having been destroyed, they are compelled to stay at a cheap motel called the Safe Haven. The moralistic manager suspects that they are furtive lovers in rendezvous, and threatens to refuse them a room. Rabbit and Janice are thus made to *pose* as the married couple they ineluctably *are*. Assuring the motel owner that they are tired and need only a place to sleep, they keep their promise: they do not seek sexual solace from each other but the companionship of rest. Rabbit strokes Janice's flesh with an affection that only matrimonial love can know:

> He slides down an inch on the cool sheets and fits his microcosmic self limp into the curved crevice between the polleny offered nestling orbs of her ass; he would stiffen but his hand having let her breasts go comes upon the familiar dip of her waist, ribs to hip bone, where no bones are, soft as flight, fat's inward curve, slack,

his babies from her belly. He finds this inward curve, and slips along it, sleeps. He. She. Sleeps. O.K.?[55]

So jaunty an ending may tempt the reader to dismiss it as inconsequential. Our skepticism would be justified had Updike suggested that all has been made well. The ironic question hints, quite to the contrary, that trouble is still at hand. The Angstrom's renewed marriage will again be filled, we must surmise, with the same difficulties that have nearly destroyed it. Yet Janice and Rabbit are at least willing to take the risk of fidelity. Their life together may finally prove impossible. Even if they remain married, other ills will surely plague them. Yet is better to fail while staying, they have learned, than to succeed while fleeing. No longer does Rabbit believe that his life can be enlarged only by slipping the noose of loyalty to everything but himself. Such freedom has proved, in fact, to be bondage.

The novel's dénouement would be more compelling if it dramatized—rather than merely suggested—the truth Rabbit has learned. This sunny outcome to events that have been so darkly depicted would seem more credible had it occurred amidst the same social Armageddon where husband and wife were first driven to distraction and alienation. Updike may believe that the times were too troubled for any such public version of moral sanity. Yet the novel itself hints otherwise. The hapless Jill tells Rabbit that, if he truly loved his country, he would want not merely to defend it but also to make it better. "If it was better," Rabbit replies, "*I'd* have to be better."[55] The fault lies not chiefly with the age, apocalyptically crazed though it may have been, but with Rabbit himself. Rather, it lies with the human condition which Rabbit embodies and which in all ages is sinfully the same. Tempting though angelic irresponsibility may be, there is no escaping time and its burdens. They are our essential milieu, Angstrom is gradually and graciously discovering. *Rabbit Is Rich* will demonstrate the difficulties of the long temporal haul, yet also the serendipities which make time a realm not merely to be endured but enjoyed.

III. From Furious Running to Gracious Plodding: *Rabbit Is Rich*

Updike's latest report on the moral and religious pilgrimage of Harry Angstrom is found in his novel of 1981, *Rabbit Is Rich*. It is a much more leisurely book than the other two Rabbit novels. The present-tense narration does not rush forward quite so rapidly. As Updike's account of the late seventies, the novel reflects the relative tranquillity of the time. The apocalypse of the sixties, even the shame of Richard Nixon's resignation, seem to be remote events. Economic inflation and the oil crisis are the only public cataclysms affecting Harry's life. Spiritually, however, it is a stagnant age. Updike's coarsened diction and blighted landscape reveal an unmistakable cultural ugliness. Nor is the outward calm able to still Rabbit's inward tumult. The old conflict between private desire and public obligation is rendered all the more intense with the passing years.

Rabbit's new problem is not chiefly marital or political but financial. He has inherited his father-in-law's Toyota dealership and thus become rich. Yet Angstrom is hardly at ease in the Zion of financial prosperity. His new money—because he dreads losing it—increases his old anxiety. First he buys South African gold as a hedge against the falsely inflated value of Susan B. Anthony dollars. Then he swaps his Krugerrands for silver in fear that the price of gold will fall. In the novel's funniest scene, Janice and Rabbit lug huge satchels of silver from the exchange office to the bank, only to discover that the cache of coins will not fit into their safety deposit box. The silver rolls wildly about the vault, until Rabbit finally gathers up three hundred of the heavy metallic pieces and lugs them home. There he ponders the crazy ambiguity of his new wealth:

> His overcoat, so weighted, drags his shoulders down. He feels, as if the sidewalk is now a downslanted plane, the whole year dropping away from him, loss after loss. His silver is scattered, tinsel. His box will break, the janitor will sweep up the coins. It's all dirt anyway. . . . through the murk he glimpses the truth that to be rich is to be robbed, to be rich is to be poor.[57]

There is more than a little self-pity in this scene, but it points up Updike's fundamental contention that all people, whether rich or poor, have their own suffering. Harry is troubled by middle-age decline. The once-lithe athlete is now growing paunchy at forty-six. Not only is America running low on gas; so is Rabbit. He is more death-conscious than ever, thinking constantly of all the corpses that lie buried under the ground he treads. Reading of Skeeter's death in a shootout with police, remembering Jill's death in the fire, recalling Becky's drowning and Ruth's abortion, Rabbit ponders the inescapable guilt of his life: "There's no getting away: our sins, our seed, coil back."[58]

The scent of mortality pervades the whole novel. Like the doctors who call life an incurable disease, Rabbit often envisions human existence as but preparation for the grave. He seems to expect no final judgment or resurrection of the dead. Even our personalities, he argues, must be understood as a series of perishing selves: "Our lives fade behind us before we die."[59] In a poignant bedroom scene, Rabbit confesses to Janice that they are caught in an inescapable contradiction. It is, for Updike, the fundamental human dilemma: "Life. Too much of it and not enough. The fear that it will end some day, and the fear that tomorrow will be the same as yesterday."[60] Yet this very paradox is what keeps the romantic flame alight in Harry. He is still willing to seek sexual adventure in order to overcome the tedium of the predictable. We humans cannot live, Rabbit believes, without benefit of passion, without erotic expectation—"that cloudy inflation of self which makes us infants again and tips each moment with a plain excited purpose."[61]

The carnality in *Rabbit Is Rich* is described with unprecedented rawness. Yet it is at once a funnier and sadder kind of sex than we have previously seen in Updike's fiction. The newly rich Angstrom keeps thinking of *Consumer Reports* when he ought to be concentrating on more erotic matters. He pours his Krugerrands over his naked wife in the hope that money might arouse them as fading desire will not. The spouse swapping that occurs at the end of the novel contains none of the usual Updikean ecstasy over the joys of illicit sex. On the contrary, there is something deeply nihilistic about Rabbit's final descent to anal intercourse with the menstruating, lupus-ridden Thelma. As an act that has no chance of producing—nor even *imitating*—the production of life, it is a deathly kind of penetration, an entry into "a void, a pure black box, a casket of perfect nothingness."[62]

Yet neither sex nor death, the coinciding opposites that are the pattern woven through the carpet of Updike's work, has its old enthralling power over Rabbit. The main obstacle to Harry's acceptance of midlife decline lies in neither external circumstances nor internal hardness of heart. The real troubler of Rabbit's peace is his son. Nelson resembles many other youths who came of age during the 1970s. Though old enough to establish his own independence, Nelson still lives at home, struggles to finish college, and gets his girlfriend pregnant before marrying her. His irresponsibility is exceedingly irksome to the elder Angstrom. The father waxes tart at the son's wastrel generation. Having been reared on television, they know nothing firsthand. All of reality is filtered for them through this sorry medium:

> Rabbit grunts. Spineless generation, no grit, nothing solid to tell a fact from a spook with. Satanism, pot, drugs, vegetarianism. Pathetic. Everything handed to them on a platter, think life's one big TV, full of ghosts.[63]

Angstrom is all the angrier for seeing that Nelson is repeating his own squalid history. They seem to prove the biblical contention that the sins of the parents are visited upon the children. Nelson is indeed Rabbit but one generation removed, heedlessly committing his father's old mistakes. Just as Rabbit brought death into the world with his abandonment of Janice and Ruth, so does Nelson almost kill the baby that his wife Pru is carrying. In a siege of anger at the drunken and pregnant Pru, Nelson half pushes her, half watches her, fall down a steep flight of stairs. Although both mother and new child are spared, Nelson flees as his father had done, leaving his new bride and daughter to be cared for by Janice and Rabbit. Thus do the years circle upon one another, life seeming to repeat itself endlessly. We plunge desperately ahead, Updike suggests, in order not to slide backward, and thus to keep circling in the same place.

There is no denying the pathos of Harry Angstrom's condition. Thelma, the pathetic woman with whom he has the desperate fling at the end, says that Rabbit's energetic embrace of life makes him both radiant and sad. The sadness becomes ever more evident. Angstrom's new sobriety appears, in fact, to be more secular than theological. Religion is still treated reverently, but it has no transforming power. It provides questions rather than answers. At most, it serves to link Rabbit with the silent majority who, like the absent God, haunt his life. Whereas the young Rabbit had a mystical sense of himself as divinely sought, the mature man encounters God more as memory than as living reality. The God who had hovered watchfully over Rabbit's childhood sleep has gradually absconded:

> Now he had withdrawn, giving Harry the respect due from one well-off gentleman to another, but for a calling card left in the pit of the stomach, a bit of lead true as a plumb bob pulling Harry down toward all those leaden dead in the hollow earth below.[64]

Although *Rabbit Is Rich* exudes a melancholy found in neither of the other Angstrom novels, there are also unprecedented signs of hope to be discerned amidst the gloom. The pattern of life described by the novel is not merely circular and downward toward death. It is also linear and upward toward newness of life. The son is not finally a replica of his father. Not only does Nelson marry the pregnant Pru; they also elect to give birth to their child, rather than conveniently aborting it, as it is now their legal right to do. Nelson does, alas, abandon his family as Rabbit had once done, but his running is not altogether selfish. He has returned to Kent State in order to finish his degree and, one must presume, to rejoin his wife and daughter later. Life has not merely gone repetitively around; it has also advanced at least a small pace forward.

The real signs of redemption are found in Rabbit's comic relation to his son. When Nelson tries to "prove" himself as a salesman at the family Toyota agency, by remarketing ancient gas-guzzling convertibles, the results are at once uproariously funny and tearfully pathetic. The father is enraged at his son's commercial ineptitude, and the son is infuriated at his father's repeated attempts to humiliate him. In a fit of pique, Nelson smashes the old clunkers into a great heap of crumpled metal, prompting Rabbit to even crueler attacks on the boy's many failures. Yet finally it is not rage but pity that Angstrom pours out upon Nelson. That his son's prospects are blighted from the start, that he is trapped in his father's own history, that his world is already worn out before he can find a place in it—these sad facts move Rabbit to humble confession. "I just don't like to see you caught," he blurts out to Nelson. "You're too much me."[65]

Such freely acknowledged pathos marks the real moral and religious progress of Harry Angstrom's life. The truth that Rabbit was driven reluctantly to acknowledge in *Rabbit Redux* he willingly embraces in *Rabbit Is Rich*. With the middle-aged calming of the soul's turbulent waters, Harry is learning that it is better to suffer what he calls the "daily seepage"[66] than to let life rush out in a single foolish passion. Despite his murderous misgivings about Janice, he is bound to her by all the trouble they have endured together. They are inveterately *married*. The presence of Mrs. Springer, Angstrom's elderly mother-in-law, also serves to remind them that their lives are not merely their own. Harry still chafes, of course, at the way the world is closing him in ever more tightly. But his fury lacks its old bitterness and desperation.

Rabbit has taken up golf again—always a redemptive sign in Updike's fiction—now that he no longer dwells on the raw edges of life. But he plays the game neither in desire to hit the perfect mystical drive down the center of the fairway, nor in conformity to the leisured life he now has the money to cultivate. He enjoys golf because it echoes the elusive mystery of human existence. It is like life itself, says Rabbit, "its performance cannot be forced and its underlying principle shies from being permanently named."[67] Angstrom is not mellowing into mildness and inanity, therefore, but into suppleness and widsom. The surprise graciously dawning on Rabbit is that his "inner dwindling"[68] contains a new freedom. To be obligated, he discovers, is to be liberated. And gracious plodding is better than furious running.

This new dispensation of hope is nicely figured in the novel's final scene. There Harry holds his new grandchild in his arms, complaining that she represents still another nail driven into his coffin. Yet his self-pitying protest is unconvincing. There is no denying Rabbit's obvious pleasure in cuddling the first member of the next Angstrom generation. Thus has Updike brought his epic American character a very long way indeed: from Rabbit the scared and solipsistic youth fleeing life's limits to Harry the middle-aged grandfather embracing his mortality. In one of the novel's most poignant passages, Rabbit ponders the significance of his life: "In middle age you are carrying the world," Angstrom thinks silently, "and yet it seems out of control more than ever, the self that you had as a boy all scattered and distributed like those pieces of bread in the miracle."[69]

This metaphor is not conveniently religious; it is profoundly gracious. Rabbit sees that his life is broken in order that others might find sustenance in him. His failure to hold fast to his youthful vision of himself as hero and ace is much more a blessing than a curse. It is true that

Rabbit does less praying in this novel than in the first two books. Only once does Angstrom utter his old Gnostic confession of guilt for the crime of mere existence. Yet this may not be a sign of unbelief so much as a mark of maturity. What the novel implicitly acknowledges is that true religious life consists not in an anguished inner consciousness but in self-forgetting service and gratitude and acceptance. Harry may not attend church much any more, but he is learning that ordinary responsibility is not the hell he once thought it was. It is, on the contrary, his true home.

This is not to suggest that, in Updike's promised ten-year installments of Rabbit's continuing saga, Angstrom is guaranteed a happy end. He may emerge again as an egregious sinner in deed no less than word and thought. He could wither away, instead, into inertia and insignificance, though it is doubtful that Updike would write about him if he did. Angstrom might become, though this is even less probable, a saintly old man. Such, at the very least, are the options open to human life under the pressure of divine grace, external circumstances, and hardness of heart.

Whatever Rabbit's future may hold, Updike has shown that the Angstrom we now know differs significantly from the character we first met in 1960. His life has changed with the glacial slowness that marks most alterations for the good, and his new existence is cast, realistically, within its original limits. Yet Rabbit *is* something of a new creation. Though still cowardly and cruel, he is also forgiving and willing to receive forgiveness. Though still obsessed with Gnostic longings to escape the confines of the flesh, he now lives for more than merely his own private delight. He also gives himself in public obligation to others. This glad affirmation of life's moral burden is, for Updike, the real ballast of faith.

So to describe Updike's work is not to claim that the Rabbit novels are imbued with the comedy of divine redemption revealed in Jesus Christ. The world remains too ambiguous a realm for Updike to call its underlying principle *sola gratia*. Yet neither can he make it the realm of unmitigated tragedy. Our fault lies in ourselves, Rabbit learns, far more than it does in life. This is why, despite his affinity for the *New Yorker's* elegance of style and insouciance of spirit, Updike does not advocate its genteel hedonistic philosophy as described by Brendan Gill:

> Not a shred of evidence exists in favor of the argument that life is serious, though it is often hard and even terrible. And, saying that, I am prompted to add what follows out of it: that since everything ends badly for us, in the inescapable catastrophe of death, it seems obvious that the first rule of life is to have a good time; and that the second rule of life is to hurt as few people as possible in the course of doing so. There is no third rule.[70]

Updike's Rabbit Angstrom novels attest that the surest way to hurt oneself and others is to live as if the purpose of life were to have a good time. Laughter and enjoyment are nearly always derivative, Harry discovers, and but rarely intentional. They are serendipitous byproducts that issue from an acceptance of life's fundamental paradox: the inescapable linkage of joy and sadness, comedy and tragedy, carnival and labor, faith and doubt. When held together in unity and complementarity—and this requires a deep religious trust, a willingness to forego the idolatry of extremes—these dialectical opposites can be the means of grace. Such contraries are reconciled, for Updike, by the enabling irony of life itself—and thus by the gracious God of life.

11

PETER DE VRIES AS A HUMORIST OF BACKSLIDDEN UNBELIEF

Peter De Vries is so funny a writer that it may seem inappropriate to take him seriously. His puns are unabashed. Like the cleaning lady, he says, we all come to dust. The mere thought of cremation turns one of his characters ashen. De Vries's aphorisms are no less outrageous. The American home, we are told, is an invasion of privacy. Never put off until tomorrow, we are advised, what you can put off indefinitely. What is an arsonist, we are asked, but someone who has failed to set the world on fire? De Vries's vignettes are even more discerningly surreal. A chiropractor attending a patient throws out his own back. A husband who demands that his wife explain why she bought a mink coat is told that she was cold. Another wife sues her husband's mistress for alienation of his affections, and asks for $65 in damages.

To regard De Vries's wildly comic fiction as a parable of the Gospel may seem to do violence both to theology and to art. De Vries himself is unapologetic about his own unbelief. In both his fiction and his public statements, he has made his skepticism plain. As the scion of a Dutch Calvinist family firmly rooted in the twin doctrines of human depravity and divine grace, De Vries claims now to profess only the former. Prayer, he adds, is a comforting exercise in auto-suggestion for those who, like himself, believe no one is listening. Yet the salient fact about De Vries's fiction is its near obsession with characters who cannot rest at ease in the Babylon of their secularism. They keep backsliding out of their unbelief, stumbling into Zion, lapsing into faith.

This is not to suggest that De Vries is an inadvertent apologist for Christian faith. My thesis is far more modest: I contend that De Vries mocks our culture's mockery of God. He laughs at our laughing riddance of redeeming grace. In the mathematics of the good God, as Barth calls him, two negatives make for a great deal more than a bare-naked positive. De Vries's kind of laughter constitutes, in fact, a comic parable of divine reconciliation, a distant echo of eschatological joy. His work forms an unintentional comic analogue of the Gospel's claim that God in Israel and Christ has negated our attempted negation of his mercy.

Not always, one must admit, does De Vries give lasting artistic expression to his almost farcical sense of life. It is difficult to keep his protagonists distinct. De Vries is the master of caricature rather than character. His anti-heroes and heroines are nearly all weary worldlings who have discovered how enslaving the liberated life can be. De Vries's plots are almost as indistinguishable as his characters. They exemplify his own stated motto that fiction should contain a beginning, a *muddle*, and an end. One suspects, indeed, that both character and plot are often but occasions for De Vries to display his splendid gift for gags and wisecracks. A suave suburbanite named Mr. Shrubsole appears briefly in *Sauce for the Goose* for no other discernible purpose than to explain why he must take early leave from a luncheon party. He has premises to keep, he laments, and miles to mow before he sleeps. These brilliant Frostian take-offs serve to satirize our enthrallment to houses and yards, but the scene forms no integral part of the novel itself. More alarming still is De Vries's tendency to plagiarize himself by repeating witticisms he had used in earlier works. At their worst, therefore, De Vries's novels consist of very funny scenes strung haphazardly together.

So to admit De Vries's artistic weaknesses is not to sanction the snubbing he has received from the official literary establishment. Perhaps De Vries is attempting to make fiction encompass more than it is able—namely, the envisioning of human life as at once absurdly meaningless and yet also strangely fine, even divinely wonderful. If this judgment be true, then De Vries is something more than a poor successor to Twain and Thurber, to Wodehouse and Beerbohm and Waugh. He is a religious wit whose measure is not fully taken until the theological dimension of his work is seriously considered. To make this case, I propose to deal not with all of the twenty-odd novels De Vries has written, but only with those works where he succeeds in uniting comic vision with fictional form. With the exception of *Sauce for the Goose* (1981), his best novels were written in the early years of his career: *The Tunnel Love* (1954), *Comfort Me with Apples* (1956), *The Mackerel Plaza* (1958), *The Tents of Wickedness* (1959), *Through the Fields of Clover* (1961), *The Blood of the Lamb* (1962), *Let Me Count the Ways* (1965), and two sequential novellas published together in 1968, *The Cat's Pajamas* and *Witch's Milk*.

In the first of these chapters, I propose to examine the nature of De Vries's comedy in what it negates, and in the second to investigate what it affirms. Though sometimes accused of being a black humorist, De

Vries is in fact the opponent of nihilistic laughter. The belief that life has no ultimate meaning but remains an absurd cosmic joke is indeed alluring to De Vries. His characters are often obsessed with the world's absurdity. Yet they but rarely respond to the unanswering welkin with the cachinnations of black humor. Like Ted Peachum in *Consenting Adults* (1980), De Vries's would-be nihilists cannot laugh at the empty cosmos for laughing at their own empty selves. Peachum is, as he says, a self-pitying Stoic and a jilted Narcissus: he has a crush on himself, but the feeling is not returned. So it is with De Vries's aesthetes and libertines. They rightly despise the madding crowd and the world that is too much with us. They know that style and sophistication can produce an enlivening triumph over dull conformity. Yet De Vries is not content to make such an obvious critique of the conformist world. He turns his wit upon his own kind, showing how aesthetes make an unaesthetic mess of their lives, and how libertines find the liberated life terribly wearying.

I. The Heavy Yoke of Satire and the Light Burden of Humor

At the center of De Vries's focus as a writer is his fascination with the question of comedy itself. So notoriously difficult is comedy to define that De Vries parodies (in *The Vale of Laughter*) the attempts of Kant, Schopenhauer, Bergson and Freud to explain why people laugh. Yet De Vries is not without his own rudimentary theory of comedy. He insists, for example, on calling himself a humorist rather than a satirist. "Humorists are more easily housebroken," De Vries confesses.[1] They are too busy laughing at themselves to be angrily wetting the carpet of life:

> I would say, very roughly, that the difference between satire and humor is that the satirist shoots to kill while the humorist brings his prey back alive—often to release him again for another chance. Swift destroyed the human race, Thurber enables it to go on. . . . I don't think I shoot to kill. If I did I'd been dead long ago, since, like most humorists, I'm my own best butt. I don't think I have enough lemon in me to be a satirist.[2]

In his most important single declaration, De Vries confesses that "Humor is more charitable [than satire], and, like charity, suffereth long and is kind."[3]

This allusion to I Corinthians 13 is not gratuitous. It accounts for what is residually Christian in De Vries despite his professed unbelief. He cannot accept the graceless moralistic assumption underlying most secular satire—the notion, namely, that the object of ridicule and deflation lies outside oneself. The satirist is notoriously a reformer, a spiritual smith who wants to pound the world into shape by dint of hammer-like blows. A humorist like De Vries, by contrast, cannot regard life as so readily malleable. Original sin and innate depravity—to cite the most familiar theological descriptions of our condition—make human nature fundamentally intractable to moralistic remedies. Our misshapen lives require something at once harsher and gentler in order to be made whole. The judgment and grace of God—even if De Vries cannot attest to them in an unqualified way—are the stuff of real transformation and thus of true laughter. De Vries does not attempt, therefore, to shake humanity by the nape of its neck. His comedy is far more confessional and benign than either Percy's or O'Connor's. Rather than poking wicked fun at human stupidity, De Vries laughs in sympathy with a species whose foolishness is irrevocably his own.

Like Updike and Percy, De Vries believes that our lives are caught in the contradiction of being both animal and angel. This paradox makes human existence at once funny and sad, both comic and tragic. In his public pronouncements no less than in his fiction, De Vries insists upon the nearness of the ludicrous and the solemn. "You can't talk about the serious and the comic separately and still be talking about life, any more than you can independently discuss hydrogen and oxygen and still be dealing with water."[4] De Vries cites Aristotle as the thinker who first saw the inextricable involvement of comedy and tragedy. But he then adds his own dark un-Aristotelian corollary: "You laugh at that which, if there were more of it, would be painful. Humor deals with that portion of our suffering which is exempt from tragedy."[5]

Not only do the laughable and the mournful often stand in close relation, but so does the comedian often probe the depths of human woe more deeply than does the tragedian. By taking life with too much solemnity, the serious writer may miss its real significance. De Vries thus chooses his epigraph for *The Tents of Wickedness* from Sydney Smith, the nineteenth-century Anglican divine: "You must not think me necessarily foolish because I am facetious, nor will I consider you necessarily wise because you are grave." The most saturnine seriousness may in fact be silly, while the most farcical comedy may be incisive and revealing. This explains why De Vries is not ashamed to be a gagster and stuntman, pitching for the guffaw no less than the sly grin: "I'd rather offer the reader an honest surfboard ride than pack him into a diving bell and then lower him into what turns out to be three feet of water. As many so-called 'serious' writers do."[6]

De Vries at his best is a humorist whose art serves not to darken life with bitter laughter, but to let it shine in all its crazy glory. True comedy issues not from a conviction that life is absurdly worthless, but from the odd kind of sense often found in nonsense. Harry Mercury, a professional comedian who appears in *Through the Fields of Clover*, says that there is a curious logic hidden within the illogic of real humor. When, for example, an outraged husband questions his wife about her purchase of a mink stole, she explains that she was cold. "Whoever heard of that," Harry asks, as "a reason for buying a fur coat? It's the most unheard-of thing he has ever heard of. *Non sequitur*, you see, with the grain of sense in it."[7] Humor's "grain of sense" lies in its sympathy rather than its accusation. It accepts even as it laments.

De Vries's compassion for the very things he mocks makes him a humorist in the medieval as well as the modern sense. The term *humour* originally had little connection with laughter as such, but referred to the four bodily liquids which were believed to determine human personality and character: blood, phlegm, and bile both yellow and black. Disease was thought to result from a disproportion of these elements, and health to issue from their proper equilibrium. It is humor's salubrious balance that Osgood Wallop has in mind when he says that "laughter must have an honest root in reality, and that means a necessary melancholy undercurrent. Anything else is false."[8] De Vries honors this dark side of reality by making his comedy acknowledge the metaphysical abyss over which everything hangs. Yet finally his humor does not leave us suspended in the void. It sets us down jauntily on the *terra firma* of affirmative, sometimes even redemptive, laughter.

Fearful though he is that all of life's opposites are really one, comedy and tragedy included, De Vries declines the nihilist temptation. Perhaps it is mere literary courtesy and moral kindness that restrains him. My own conviction is that something deeper prompts De Vries's confession that satirists like Swift destroy humanity while humorists like Twain and Thurber enable it to stumble forward. The heart of De Vries's faith as a humorist is to be found in his declaration that the humorist "does not laugh so much at mankind as he invites mankind to laugh at itself."[9] We can chuckle at ourselves only from a perspective not wholly our own. Whether wittingly or not, such laughter requires a suprahuman vantage point from which human folly can be seen, perhaps even seen as redeemed. Stew Smackenfelt, the narrator-protagonist of *Forever Panting*, is onto this truth when he insists that "Christ may have been a superb mimic, not just a satirist." He was "really taking the scribes and Pharisees off," Stew insists, "about straining at a gnat and swallowing a camel and so on. Burlesquing them with his impressions. Mugging like hell."[10]

Satire and humor, anger and compassion, are not ultimately trapped in a coincidence of opposites. For De Vries there is no deadly equipoise between comedy and tragedy because real humor can turn back upon itself and ironize its own ironies. "Professions, like nations," says Jim Tickler in *The Glory of the Hummingbird*, "are civilized to the degree to which they can satirize themselves. England and Literature occupy, by this yardstick, their respective eminences."[11] De Vries is not here proposing a literary or cultural way to salvation; he is merely affirming the transcendent character of comedy, the power of laughter to deny its own denials. Not only does human wit thereby step beyond criticism into self-criticism; it also finds, at least in De Vries's fiction, that self-mockery need not lead to fury and futility. Comedy of his kind can be binding and healing, even as one's sides ache from laughing.

De Vries knows, of course, that comedy often serves as a cruel release for hostility. This desire to laugh at the expense of others helps explain both the popularity of satire and the relative rarity of true humor. The narrator and namesake of *Mrs. Wallop* observes that many attempts at humor arise "as much from inner bitterness as from the sunniness they [may seem to have] celebrated."[12] Joe Tickler makes a similar declaration in *The Glory of the Hummingbird*. Witticisms spring, he says, "from some deep-seated maladjustment in the jokester, perhaps inner misery, with which one must be patient and understanding, however irksome the end-product endured as a string of wisecracks. A need to evade reality may motivate such people, to fend off life's slings and arrows with a protective mechanism at once shield and weapon."[13]

Such bilious humor need not have a personal or social object for its scorn. Life itself provides sufficient cause for derision. Osgood Wallop reminds a friend not to "ask too much of comedy. There's only so much futility to go around."[14] Wallop is one of several "black" humorists who populate De Vries's fiction. As with Beckett and Kafka, they are obsessed with the metaphysical emptiness of modern life, and they are determined to answer the world's absurdity not with tears but with howling cachinnations. Yet De Vries does not deal with these absurdists very sympathetically. Mrs. Wallop addresses her son's nihilistic comedy from what would seem to be De Vries's own viewpoint: "You don't have to empty a bucket of slops on my head, beat me about the ears with bags of garbage, and set off a stink bomb under my chair to show me life can be nasty."[15] Cheerless comedy offends not by its untruthfulness but by its obviousness. It tells us what Job discovered long ago—that the world is a sorry sphere, that "man . . . born of a woman is of few days, and full of trouble."

Unlike Job, who protests against God for not behaving as God, black humor makes bleakness and blankness its own justification. It cannot explain why a denial of life's value is itself valuable. In *Madder Music* De Vries confronts the inadequacy of disconsolate comedy as a response to cosmic absurdity. Bob Swirling, the protagonist, is plagued with an illness which, though described by the psychiatrist as a fugue state, is also a metaphysical malaise. Swirling wishes to flee not only the frustrations of his own life, but the futility of life itself. As his name reveals, Swirling finds human existence too much like a vortex ever to gain any permanent footing within it. His reflexive consciousness, always doubling and tripling back upon itself, combines with the world's own evident lack of logic to make him a man devoid of identity except as he can act as if he were someone else. He remains sanely aloof from the world's madness by impersonating Groucho Marx, thus descending into a madness all his own.

Swirling's analyst, a Dr. Josko, pronounces the harsh truth about his patient's antic dementia: "What a smug haven to curl up in, safe from the winds that buffet this cold world."[16] The doctor seems also to agree with Freud's famous declaration that the purpose of psychoanalysis is to reduce screaming rage to ordinary unhappiness. Dr. Josko describes therapy as an attempt to "get the patient to purchase back his reason at the price of his tranquillity."[17] Swirling may be right in believing that the world is but a "mote spun out of a delirium of gas and dust five billion years ago,"[18] but such apparent absurdity is no excuse for robbing life of the fragile and tenuous meaning it has.

At the end of the novel Swirling makes yet another descent into an assumed personality, "the envelope of abstraction thickening rapidly about him, like an invisible cocoon; a mental sheath within which he would in a few minutes be encapsulated and inaccessible."[19] Such willed idiocy may be a funny response to the spinning senselessness of life; perhaps, in fact, it is the only way Swirling can continue to exist. Yet such an abdication of reason is no answer to our spiritual predicament. For all his splendid foolery, Swirling lacks the humor that enables one to embrace the ambiguity of human life. He cannot accept our droll likeness to the contradictory condition of the platypus:

> . . . that whimsically improbable little creature that is both aquatic and terrestrial and yet not comfortably either, and so an amphibian *manqué* into the bargain. It kills its water prey and then slinks off with it, stored in cheek pouches, to eat it on dry land, perhaps out of a sense of guilt over the element to which it has been disloyal—certainly out of insecurity of some sort. Its domiciling is equally muddled. The female cohabits in a burrow with her mate but only until it's time to have her young, precisely when one would think an adult male around the house would be welcome, at least a stabilizing factor. But no, off she waddles to lay her eggs in a separate burrow of her own building—leaving the male with still more on his conscience. . . . To lay her eggs? Yes, for the platypus is, finally, further biologically scrambled in being an oviparous mammal.[20]

As this declaration ruefully indicates, most hard definitions do violence to the thing defined. The divide between healing and hurtful humor is also exceedingly fine. De Vries knows, far more acutely than Updike, that human self-contradiction, far from being proof that God has set us here, may reveal that there is no God. Though De Vries shares nothing whatever of Sartre's humorless spirit, he does appreciate Sartre's conviction that human life may be nothing more than nature's gigantic mistake. The hominoid brain, in leaping out of animal self-contentment into human self-awareness, may have achieved something radically different than self-consciousness before God.

The problem of nihilism haunts, in fact, the whole of Peter De Vries's fiction. In *The Vale of Laughter*, for example, he has Joe Sandwich ask his computer whether life is worth living. The machine refuses to answer, "like the television network Vote Projection Indicators on election night when it is still too early to tell."[21] Joe's fear, perhaps arising out of De Vries's own dread, is that there will never be sufficient data to render a final decision about the ultimate value of life. It will always be "too early to tell," and thus also terribly too late. We remain caught, Sandwich believes, in an unresolvable ambiguity wherein the contraries of life coincide, threatening thereby to cancel the significance of their seeming opposition.

Joe concludes that tragedy and comedy, perhaps like love and hate, are basically the same. "Shelley regarded *King Lear* as a comedy. So did Yeats. He said *Lear* was gay. Coleridge said *Hamlet* verges on the ludicrous."[22] What is true in literature Sandwich finds even more evident in life. An automobile driver is killed while fastening his seat belt. A mass meeting held to protest student apathy attracts four people. A house is set ablaze by a short in the fire alarm. A man works himself to death paying off his life insurance policy. Are these incidents funny or sad, gloomy or hilarious? Sandwich has the awful suspicion that they are both, that comedy is but tragedy without tears, and that we blink back desperation with laughter. De Vries has no ready answer to this dark dilemma. Yet he remains convinced that it is better to *think* nihilism than to live it.

II. How to Commit Suicide without Killing Oneself: Nihilistic Humor in *The Cat's Pajamas* and *Witch's Milk*

The Cat's Pajamas is De Vries's fictional attempt to show what happens when humor turns nihilistic. Hank Tattersall, the novel's central character, is obsessed with the antipodal character of both human and natural life. He is a latter day Nietzschean who finds evidence of the Eternal Return everywhere:

> "For one cheek of this old world is always enshadowed whilst the other twinkles in full sunshine. . . . We no less than the stars in their courses swing in our eternal orbit of contradictions: love and hate, hot and cold, birth and death, yes and no. The principle of contrariety is built into the very bricks of the universe. It whizzes in the merry molecules, it boils in the unthinkable vats of galactic space. Peer into the microscope and you will find it. Gaze out

through the telescope and it is there. If you take the wings of the morning and fly to the outermost parts of the earth, lo, it is there. You eat it and you drink it, you sneeze it and you sweat it. Socrates rightly said that the talent for tragedy was the same as the talent for comedy. Tragedy and comedy have a common root, whose name at last I think I know. . . . Mirth and grief have a common manifestation, the convulsion, and of course they share your tear ducts, like good neighbors sharing a well. . . . The whole cosmos is a contradiction balanced as delicately as a stick on a clown's nose. The thing anything is most closely wedded to is its opposite. The relativity scientists of the day tell us that the quality that most nearly resembles Everything is—Nothing. That is why life is always half promise and half threat. It is like Walter Cronkite giving us fair notice that he will be back with more news in a moment. . . . "[23]

Tattersall's long speech is worth quoting, if only for its sardonic eloquence. Yet it also reveals De Vries's clear grasp of the mythic vision of life as a *coincidentia oppositorum*. To believe that finally all things belong to an undifferentiated unity devoid of real distinctions is to make a grim admission indeed. The marvel of De Vries's fiction is that, while he seems to share the philosophical nihilism of his protagonists, he does not sanction it as a guide and basis for life. Hank Tattersall is a character who reveals the terrible cost, both to oneself and to others, of making the pointlessness of life a rationale for living. *The Cat's Pajamas* is at once a funny and chilling account of what happens when one attempts to act as if nihilism were not only funny but true.

Tattersall shares Bob Swirling's conviction that, because a single lifetime is too brief a span for assuming all the identities of which our protean natures are capable, he will be no self at all. By embracing no permanent role, he will thus parody the endless flux of the universe itself. If we have no character except that which we create for ourselves, and if the self is but a mask which we arbitrarily wear, why not put on a random series of personalities? Taking the logic of self-invention to its absurd end, Hank ceases being a professor and becomes, successively, an ad man, a German gardener, and a Negro lackey. "To be a misfit in a tale told by an idiot," he bleakly consoles himself, "is after all hardly the worst of fates."[24]

As the professed "exponent of futility," Tattersall's revised Cartesian motto is "I stink, therefore I am."[25] "Self-esteem," he declares with dark deflation, "is what others think of you."[26] The trend of all things being irrevocably downward, Tattersall determines to push the world's pointlessness to its logical limit. He sells cans of fresh air, bakes beef Stroganoff in bedpans, and peddles signs which read "NO PEDDLERS ALLOWED."[27] Hank's room is the perfect expression of life's randomness, a pure illustration of Dadaistic despair:

A drip-dry shirt hung from the chandelier, from one of whose sockets depended also a length of electric cord ending in no visible appliance, but just vanishing under the piano among an assortment of empty bottles. It was like a strand of vine in an untended yard. . . . Half-finished tongue twisters lay everwhere. In one corner the dog was sleeping off a drunk. An electric razor seemed plugged into a can of lard. That was an example of something not the product of neglect, but only of a conscious intelligence. There might have been lurking about the premises someone waiting just to be asked about it, in order to be able to answer, "Oh, I forgot to disconnect it."[28]

"The product . . . only of a conscious intelligence"—there lies the rub. The faculty that elevates us angelically above the apes can also plunge us demonically into misery, however comic our descent into hell. So completely does Tattersall live amidst hypertrophied self-awareness, determined to remain totally skeptical and undeceived by life, that he scorns all counterclaims against the irrationality of the universe. He despises, for example, his wife Sherry's "irritating view that the sun rose and set on him."[29] To keep their union ever new, Hank insists on repeated remarriages and honeymoons. Yet nothing galls him more than success. He is able to devote himself to his work only after his job is doomed. Like a latter-day Samson, Tattersall wants to pull down the Dagonic temple of value and meaning, burying himself alongside its naive worshippers. He furiously rejects, therefore, a Christmas bonus presented by his boss dressed as Santa Claus. For Hank can be happy only when he is turning "himself steadily on the lathe of self-torment."[30]

Although Tattersall does not narrate his own story, he is not without insight into his predicament. In one of his periodic letters to himself, he complains about his masculine tendency to follow "the long, tortuous odyssey of self-justification," and thus to think himself "the cat's pajamas."[31] It is not mere egoism that Hank is describing, but a deep refusal to live within the limits of the given. Theologically speaking, he is tempted to exist without grace. For De Vries, such an overwrought intellectuality is the peculiar failing of men. As he explains in an interview, the cosmos generally inhabited by women "is human, not galactic. In the end, they bring everything back down to earth where it really belongs, like Molly Bloom in *Ulysses*. They don't deal in things like categorical imperatives and windowless monads. They don't know what the hell you're talking about, and they'd be damn fools if they did.[32]

The noteworthy point is not De Vries's apparently unreconstructed male chauvinism, but his refusal to sanction a self-sufficient life devoted to omnivorous consciousness, however witty. That Hank finds himself all in tatters is, as his name indicates, the salient fact. In the end he alienates his wife, begins drinking with his dog, and moves in with a wretched woman and her mongoloid son in order to embrace "the purposeless squalor of human existence."[33] On a snowy November night, having accidentally locked himself out of his house, Tattersall tries to call for help through the doggy door. No one comes. We last see Hank as he remains bent over on all fours, his strangely warmed head caught in the narrow opening, his wagging body gradually succumbing to the cold. Perhaps the moral of the story is this: See what trouble your head will get you into. Or else this: Cynics become literally doglike. Proud that such an ignominious dying proves the absurdity of things, Hank is visited one last time by his antagonistic alter ego. It insults him with a final pun: "Your end is in sight."[34]

Never the moralist wanting to chastize or lecture, neither is De Vries merely neutral about Tattersall's fate. In the figure of Tillie Seltzer, he provides an even clearer assessment of Hank than the judgment already implicit in the sorry end which Hank meets. As a social worker who comes to visit Tattersall and the down-and-out family he lives with, Mrs. Seltzer charges that Hank's absurdism, for all its apparent tough-mindedness, is a covert form of self-indulgence. She accuses him of "biting down on an aching tooth," of playing the game called "instant despair," of attempting to create "surrealism in everyday life," and thus of being "a black humorist [who is] living it up."[35]

De Vries's implied assessment of such self-interested nihilism is made evident in an important speech by Tillie. She tells Hank that "misanthropes all hate themselves." The nihilist grievance against life makes one opaque, says Tillie, to both the grief and the glory that the world mysteriously grants to us:

> "I think the truer it is that Everything Stinks the less one should call it to others' attention. Quiet is requested for the benefit of other patients. These people [like Tattersall]—they can't forgive God for not existing. . . . They gorge themselves on Nothing. They can't get enough of Nothing. They can't suck enough out of that Existentialist tit. They cozy up to it till they're glutted, they're drooling, it's running down their chin. . . . But this Someone they can't forgive for not existing, neither can they stop going on to him, or it. Don't try to divert me with beauty, they say. Don't try to buy me off with spring flowers, or young May moons, or falling snow. I want to stay mad."[36]

The noteworthy fact here is that De Vries does not have Tillie Seltzer refute absurdism by denying life's irrationality. She observes, simply but acutely, that the nihilist often makes the world's suffering and chaos a convenient excuse for self-absorption. Like Ivan Karamazov, Hank Tattersall is unable to worship God because of life's apparent illogic and injustice.

Yet the awful absence of ultimate order and meaning, rather than humbling Hank, serves to justify his descent into sweet misery and bitter self-love. His Ivanesque obsession with God's cruelty blinds him to the suffering existence of others. Tillie quickly discerns that Tattersall cares not at all for the mongoloid child he proposes to adopt, except as the pathetic creature provides further documentation for his case against life.

Rather than lighting a candle amidst the darkness, as Tillie does, Hank prefers to "stay mad." Cosmic idiocy becomes the excuse for his own self-indulgent spite. In one of his most brilliant comic reversals, De Vries has Tillie invert Nietzsche's notion that believers in God harbor a deep grudge against the harshness of human existence. Perhaps it is nihilists like Hank, she suggests, who are filled with real *ressentiment*. They would rather bear a lingering grudge against the whole of existence than confirm the world's absurdity through self-murder: "Some rub it out. That's suicide. The other type wants to do the opposite. They want to rub it in. They want to live as long as possible, to rub all of it in they can." Tattersall is self-destructive only "up to a point." In a deadly accurate thrust, Tillie accuses Hank of wanting to "commit as much suicide as possible without killing himself."[37]

Witch's Milk, the novella printed alongside *The Cat's Pajamas*, is De Vries's attempt to provide more than a mere verbal critique of Tattersall's darkly comic end. In the character of Pete Seltzer, he offers an alternative to Hank's embittered unbelief. Pete is indeed a benign absurdist, a nihilist willing to laugh at his own futility, and thus an unbeliever who is partially delivered from his unbelief. Tillie is drawn to Pete because he possesses what Hank lacks—a love of the ludicrous for its own sake, and not as a weapon against life. "He ridicules everything, and nobody," Tillie observes. He relishes "the absurdities in which life happily abounds, and of which it may in fact be made."[38] When their child Charlie contracts leukemia—a real cause for personal distress, and not one of Hank's impersonal demonstrations that the world is senseless—Pete does not succumb to an angry absurdism. Instead, he uses his foolery as a means of holding madness at bay. Pete cheers up both himself and the dying boy by imagining such goofy products as collapsible popcorn, dehydrated water, fireproof pickles, and odorless cologne.

At its worst, such manic drollery is but a desperate whistling in the void. Seltzer's zany kind of Stoicism pretends to take nothing seriously by regarding everything jokingly. Pete can banter even about Charlie's fate beyond death: "I was reading the other day where astronomers have discovered some strange blue particles in the Milky Way they didn't know were there. So cheer up. . . . I mean if nothing is certain, then everything is possible." The universe "expands and contracts," he continues, "at intervals of eighty-two billion years. Isn't that terrific? So buck up. What the hell."[39]

At the child's funeral, the Seltzers ask the minister to read a prayer by Robert Louis Stevenson. Like De Vries himself, they regard it as a petition "that might validly be uttered by people who didn't really think anyone was listening":

> "Purge out of every heart the lurking grudge," it ran. "Give us courage and gaiety and the quiet mind. Spare us to all our friends, soften us to our enemies. Bless us, if it may be, in all our innocent endeavors. If it may not be, give us the strength to encounter that which is to come, that we may be brave in peril, constant in tribulation, temperate in wrath, and in all changes of fortune, and down to the gates of death, loyal and loving to one another."[40]

Pete and Tillie's brave Stevensonian declaration of faith without God rings empty; it is a bell tolling in an abyss. On literary no less than theological grounds, it fails to convince. Nothing within the novel's own action reveals human endeavor to be an exercise in innocence, nor bravery and constancy and loyalty to be self-generated commodities, nor gaiety and quiet and temperance to be gifts which have no Giver. That Hank lacks these graces while Pete possesses them is a mystery perhaps better explained by De Vries's native Calvinism than by the pathetic autosuggestion of the Stevenson prayer.

As if in covert confession that the Seltzers' Victorian humanism is a hollow thing, De Vries ends *Witch's Milk* with an almost Calvinistic turn, a peripety whose implicit affirmation is all the more convincing for being funny. Temporarily alienated by their grief over little Charlie's death, Pete and Tillie come finally to recognize that their common experience of life's joy and sadness is too strong for them to be driven apart. Yet it is not in somber apologies but in rollicking jibes that they are reconciled. Pete tells his wife that she must hold her chin especially high—now that she has not one but two. Tillie replies that Pete is the only husband who could shepherd her through the disillusionments of marriage. The Seltzers possess an effervescence that they cannot deny. They seem comically predestined for each other, wackily elected to a happiness that has been bestowed on them despite all their bungling. Nihilism is not only unfunny, therefore, but perhaps untrue. Life may force us to drink the witch's bitter milk, the Seltzers discover, but true laughter can make it taste strangely sweet.

III. Bathed in Swank, Gliding on Suavity: The Glories of Aestheticism in *Comfort Me with Apples*

Peter De Vries's comic characters are almost all cosmopolitans—even when they come from such places as Slow Rapids, Indiana, and Ulalume, North Dakota. Humor springs largely from the distance one gains on oneself and the world by way of a cultured consciousness. Throughout nearly all twenty of his novels, De Vries's characters seek diligently for the freedom of an urbane mind, for liberation from the conformity of small towns and small souls. Yet no sooner have they been thus set free than the limits of mere suavity become evident. The cultivated life proves altogether as predictable and exhausting as the most unthinking conventionality. The comic burden of De Vries's fiction is to show how dull can be the products of refinement, how strict the conformities of the epicure, how laborious the leisures of the flesh. His willingness to gouge friendly fun out of the bloated carcass of culture reveals, once again, that De Vries is a humorist of a rare kind. For it is chiefly himself and his fellow sophisticates that he parodies, thus graciously freeing his readers from the trap into which his own books might lead them.

In his novel of 1974, *The Glory of the Hummingbird*, De Vries has Jim Tickler announce what might be considered the motto for his entire work. Tickler declares that he has embarked upon a backward quest, a renunciation of sanctity for the world's sake, "a sort of Pilgrim's Progress in reverse; as though our young Christian, his back turned on the City of God, sets his face like flint for the beckoning glamors of Vanity Fair."[41] This is a personal no less than a literary confession. There is much of De Vries himself in his many protagonists who struggle valiantly to quit the heavenly Jerusalem for the earthly Babylon.

In *The Blood of the Lamb*, Don Wanderhope's rebellion against his narrow Dutch Calvinist upbringing seems clearly reminiscent of De Vries's own childhood. The youthful Wanderhope recalls that his forbears regarded themselves as "a chosen people, more so than the Jews, who had 'rejected the cornerstone.'" His mother "sometimes gave the impression," says Wanderhope, "that Jesus was a Hollander."[42] Having fallen in love with his first girlfriend, Don is commanded by his father to have her pass the ultimate muster: "Any girl you go out with you take here, *verstaan*, because I want to see what Jesus would say."[43] It is not surprising to learn that Sunday afternoon at the Wanderhopes was spent discussing Biblical Infallibility and Total Depravity.

It is meet and right that De Vries's characters should want out of such a constricting and repressive world. Nor is their desire for secular experience a mere matter of adolescent rebellion. They want to be numbered among the Smart Set because they regard sophistication as the way to liberty and style, the means for savoring the glories and serendipities of life rather than squashing them under the heel of a rigid morality and religion. De Vries's protagonists are unapologetic romantics who, like Chick Swallow in *Comfort Me with Apples*, want to relish all the possibilities latent in the human no less than in the natural world. "What infinities are in the mind!" Swallow exclaims. "The idlest thought teems like a waterdrop with microscopic life, and no day's wakening but renews the long symbolic dream that is as dense and haunting as the sequences we know to be compressed into a wink of sleep."[44]

The attractiveness of the aesthete's life is a motif running throughout De Vries's fiction. It is nowhere more apparent than in the two novels devoted to the career of Chick Swallow, *Comfort Me with Apples* (1956) and *The Tents of Wickedness* (1959). The aim here is not to follow Swallow's development as a character through the zany convolutions of De Vries's plot, but to examine his cosmopolitan vision of reality. Swallow comes by it naturally, having been "read to sleep with the classics and spanked with obscure quarterlies."[45] His father was a writer so fastidious about punctuation that he suffered, appropriately, from colon trouble. So does the younger Swallow seek nothing other than the sleekest urbanity. What he observes of his friend Pete Cheshire is no less true of himself: "As young men plan to go into medicine or law, he planned to go into suavity. . . . It was after all but the simple wish for worldly patina . . . movie-nourished, woman-haunted, bathed in swank."[46] It is a dream world of the purely effete that Swallow inhabits. He and his friend Nickie Sherman are fond of imagining themselves as barons of an English country estate called Wise Acres, where the pursuit of paradox and nuance is so avid "that the cook complained the upside-down cakes came out right-side-up."[47]

Chick Swallow pursues the career of a *boulevardier* in order to escape the inanity of middle-class life. He wants to avoid a naive hopefulness and sincerity—the "readiness for trite philosophy that the slightest sign of rhythm or pattern in our lives inspires."[48] The alternative to such spiritual banality is *style*—a manner of speaking and dressing, of eating and acting, that is more distinguished than what obtains in Decency, Connecticut. Life there is all too decent indeed. It is populated, Swallow laments, with "new owners of old shore properties, people with allergies and two-toned cars," and builders of "swimming pools on the beaches."[49] The problem is not merely local but national. The whole of American society is blind, in Chick's estimate, to the higher things of the spirit:

> It was simple to tell the British from the Americans, even without the clues of speech and through the dense thickets of disguise. The English ate as they talked; the Americans merely talked while they ate. It was churlish to note the trick of style—there was a thousand years of history behind the one; no doubt a millennium would suffice for the raw young country straining in its materialist traces, sweating to produce more air conditioners, more snorkels and ballpoint pens than any other, while its parent would go on from prime to senility, dribbling her gruel and owing all the world. Meanwhile the hog bestrode the world, scattering its billions to all

who wanted. It had not yet learned the civilized knack of the French to nick you for just what the traffic will bear.[50]

De Vries is hardly at one with Chick Swallow's overwrought aestheticism. On the contrary, he mocks its preciosity. Yet Swallow the romantic is onto a truth which the dull masses largely ignore. However effete his manner, he is right in wanting to celebrate the world's shimmering beauty and glory—the "tinkling pleasures" and "caught felicites, for which we are so sumptuously cued by nature."[51] Amidst a particular moment of transport, Swallow says that "the stars struck me as a handful of hot rivets precariously holding together a night threatening to burst under the strain of too much ecstasy."[52] For all of his effete excess, Swallow gives voice to the permanent truth embodied in the romantic vision of imagined wonder: "If a man acted on every instinct normal to the yearning to make a sacrament of life, he would soon be put away."[53] There is indeed a deep strain of aesthetic religion undergirding De Vries's entire work, a belief in the power of sensibility to overcome what George Eliot called the tragedy of frequency and familiarity: "If we had a keen vision and feeling of all ordinary life, it would be like hearing the grass grow and the squirrel's heart beat, and we should die of that roar which lies on the other side of silence. As it is, the quickest of us walk about well wadded with stupidity."[54]

It is not only the sense of worldly wonder that Chick Swallow and his fellow sophisticates seek to cultivate. They also have a sniffing contempt for all the species of humbuggery. They specialize, therefore, in the withering epigram, the anti-moralistic apothegm that seeks to shrivel the regnant sentimentality. Many of Swallow's *bon mots* verily exude the world-weariness of the Mauve Decade: "Relax," Chick tells himself, "everything is hopeless."[55] His friend Nickie Sherman assures him, "Of course I want a home, children, all that sort of thing. You know—the eternal severities."[56] "Life is a carnival," Swallow laments, "at which one should throw balls at the prizes."[57] "Love," he sighs, "is the lotus that turns into lettuce."[58] Seeing worshippers hurrying toward church, Chick gives complacent thanks: "There, but for the grace of God, go I."[59] Perhaps the darkest maxim of all is his description of life as "a tragedy perpetuated by the passion that relieves it."[60]

Such waggish asperities have given De Vries a reputation as a wit and prankster who is more clever than profound. Yet he is also an aphorist who penetrates as deeply as a Chesterton or a Johnson, a Lichtenberg or a Kierkegaard. "Platitudes have their place," Swallow observes wisely. "They are like the lower teeth in a smile."[61] Even his puns often hit the mark: "A man is made of chalkstone—don't take him for granite."[62]

For all of his apparent ennui and cynicism, Swallow can be both confessional and compassionate. He is himself an aficionado of nuance, but he admits that there is something self-negating about an excessive subtlety: "It is like being winked at with both eyes."[63] Angered at Nickie Sherman's bungling of a criminal case that could have secured his career as a detective, Chick soon retracts his harsh judgment. "The worse people are," he allows, "the easier it is to be objective with them. We fuss at what irritates us," he concludes, "but try to understand real breaches of behavior."[64] Swallow also shares Dostoevski's conviction that gifts are often given in order to put their recipients at the mercy of the giver: "It's easy enough for a man to love his enemies. The question is whether he can forgive his benefactors."[65]

Swallow's crackling conceits are not motivated by a merely cynical self-regard. They are prompted by a deeper sense of value than conventional sincerity and sobriety are able to perceive. He gives profundity, for example, to an otherwise hackneyed piece of conventional wisdom: "Children do indeed hold two people together, but as the mortar does the bricks, by also keeping them a little apart."[66] Swallow has a concern for true literacy when he protests against the superficial learning acquired in much of modern education: "If there's any one major cause for the spread of mass illiteracy," he opines, "it's the fact that everybody can read and write."[67] There is also considerable truth in Swallow's Hawthornian conviction that worldlings may be less prurient than Puritans. "What is chastity," he asks, "but an overemphasis on sex?"[68] Perhaps most surprising of all, for a professed unbeliever like Chick, is his theological astuteness. "We know God will forgive our sins," he declares brightly to his mistress. But then he confesses darkly that "the question is what [God] will think of our virtues."[69]

It is not only the droll epigram that Swallow has mastered; he also has a keen ear for the malapropism and solecism. Again, his motives are not merely self-serving; he does not want to ridicule the ignorant so much as to celebrate the wackiness of their mistakes. As an advice columnist, he receives a letter from a woman who suspects that something is missing from her seventeen-year marriage, since she has never experienced an "organism" and wonders what one is. Another letter comes from a lady with eight children who, much to her consternation, has found out that her husband is "heterosexual." "Everywhere you turn these days," she complains, "you hear of some new kind of perversion or abnormality. How can a person keep up with these big words, the curse of our time? Homosexual, asexual, bisexual—now heterosexual."[70] Swallow's Greek bartender, who has "Americanized" his name from Andropoulos to Nachtgeborn, is not at all put off by Chick's use of such forbidding locutions as "existential." He thinks it is the name of an insurance company. So innocent and artless are these mistakes that an aesthete like Swallow can extol naivety even as he exposes it. Long before the term was invented, he is the connoisseur of Camp. He describes this back door appreciation of the ordinary as being "like one of those Currier and Ives prints which, having outgrown them, one then laps the field of Sensibility to approach again from behind and see as 'wonderful.'"[71]

Yet if De Vries's protagonists must undergo an aesthetic liberation from deadening convention and conformity, so must they also learn the narrow constrictions of the libertine life. Living it up in Vanity Fair proves to be a terrible strain. De Vries's worldlings learn that there is nothing quite so time-consuming as seizing the day. To devote oneself to endless playfulness turns out to be very hard work. Even Nickie Sherman confesses the utter monotony of "unrelieved novelty."[72] It is not the emancipated life but humdrum existence that affords the true challenge. For there, amidst ordinary responsibilities and commitments, one cannot play the aesthete's game of eternally juggled possibilities. This is not to say that De Vries's protagonists repent their worldly-wiseness and embark for the Heavenly City. But most of them do, in fact, return to a secular version of it—to the wives and work, the families and obligations, they once thought so enslaving. An epigraph from Ben Hecht sums up the deep irony which De Vries's shallow ironists come reluctantly to acknowledge: "Convention has always more heroes than revolt."[73]

Chick Swallow learns the pleasures of convention only after he has first sought to elude the constrictions of marriage, forsaking his pedestrian wife Crystal for the elegant Clara Thicknesse. She kindles in Chick an ardor for what he calls "a citified communion," a desire to breathe the *Zeitgeist* that has been stifled by matrimony.[74] So sophisticated is Mrs. Thicknesse that she has become skeptical about science. And so thoroughgoing is her negativism that she rejects Chick's affirmations even before he can make them. He thus compares her to a wing shooter who aims, "like a hunter, a little ahead of the ducks in flight so they would be there when her shot arrived."[75]

It is little wonder that Mrs. Thicknesse should prove less delectable than Swallow has dreamed. As is often true of De Vries's womanizers, Chick is impotent once he gets the long-desired Clara in bed. Although he recalls a line from the Song of Solomon—"Thy belly is an heap of wheat"—his languor persists. Even more dispiriting is Mrs. Thicknesse's query, "What ails thee, knight at arms?"[76] It is the human condition that plagues Swallow—not only the guilt of betraying his wife, but also the absurdity of his exquisite dalliance's having so ordinary an aim. To compound Swallow's sexual difficulties there is a cameraman setting up his equipment nearby, declaring that "this will be the first time I've ever shot a man in bed."[77] The photographer is in the employ of Mr. Thicknesse, not because the husband fears his wife is unfaithful, but because he wants to secure the divorce she has long denied him. Chick Swallow and Clara Thicknesse end their rendezvous by having a genial conversation, the latter consoling the former that he can take moral pride for having been "good in bed."[78]

De Vries's aesthetes are comically caught in this same gracious irony: their attempt to suffice pleasurably unto themselves backfires, and they are propelled against their wills into a happiness unknown to mere sophistication. In *The Tunnel of Love*, for example, Augie Poole and his wife, being childless, seek to adopt an infant. The adoption agency questions Augie's moral probity, and he confirms their suspicions by getting his mistress pregnant. Yet life can never, in De Vries's fiction, be assessed according to any easy, convenient moral calculus. Scared into responsibility by this accidental creation of human life, Augie breaks off the affair and becomes utterly faithful to his wife. The mistress, for her part, puts the infant up for adoption, and the baby is unwittingly assigned to the Pooles. This is De Vries's goofy version of the Gospel's own comedy—the good news that we are saved in spite of ourselves, that we may do inadvertent good when we are most selfish, and that (to quote De Vries's own epigraph from T. S. Eliot) "virtues are forced upon us by our impudent crimes."

One need not read these grimly happy endings as having theological import. They may be seen, instead, as grin-and-bear-it resignations to the absurdity of Fate. These dreamers who long for an ideal beauty must, according to this darker view, surrender their high vision and accept the lesser satisfactions of life. Like the author of Solomon's Song, they are sick with love's insatiable desire. They cry out to be "stayed with flagons and comforted with apples." Were romantics like Swallow to obtain their long-sought liberation from the hackneyed and the habitual, and thus be freed to live wholly under the inspiration of the moment, they would find their new joy strangely disappointing. This is Swallow's own melancholy conclusion, and De Vries does nothing to undermine it. On the contrary, he allows Swallow to state his defeatist philosophy with powerful unironic poignancy:

> There is a bird we've all heard singing but none has ever seen; not even the completest apparent success fulfills the visions entertained for it. We return from journeys on which we have set out hunting unicorns, glad to have bagged a boar. . . . So, enjoying ourselves as best we can—which is often enough quite considerably, if we would be honest about it—we spend what time we have of Time, that river down whose chuckling waters we are carried to the sea.[79]

The eloquence of this Housmanic hedonism notwithstanding, it does not reveal the real bent of Peter De Vries's fiction. Swallow's conscious philosophy is sad and sardonic, but the vision implicit in the novel's tone and action is deeply comic. The real significance of a novel like *Comfort Me with Apples* is to be found in Swallow's wacky recovery of his marriage to Crystal. The redemptive turn so typical of De Vries's entire work is signalled early in the narrative when, fearing that Crystal is pregnant but learning that she is not—and thus being liberated from the shackles of hated domesticity—Chick immediately proposes marriage. "I could have kicked myself," Swallow moans. "Here I'd had freedom in my grasp and let it go, victim of my passions again. For I'd lost my head in a passion of thanks scarcely worthier than its more sensual counterpart of a few weeks ago, judged as a gauge of self-control. What a jackass!"[80] The irony is too patent to miss. Swallow's inability to live merely out of his own self-regard is what makes him so winsome a character, even as it also gets him into the "trouble" of marrying Crystal Chickering. It is not toward a solemn Stoic serenity that his life is fatefully inclined. He is launched willy-nilly toward a redemptive marriage. He is delivered from evil not by a moralistic fear of hell but by a comic granting of grace.

It comes as no surprise that Chick should be drawn back to Crystal in the end. No sooner, in fact, does he forsake her for Mrs. Thicknesse than Crystal begins to acquire all the elegance he has previously complained that she lacked. As an imperfect lecher, moreover, Chick devotes his sexual fantasies to his wife rather than his mistress. The more furiously Chick and Crystal fight, the deeper their reconciliation. Indeed, it is while they are screaming at each other that Swallow discovers their total compatibility: "As she threw a suitcase on the bed and began flinging things into it with the declaration that she was leaving me and never wanted to see me again as long as she lived, then ordered me out and slammed the door after me, I knew, as I had never known before, that she was the woman for me."[81] Not to be outdone, Crystal threatens to sue Mrs. Thicknesse for alienation of her husband's affections. Yet, not wanting to overestimate Chick's worth, she plans to ask for only $65 in damages. Thus does the husband who set out to be the perfect man-about-town find himself ruefully but happily domesticated.

IV. Imaginative Conformity vs. Predictable Revolt: *The Tents of Wickedness*

In *The Tents of Wickedness*, De Vries makes an even more telling critique of life amidst the *avant garde*. In this novel Charles Swallow has become so infatuated with literature that he cannot think in his own images or speak his own idiom; he is forever imitating one or another of his literary masters. Faulkner is his special favorite. Describing Sweetie Appleyard, his old school chum who is soon to become his new lover, Swallow cannot resist Yoknapatawpha orotundity. She has lost herself, he insists, in a "lute-embodied, verse-bemused, high gutless swooning

based on the illusion and maybe even belief that flesh could be repro-
duced without recourse to flesh; that you could multiply arms and legs
and smiles and tears and hands and feet without sex organs."[82] Little
right does Swallow have to call Sweetie a dreamy Gnostic. He is himself
a ghostly figure. As Roderick Jellema notes, Swallow "moves from
atrophied Marquandian hero to a Faulknerian haunted by memory,
through a Kafkaesque nightmare of metamorphosis to a state of delirium
borrowed from *Finnegan's Wake*."[83]

A purely artistic life, in De Vries's estimate, often makes for an un-
artistic chaos. Chick's exquisitely literary existence reduces him to gibberish and finally to confinement in a mental hospital. Both his wife and
his mistress having insisted that he is a swine, Swallow becomes one—
rooting about on all fours, developing beady little eyes, climbing upon a
dresser to see if he has a curly tail, and even thinking of piggish puns:
"Nobody knows the truffles I've seen."[84] It turns out that Swallow is
afflicted with no esoteric psychosis but with ordinary trichinosis.
Neither is it a highfalutin literary reconciliation that brings him back to
Crystal; he appeals to her love through a sentimental song entitled "Jest
a-wearyin' fer you."[85]

Swallow may not, like the Psalmist, be a doorkeeper in the house of
God, but neither can he dwell at home in the tents of wickedness. The
humbler terrain where he takes up his final abode lies, paradoxically, not
below but above the territory of the suave. "The conformity we often
glibly equate with mediocrity," Chick observes, "isn't something free
spirits 'transcend' as much as something they're not quite up to. . . . Convention calls for broader shoulders—and, for all I know, more imagination—than revolt."[86] It also demands a greater sense of grace, however
obscurely one may recognize it. That Swallow has comically found such
mercy amidst conformity is revealed in the wildly self-deflating conclusion to the novel:

> Crystal's emotions were shaken and her temper was really in-
> flamed, for a good while there. But passions have cooled now, and
> we are again sleeping together in the great double bed which is also
> an heirloom of mine. I have had, for the record, one clear-cut in-
> stance of physical temptation since the events put down here. I
> don't imagine I need add that I resisted it. It concerned a woman I
> have known for years, freshly divorced when I came across her in a
> New York bar one night when I was staying in town. "Thanks just
> the same," I told her, "but I don't want any pleasures interfering
> with my happiness."[87]

This, then, is De Vries's brilliantly funny assessment of people who
are satiated with sophistication. He does not call for any reactionary return to the simple old-fashioned virtues. The cultured life is, as we have

seen, an important means for transcending dull sentimentalism and trite moralism. To live with style and flair is to acknowledge the great fact that life is not an obvious and straightforward proposition. It is, instead, an ironic, paradoxical, and even grace-laden business. In De Vries's work, there is no respite in the battle against banality and cliché.

Yet if one achieves too great a distance from the ordinary round, the result is affectation and pretense. Hence the necessity of ribbing the advanced and the emancipated. However far he may be removed from the Calvinist orthodoxy of his youth, Peter De Vries remains a prophet and witness to his fellow sophisticates. "O my people," cries Chick Swallow at a cocktail party, "why are ye not at home in groups of four and six, giving and taking in easy communion all that is pleasant and foolish and lovably human? Why stand ye here in this woman's house taking meat and drink in such wise that what cometh out is no better than what goeth in?"[88] Yet finally it is not a hectoring message that De Vries's fiction proffers. It is rather the good news that we can loop all the way around past sophistication into simplicity, past mere pleasure into real happiness, past the slavery of self-emancipation into the freedom of bemused acceptance and ironic conformity.

12

THE COMEDY OF
UNCONDITIONAL ELECTION
AND IRRESISTIBLE GRACE

Peter De Vries is not chiefly a comedian of the *via negativa*. He laughs at nihilistic laughter and out-sophisticates the most effete sophistication in the name of something essentially positive and redemptive. His best work is concerned not with condemnation but with affirmation. It rests on a grace that is amazingly human because it is first of all transhuman. De Vries lampoons and satirizes only in order to confess and forgive. His comic art constitutes a most vivid parable of the Gospel when he writes about three subjects in particular: marriage, doubt, and faith.

Like nearly all of De Vries's novels, *Through the Fields of Clover* (1961) deals with the proverbial battle of the sexes. It also ends in the truce wherewith De Vries nearly always concludes the ancient war: marriage. Yet this novel makes marriage not only its conclusion but also its starting point. How, De Vries asks, can so fierce and fragile a relation be permanently sustained? Alma and Ben Marvel are bound crazily together, we discover, by a grace that is even more prevenient than Calvin's eternal decrees. It is a grace that is mediated, moreover, by the failures rather than the successes of family life. In *The Blood of the Lamb* (1962), De Vries wrestles powerfully with the problem of religious doubt, especially as it is provoked by innocent suffering. The novel contains passages of such rending anguish that, like certain scenes in *King Lear*, they are almost too painful to behold. Yet the reader is made to experience, at least in two surprising moments, a vision of transcendent faith rather than final doubt. *The Mackerel Plaza* (1958) combines De Vries's concern with both marriage and religion into a magnificent comic unity. Andrew Mackerel is an anti-Calvinist minister who proudly denies the reality of a personal and providential God. Yet, for all his protests to the contrary, he keeps backsliding out of his unbelief.

By means of an irresistible feminine grace, he is made to acknowledge his unconditional election.

I. Shipwrecked in the Haven of Marriage: *Through the Fields of Clover*

The plot complications of De Vries's novels are repeatedly resolved by way of marriage, and in this regard he is a comedian in the classic mold. Yet these matrimonial resolutions imply no easy answer to sexual conflict and human alienation. De Vries is not a facile optimist who believes that things cannot go fatally awry between men and women. Especially in his later works, husbands and wives often drift apart or reach a largely pragmatic accommodation. Yet the institution of marriage is itself preserved, however precariously. Domesticity is still the rule, if only in the debased metaphor of "shacking up." Rarely, therefore, do De Vries's couples separate into solitary self-sufficiency. Inadvertently, often even against their wills, they discover that they cannot live without the grace enabled by life companionship. Husbands and wives keep stumbling into love, backpedaling into hope, and thus recovering faith in each other despite themselves.

This is not to say that De Vries is a mere traditionalist in making his humorous defense of marriage. Although his fictional couples are usually reconciled rather than estranged, their reunions are not morally predictable or psychologically necessary. It is the surprising and even outrageous character of these reconciliations that makes them at once comic and gracious. De Vries's connubial partners are delivered from mutual suspicion and hatred not by human engineering—via marital counseling and similar nostrums—but by utterly odd turns of events and attitudes. They discover their compatibility while shouting imprecations at each other. They are reunited amidst wildly honest confessions: "You're the salt of the earth, you louse." One particular De Vriesian wife vows never to divorce her spouse even if he were the last man on the earth. Another declares that her husband is one of the many men to whom she would like to say, "Only a woman would marry you." I contend that these back door affirmations of marriage form still another significant parable of our comic redemption; they serve funnily to echo the happy tidings that we are saved not by solemn works but by serendipitous grace.

Given this high comic regard for marriage as an emblem of our fundamental mutuality, it is not surprising that De Vries should mount his own counterattack against its attackers. But he does not suggest, in pure comic fashion, that the bare act of marriage itself will make for peace between the warring sexes. In *Through the Fields of Clover*, he examines the state of marriage after four decades of family life. The novel's action centers around Ben and Alma Marvel's celebration of their fortieth wedding anniversary. Theirs has hardly been an exemplary American household. The Marvels have just cause for observing their golden jubilee a decade in advance: they fear that their family will be hopelessly scattered and sundered ten years hence. All four of their children have already had at least one divorce, and their assorted grandchildren are a collocation of all the ills plaguing our culture—obesity, sexual vagary, cultural deracination, loss of identity, and the like. These modern Marvels are, in short, an alienated lot, a wretched gaggle of ex-wives and ex-husbands, boyfriends and girlfriends, all gathered to acclaim an ideal which even the father himself has begun to doubt:

> "Why summon people for miles around," he asks, "to crow about something they simply no longer believe in? People don't care any more about their sisters and their brothers, let alone their cousins and their uncles. There's been a social revolution going on for just about the forty years you want to commemorate. The family is going and the clan is gone."[1]

It is false to assume that De Vries devalues marriage and the family merely because these institutions lie in shambles. On the contrary, his comic portrayal of the collapsed ideal forms a cautionary tale that we are meant to heed even as we bend double with laughter. These up-to-date sons and daughters of Ben and Alma Marvel have made a mess of their lives because they have embraced all that is banal and silly and destructive in contemporary American life. Marriage is the first thing to fall apart when the center no longer holds. It is not morality and religion so much as it is irony that the Marvel epigoni lack. Unable to laugh at the fads and follies of our time, they become their victims. They cannot howl in derision at the footling values which are being proposed as replacements for so venerable an ideal as life companionship.

The Marvels' son Cotton, for example, has rudely rejected his parents' religion by scorning the Puritan name they have given him. This latter-day Cotton Mather refuses to attend church, taking the Psalmist's ejaculation of praise as a cynical complaint: "a day in [God's] courts is as a thousand."[2] Religion is not only a bore, in his opinion, but also an illusion. It fails to acknowledge the emptiness and capriciousness of life. The ultimate trick of nature, Cotton says, is to make us reproduce ourselves before discovering that we should never have been born.[3] Yet Cotton is not as swift a skeptic as he would wish. When he announces to his mother that the cosmos is a gigantic joke, she skewers him with a question: "Is that why you never laugh?"[4] Cotton turns out to be, in fact, a sentimental cynic who blubbers his way through maudlin plays he later condemns in his official capacity as a reviewer.

Unlike his brother, Bushrod Marvel is not a cynic convinced that the world is a sham; he is, instead, a humanist ready to reform it according to his own image of what is good and right. He agrees to return home for his parents' anniversary only because there is a local civil liberties case needing his attention. It turns out that the storeowner being "persecuted" by the local WASPs is not a Jew at all, as Bushrod believes, but a Swede who thinks that Bushrod himself might be a Semite. "You a Yew?" he asks Marvel with his imperfect immigrant's pronunciation.[5] Bushrod the illiberal liberal is indignant at such a suspicion.

This second Marvel finds nothing unseemly in his own affair with the family's Negro maid. Bushrod's fury is set off, instead, by his wife's objection to such an interracial tryst. All his years of giving her current events quizzes, all his attempts to instill her with civic virtues and ethical ideals—they are all in vain: "Prejudice!" he cries out at his benighted spouse. "To think I should find it in my own family. My own wife."[6] Such is the higher morality of one who believes that crime should be combatted not with punishment but with rewards. When his son Beaumont burns down the elder Marvel's gazebo, Bushrod insists that the boy was releasing pent-up hostility, and that he should be given sweets to compensate for his anger. De Vries's narrator comes much closer to the truth when he asks, "What is an arsonist but someone who has failed to set the world on fire?"[7]

If Bushrod and Cotton Marvel have cut themselves off from their parents' world by way of a graceless cynicism and a humorless righteousness, their sister Elsie has severed her familial ties by recoiling against the burden of being both a woman and a wife. She despises what she calls the unnatural act that marriage forces upon her: sexual intercourse. Elsie is disgusted that her former husband Harry Mercury should have loved her so bodily, worshipping her with "all his five senses," and turning the act of love into a brusque seizure and ecstatic easement. She calls it "breaking and entering." Elsie "bore him two children," we are told, but also "a good deal of resentment."

> The passing years confirmed her opinion, bolstered by additional reading matter, that Woman is the victim of a culture which requires educated attainment of her while obstructing its fulfillment and keeping her at best an economic asset and at worst a physical entity, or what's-on-the-menu as Harry called her body, the frenzied consumption of which seemed an extension of his life as a gourmet.[8]

De Vries does not sanction the harsh and often heedless physicality of masculine desire, nor is he slighting the feminine plight of having to serve at once as spiritual subject and sexual object. But the far firmer judgment falls on Elsie's resentment of her womanhood than upon the men who would honor it with physical urgency. Art Trautwein, Elsie's third and current husband, provides still another instance of her general loathing for men. She is bound to him not by mutual respect or regard, but by a tight-lipped determination to martyr herself to his male insensitivity. So graceless and equalitarian is their marriage that the only way they can fight is by performing each other's chores, even polishing one another's shoes. "She would mount the ladder and put up storm windows he had been badgered in vain to get at; coming home to find that all [was] shipshape, he would tramp inside and wash dishes [she had] let accumulate in the sink."[9] Even Elsie's love affairs are passionless. Her many extramarital attempts to overcome sexual frigidity result in a wild irony: Elsie becomes known as a nymphomaniac. Such is the world's vengeance on a creature so self-protective and self-absorbed that she cannot give herself to another in either love or lust.

The one Marvel offspring who does not currently suffer from personal and marital disaster is the daughter Evelyn. Though twice previously wed, she now seems happily married to Johnny Glimmergarten. As an advertising manager in a large Chicago firm, he is generally miserable in his work. Evelyn and Johnny make a viable pair if only because they recognize that, as De Vries says in an interview, life is not a matter of equal rights but of equal wrongs. The husband may be as maddeningly trapped in his office as the wife is in her kitchen. Marriage can issue in something other than a nursed bitterness only through a humble and humorous acceptance of what De Vries calls "the general human ordeal."[10] The Glimmergartens have recognized their partnership in the common fray and thus have found relative happiness amidst it. Not for them Ibsen's naive notion that women should be liberated from the injustices of marriage. Inequity is the chronic human state, whether within marriage or without. And as Glimmergarten rightly complains, the ancient woe may now fall as fully on the husband as the wife:

> "Eighty years ago Nora walked out of the Doll's House—where to? Nobody knows, least of all Ibsen. It is one of the puzzles of our time, which he ducked. But there is now a strong body of evidence that she is at a club meeting, or the PTA, or the board of the Friends of the Library while her husband tidies up the Doll's House. And now let us stop and consider what Ibsen would think of the male tyrant [whom] Nora fled, standing at the kitchen sink with his arms to his elbows in suds, or, an apron over his trousers, giving the children their evening baths. Oh, Jesus, spare us yet. Deliver us we pray."[11]

Roderick Jellema argues that the sins of the Marvel children have been visited upon them, at least in part, by "the rootlessness of the old homestead." The elder Marvels "have no answers for their progeny," no defenses against the "over-civilized complications spun by the children and grandchildren."[12] It is true that Ben and Alma Marvel possess no self-conscious set of values that could cure the ills suffered by their offspring. But they do embody—especially Mrs. Marvel—certain unmistakable virtues. When the embittered Elsie calls her own husband a beast, for instance, Alma chides the daughter for speaking so rudely about her son-in-law. But when Elsie enlarges her claim by calling all men beasts, Alma is satisfied: "That's better. But don't single him out."[13] One could hardly ask for a clearer understanding of the distinction between individual and original sin, nor for a greater patience with the human carnality consequent upon it.

There is also something immensely endearing about a woman who, despite her aspirations for the tonier social climes, remains an inveterate master of malaprop. Alma Marvel declares herself, for example, to be "a stout advocate of regular exercise."[14] When her son Cotton tells her he is reading a novel about a woman with three breasts, she laments the evils of modern realism. Communism she has already dismissed because it "smacked of socialism."[15] She also complains that the fee for joining the Mayflower Society is "nominal in name only."[16] When Harry Mercury tells her that one of his show business friends is a philatelist, Mrs. Marvel replies that the theater has more of those than the other arts, and wonders if he has ever sought treatment for his ailment. Upon learning that this same friend's father is a podiatrist, Alma is sure that the illness runs in the family. She also admires Proust for his command of the English language, and praises Beethoven for his "Erotica" Symphony.[17] Stories whose veracity is doubtful she calls "prophylactic."[18]

It is not mere naivety that underlies such unsuccessful striving to be chic. Ben and Alma Marvel are more than lovable naifs, more than amiable fools befuddled by modernity. They are also people of real substance and character who pass discerning judgment on the smart secular society which has tangled them and their children in its tentacles. Alma says, for instance, that sophisticated poets like Wallace Stevens remind her of "highly seasoned dishes on which it is still necessary to spread salt."[19] And when, at last, she is accepted into the Mayflower Society, Mrs. Marvel is not flustered by the aristocratic demeanor of its president, Mrs. Wetwilliam. Instead, she learns to return gelid gestures in kind: "The smiles the two women exchanged might have given an onlooker the idea that they were baring their teeth in a comparison of dentrifices to which they were individually loyal."[20]

Neither is Mrs. Marvel unduly impressed by the fact that her children have become overwrought, hypersensitive, exquisitely distilled egotists and malcontents. Another character voices Alma's complaint: being complicated does not prevent one from being shallow. The younger generation's ability to turn everything inside out, irony toppling irony, does not absolve it from the larger obligations and burdens of life. "It's all too easy!" Mrs. Marvel explodes at Elsie. "Because if your generation wants to blame us for everything, we can blame our parents, and they can blame theirs, and nobody will ever take responsibility for anything."[21]

This is the heart of the matter. Their many sufferings notwithstanding, the elder Marvels know that there is no shirking the burden of one's own life. As Abraham Lincoln is supposed to have said, there comes a time when one must assume responsibility for one's own face. The key to such plain virtue is belief in the transcendent God whose goodness is the norm of both faith and morality. Once the theological categories of sin and salvation are replaced with phobias, complexes, and the like, there is an ethical no less than a religious loss. Alma Marvel's diatribe against our psychological mushiness is thus justified, even as she malaprops her way into fury:

> "Oh, mature! Is that all anyone is ever to hear these days? Why can't they see children as bad any more, instead of maladjusted or insecure or whatever, and give them a good whaling instead of more confidence. All this psychological stuff, tension spans and one thing and another— what they need is discipline! Good old-fashioned discipline!"[22]

However jumbled their values may be, Ben and Alma Marvel have not succumbed to our culture's glib disregard for what remains both horrible and wonderful about human life. When they conclude their disastrous anniversary festivities with an awful verbal fight, they know that something precious has indeed been sullied. They cannot hide the fact that their four decades together are shadowed by failure: "Marvel felt something from the young people's lives like a stain spreading into theirs, like a poisonous mist curling slowly up the stairs and under the door, to infect them in the very bedroom that he had always thought of as a haven, and that had once been a bower."[23] Yet it is precisely this recognition of evil that makes the Marvels' marriage serve as a critique of what is "gummed up" and narcissistic about the lives of their children. Their forty year companionship is built on something more than a vapid bliss; they are bound together not chiefly by romantic love but by the mutually endured pain of disappointment and unsuccess.

There is an immense poignancy in Ben Marvel's silent survey of the rooms where, for once, all his grandchildren lie sleeping under his own roof. Inspecting them one by one, discerning in each child the pathos of life itself, he kisses their cheeks and smooths "the hair back from their damp brows."[24] Even the overweight arsonist receives Ben's blessing, a smile of benediction, "as though by an effort of sheer yearning he might distill into the boy some current of the love he could not consciously and by daylight extend."[25] This is a scene worthy of a tragic writer like John Cheever. It shows the somber depths which De Vries's larky fiction is able to plumb. Yet finally it is not the tragic vision which animates his work. The comic truth, for all its apparent flippancy, is profounder.

What matters ultimately is not that the Marvel children have fouled up their lives, but that Ben and Alma are reconciled to each other and to life itself. Their brief alienation is overcome as Alma comically invents a neurosis in order to throw off Patchkiss, the marriage expert to whom she has been sent for counsel. She tells him that she sees ping-pong balls bouncing, syllable by syllable, over the words that people speak. The psychologist thinks he has thus fathomed the secret springs of the Marvels' marital trouble. Yet Patchkiss himself starts to see the little white spheres doing their dance over Alma's words. The Marvels' final deliverance takes an even funnier form. Driving back home from New York City, whence they had gone to work things out, Alma thinks wearily "of all they'd been through, of all of the Twentieth Century that had been brought to their old door. What was happening in and to the world?" she muses. "What," she solemnly queries her husband, "are we coming to?" "Connecticut," he replies with a deeply truthful jibe.[26]

This brave new world of ours, despite its wretched discontent, is still the ancient Adamic realm which our species has inhabited for millennia. Its sins and miseries have been but transposed, De Vries suggests, into a new key. While he declines so to state the matter theologically, he holds nonetheless to a truth which is more profoundly religious than secular—the comic conviction that we dwell not, at least yet, amidst the apocalypse but only in "Connecticut." Our disasters are no worse than those that have afflicted other ages. Our lives may not be a bed of roses, but neither are they doomed to the ditch wherein they seem inevitably cast. The novel's title is less bitterly ironic, therefore, than it is oddly affirmative. We pass not through the fires of hell but, by an unaccountable grace, "through the fields of clover." Marriage and family life, assaulted and beleaguered things though they are, remain the most revealing human embodiments of this redemptive passage.

II. Within the Shadow of Doubt: *The Blood of the Lamb*

Peter De Vries comes close to granting marriage a metaphysical status. It is the one unchallenged moral norm, the only social stay against the surrounding void, the single human reality that crosses cultural boundaries and that thus can be accorded virtually religious sanction.[27] Yet as a vestigial Calvinist, De Vries can give final authority to nothing humanly conceived and achieved. While the matrimonial state serves as an enduring metaphor of an unaccountable grace, it can suffice no more than black humor or suave sophistication as an answer to the question of the world's ultimate order and shape. It serves De Vries as a means for confronting the only thing that finally matters: the presence or absence of God.

The fact that De Vries is a comedian does not lessen the gravity of his obsession with the reality of faith. A laughing atheism is indeed all the more chilling than a sober unbelief. In *The Blood of the Lamb*, a character named Stein summarizes most cogently the doubt that is the central concern of De Vries's entire work: "What baffles me," Stein confesses both for himself and for a host of other De Vriesian characters, "is the comfort people find in the idea that somebody dealt this mess. Blind and meaningless chance seems to me so much more congenial—or at least less horrible. Prove to me that there is a God and I will really begin to despair."[28]

Such Karamazovian antitheism lies at the heart of De Vries's fiction. The mere atheistic denial that life has ultimate meaning seems vapid compared to De Vries's concern with the far more troublesome problem of God's conniving cruelty and bungling indifference. If the universe reflects the divine intelligence—so reasons Joe Sandwich in *The Vale of Laughter*—then the only petition worthy of such a God is the one Joe prays: "Give us a break, will Ya!"[29] The atheism of a Camus or a Sartre can seem strangely bracing, but there is no Sisyphean courage to be garnered from De Vries's work. Witness Sandwich's deflating (if also hilarious) description of our evolutionary ascent up from microscopic life:

> "Man is trapped in a biochemical riddle about which he was not consulted, and through which he is hustled to the same oblivion from which he was summoned. That is his lot. He cannot win. He spends a billion years dragging his misbegotten guts across dry land, sometimes in pouring rain, goes up into trees, comes down again, puts on coat and pants, staggers at last into Philharmonic Hall—to find Bruckner a bag of wind. . . ."[30]

Unlike many of his fellow artists and intellectuals, De Vries cannot accept the common secular ploy for dealing with the death of God. The eclipse of transcendent faith is not, for him, the assumed and accepted background against which modern life can be made to trip along as usual. For De Vries as also for Nietzsche, the absence of God is not merely an added difficulty with which our species must learn benignly to cope. It is the single most devastating fact of our existence, a terror beyond any human solution. Yet, unlike Nietzsche, De Vries cannot believe only in nothingness. His doubts are far closer to Job's than to Zarathustra's, and thus far more troublesome.

The suicidal poet McGland puts the matter succinctly in *Reuben, Reuben*: "Worse than Nothing," he says, is the evidence that there "might very well be a malevolent intelligence to whom all our humiliations offer an eternally unfolding comedy."[31] According to McGland, the welkin resounds not with the music of the spheres but with a raucous rendition of "There Is a Fountain Filled with Blood." In this cosmic caprice, the life fluid is drawn from humanity's rather than Immanuel's veins. As a final defiant gesture of despair on the brink of his suicide, McGland thus offers himself his own unholy communion: "This is my body which is broken for some reason [that is] apparently none of my cotton-pickin' chicken-pluckin' goddam business."[32]

De Vries offers no easy religious answers to such radical irreligion. Yet he does treat the problem of unbelief in ways that are comically refreshing. His humorous regard for ultimate questions is revolutionary, I maintain, because it turns the tables on the complacent atheism of our time. Unlike Percy and O'Connor, who satirize naive secularists and believers from an enlightened Christian point of view, De Vries directs his humor against his own convinced apostasy. He parodies paganism from within, in an act of secular self-negation rather than Christian apologetics.

It is unfortunate that *The Blood of the Lamb* should have become De Vries's most famous book, for in many ways it is his least typical novel. Not only is it written in a semisolemn tone that is uncharacteristic of his fiction as a whole; neither is it artistically as well unified as his best novels. Its alternately comic and tragic emphases do not really mesh. The zany beginning jars violently against the elegiac ending, breaking the story into an unreconciled division of parts. Even if the novel's disunity is meant to demonstrate the world's absurdity, De Vries might well have remembered Kafka's dictum that chaos is discernible only amidst order.

Such serious defects notwithstanding, this deeply autobiographical narrative remains an affecting piece of art. Its great power derives, I believe, not from the poignancy wherewith it renders the death of a young girl, nor from the Stoic response it makes to her outrageous dying, but from its Job-like insistence on attributing this outrage to God himself. De Vries's novel thus stands curiously faithful to the revelation which it would seem, and perhaps is intended, to repudiate. Like Job, this writer will not let us escape the terrible fact that it is God with whom we must deal, even if it be God in his hostility. And there is at least one stunning suggestion in *The Blood of the Lamb* that the God who slays is preeminently the God who blesses and resurrects.

Despite the unforgettable quality of little Carol's death, the novel is concerned not chiefly with her but with her father, Don Wanderhope. The daughter is born after the story is already half told, though it is her dying that all of Don's life points toward. If the novel can be said to have a thesis, it is uncheering truth that Wanderhope is woefully unready for what the world does to him; and that, errant as his life may have been, there is nothing he could have done to withstand the awful thing that occurs. This Dutch-descended disciple of Don Juan turns out to be man whose hope has indeed gone wandering. Yet his fate takes several amusing twists before reaching its grim conclusion. His history seems, in fact, to trace the course described in a later aphorism: "There is a point when life, having showered us with jewels for nothing, begins to exact our life's blood for paste."[33]

The Wanderhope of the novel's beginning is a familiar De Vriesian figure: the young blade who has set his face for the boulevards of Babylon and turned his back on the narrow Jerusalem of his Calvinist upbringing. He is another backwards pilgrim toiling downward from the City of God toward the City of Man: "The urbane drawl, the prattled wit, the indifference to the answers at the other end—supplying just the right tincture of snobbishness—were the sort of thing one had in mind."[34]

He wants off South Halstead Street and into the intellectual chic of Hyde Park and the University of Chicago. His brother Louie is a student there. He is also a hero of the skepticism which Don already espouses and which he will find life repeatedly vindicating. The first confirmation of Wanderhope's incipient atheism comes when Louie dies a rapid death from pneumonia, or rather when the minister intercedes for Louie in the name of a God who strikes Wanderhope as a monster:

> My sensation, rather than fear or piety, was a baffled and uncomprehending rage. That flesh with which I had lain in comradely embrace [was] destroyable, on such short notice, by a whim known as divine? . . . Who wantonly scattered such charm, who broke such flesh like bread for his purposes? In later years, years which brought me to another such vigil over one more surely my flesh and blood, I came to understand a few things about what people believe. What people believe is a measure of what they suffer. "The Lord giveth and the Lord taketh away"—there must be balm of some sort in that for men whose treasures have been confiscated. These displaced Dutch fisherfolk, these farmers peddling coal and ice in a strange land, must have had their reasons for worshipping a God scarcely distinguishable from the devil they feared. But the boy [young Don himself] kneeling on the parlor floor was shut off from such speculatory solaces. All the theologies inherent in the minister's winding drone came down to this: Believe in God and don't put anything past him. Or another thought formed itself in the language of the street in which the boy had learned crude justice and mercy: *Why doesn't He pick on somebody his size?*"[35]

Because human existence is not long endurable at the precipice of such an abyss, we are given respite from Job's quandary by means of Don's comic progression through the stages along life's way. Perhaps the funniest of these episodes occurs amidst his adolescent entanglement with a girl named Greta Wigbaldy, who is later to become his wife. Finding them in bed together, Mrs. Wigbaldy fumbles at first in her native Dutch and then shrieks malappropriately in her borrowed tongue. "Prude!" she calls the villainous Wanderhope. "Slut!" she adds with even more inaccurate gratuity.[36] Even these wildly errant epithets contain a poignancy typical of De Vries's humor as a whole. Mrs. Wigbaldy is a woman made to face a reality for which she is hopelessly unprepared. Her furious stray shots are not mere non sequiturs; they are eloquently misfired confessions of the same human helplessness which Wanderhope will himself have to confront in a far more terrible form.

A similarly affecting humor underlies Wanderhope's adventures as a garbageman. Having enrolled at the secularized Baptist university on the Midway, Don spends his youthful summers and Saturdays helping pay his expenses by assisting his father. The elder Wanderhope has graduated from ice hauling to garbage collection. Much to Don's displeasure, Ben Wanderhope has redundantly named his company "Sanitary Sanitation." In a scene that outdoes anything in either Kafka or Beckett for bleak metaphysical humor, the father backs their truck too near the edge of the garbage dump. It is indeed a fetid Gehenna into which they fall. Perhaps it was this event that unhinged Ben Wanderhope and landed him in an insane asylum known popularly as "Chock Full o' Nuts." As father and son sink with their machine into the rubbish, the once-skeptical Ben finds himself reverting to the Psalmist's faith: "I will lift up mine eyes unto the hills," he affirms amidst their descent into offal. "He will save Israel, and that right early." The elder Wanderhope finally surfaces wearing a cantaloupe rind like a beret. Though Don and Ben are both saved, this scene remains one of De Vries's most arresting Conradian images of what is deeply comic in our human desperation:

> We had to call to one another (and my father to the Lord) above the noise of the truck, the engine of which had all this time continued to run. Now it stopped, asphyxiated by refuse, and rolled over on its back. An overturned motor vehicle is an unnerving sight, in some ways more so than a demolished one. Its exposed wheels and underside make it resemble some monstrous helpless beast, and it is this "helplessness," paradoxically, that gives it for the moment the look of something other than mechanical. Our truck lay in this position for only a few seconds. Then it began to roll and tumble down the slope in the avalanche it had itself unloosed. The horror of this was followed instantly by a worse. The box on which my father stood was sucked away in the landslide—or perhaps I should say garbageslide—and he disappeared from view, singing the doxology.[37]

Such an apt metaphor of the human plight might have been the means for a proper transition to the novel's ever darkening latter half. Instead, De Vries has Wanderhope contract tuberculosis and undertake his recovery in a Colorado sanatorium. There he meets still more instances of the unexplained suffering that will soon fall upon him with Hardy-esque fatality. Yet the shift from comedy to tragedy is too sudden, and this gallery of the fated seems too obvious a foreshadowing of things to come. Wanderhope falls quickly in love with tubercular Rena Baker, and they engage in brittle Arnoldian meditations on human affection as the only answer to universal extinction. When Rena dies, Don likens her passing to the death of an animal he hears cry in the brush, "where nature was also keeping itself in balance. 'Thou shalt not kill.' This was advertised as the law of someone who had also created a universe in which one thing ate another. Were not believers aware of the holes a single thought tore in their fabric? Perfect love did not quite cast out fear, but rage did grief, or nearly so."[38]

A man cannot live by rage alone, however justified. Thus does Wanderhope find himself falling in love again with Greta Wigbaldy. He meets her (all too improbably) at the same mental hospital where his father had also been sent. Whether out of pity or love, Don marries her. Like his father, Greta remains distracted by religion. The Calvinist obsession with total depravity fills her with a guilt that neither repeated affairs nor repeated conversions can assuage. She ends by killing herself, but not before she has given birth to their precious Carol.

As sole parent to this child, Wanderhope finds his whole life centering around her. It is indeed a sentimental situation from which De Vries is able to extract the maximum emotional power. This effect is enormously heightened when Carol falls ill and dies of leukemia. Yet it is not the pathos of her suffering that is the novel's chief concern. De Vries depicts Carol's death, instead, as a metaphysical injustice of Dostoevskian proportions. And he makes Don Wanderhope ask why, like Ivan Karamazov, one should not return one's ticket to life in the face of such an outrage.

So lovely a girl is Carol that Wanderhope virtually idolizes her. "This was a dream of a child," he says. "Hair like cornsilk, blue bird's-wings eyes, and a carriage that completed the resemblance of a fairy sprite. One would not have been surprised to see her take off and fly away in a glimmer of unsuspected wings."[39] Had De Vries centered his dénouement on the dying girl, the result would have been an embarrassing effusion of sentiment. He chooses wisely to focus the narrative on Wanderhope himself. Against Carol's death, the desperate Don can throw up no stronger bulwark than a modern Stoic creed he writes during a time when Carol's leukemia has gone into remission. As a final gift to her father, the dying daughter makes her own tape-recorded version of this somber paean to human sufficiency. Wanderhope quotes it again in full upon discovering Carol's declaration that it enabled her to face death. Perhaps De Vries wants thus to emphasize how fully this is his own testament of faith:

"I believe that man must learn to live without those consolations called religious, which his own intelligence must by now have told him belong to the childhood of the race. Philosophy can really give us nothing permanent to believe either; it is too rich in answers, each cancelling out the rest. The quest for Meaning is foredoomed. Human life 'means' nothing. But that is not to say that it is not worth living. What does a Debussy *Arabesque* 'mean,' or a rainbow or a rose? A man delights in all of these, knowing himself to be no more—a wisp of music and a haze of dreams dissolving against the sun. Man has only his own two feet to stand on, his own human trinity to see him through: Reason, Courage, and Grace. And the first plus the second equals the third."[40]

The remarkable thing about this humanist manifesto is not its content—an eloquent amalgam of secular wisdom—but the pressure and opposition to which De Vries subjects it. He does not allow it to stand as an all-sufficient answer to the problem of suffering and evil. On the contrary, Wanderhope remains obsessed with the God whom he claims not to believe but whom he rightly blames for Carol's death. Persuaded by the child's nurse, Mrs. Brodhag, to pray for his dying daughter before a shrine to St. Jude, Don "sank to the floor and, squeezing wet eyes to hands clenched into one fist, uttered the single cry, 'No!'"[41] This is not the acceptance of a serene Stoic but the protest of a latter-day Job.

Don meets still more opposition to his humanist faith when he and Carol go to visit the addled Ben Wanderhope for the last time. The sanatorium doctor confronts Wanderhope with unanticipated faith by asking God's blessings on him and his leukemic daughter. "You believe in Him?" Don asks. "And in man," replies the psychiatrist, "which is a hell of a lot harder. Still there are times when we can, for which one is glad."[42] For a novel whose theme is the necessity of unbelief, this is a strangely Pauline confession about the trust in God which enables faith in one's fellows.

Wanderhope's humanism meets an even fiercer test in an atheist Jew named Stein. This man has been so embittered by his experience of senseless suffering that he has turned sour and nihilistic. He has no more faith in science than in religion. Science reveals that cancer is nothing other than nature's prolific anarchy: "A souvenir from the primordial ooze. The original Chaos, without form and void. In de beginning was de void, and de void was vit God. Mustn't say the naughty void."[43] Such raucous nihilism makes Hemingway's famous invocation of "Our father who art in nada" seem pious by comparison. Like Hank Tattersall, Stein bites down on the aching tooth of his own unbelief, declaring that there is no difference between "a martyr giving his life, [and] a criminal taking one. It's all the same to the All."[44]

Though Stein has grimly restated Wanderhope's own atheist creed, Don will not accept it in this misanthropic form. "I can't believe that," he replies.[45] Wanderhope's spiritual task is the one faced by all humanists: how to retain Stein's tough-minded skepticism while avoiding his disillusionment with life. This is why Wanderhope calls Stein "the goalkeeper past whom I must get my puck."[46] Stein represents pure unillusioned truthfulness, an unblinkered candor about nature's ruthlessness. Wanderhope wants to combine such human reason with a no less human courage in order to produce a distinctively human grace. Rationality alone issues in Stein's anger and hatred. Courage alone results in a cold Stoic pride. But when the two are suffused with a gracious acceptance and humility, a new secular trinity is born. Reason plus courage equals grace.

Such an antitheistic humanism explains why De Vries has Wanderhope invert the central Christian affirmation. It is not Christ who is the Lamb slain from the foundation of the world, but little Carol herself who is the innocent creature needlessly destroyed by Nature. Don addresses her, in fact, as his "lamb." He strokes her hair as "precious fleece." And he calls her needle marks and incisions "stigmata." De Vries has Carol die, as James Bowden notes, not only at the hour when children are frolicking their way home from school, but also when Jesus dies: three o'clock in the afternoon.[47] The abandonment which occurred at Calvary is not a substitutionary atonement wrought by Christ, De Vries suggests, but a fearful sign of God's perpetual truancy in the hour of human anguish.

There are moments when Wanderhope attempts to put a religious construction on Carol's death. Left alone briefly with her just before she dies, Don whispers a biblical benediction over Carol. On the whole, however, her dying is a terribly secular event. Its only apparent meaning lies in inconsolable," he concludes, "thanks to that eternal 'Why', . . . that Carol dies, he angrily flings away the crucifix he has been carrying in his pocket, as if in final recognition that he must suffice unto himself. "Man is inconsolable," he concludes, "thanks to that eternal 'Why?', . . . that question mark twisted like a fishhook in the human heart." Once again Don reverses the place of humanity and divinity. We mortals cry "Let there be light," only to discover another dawn.[48] Absent any ultimate answers, Wanderhope finds it necessary to make an ironic inversion of the Reformers' claim that salvation is given *sola gratia*. "We are indeed saved by grace in the end—but to give, not take."[49] The only goodness is what we engender and sustain ourselves, not what we receive from the bloody-minded God.

For Wanderhope, as it would seem also for De Vries, there is something other than bitterness to be gained from such bitter experience. Don finds consolation in remembering that Carol gave him "a dozen years of perfection," that a poem is no less a poem for being short rather than long, and that most people never experience so wondrous a gift as was his. Though God seems absent, or perhaps present in a demonic way, Wanderhope concludes that we humans can generate at least a modicum of the mercy which the universe lacks. The memory of Carol herself, the innocent slain lamb, will be his sufficient grace. She is the golden-haired angel who now bars his entrance to the Western Gate of suicide, as he calls it. For her sake he must resume the burden of life. He must make her death an occasion for sympathy rather than despair. He must join the myriads of other mourners who sit on the long bench of sadness, "arms linked in undeluded friendship, all of us, brief links, ourselves, in the eternal pity."[50] On such a somber note does this very somber novel end.

De Vries's portrayal of Carol's death makes for a wrenchingly powerful antitheodicy. Wanderhope describes his dead child, almost too painfully, as looking "like some mangled flower, or like a bird that had been pelted to earth in a storm." He frankly confesses his inability to sustain his Stoic self-mastery when Carol dies. He cannot remain impassive and unruffled before the extinction of his own daughter: "As for the dignity of man, this one drew forth a square of cloth, and, after honking like a goose, pocketed his tears."[51] Yet the effect is not gruesome or macabre. Here is a man, we are made to feel, who is responding with rightful rage and grief at an event of surpassing sadness. Any theodicy worthy of the name must able to confront the awful reality of human suffering as De Vries has so unforgettably described it. The fact that De Vries has Wanderhope sentimentally idealize the dying Carol into a virtual Christ does not diminish the power of his anti-Christian critique.

The extraordinary irony implicit in the novel is that one does not have to look beyond it to glimpse an answer to its own dark denial of God's goodness. For there is a single scene where De Vries has Wanderhope forsake his self-obsessed grief. It is a moment carefully foreshadowed by a discussion Carol has with her friend Omar about the stylized character of slapstick comedy, and especially the ceremony of pie throwing. The comic who throws the first pie, Carol explains, makes no attempt to defend against the pie he must surely receive in return. Wanderhope italicizes his daughter's explanation of the comedian's act: "*He just stands there and takes it. He even waits for it. . . .*"[52]

Nor is the event ended once the villain becomes the victim. "Then when he gets it, he still waits a second before wiping it out of his eyes, doing it deliberately, kind of solemn, as though the whole thing is a ———" Her friend Omar supplies the crucial word: "ritual."[53] The point of comedy's ceremonial swap, De Vries makes clear, is to acknowledge that life is never a single-sided business, never an affair of simple good vs. simple evil. Victims rightly protesting their suffering—whether by flinging a Jobian taunt or a meringue pie—may also be committing an injustice. There is no easy calculus of right and wrong. The accuser must be prepared thus to become the accused.

Such is the essence of the exchange Wanderhope has with the figure of Christ on the day of Carol's death. Staggering with both grief and drink, Don remembers the cake he had brought for Carol but accidentally left behind in a Catholic church where he had stopped to say one last desperate prayer for her recovery. In a gesture of pure fury, Wanderhope flings the confection at the crucifix hanging over the church door. Yet this final sacrilege is mysteriously transformed into a momentary image of the grace that Wanderhope otherwise misses. Perhaps it is Wanderhope who, in his justified anger, also stands accused. He has himself inflicted injury out of his justified grief at so grievous loss. And yet God in his mercy blesses this revolt against his own seeming monstrousness. In what is surely the novel's most discerning scene, Don envisions Christ as a comedian observing the slapstick ceremony of thrown pastries. He wipes the icing from his eyes "very slowly, very deliberately, with infinite patience. . . . Then the cheeks were wiped down with the same sense of grave and gentle ritual, with all the kind sobriety of one whose voice could be heard saying 'Suffer the little children to come unto me . . . for of such is the kingdom of heaven.'"[54]

Here De Vries approaches, whether by intention or inadvertence, the wisdom of Ecclesiastes, the Psalms of lament, and the Book of Job. The last does not concern the patience of Job—as conventional piety would have it—but the patience of God. The divine grace is displayed not only in permitting, but actually in sanctioning, Job's fearful complaint against the suffering that God himself causes. Job's enemy is not the Adversary who wagers that Job's faithfulness will last only as long as his prosperity. Job's disheartenment comes from God himself, from the good God who has become wicked: "Thou hast turned cruel to me; with the might of thy hand thou dost persecute me" (Job 30:21).

Were Job a mere pagan, his problem would not thus be compounded. It is his very faithfulness which, paradoxically, increases both his misery and his hope. Job can neither curse God nor die by his own hand. In either case, he would be cutting himself off from the One with whom, for good or ill, he must deal. Like Wanderhope, Job would have been faithless had he not raised his bitter objection. In the name of the revealed God, he protests against this unknown deity who rejects and assaults him. Finally, therefore, the faithful Job is vindicated as his faithless friends are not. They are wrong for denying that God has done awful things to Job without apparent cause. Job is right for insisting that human misery and human desert have no necessary connection.

Job is justified, Karl Barth argues, not only as he repents in dust and ashes, but also as he rails against the God who proclaims himself merciful but seems altogether monstrous. Just as the Christ over the church door patiently wipes away the cake Wanderhope has flung in his face, so is God long-suffering with those who, like Job, are willing to contend with him. And just as Yahweh prompts Job's fury by acting in an alien manner, so does the same Yahweh answer and justify Job on his own terms rather then Job's. Job is not obliterated with a sense of his own worthlessness. Instead, God honors Job's freedom by asking him to serve (as the Adversary contends Job will not) *for nought*—with no prior claim that God's world rule must conform to Job's own idea of it. As Barth explains:

> In [God's autonomy of will and purpose] He always in some degree encounters, confronts and opposes man in a way which is sinister, strange, disquieting and even terrifying. He does not ask for his understanding, agreement or applause. On the contrary, He simply asks that he should be content not to know why and to what end he exists. . . . that he should admit that it is not he who plans and controls. . . . that he should concede that he has nothing to do with his course and direction. . . . What is brought forward in these speeches of Yahweh is not His blind superiority to man, but His questioning whether man can really think that the cosmos is his cosmos and belongs and listens to him. Can he really think that it is ordered according to his ideas, wishes, purposes and plans, that it must be the *theatrum* of his *gloria* and guarantee of his *felicitas* or at least of his *securitas?*[55]

These are difficult sayings even as Job is a difficult book. To live amidst the mystery and pain of creation, the Book of Job suggests, requires the humility of faith. That a work of literature should contain no such call to divine trust and obedience is not surprising. It is not the function of fiction to serve as the revelation of God—to have the Lord speak directly to Don Wanderhope as he does to Job: "Gird up your loins like a man; I will question you, and you declare to me. Will you even put me in the wrong? Will you condemn me that you may be justified?" (Job 40:7–8). De Vries does indeed have Wanderhope "put God in the wrong." Repeatedly, and altogether like Job, his characters declare that God is not himself a Christian. They join Job in darkening "counsel by words without knowledge" (Job 38:2).

Yet in his insistence on holding God accountable to his own divine character and promise, Don Wanderhope remains one of Yahweh's servants. He does not seek to justify his own goodness. On the contrary, he sinks down beneath the crucifix he has just splattered with cake, confessing that "the only alternative to the muzzle of a pistol [is] the foot of the

Cross."[56] This is not a vision that Don Wanderhope can long sustain. Yet, if only for the briefest moment, he glimpses the comic truth that Peter De Vries's fiction serves unwittingly to attest: Christ can take all the flung pies of human fury because he is the Clown who has borne our griefs and carried our sorrows, the Jester who is smitten of God, the Fool who, knowing no evil, was made sin that "we might become the righteousness of God" (II Cor. 5:21).

III. Calvinistic Anti-Calvinism: *The Mackerel Plaza*

Peter De Vries's comic sense is deeply muted in *The Blood of the Lamb*, perhaps because it was written in painful remembrance of his own daughter's leukemic death. Although *The Mackerel Plaza* (1958) is an earlier book, it is much more typical of De Vries's work as a whole, and especially of his comic attitude toward religion. Yet it is a book which is easy to misread. De Vries's satire of the Reverend Andrew Mackerel's tepid liberalism is so blistering that one might think the author to be an orthodox apologist for Christianity. The truth is that Mackerel's creed is not far removed from the humanist faith which Don Wanderhope advocates and which De Vries seems personally to espouse. Both men are secularists haunted by traditional belief and yet unable to affirm any of the central Christian claims.

Why, then, is the one treated sympathetically and the other satirically? I contend that Mackerel is the object of De Vries's comic attack because he is a humanist without any real humanity, an atheist undoubtful of his doubts, a cynic unwilling to turn sour on his sourness—which is also to say that Mackerel has no real sense of humor. He is an unskeptical skeptic who is thus fair game for De Vries's comic art. But De Vries does more than negate Mackerel's negativism. Whether intentionally or not, the novel makes an oblique affirmation of the very faith which author and character alike would seem to have abandoned.

Like Don Wanderhope, Andrew Mackerel is the teller of his own tale. They are both sufficiently self-aware and articulate to narrate the recent events around which their respective novels center. But there the resemblance ends. Wanderhope's first-person narration takes the form of a confession, a poignant personal memoir about the way his life has come unravelled. Mackerel, by contrast, writes an *apologia pro vita sua*, a testy vindication of his own sanity and an angry accusation of the world's madness. De Vries's authorial stance toward the two narrators is thus quite different. Since Wanderhope's self-description is essentially straightforward and true, there is no need to undercut him. But since Mackerel's personal account is defensive and self-justifying, De Vries conspires with his readers to subvert nearly everything Mackerel says and does. Indeed, the whole novel is a witty unmasking of Mackerel's delusions about himself and the world.

We know something is awry upon discovering that Mackerel sometimes speaks of himself in the third person. The problem is not excess modesty but its opposite. He describes himself objectively, he confesses, "in relating things about which I am a trifle self-conscious."[57] Chief among the matters which make Mackerel proudly self-aware are the accomplishments of his church and its ministry. He is the pastor of People's Liberal Church, "the first split-level church in America." As a congregation long on relevance and short on belief, their church is designed to meet the needs of "the whole man." Its physical arrangements include a ballroom, a parlor, a gymnasium, a theater, an expandable psychiatric wing, but no sanctuary at all—only "a small worship area at one end." In deference to higher biblical criticism, the pulpit is built of four differing fruitwoods—a witness to the failure of the Gospels to harmonize. A huge interdenominational mobile has been placed in the foyer of the church, less in fear than in celebration of "the Pauline stricture against those 'blown by every wind of doctrine.'"[58]

This swinging congregation does not tremble at the thought of heresy. Its only dread is that it might be something less than totally current. These latter-day religiosi want their faith to accord with their lives: up-to-date, suave, sophisticated, and utterly without offense. They dwell in Avalon, Connecticut, amidst what Mackerel calls "hand-to-mouth luxury, never knowing where their next quarterly installment of taxes or the payment on their third car is coming from."[59] When a flood strikes a nearby town, these uncomprehending party-goers send cocktail snacks to the victims: "vichyssoise, artichoke hearts, smoked clams and even trout *paté*."[60] For all that is avant-garde about the Reverend Mackerel, even he is taken aback by the vision of the distraught flood victims sitting on the roofs of their floating homes while eating tomato aspic and calf's-foot jelly.

About the adequacy of his own theology, Mackerel has no misgivings whatsoever. More than a decade before the death-of-God phenomenon, he is already a convinced necrotheologian. "The final proof of God's omnipotence," he announces unironically, is that "he need not exist in order to save us."[61] It is the idea and not the reality of God that matters. The grand abstraction called God enshrines, for Mackerel, the noblest values of the human species. It represents all of humanity's skull-cracking attempts to explain the universe and to project mundane meaning into cosmic terms. Like Feuerbach, Mackerel believes that the calling of true Christianity is to declare its own bankruptcy: "theology, by annihilating itself, sets religion free."[62]

It's as if Mackerel had made a positive slogan out of Karl Barth's

scandalous declaration that "religion is unbelief." For while this modernist minister has great regard for religion as a human thing, he has no use
at all for Jesus as the true revelation of God. Mackerel's prophetic ire can
be kindled only when a church member has a "Jesus Saves" billboard
erected outside the pastor's window. Furious at this threat to aesthetic
and economic values, Mackerel screams at the Zoning Board recep-
tionist: "How do you expect me to write a sermon with that thing staring me in the face? How do you expect me to turn out anything fit for
civilized consumption?"[63]

De Vries's parody of what is banal and vapid in mainline American
Protestantism is so wildly comic that we are tempted to regard Mackerel
as a mere caricature. He is in fact an uncanny proleptic version of those
Protestant theologians who, upon discovering Nietzsche as if stumbling
upon a fifth Gospel, began in the mid-1960s to speak of God as having
died in our time, and of true faith as the willingness to affirm this demise
of the late deity. Surely the most celebrated of these "Christian atheists"
is Thomas Jefferson Jackson Altizer. He speaks in Mackerel's very mode:

> Only by accepting and even willing the death of God in our ex-
> perience can we be liberated from a transcendent beyond, an alien
> beyond which has been emptied and darkened by God's self-annihi-
> lation in Christ. To the extent that we attempt to cling to a trans-
> cendent realm, a realm that has become ever darker and emptier in
> our actual experience, we must be closed to the actual presence of
> the living Christ, and alienated from the contemporary movement
> of the divine process. . . . We know the finality of the Incarnation by
> knowing that God is dead; and once we fully live the death of God,
> we will be liberated from the temptation to return to an epiphany
> of deity which is present only in the past. . . . A truly contemporary
> Christ cannot become present to us until we ourselves have died to
> every shadow and fragment of his transcendent image.[64]

It is tempting to dismiss such vaticinations as gibberish worthy
only of satirical derision. But Altizer is no mere atheist, and neither is
Mackerel. As Langdon Gilkey has noted, Altizer "does not believe for a
moment that the divine is unreal or nonexistent. By no means a
naturalistic, humanistic theologian, Altizer is inspired by a mystical
awareness of, dependence on, and waiting for the divine power that manifests itself in current life and in history."[65]

Just as Altizer believes in a wholly immanent God, so does Mackerel's deity reside totally within the human sphere. Yet there is a stark
difference between the two theologies, and the difference redounds to
Mackerel's credit. He has the courage to admit that, when the transcendent God is eclipsed, we are left not with a new immanent deity who
somehow saves us through the dialectical processes of history, but with

an Idea which we ourselves are obligated to keep desperately afloat. Mackerel's aim is thus to preserve the cultural and moral core which lies at the heart of Christian faith, while sloughing off the rind which encases it:

I believe in belief. I believe that some binding ethic and some informing myth are necessary to any culture, the myth being to the morality what the wooden forms are to the concrete that is poured into them, in building construction. When the concrete is hard you can remove the forms (or they will rot away) and the walls will stand of their own. Has Western man reached the point where his ethical walls will stand without the forms of his faith? You tell me, after thinking a moment about our sexual, drinking, and crime records, our political and business practices, and the present behavior of a crop of teen-agers raised without religious instruction. But I believe that a faith is a set of demands, not a string of benefits, that a man is under some obligation to better himself, not sit around and wait for Jesus to save him.[66]

The comedy implicit in such a passage is at once sardonic and sympathetic. It is indeed silly to call for belief in belief, and to speak of Jesus as the lord of loafers. Yet it is also true that a culture without ethics cannot long stand, and that humanists must place their faith in something akin to an "informing myth" if there be no redeeming God. De Vries is not satirizing Mackerel's humanism so much as his ludicrous overconfidence in it. Like the death-of-God theologians during the succeeding decade, Mackerel immodestly turns necessity into virtue. What should remain at best a reluctant confession—namely, that humanity can rely only upon the light it generates for itself—becomes an evangelical call to arms. "Dearly beloved," Mackerel begins one of his sermons, "the Bible is at worst a hodgepodge of myths, superstitions and theologies [which are utterly] repugnant to a man of taste and sensibility, let alone a true Christian. . . . "[67] Yet the illusory character of our fondest beliefs does not diminish their ethical and psychological value. "Indeed, the more void the universe may be of meaning, the more precious the lanterns by which man picks his little way through it."[68] Hence Mackerel's conviction that evolution does not occur as a biological inevitability. He has written a book arguing the thesis that humanity has a moral *obligation* to evolve. Its title is revealingly, but of course unconsciously, redundant: *Maturity Comes of Age.*

Gradually and ever so comically, this overardent humanist is cooled down to the humble recognition that humans cannot live by humanism alone. Among the instruments of Mackerel's return to sanity is a character named Frank Turnbull. He is a lecher who fears that, in punishment for his sins, he may have bequeathed his obsessive sensuality to his son. He is a preppy young educationist-cum-psychologist who has written and privately published a term paper entitled "*Some Notes Toward an Examination of Possible Elements of Unconscious Homosexuality in Mutt and Jeff.*"[69] Chiefly, however, it is his own sin that Turnbull wants to confess to his pastor. Mackerel will hear none of it. He explains Turnbull's fornications as mere "carnal peccancies" which spring from middle-aged terror at the loss of libido. But Turnbull, as his name indicates, is not to be averted. He insists that the fashionable emphasis on guilt misses the real horror of sin: the violation of God himself.

Turnbull believes, indeed, that the human condition requires salvation and not mere medication. Jesus—so Turnbull catechizes his own minister—saves us from sin, which otherwise damns us to hell. But Mackerel remains heedless. "Forget about Jesus," he tells this poor penitent. "Try to get a whole new viewpoint."[70] When Turnbull pleads that he is a miserable offender, a "guilty, life-long, rotten, damnable sinner," Mackerel accuses him of putting on "airs."[71] "Poor man, that he needs the doctrine of the Fall to invest him with a little glamour! Pitiful ego, that must sit in sackcloth and ashes and fancy itself the butt of Reprobation."[72] Thus does this minister of the Gospel count his sin-laden parishioner as hopelessly lost in faith:

> "Another backslider," I thought wearily. It was this damned religious revival. They were everywhere, these converts, defecting to pie-in-the-sky from the hard-won positions to which they have been urged and hauled by rational and honest men. Looking at the codger, I thought, Can this man be educated? Or is he beyond salvation?[73]

The real question is, of course, whether Mackerel can be salvaged from his foolish complacency about human self-rescue. As is ever the case in DeVries's fiction, women are the means for Mackerel's recovery of the truth. First there is Molly Calico, a secretary who would appear to be no more than a delectable dunce. The recently widowed Mackerel finds her so desirable that, though ordinarily an unbiblical minister, he is forced to quote Scripture. "Hope deferred maketh the heart sick," he laments.[74] With the Psalmist he cries, "How long, O Lord, how long?"[75] Yet Molly has sense enough to know that Mackerel does not desire her so much as what she symbolizes. Like Kierkegaard's Seducer, Mackerel cares for Molly only as she forms an instance of the romantic ideal, a Hollywood fabrication best presented by Kim Novak. The actress's appeal, says Mackerel, lies not in her gorgeous body but in her "sheer incorporeality. She was impalpable. She was a soft gold cloud of a girl, who drifted through scene after scene of the utmost intimacy without being *there*. . . . She was flawlessly present, weaving an abstraction called love."[76]

No wonder that Molly refuses to play Isolde to Mackerel's Tristan. She is no mere impersonal embodiment of the male dream, but a woman filled with real passion—with the suffering and ache that make her irreducibly human. It is not surprising, therefore, that their long-awaited rendezvous turns out to be a comic misadventure. Mackerel, forgetting to take a key, leaves their hotel room in search of something to eat. Molly, made nervous by the impropriety of the whole affair, takes a sedative and falls into deep sleep. All of Mackerel's attempts to reenter the room prove fruitless.

What was to have been their luscious first night in bed Mackerel spends watching a third-rate movie and eating stale pastrami sandwiches in the seedy hotel lobby. When Mackerel finally awakens Molly the next morning, he is too weary for amorous play. So there they lie chastely in bed, "cherishing the carnal jewel of purity," as Mackerel calls their erotic failure.[77] In the end, Molly leaves Mackerel for a new career in Florida, where she sings underwater television commercials through a snorkel. Yet she departs only after a final blast at the childish pretension that passes as moral and religious "emancipation" among such sophisticates as Mackerel. "Oh, Jesus, you intellectuals," she shouts.

> "You with your Baudelaires, all of you, and your infinite weariness, and your cultural patterns and your Voltaires and your Rimbauds and [your] recurring symbols in Faulkner and now it's Dylan Thomas. Oh you intellectuals," she cried again, "smoking your literary cornsilk behind the barn of——of——I don't know what," she said, letting the metaphor collapse.[78]

The other woman who enters Mackerel's life is Hester Pedlock, the housekeeper who also happens to be the sister of the minister's deceased wife. Although, as her name suggests, Hester possesses the sexual vitality of her Hawthornian namesake, she is no lascivious live-in maid. She insists that the carnal life be lived within the bounds of marital fidelity. She wills, in short, to padlock Mackerel in wedlock—the institution which would, perhaps, give substance to his abstract lust and his abstract religion. De Vries's hilarious plot convolutions trace Mackerel's failure to escape this marriage, even as he failed to maneuver Molly into bed. Like Ms. Calico, Ms. Pedlock is also a woman of real spiritual substance. In a very uncomic scene toward the end, she confesses that she secretly hated her sister, that she was jealous of her from the day she married Mackerel, and that she welcomed her death. Hester makes Andrew discern the nihilism that lurks beneath the frivolity of their lives:

> "I had this overwhelming need to——to heap the awful truth over, to bury it as deep as possible, smother it the way we do death with flowers anyway. It's the same as your drive to *believe*

when you know there really isn't anything to believe. Like in that awful poem of MacLeish's where the top of the tent blows off and there's nothing—nothing, nothing at all. Well, let's *make* something. Let's bury the awfulness and the nothingness with [a] something-ness we've made with our own two hands. Let's make the lie so big and convincing, and worship it so bitterly, bitterly much, that it becomes a truth."[79]

This is an uncommonly somber confession for an uproariously comic novel. It shows how serious a writer De Vries really is, despite the popular view that he is a mere stuntman. Yet even as he confronts the ugly truth, De Vries insists on dealing with it comically rather than tragically. Hester and Andrew escape their slide into the Void, not by desperately clawing their way out, but by humorously falling into freedom. Their serendipitous deliverance is provided chiefly through Mackerel's dead wife Ida May, and through the memorial which his parishioners have erected in her honor.

Having preached to his flock from the semanticist Korzybski rather than the Apostle Paul, Mackerel has repeatedly stressed the importance of "time-binding"—the human ability to transfer cultural values from one generation to the next. Thus does Mackerel make evolutionary progress take the place of eschatological hope. Faithful to their pastor's worldly gospel, his congregation has persuaded the town fathers to erect the Ida May Mackerel Memorial Shopping Plaza. Its aim is to preserve the value-laden memory of their minister's dead wife. Prophetic as always, De Vries hilariously heralds—a quarter century in advance—the coming of the "wellness" movement. For at the Plaza's center there is a wishing well where visitors may toss in coins and make remembrance of the extinct Ida May. This memorial cistern has as its premise the conviction that "if there were more well wishers (that is, people wishing others well) the world would be more well and less sick than it is now."[80]

The Reverend Mackerel refuses, of course, to admit that the memorial plaza is a comic revelation of his own ministerial inanity. He cannot see that his unreconstructed humanism, when preached as a positive gospel, translates into something as trite and literal as well-wishing. His congregation is frantic for a heroine because it has been denied a Savior. Nor does the late Mrs. Mackerel prove a worthy paragon. She was originally believed to have drowned while trying to save a sinking man, and to have leapt into the water though unable to swim. Later evidence indicates that she may have fallen through her own fault, or even that Mackerel may have pushed her. Yet the pastor of People's Liberal remains opaque to the webbed connection of it all: his own moral bankruptcy, his parishioners' spiritual vapidity, and his sermons preached on such topics as the superiority of American over British pronunciation. To this last, an enthusiastic Harvardian responds not with an "Amen" but with "Hyah! Hyah!"[81]

With his every attempt to elude the truth, Mackerel ensnares himself more tightly in it. At first he tries to make himself a martyr to the philistinism of the city councilmen who approved the building of the Mackerel Plaza. But the more he comports himself as a Marxist enemy of the capitalist myth, the greater their tolerance and understanding.

> "Social elements thus in opposition," [Mackerel pontificates], "enact dramatico-metaphoric embodiments of tribal drives which are at the same time religious in nature. . . . The Mackerel Plaza is an example of such a myth in our time and in our place. . . . It unites your material with your instinctual interests, and having embraced it as sacrosanct, you will defend it with every resource at your command."
>
> "We will?" the mayor said, screwing his face up.[82]

So all-approving are the sheep of Mackerel's flock that they are not a whit scandalized when their minister is thrown in jail for fighting with a street-corner evangelist. Like their leader, they oppose vulgarity in all its forms. Indeed, they welcome him back into the pulpit, raising "their voices in the strains of 'Funiculi-funicula.'"[83] Mackerel finally oversteps his bounds by indulging in outrageous sexual word play from the pulpit. Even then, he is not fired but remanded to the church's mental health clinic. Far from being the end of Mackerel's troubles, this therapeutic retreat proves to be yet another stage in his comic undoing. There he confronts a psychiatrist named Von Pantz, who has recently been converted from believing that people need to be cured to believing that they need to be saved. Announcing to the startled Mackerel that he is "in the grip of sin," Von Pantz transfixes his preacher with the question he least wants to hear: "Reverend Mackerel, do you now and before God, accept Jesus Christ as your personal savior?"[84]

Mackerel will have none of this "godforsaken theology," as he wildly misnames it. He prefers his own gospel of ethical evolution—the sweating trek "up from the muck on this rotten ball and . . . into something resembling human grace and wit and beauty."[85] As a doubter of divine providence, Mackerel vehemently opposes an ecumenical prayer service beseeching God to end the terrible drought afflicting their region. This hater of all things religious snidely disdains the prayer effort as "the community rain dance."[86] When the Lord provides an all too miraculous flood—a cloudburst from a cloudless sky—Mackerel dismisses it as "Jehovah's wetness."[87]

Such cynicism is of little avail. His secular confidence has been crushed by a miracle. "I have no more faith," Mackerel laments.[88] As long as he was assured that humanity can rest only upon its own cultural achievements, he could call himself a religious secularist. "If there was Nothing," he had reasoned, "so much the more need to tend to your own visions of truth, beauty and goodness."[89] Now that he has been made to face the "personal God whose nonexistence was the mast to which I nailed my flag,"[90] Mackerel is ready to despair. A God who answers the prayers of bores and dullards and bigots is definitely not of Mackerel's class. He might *believe* in a God who sends alternate droughts and floods, but Mackerel refuses to *worship* him. Such a God is an offense against good taste, a threat to property values, and a peril to humanity itself. The proper question is not whether Jesus is the Son of God, Mackerel insists, but whether Christ would claim so unpaternal a Being as his Father. Mackerel doubts it.

Mackerel's one consolation is that, since his original faith was a mere "workable illusion," its death is no great loss. He compares it to "losing a wooden leg in an accident."[91] Yet it is a barren Candidean garden that Mackerel finally cultivates. He can rest upon nothing other than the solid rock of unyielding despair. Mackerel glumly admits, therefore, that the sum total of his wisdom amounts to an empty truism: "To be as humane as humanly possible."[92]

Even so, Mackerel has come a far distance from his original naivety and presumption. Not only has his humanistic faith been properly chastened; so has his regard for revealed religion been oddly enhanced. Though he still cannot admire it, neither can he dismiss it. The Christian insistence on the bondage of the human will and the freedom of Jesus Christ provides a radical alternative to Mackerel's secular self-sufficiency. He knows, at last, that the two cannot be synthesized, that it is either one way or the other. As Hester acutely discerns, Mackerel is an instinctive Calvinist even in his unbelief: "This all-or-nothing idea. Whole hog. It's got to be one thing or another, splitting hairs right down to the finish. All right, not hairs—essentials. . . . Even your anti-Calvinism is the most Calvinistic thing I've ever seen."[93]

Here, perhaps, Peter De Vries is poignantly describing himself. His entire career may be read, in fact, as a sustained attempt to exorcize the specter of Dutch Calvinism from his life and work. His blessed failure remains, I believe, the real source of his success as a comic writer. The past that haunts De Vries is no mere ethnic narrowness; he is hounded by nothing less than belief in the transcendent and redemptive God. It gives his fiction a clear sense of Christian revelation as a drastic counterproposal to all secular nostrums, both ancient and modern. It also makes his humor more than a guffawing in the graveyard.

De Vries may consciously intend to create a comedy of human sufficiency. He provides, in fact, a parable of divine redemption. "You *can't* say there isn't *design*," Hester reminds Andrew. "You can't say you don't see that everywhere you look, everywhere in the universe. You can't say there isn't such a thing as a designing intelligence." Staring across the table at the woman whom he knows he cannot avoid loving and marrying, Mackerel admits, "I'd be a damn fool if I denied that."[94] However much Mackerel may be determined to tend his bleak little Voltairean garden, he will not be allowed the consolation of solitary unbelief. Hester Pedlock has unconditionally elected him, and her grace, like God's, is irresistible.

CONCLUSION:
HOW COMIC VISION SERVES
THE CHURCH AND THE WORLD

This essay in theology and literary criticism has been premised on the assumption that the clamant need of the hour is to recover genuine Christian faith for post-Enlightenment culture. The contemporary church faces what I believe to be twin temptations: either to recoil in disgust at the unprecedented apostasy of modern secularism, or else to embrace secular values as covertly Christian in content if not in form. These represent, respectively, the conservative and the liberal agenda. Theological conservatism, whether it takes the form of Protestant fundamentalism or Catholic traditionalism, rightly refuses to abandon biblical language and church tradition for the sake of contemporary relevance. Yet what conservatives maintain in the way of Christian integrity, they often squander in an inbred isolation. Religious liberalism, whether in the mainline Protestant churches or in post-Vatican II Roman Catholicism, is equally correct in wanting to engage modernity on its own terms. Yet what liberals gain in cultural relevance, they often surrender in Christian distinctiveness.

My task has been to sketch a new theology of culture that would open a way beyond both conservatism and liberalism. Against the conservatives who would limit the revelation of God in Christ to Scripture and tradition, I have sought to show that there are genuine analogues of the Gospel in the secular world. Against the liberals who would baptize all moral heroism and tragic wisdom as anonymously Christian, I have tried to demonstrate that the secular signs of grace are usually comic and not always moral, and that they can be discerned only from the vantage point of God's redemptive activity in the Jews and Jesus.

That extrabiblical parables of the kingdom are fundamentally comic in character cuts against the grain of both liberals and conservatives, who are usually united in their reading of the Gospel in essentially tragic terms. Conservatism regards the Kingdom of God as a proposition which must, by an act of either the will or the intellect, be bravely received or rejected. What God does in history thus depends on burdensome human decisions. Liberalism seeks to make Christian contact with secular culture through the moral seriousness of the noblest human projects. The fact that human beings are natively capable of transcending their own immediate interests, if only partially and tragically, gives liberals a tenuous assurance that God is at work in the world. Both liberal and conservative Christians are equally heavy and somber, therefore, in their understanding of the Gospel.

I have turned to the theology of Karl Barth as a way out of such a solemn impasse. Precisely because he begins (as do conservatives) with the Gospel heard in Scripture and announced in the church can Barth discern (with liberals) the secular signs of the world's redemption. But the Gospel Barth begins with is not the dour proposition (as conservatives would have it) that God's grace must be fearfully accepted or rejected. Barth's understanding of Christian faith is imbued with a radical eschatological joy over the fact that God in Christ has already decided about us—and that his decision is revealed in the Glad Tidings of our gracious acceptance despite our deserved rejection. God's unilateral reconciliation of the world unto himself is best mirrored in surprising and unexpected parables of the Gospel: not (as liberals insist) in the tragic ambiguity of human self-transcendence, but in the comic irresistibility of divine grace.

This explains my willingness to be more critical of professed Christians like O'Connor and Percy and Updike than of an avowed skeptic like De Vries. Christians ought to know better than to skimp and trim the total unconditionality of God's mercy. The unbeliever, by contrast, remains understandably oblivious to what is incommensurable about divine and human truth. The gladness of the Gospel will not fit within the fallen and mortal confines of art. Thus have I sought to show how O'Connor threatens to turn redemption into a baleful cornering by the Hound of Heaven; how Percy dallies with an aesthete's satire that is more Catonist than Christian; how Updike verges on an outright tragic vision wherein life's oppositions prove irredeemably contradictory and paralyzing.

At their best, however, our authors observe the crucial distinction between art and faith. Percy has repeatedly described his work as cautionary rather than proclamatory, and O'Connor creates characters who are just barely able *not* to escape the tentacles of divine grace. Though Binx Bolling and Francis Marion Tarwater are ultimately converted to Christian faith, their conversions come only at the very last, by uncertain means, and with unsure consequences. Responsible readers will not confuse such fictional deliverances with their own salvation. Perhaps this is why Updike and De Vries make their protagonists such minimal believers. At the end of the third novel recounting his life and times,

Rabbit Angstrom is overtly less Christian than when we first met him. And the Reverend Andrew Mackerel, far from being won over to orthodox faith, is merely bereft of his confident unbelief.

What I find most salutary in these four writers is that they do not make their art into a pseudosalvific means to either belief or doubt. Christians are not converted and sustained in their faith chiefly through art and culture, but through the community of worship and witness called the church. So are atheists and skeptics similarly confirmed in their unbelief: not through a literary and cultural discovery that the world in devoid of God, but through their denial that the church and the synagogue are communities of saving faith.

This insistence on the scandalous uniqueness and offensive exclusivity of God's self-disclosure in the Jews and Jesus does not lead to a Christian devaluation of literary art. Quite to the contrary, the believer who does not look to culture for salvation can gladly affirm and celebrate worldly echoes and parables of the Gospel, especially in those comic places where culture does not take itself with a tragic overseriousness. The remarkable irony must not be missed: precisely because he starts with the Gospel message heard in Scripture and the church, Barth can discern surprising signs of the world's already accomplished—through blasphemously denied—redemption. He can hear, in even the most vigorous denials of God, a certain echo of this undialectical word: not the duplicitous tidings of both darkness and light, cursing and blessing, damning and saving; but the singular message of salvation without strings, blinders, or halters.

Human existence remains, of course, a calamitously sorry story, as our species persists in the delusion of its own sufficiency. Yet the world cannot be summoned back from annihilation by a church that speaks merely its own language (as conservatives tend to do), nor by a church that identifies the Gospel with the deepest worldly wisdom (as liberals are wont). What we need, I believe, is a church that will declare the full scandal of the Gospel, not the better to insure its irrelevance, but precisely in order to understand post-Enlightenment culture better than it understands itself.

This is why Barth insists that all strictures and admonitions against sin and evil must be issued only in the joyful context of God's gracious promise: the covenant that he first made with the Jews, that he consummated in the crucified and risen Messiah, that he is now establishing on earth through synagogue and church, and that he shall fully realize in his eschatological kingdom. But the community summoned to proclaim and perform this Gospel of unalloyed Good News does not act for its own sake. It is called, instead, to offer the world a parable of redemption. And this it does by pointing not to itself but to the Lord whose grace is echoed in worldly resonances.

Barth detects reverberations of God's unmuted mercy in the music of Mozart. So have I also discerned a distant glimmer of the Gospel in the work of these four contemporary American writers. Often against their own willful purpose, I have heard the rumor of comic redemption re-sounding in their fiction. Authorial intent cannot count for everything in a work of literary art. Unlike the Deconstructionists who argue that literature always says less than it intends, I believe that it can also say more. Serendipitously, unintentionally, and thus ever more graciously, a writer can offer analogues of the Gospel unawares. This surprising power is not something inherent in comedy itself, I believe, but in the often un-witting gestures it makes at a Reality beyond itself. Providence is not content to let Mozart's music suffice merely unto itself. The good God, says Barth, turns the good things of his good creation to his own good uses. As much by inadvertence as by intent, therefore, our four novelists body forth convincing fictional parables of what is irreducibly comic in the Gospel of redemption.

O'Connor's boy prophet, Francis Marion Tarwater, is not finally forced to make a dread existentialist choice between God and the Devil—as if they were dualistic polarities between which his solitary will is miserably stretched. The Kingdom of Heaven lays gracious hold on him even as he struggles furiously against it. He will thus awaken the sleeping children of God to alarming but happy tidings: not that fiery wrath is coming next time, but that divine mercy hurries graciously near. Walker Percy's jaded aesthete, Binx Bolling, is also brought out of his self-indulgent despair and into comic newness of life. Having re-ceived God's own "importunate bonus" in spite of himself, he seeks in the end not only to devastate but to edify. It will not suffice to be a profes-sional "ass-kicker" who jolts the spiritually dead into self-awareness; he must also become a fellow pilgrim who guides his wounded wife-to-be along the path toward ultimate hope.

John Updike is the hardest case to make as a parabler of comic re-demption. Yet at the end of the third novel chronicling the life of Harry Angstrom, Rabbit is no longer a romantic Blakean rebel shouting "Damn braces, bless relaxes." He finds himself strangely upheld rather than oppressed by mortal limits and responsibilities. No longer obsessed with the vagaries of his own sweet self—indulging them lest his soul die of neglect—Angstrom learns to save his own life only as he loses it in duty and service to his family and friends. Although Updike's fiction acknowledges this paradox of grace as a wry and rueful necessity more than a celebrative discovery, it remains deeply redemptive nonetheless.

Peter De Vries has the slenderest literary reputation and the least orthodox theology of the four authors we have here examined. Yet I be-lieve that his fiction, despite the bleak aestheticism of its avowed inten-tion, constitutes our largest parable of the divine comedy. Setting out to vindicate a sardonic skepticism, De Vries often ends by creating a won-derfully comic analogy of salvation *sola gratia*. His redeeming comic vision is nowhere better illustrated than in a scene from his most recent novel, *Peckham's Marbles*. Near the end, in what would appear to be a deliberate attack on the shallowness and presumption endemic to fun-damentalism, De Vries shows Peckham being confronted by a street-corner evangelist who asks him whether he will make "a decision for Christ." Perhaps with secular cynicism, but perhaps also with serpen-tine Christian wisdom, Peckham replies: "Can't he make it for him-self?"

Where else in our literature is there such cackling acknowledg-ment of the fact that what God decides about us is infinitely more impor-tant than what we decide about him? Whether wittingly or not, De Vries gives the ultimate Augustinian-Calvinist answer to all Pelagian and Ar-minian exaltation of human autonomy. The comedy of our redemption is that the God of Jesus and the Jews can indeed make a decision for him-self, that he has made for us the only decision that counts, and that his work in the world is not confined to the pathetic little decisions we make for him. He has decided from the foundation of the world to seek and to save the lost, to salvage sinners rather than to help self-helpers, to restore and redeem his fallen creation, and thus to bring in his Kingdom despite all our furious and foolish attempts to stave off its coming.

As we have heard, Voltaire called God "the comedian whose audi-ence is afraid to laugh." For the author of *Candide*, the author of the uni-verse is indeed a Bungler. Being too cowardly to guffaw at this botched job called the world—so Voltaire thought—we pay dutiful homage to its Creator. Seen from a human point of view, Voltaire is right. Humanly speaking, tragedy is indeed the highest of the arts. It rightly protests the awful state of things. It reminds us of the world's inexorable sadness and calamity, the harsh immutability of life, the inconsolable fact that it cannot be drastically other than it is—relentless and absurd, irrational and unforgiving, punishing and unjust. Tragedy would have us see that the universe is a dialectical affair of opposites that circle endlessly around, colliding and coinciding and finally collapsing into the great nothing whence it all came.

What eye has not seen, what ear has not heard, what has not en-tered into the human heart by our own imagining and inventing is the counterproposition that the Apostle calls "the Gospel of God" (Rom. 1:1). It is not a Feuerbachian projection of our own desires and de-vices—if only because a God who is so unstintingly gracious cannot be morally managed according to our own terms. Hence the grim offence and the dour scandal that we bring to the absolutely free grace that is shed abroad in Christ Jesus. For sinful reasons wholly beyond Voltaire's fathoming, we are indeed afraid to laugh: because we have stopped our ears to the message of the Comedian who calls us to live out our lives in redemptive laughter. Literary art cannot itself generate such holy hilarity. But the ear of faith, having first heard the redeeming Comedy in Scripture and the church, can also hear its parabolic echo in certain kinds of comic art. In the fiction of Flannery O'Connor and Walker Percy, of John Updike and Peter De Vries, there resounds, however distantly, this same Good News: that we do not flail in a void, that the universe has a final floor, that we are upheld by sheer grace, that we stand on Christ the solid rock, that all other ground is sinking sand.

NOTES

INTRODUCTION

1. See Reinhold Niebuhr, *Beyond Tragedy: Essays on the Christian Interpretation of History* (New York: Charles Scribner's Sons, 1937), pp. 155–69.

2. Niebuhr, "Humour and Faith," in *Discerning the Signs of the Times* (New York: Charles Scribner's Sons, 1946), p. 112.

3. G. K. Chesterton, *Orthodoxy* (London: Collins Fontana Books, 1961), pp. 118, 120.

1. REINHOLD NIEBUHR AND THE TRAGIC VISION

1. G. K. Chesterton, "The Three Tools of Death," in *The Complete Father Brown Stories* (New York: Penguin, 1981), p. 160.

2. James M. Redfield, *Nature and Culture in the "Iliad": The Tragedy of Hector* (Chicago: University of Chicago Press, 1975), pp. 91, 83.

3. Ibid., p. 87.

4. James M. Gustafson, *Ethics from a Theocentric Perspective*, vol. I: *Theology and Ethics* (Chicago: University of Chicago Press, 1981), p. 341.

5. Stanley Hauerwas, *The Peaceable Kingdom: A Primer in Christian Ethics* (Notre Dame, Ind.: University of Notre Dame Press, 1983), p. 22.

6. Stanley Hauerwas, *Truthfulness and Tragedy: Further Investigations into Christian Ethics* (Notre Dame, Ind.: University of Notre Dame Press, 1977), p. 69.

7. Hauerwas, *The Peaceable Kingdom*, p. 145.

8. Reinhold Niebuhr, *The Irony of American History* (New York: Charles Scribner's Sons, 1952), pp. 156–57.

9. Niebuhr, *Beyond Tragedy*, p. 156.

10. Ibid., p. 169.

11. Ibid., pp. 27–28.

12. Reinhold Niebuhr, "The Truth in Myths," in *Faith and Politics: A Commentary on Religious, Social and Political Thought in a Technological Age*, ed. Ronald H. Stone (New York: George Braziller, 1968), p. 30.

13. Reinhold Niebuhr, *Faith and History: A Comparison of Christian and Modern Views of History* (New York: Charles Scribner's Sons, 1949), p. 147.

14. Quoted in Richard W. Fox, *Reinhold Niebuhr: A Biography* (New York: Pantheon, 1985), p. 215.

15. Ibid., p. 182.

16. Reinhold Niebuhr, *The Nature and Destiny of Man: A Christian Interpretation*, 2 vols. (New York: Charles Scribner's Sons, 1949), II: 63.

17. Ibid., I: 265.

18. Ibid., II: 63.

19. Niebuhr, *Beyond Tragedy*, p. 190.

20. Ibid., p. 95.

21. Fox, p. 183.

22. Niebuhr, *Nature and Destiny*, II: 207.

23. Ibid., II: 156.

24. Ibid., I: 263.

25. Ibid., I: 251.

26. Ibid., I: 185.

27. Ibid., II: 21.

28. "Intellectual Autobiography of Reinhold Niebuhr," in *Reinhold Niebuhr: His Religious, Social, and Political Thought*, ed. Charles W. Kegley and Robert W. Bretall (New York: Macmillan, 1961), p. 18.

29. Niebuhr, *Nature and Destiny*, I: 181, 253; II: 73.

30. Ibid., I: 182–83.

31. Ibid., II: 73.

32. Ibid., I: 263; II: 80.

33. Ibid., I: 183.

34. Ibid., II: 258.

35. Dietrich Bonhoeffer, *No Rusty Swords: Letters, Lectures and Notes, 1928–1936*, trans. Edwin H. Robertson and John Bowden (New York: Harper and Row, 1965), p. 104.

36. Ibid., p. 108.

37. Quoted in Paul Merkley, *Reinhold Niebuhr: A Political Account* (Montreal: McGill-Queen's University Press, 1975), p. viii.

38. Karl Löwith "History and Christianity," in Kegley and Bretall, p. 283. I owe this citation to an unpublished paper by Stanley Hauerwas, "History as Fate: A Critical Presentation of Reinhold Niebuhr's Anthropology."

39. Stanley Hauerwas, "On Keeping Theological Ethics Theological," in *Revisions: Changing Perspectives in Moral Philosophy*, ed. Stanley Hauerwas and Alasdair MacIntyre (Notre Dame, Ind.: University of Notre Dame Press, 1983), p. 25.

40. Niebuhr, *Nature and Destiny*, II: 49.

41. Löwith, "History and Christianity," p. 286.

42. Niebuhr, *The Irony of American History*, p. 174.

43. Niebuhr, *Discerning the Signs of the Times*, pp. 119–20.

44. Ibid., p. 120.

45. Ibid., pp. 122–23.

46. Niebuhr, *Nature and Destiny*, I: 92.

47. Ibid., II: 56–57.

48. Ibid., II: 118.

49. Lionel Trilling, *The Liberal Imagination: Essays on Literature and Society* (Garden City, N.Y.: Doubleday Anchor, 1950), p. xii.

50. Niebuhr, *Discerning the Signs of the Times*, p. 130.
51. Stanley Hauerwas, *Against the Nations: War and Survival in a Liberal Society* (Minneapolis: Winston Press, 1985), p. 77.

2. COMIC VISION AND CHRISTIAN FAITH

1. Quoted in Ramon Fernandez, *Molière: The Man Seen through the Plays*, trans. Wilson Follett (New York: Hill and Wang, 1958), p. 137.
2. F. M. Cornford, *The Origin of Attic Comedy*, ed. Theodore Gaster (Garden City, N.Y.: Doubleday Anchor, 1961), p. 23.
3. Gaster, editor's "Foreword" to *The Origin of Attic Comedy*, p. xxiv.
4. Augustine, *The City of God*, book VII, chapter 26, trans. Henry Bettenson (New York: Penguin, 1972), pp. 286–87.
5. Susanne Langer, *Feeling and Form: A Theory of Art Developed from "Philosophy in a New Key"* (New York: Charles Scribner's Sons, 1953), p. 330–31.
6. Ibid., p. 333.
7. Ibid., p. 331.
8. Ibid., p. 335.
9. Ibid., p. 342.
10. Ibid., p. 349.
11. Ibid., p. 334.
12. Cornford, p. 186.
13. Ibid., p. 184.
14. Robert M. Torrance, *The Comic Hero* (Cambridge, Mass.: Harvard University Press, 1978), p. 1.
15. Quoted in Fernandez, p. 104.
16. Ibid., p. 117.
17. Ibid., pp. 59–60.
18. Ibid., p. 154.
19. Ibid., p. 156.
20. Ibid., p. 113.
21. Ibid., p. 117.
22. Karl Löwith, *Meaning in History* (Chicago: University of Chicago Press, 1949), p. 201.
23. Ibid., p. 188.

3. KARL BARTH AS A THEOLOGIAN OF THE DIVINE COMEDY

1. Karl Barth, *Church Dogmatics*, 4 vols., ed. G. W. Bromiley and T. F. Torrance (Edinburgh: T. & T. Clark, 1934–69), III, 1: 215.
2. Ibid., IV, 1: 427.
3. Ibid., II, 2: 111.
4. Ibid., II, 2: 134.
5. Karl Barth, *Letters 1961–1968*, ed. Jürgen Fangmeier, Hinrich Stoevesandt, and Geoffrey W. Bromiley (Grand Rapids, Mich.: Eerdmans, 1981), p. 258.
6. Barth, *Church Dogmatics*, II, 2: 101.
7. Ibid., II, 2: 56–57.

8. Karl Barth, *Dogmatics in Outline*, trans. G. T. Thomson (New York: Harper and Row, 1959), p. 107.

9. Robert McAfee Brown, "Introduction" to George Casalis, *Portrait of Karl Barth* (Garden City, N.Y.: Doubleday Anchor, 1964), p. xvi.

10. Barth, *Church Dogmatics*, III, 3: 293.

11. Quoted by Hans Dieter Betz, "On Academic Integrity," *Criterion* (University of Chicago Divinity School) 22, no. 3 (Autumn 1983): 19.

12. Barth, *Church Dogmatics*, IV, 1: 412.

13. Karl Barth, *Natural Theology: Comprising "Nature and Grace" by Professor D. Emil Brunner and the Reply "No!" by Dr. Karl Barth* (London: Geoffrey Bles, 1946), p. 120.

14. Barth, *Church Dogmatics*, IV, 1: 416.

15. John Hick, *Evil and the God of Love* (New York: Harper and Row, 1966), p. 142.

16. Barth, *Church Dogmatics*, II, 1: 503.

17. Ibid., III, 3: 342.

18. Ibid., III, 3: 355.

19. Ibid., III, 2: 616–17.

20. Ibid., III, 3: 296–97.

21. Ibid., III, 4: 373.

22. Quoted in Eberhard Busch, *Karl Barth: His Life from Letters and Autobiographical Texts* (Philadelphia: Fortress, 1976), p. 311.

23. C. S. Lewis, *The Problem of Pain* (New York: Macmillan, 1962), p. 93. Lewis held to this view even after his wife's agonizing death from cancer: "The terrible thing is that a perfectly good God is in this matter hardly less formidable than a Cosmic Sadist. The more we believe that God hurts only to heal, the less we can believe that there is any use in begging for tenderness. . . . If [tortures] are unnecessary, then there is no God or a bad one. If there is a good God, then these tortures are necessary. For no even moderately good Being could possibly inflict or permit them if they weren't." C. S. Lewis, *A Grief Observed* (New York: Bantam, 1976), pp. 49–50.

24. Barth, *Church Dogmatics*, III, 4: 366–67.

25. Karl Barth, *Epistle to the Romans*, 6th ed. (New York: Oxford, 1968), p. 362.

26. Barth, *Dogmatics in Outline*, p. 56.

27. *Karl Barth's Table Talk*, ed. John Godsey (Richmond, Va.: John Knox, 1963), p. 37.

28. Barth, *Church Dogmatics*, III, 3: 315.

29. Ibid., IV, 1: 448.

30. For a very similar soteriology, see Arthur C. McGill, *Suffering: A Test of Theological Method* (Philadelphia: Westminster, 1982).

31. Barth, *Dogmatics in Outline*, p. 49.

32. Joseph D. Bettis, "Is Karl Barth a Universalist?" *Scottish Journal of Theology* 15 (1967): 432.

33. *Church Dogmatics*, III, 3: 356–57.

34. Ibid., III, 3: 357.

35. Ronald Goetz, "The Suffering of God: The Rise of a New Orthodoxy,"

Christian Century 103 (April 16, 1986): 385–89.

    36. Barth, *Church Dogmatics*, III, 1: 380.

    37. Ronald Goetz, "The Karl Barth Centennial: An Appreciative Critique," *Christian Century* 103 (May 7, 1986): 460.

    38. Barth, *Church Dogmatics* III, 1: 383.

    39. Ibid., III, 1: 384.

    40. Bettis, p. 434.

    41. George Lindbeck, *The Nature of Doctrine: Religion and Theology in a Postliberal Age* (Philadelphia: Fortress, 1984), p. 60.

    42. Barth, *Dogmatics in Outline*, p. 136.

    43. Barth, *Church Dogmatics*, IV, 3, i: 477–78.

    44. Barth, *Dogmatics in Outline*, p. 134.

    45. Barth, *Church Dogmatics*, III, 2: 609.

    46. Ibid., III, 2: 605.

    47. Ibid., IV, 2: 781.

    48. Ibid., I, 1: 247.

    49. Ibid., II, 2: 632–33.

    50. Barth, *Dogmatics in Outline*, p. 138.

    51. *Karl Barth's Table Talk*, pp. 16–17.

    52. Barth, *Dogmatics in Outline*, p. 123.

    53. Barth, *Church Dogmatics*, IV, 3, i: 376–77.

    54. Ibid., IV, 3, i: 378.

    55. Ibid., IV, 3, i: 397.

    56. Karl Barth, *Deliverance to the Captives* (New York: Harper and Row, 1978), p. 47.

    57. Barth, *Church Dogmatics*, III, 4: 375.

4. BARTH'S EVANGELICAL THEOLOGY OF CULTURE

    1. Barth, *Church Dogmatics*, IV, 3, i: 91.

    2. Karl Barth, *God Here and Now*, trans. Paul M. van Buren (New York: Harper and Row, 1964), p. 106.

    3. Ibid., IV, 3, i: 101.

    4. Ibid., IV, 3, i: 102.

    5. Barth, *Dogmatics in Outline*, p. 84.

    6. Barth, *Church Dogmatics*, III, 2: 453.

    7. Ibid., II, 2: 13.

    8. Barth, *Deliverance to the Captives*, p. 36.

    9. See David Kelsey, *The Uses of Scripture in Recent Theology* (Philadelphia: Fortress, 1975), pp. 64–85.

    10. Lindbeck, *The Nature of Doctrine*, pp. 16, 47, 49, 51.

    11. Ibid., pp. 23, 32, 34.

    12. David Ford, *Barth and God's Story: Biblical Narrative and the Theological Method of Karl Barth in the Church Dogmatics* (Frankfurt am Main and Bern: Verlag Peter Lang, 1981), p. 22.

    13. Van A. Harvey, *The Historian and the Believer: The Morality of Historical Knowledge and Christian Belief* (New York: Macmillan, 1969), pp. 157–58.

    14. Barth, *Church Dogmatics*, IV, 1: 227.

15. James M. Robinson, "Hermeneutic since Barth," in *The New Hermeneutic*, ed. James M. Robinson and John B. Cobb, Jr. (New York: Harper and Row, 1964), p. 27.

16. *The Resurrection*, a dialogue arising from broadcasts by G. W. H. Lampe and D. M. MacKinnon (London: A. R. Mowbray, 1966), pp. 10–11.

17. Rachel Trickett, "Imagination and Belief," in *God Incarnate: Story and Belief*, ed. A. E. Harvey (London: SPCK, 1981), pp. 35, 38.

18. Lindbeck, p. 34.

19. Karl Barth, *The Faith of the Church: A Commentary on the Apostle's Creed according to Calvin's Catechism*, ed. Jean-Louis Leuba, trans. Gabriel Vahanian (New York: Meridian Living Age Books, 1958), pp. 97, 101.

20. Barth, *Church Dogmatics*, IV, 2: 248.

21. Kelsey, p. 45.

22. Barth, *Dogmatics in Outline*, p. 51.

23. Barth, *Church Dogmatics*, III, 3: 374.

24. Barth, *The Faith of the Church*, p. 98.

25. Barth, *Church Dogmatics*, III, 3: 375.

26. Thomas W. Ogletree, *Christian Faith and History: A Critical Comparison of Ernst Troeltsch and Karl Barth* (Nashville, Tenn.: Abingdon Press, 1965), pp. 157, 161–62.

27. Ford, p. 111.

28. Ibid., p. 103.

29. Lindbeck, p. 118.

30. Barth, *The Faith of the Church*, p. 31.

31. Barth, *Dogmatics in Outline*, p. 127.

32. Barth, *Church Dogmatics*, IV, 3, i: 115.

33. Ibid., IV, 3, i: 21.

34. Ibid.

35. Ibid., IV, 3, i: 119.

36. Ibid., IV, 3, i: 112–13.

37. Ibid., IV, 3, i: 125.

38. Ibid., IV, 3, i: 117.

39. Barth, *Dogmatics in Outline*, p. 132.

40. I owe this insight, as indeed the entire thesis of the book, to Warren Carr.

41. Lindbeck, p. 54.

42. Barth, *Church Dogmatics*, IV, 3, i: 125.

43. Ibid., IV, 3, i: 128.

44. Barth, *Dogmatics in Outline*, p. 138.

45. Barth, *Church Dogmatics*, IV, 3, i: 131.

46. Adam Ulam, *Expansion and Coexistence: The History of Soviet Foreign Policy 1917–67* (New York: Frederick A. Praeger, 1968), p. 24.

47. Quoted in Busch, pp. 362–63, 409.

48. Karl Barth, "Wolfgang Amadeus Mozart," in *Religion and Culture: Essays in Honor of Paul Tillich*, ed. Walter Leibrecht (New York: Harper and Row, 1959), pp. 62, 69.

49. Quoted in Busch, p. 410.

50. Barth, *Church Dogmatics*, III, 3: 298.

51. Barth, "Wolfgang Amadeus Mozart," pp. 76–77.

52. Thomas Merton, *Conjectures of a Guilty Bystander* (Garden City, N.Y.: Doubleday Image, 1968), p. 12.

53. Barth, "Wolfgang Amadeus Mozart," p. 69.

54. Ibid., p. 76.

55. Ibid., p. 69.

56. Ibid., p. 64.

57. Karl Barth, *Final Testimonies*, ed. Eberhard Busch (Grand Rapids, Mich.: Eerdmans, 1977), p. 21.

58. Karl Barth, *The Humanity of God* (Richmond, Va.: John Knox, 1960), p. 57.

59. Barth, *Dogmatics in Outline*, p. 41.

60. Barth, *Church Dogmatics*, IV, 3, ii: 866–67.

61. Busch, p. 385.

62. Barth, *Church Dogmatics*, IV, 3, ii: 868.

63. Karl Barth, *The Word of God and the Word of Man* (Gloucester, Mass,: Peter Smith, 1978), p. 75.

64. Barth, *The Humanity of God*, p. 54.

65. Barth, *God Here and Now*, p. 101.

66. Barth, *The Humanity of God*, p. 53.

67. Martin Rumscheidt, "Epilogue" to Karl Barth, *Fragments Grave and Gay*, ed. Martin Rumscheidt (Cleveland: Collins & World, 1976), pp. 124–25.

5. FLANNERY O'CONNOR AS A SATIRIST OF THE NEGATIVE WAY

1. Flannery O'Connor, *The Habit of Being: Letters of Flannery O'Connor*, ed. Sally Fitzgerald (New York: Farrar, Straus & Giroux, 1979), p. 581.

2. Ibid., p. 57.

3. Ibid., p. 258.

4. Ibid., p. 280.

5. Ibid., p. 349.

6. Ibid., p. 92.

7. Ibid., p. 163.

8. This unpublished letter is quoted with the kind permission of Fr. James H. McCown, S.J., to whom it was first addressed.

9. O'Connor, *The Habit of Being*, p. 419.

10. Ibid., p. 224.

11. Flannery O'Connor, *The Complete Stories* (New York: Farrar, Straus and Giroux, 1972), p. 282.

12. O'Connor, *The Habit of Being*, p. 326.

13. This argument was first voiced by Josephine Hendin in *The World of Flannery O'Connor* (Bloomington: Indiana University Press, 1970), a book so presumptuous in its psychologizing that it closed off all further scholarly conversations with Mrs. O'Connor about her daughter's life and art.

14. O'Connor, *The Habit of Being*, p. 19.

15. Ibid., p. 169.

16. Ibid., p. 340.

17. This incident was reported to me by the Rev. Dr. Paul W. Barrus.

18. O'Connor, *The Habit of Being*, p. 498.

19. Ibid., p. 536.

20. Ibid., p. 166.

21. Ibid., p. 569.

22. Ibid., p. 230.

23. *"The Presence of Grace" and Other Book Reviews by Flannery O'Connor*, ed. Leo J. Zuber and Carter W. Martin (Athens, Ga.: University of Georgia Press, 1983), p. 77.

24. O'Connor, *The Habit of Being*, p. 104.

25. Flannery O'Connor, *Mystery and Manners: Occasional Prose*, ed. Sally and Robert Fitzgerald (New York: Noonday Press, 1970), p. 44.

26. Flannery O'Connor, *Wise Blood*, 2nd ed. (New York: Farrar, Straus and Cudahy, 1952), p. 5.

27. O'Connor, *Mystery and Manners*, pp. 44–45.

28. O'Connor, *The Habit of Being*, p. 350.

29. Ibid., p. 518.

30. Ibid., p. 118.

31. Ibid., p. 131.

32. O'Connor, *The Complete Stories*, p. 133.

33. *The Presence of Grace*, p. 159.

34. O'Connor, *Mystery and Manners*, p. 182.

35. Henri de Lubac, S.J., *Catholicism: A Study of Dogma in Relation to the Corporate Destiny of Mankind* (New York: Mentor-Omega, 1964), p. 121.

36. O'Connor, *The Complete Stories*, p. 165.

37. Ibid., p. 241.

38. Karl Rahner and Karl-Heinz Weger, *Our Christian Faith: Answers for the Future*, trans. Francis McDonagh (New York: Crossroads, 1981), p. 79.

39. *The Presence of Grace*, p. 130.

40. Ibid., p. 87.

41. Quoted by Pierre Leroy, "Teilhard de Chardin: The Man," in *The Divine Milieu* (New York: Harper Torchbooks, 1965), p. 15.

42. Pierre Teilhard de Chardin, *The Phenomenon of Man* (New York: Harper Torchbooks, 1961), pp. 310–11.

43. Quoted in Max Bégouën, "Foreword" to Pierre Teilhard de Chardin, *Building the Earth and the Psychological Conditions for Human Unification* (New York: Avon, 1969), p. 11.

44. Teilhard de Chardin, *The Phenomenon of Man*, p. 242.

45. *The Presence of Grace*, pp. 87–88.

46. O'Connor, *The Habit of Being*, p. 365.

47. O'Connor, *Mystery and Manners*, p. 44.

48. Ibid., p. 50.

49. Cited by Sr. Rose Bowen, O.P., *Christology in the Works of Flannery O'Connor* (Florida State University Ph.D. Dissertation, 1984).

50. O'Connor, *The Complete Stories*, pp. 131–32.

51. Ibid., p. 132.

52. Jacques Maritain, *Integral Humanism: Temporal and Spiritual Problems of a New Christendom*, trans. Joseph W. Evans (Notre Dame, Ind.: University of Notre Dame Press, 1973), pp. 59–60.

53. O'Connor, *The Habit of Being*, p. 439.

54. Ibid., p. 97.

55. Ibid., p. 360.

56. O'Connor, *Mystery and Manners*, p. 193.

57. O'Connor, *The Habit of Being*, p. 90.

58. Jacques Maritain, "Preface" to *Antimoderne*, quoted in Jacques Maritain, *Saint Thomas Aquinas*, trans. and rev. by Joseph W. Evans and Peter O'Reilly (New York: Meridian, 1958), p. 1.

59. Cf. O'Connor, *Mystery and Manners*, pp. 201, 208.

60. Ibid., p. 192.

61. O'Connor, *The Habit of Being*, p. 229.

62. O'Connor, *Mystery and Manners*, p. 34.

63. John Hawkes, "Flannery O'Connor's Devil," *Sewanee Review* 70 (Summer 1962): 395–407.

64. O'Connor, *The Habit of Being*, p. 507.

65. Ibid., p. 367.

66. Terry Eagleton, *Literary Theory: An Introduction* (Minneapolis: University of Minnesota Press, 1983), p. 146.

67. André Bleikasten, "The Heresy of Flannery O'Connor," in *Les Americanistes: New French Criticism on Modern American Fiction*, ed. Ira D. Johnson and Christiane Johnson (Port Washington, N.Y.: Kennikat Press, 1978), p. 53.

68. Ibid., pp. 66–67.

69. Ibid., p. 62.

70. Ibid., p. 70.

71. O'Connor, *Mystery and Manners*, p. 168.

72. Ibid., p. 167.

73. C. S. Lewis, *Mere Christianity* (New York: Macmillan, 1960), pp. 50–51.

74. O'Connor, *Mystery and Manners*, p. 118.

75. O'Connor, *The Habit of Being*, pp. 488–89.

76. Flannery O'Connor, *The Violent Bear It Away* (New York: Farrar, Straus & Giroux, 1960), p. 19.

77. Ibid., p. 114.

78. Ibid., p. 113.

79. O'Connor, *The Habit of Being*, p. 488.

80. Ibid., p. 484.

81. *The Essential Augustine*, ed. Vernon J. Bourke (Indianapolis: Hackett, 1974), p. 181.

82. O'Connor, *The Habit of Being*, p. 486.

83. Cf. *The Jerome Biblical Commentary*, ed. Raymond E. Brown, Joseph A. Fitzmeyer, Roland E. Murphy (Englewood Cliffs, N.J.: Prentice-Hall, 1968), vol. II, p. 82.

84. W. G. Kümmel, *Promise and Fulfillment: The Eschatological Message of Jesus*, trans. Dorothea M. Barton (Naperville, Ill.: Alec R. Allenson, 1957), p. 123.

85. Ibid., p. 129.

86. O'Connor, *The Complete Stories*, p. 481.

87. O'Connor, *The Violent Bear It Away*, p. 242. Old Mason Tarwater had earlier warned the children of God against "the terrible speed of justice" (p. 159). Young Tarwater's altered summons to announce the fearful urgency of God's mercy shows a much profounder understanding of the gracious paradox inherent in transcendent salvation.

88. O'Connor, *The Habit of Being*, p. 342.

89. Cited by C. S. Lewis, "Preface" to *George MacDonald: An Anthology* (New York: Macmillan, 1978), p. xxxi.

6. FLANNERY O'CONNOR AS A COMEDIAN OF POSITIVE GRACE

1. O'Connor, *Mystery and Manners*, p. 200.

2. O'Connor, *The Habit of Being*, p. 414.

3. Ibid., p. 580.

4. Ibid., p. 329.

5. Ibid., p. 580.

6. O'Connor, *Mystery and Manners*, pp. 28–29.

7. See Robert Coles, *Children of Crisis: A Study of Courage and Fear* (New York: Delta Books, 1967).

8. Robert Coles, *Flannery O'Connor's South* (Baton Rouge: Louisiana State University Press, 1980), pp. 100–101.

9. O'Connor, *Mystery and Manners*, p. 234.

10. G. K. Chesterton, *St. Francis of Assisi* (Garden City, N.Y.: Doubleday Image, 1957), p. 75.

11. O'Connor, *The Complete Stories*, p. 255.

12. Ibid., p. 262.

13. Ibid., p. 265.

14. Ibid., p. 267.

15. Ibid., p. 268.

16. Ibid., p. 269.

17. Ibid., pp. 269–70.

18. O'Connor, *The Habit of Being*, p. 78.

19. Ibid., p. 158.

20. O'Connor, *The Complete Stories*, p. 364.

21. Quoted by C. S. Lewis, *The Screwtape Letters and Screwtape Proposes a Toast* (New York: Macmillan, 1962), p. 5.

22. O'Connor, *The Complete Stories*, p. 359.

23. Ibid., p. 360.

24. Ibid.

25. Ibid., p. 375.

26. Ibid., p. 376.

27. Ibid., p. 370.

28. Ibid., p. 379.

29. Ibid., p. 361.

30. Ibid., p. 370.

31. Ibid., p. 382.

32. Ibid., p. 361.

33. O'Connor, *The Habit of Being*, p. 518.

34. Ibid., p. 468.

35. For an interpretation of "Judgement Day" as a story of positively comic redemption, see my essay "From Fashionable Tolerance to Unfashionable Redemption: A Reading of Flannery O'Connor's First and Last Stories," *Flannery O'Connor Bulletin* (Autumn 1978): 10–25.

36. O'Connor, *The Complete Stories*, p. 490.

37. Ibid., p. 491.

38. Ibid.

39. Ibid., p. 492.

40. Ibid., p. 494.

41. Ibid., p. 497.

42. Ibid., p. 500.

43. Ibid., p. 501.

44. Ibid., p. 503.

45. Ibid.

46. Ibid., p. 505.

47. Ibid., p. 507.

48. Ibid., p. 508.

49. Ibid., p. 509.

7. WALKER PERCY AS A CATHOLIC EXISTENTIALIST

1. Quoted in Bradley R. Dewey, "Walker Percy Talks about Kierkegaard: An Annotated Interview," *Journal of Religion* 54, no. 3 (July 1974): 295.

2. Lewis Baker, *The Percys of Mississippi: Politics and Literature in the New South* (Baton Rouge: Louisiana State University Press, 1983), chapter 1.

3. Walker Percy, "Introduction" to William Alexander Percy, *Lanterns on the Levee* (Baton Rouge: Louisiana State University Press, 1973) p. xviii.

4. Walker Percy, "Stoicism in the South," *Commonweal* (July 6, 1956): 343.

5. Walker Percy, *The Moviegoer* (New York: Farrar, Straus, and Giroux, 1967), p. 54.

6. Ibid., p. 4.

7. William Alexander Percy, *In April Once* (New Haven, Conn.: Yale University Press, 1920), p. 134.

8. Baker, p. 60.

9. William Percy, *Lanterns on the Levee*, pp. 13–14.

10. T. S. Eliot, "Shakespeare and the Stoicism of Seneca," in *Selected Essays*, new ed. (New York: Harcourt, Brace & World, 1960), pp. 119–20.

11. Quoted in Frederick Copleston, *A History of Philosophy*, vol. I, part II, new rev. ed. (Garden City, N.Y.: Doubleday Image, 1962), p. 175.

12. Richard H. King, *A Southern Renaissance: The Cultural Awakening of the American South, 1930–1955* (New York: Oxford University Press, 1980), p. 51.

13. William Percy, *Lanterns on the Levee*, p. 20.

14. Walker Percy, "A Southern View" *America* 97 (July 20, 1957): 429.

15. Walker Percy, "Stoicism in the South," p. 344.

16. William Percy, *Lanterns on the Levee*, p. 315.

17. Ibid., p. 348.

18. Ibid., p. 313.

19. Baker, pp. 78–85, 165.

20. King, p. 97.

21. William Percy, *Lanterns on the Levee*, pp. 126–27.

22. Robert Coles, "Profiles: The Search—1" (on Walker Percy), *New Yorker* 54 (October 2, 1978) 48, 50, 52, 57.

23. Walker Percy, *The Last Gentleman* (New York: Farrar, Straus and Giroux, 1972), pp. 9–10.

24. William Percy, *Lanterns on the Levee*, p. 145.

25. Ibid., p. 154.

26. Ibid., p. 348.

27. Ibid., p. 321.

28. Ibid., p. 95.

29. Quoted by Dewey, p. 281.

30. Percy makes no mention of the fact that, across the street from Columbia at Union Theological Seminary, Reinhold Niebuhr was also drawing upon Kierkegaard to make a powerful critique of Deweyesque humanism.

31. Dewey, p. 288.

32. Søren Kierkegaard, "Of the Difference Between a Genius and an Apostle," printed together with *The Present Age* (New York: Harper Torchbooks, 1962), p. 90.

33. Walker Percy, *The Message in the Bottle* (New York: Farrar, Straus and Giroux, 1975), p. 145.

34. Kierkegaard, "Of the Difference Between a Genius and an Apostle," p. 94.

35. Dewey, p. 297.

36. Coles, "Profiles: The Search—1," p. 52.

37. Dewey, p. 282.

38. Walker Percy, *The Message in the Bottle*, p. 141.

39. Ibid., p. 143.

40. Ibid., p. 149.

41. Ibid., p. 148.

42. Ibid., p. 85.

43. Ibid., p. 35.

44. Ibid., p. 173.

45. Ibid., p. 263–64.

46. Ibid., p. 216.

47. Linda Whitney Hobson, "The Study of Consciousness: An Interview with Walker Percy," *Georgia Review* 35, no. 1 (Spring 1981): 56–59.

48. Walker Percy, *The Message in the Bottle*, p. 326.

49. Weldon Thornton, "Homo Loquens, Homo Symbolificus, Homo Sapiens: Walker Percy on Language," in *The Art of Walker Percy*, ed. Panthea Reid Broughton (Baton Rouge: Louisiana State University Press, 1979), pp. 184–90.

50. Walker Percy, *The Message in the Bottle*, p. 105.

51. Ibid., p. 20.

52. Ibid., p. 116.

8. PERCY AS THE SATIRIST SATIRIZED: *THE MOVIEGOER*

1. Søren Kierkegaard, *The Point of View for My Work as An Author* (New York: Harper Torchbooks, 1962), p. 25.
2. Ibid., p. 26.
3. Walker Percy, *The Moviegoer*, p. 125.
4. Ibid., pp. 69–70.
5. Søren Kierkegaard, *Either/Or*, vol. I, trans. David F. Swenson and Lillian Marvin Swenson (Garden City, N.Y.: Doubleday Anchor, 1959), p. 30.
6. Walker Percy, *The Moviegoer*, pp. 135–36.
7. Ibid., pp. 6–7.
8. Ibid., p. 101.
9. Ibid., p. 228.
10. Ibid., p. 108.
11. Ibid., p. 109.
12. Ibid., p. 99.
13. Ibid., p. 190.
14. Ibid., p. 31.
15. Ibid., p. 24.
16. Ibid., p. 25.
17. Ibid., p. 88.
18. Ibid., p. 23.
19. Ibid., p. 54.
20. Ibid., p. 3.
21. Ibid., p. 53.
22. Ibid., pp. 223–24.
23. Ibid., p. 224.
24. Ibid., p. 226.
25. Søren Kierkegaard, *The Sickness Unto Death*, printed with *Fear and Trembling*, trans. Walter Lowrie (Garden City, N.Y.: Doubleday Anchor, 1954), pp. 205–6.
26. Walker Percy, *The Moviegoer*, p. 145.
27. Ibid., p. 13.
28. Ibid., p. 146.
29. Ibid., p. 11.
30. Ibid.
31. Ibid., p. 13.
32. Ibid., p. 7.
33. Ibid., pp. 13–14.
34. Ibid., p. 146.
35. Ibid., p. 163.
36. Ibid., p. 137.
37. Ibid., p. 43.
38. Ibid., p. 194.
39. Ibid., p. 197.
40. Ibid., p. 200.
41. Ibid., p. 207.
42. Ibid., p. 231.

43. Ibid., p. 234.
44. Ibid., p. 235.
45. Ibid., p. 228.
46. Ibid., p. 237.
47. Ibid., p. 228.
48. Ibid., p. 236.
49. Ibid., p. 240.
50. Fyodor Dostoevski, *The Brothers Karamazov*, trans. Constance Garnett, ed. Ralph E. Matlaw (New York: W. W. Norton, 1976), p. 735.

9. JOHN UPDIKE AS AN IRONIST OF THE SPIRITUAL LIFE

1. John Updike, *Assorted Prose* (New York: Fawcett Crest, 1966), pp. 232–33.
2. Kierkegaard, *Either/Or*, vol. I, p. 88.
3. Ibid., p. 129.
4. Updike, *Assorted Prose*, p. 233.
5. Charles Samuels, "The Art of Fiction, XLIII: John Updike," (interview) *Paris Review* 12, no. 45 (Winter 1968): 101–2.
6. John Updike, *The Music School* (New York: Fawcett Premier, 1967), p. 141.
7. John Updike, *The Centaur* (New York: Knopf, 1963), p. 95.
8. Ibid., p. 27.
9. John Updike, *The Witches of Eastwick* (New York: Knopf, 1984), p. 210.
10. Samuels, p. 103.
11. John Updike, *Picked-Up Pieces* (New York: Knopf, 1975), p. 263.
12. John Updike, *Hugging the Shore: Essays and Criticism*, (New York: Knopf, 1983), pp. 198, 201.
13. John Updike, *Too Far To Go: The Maples Stories* (New York: Fawcett Crest, 1979), p. 198.
14. Ibid., p. 209.
15. John Updike, *Couples* (New York: Fawcett Crest, 1969), p. 12.
16. Ibid., p. 58.
17. Ibid., pp. 24–25.
18. Ibid., p. 389.
19. Ibid., p. 46.
20. Ibid., p. 81.
21. Ibid., p. 107.
22. Quoted in Updike, *Assorted Prose*, p. 222.
23. Updike, *Couples*, p. 215.
24. Ibid., p. 271.
25. Updike, *Picked-Up Pieces*, pp. 503, 505.
26. Updike, *Couples*, p. 434.
27. Updike, *Picked-Up Pieces*, p. 504.
28. John Updike, *Buchanan Dying* (New York: Knopf, 1974), p. 167.
29. John Updike, *A Month of Sundays* (New York: Knopf, 1975), p. 38.
30. Updike, *Assorted Prose*, p. 143.
31. Updike, *Picked-Up Pieces*, p. 89.

32. Ibid., p. 87.

33. *A Compend of Luther's Theology*, ed. Hugh T. Kerr, Jr., (Philadelphia: Westminster, 1966), p. 55.

34. Updike, *Assorted Prose*, p. 125.

35. Augustine, *Confessions*, trans. R. S. Pine-Coffin (Baltimore: Penguin, 1961), XI, 4, p. 256.

36. Updike, *A Month of Sundays*, p. 23.

37. Updike, *Picked-Up Pieces*, p. 91.

38. Samuels, p. 116.

39. Frank Gado, ed., *First Person: Conversations on Writers and Writing* (Schenectady, N.Y.: Union College Press), p. 109.

40. Updike, *Picked-Up Pieces*, p. 27.

41. John Updike, *Pigeon Feathers and Other Stories* (New York: Fawcett Crest, 1963), p. 99.

42. Ibid., p. 105.

43. Updike, *A Month of Sundays*, p. 209.

44. John Updike, *Verse* (Greenwich, Conn.: Fawcett Crest, 1965), p. 164.

45. Gado, p. 89.

46. Updike, *Picked-Up Pieces*, p. 514.

47. Ibid., p. 519.

48. Updike, *Assorted Prose*, p. 211.

49. Updike, *Hugging the Shore*, p. 649.

50. Arthur C. Danto, *Jean-Paul Sartre*, (New York: Viking, 1975), p. 25.

51. Updike, *Assorted Prose*, p. 143.

52. Updike, *A Month of Sundays*, pp. 102–3.

53. Ibid., p. 166.

54. Augustine, *Confessions*, X, 17, p. 224.

55. Updike, *Hugging the Shore*, pp. 644–45.

56. Updike, *Picked-Up Pieces*, p. 121.

57. Ibid., p. 112.

58. Ibid., p. 118.

59. John Updike, "Søren Kierkegaard," in *Atlantic Brief Lives: A Biographical Companion to the Arts*, ed. Louis Kronenberger (Boston: Little, Brown, 1972), p. 430.

60. Updike, *Hugging the Shore*, pp. 109–10.

61. Updike, *Assorted Prose*, p. 143.

62. Updike, *Hugging the Shore*, p. 117.

63. John Updike, *"Midpoint" and Other Poems* (New York: Knopf, 1969), p. 38.

64. Ibid., p. 32.

65. Ibid.

66. Ibid., p. 36.

67. Ibid., p. 42.

68. Ibid., p. 38.

69. Ibid., pp. 39–40.

70. Ibid., p. 40.

71. Ibid., p. 42.

72. Ibid., pp. 43–44.
73. Gado, p. 92.

10. THE STRANGE MORAL PROGRESS OF HARRY ("RABBIT") ANGSTROM

1. Quoted in Updike, *Hugging the Shore*, p. 831.
2. Ibid., p. 850.
3. Ibid., pp. 849–50.
4. Updike, *Assorted Prose*, p. 161.
5. Updike, *The Witches of Eastwick*, p. 96.
6. Updike, *Assorted Prose*, p. 236.
7. O'Connor, *The Habit of Being*, p. 420.
8. Samuels, pp. 106, 108.
9. See John Bayley, *The Characters of Love: A Study in the Literature of Personality* (London: Constable, 1960).
10. Updike, *Picked-Up Pieces*, p. 38.
11. Updike, *Hugging the Shore*, p. 864.
12. John Updike, *Rabbit, Run* (New York: Fawcett Crest, 1963), p. 12.
13. Ibid., p. 17.
14. Ibid., p. 73.
15. Updike, *Picked-Up Pieces*, p. 20.
16. Updike, *Rabbit, Run*, p. 68.
17. Ibid., p. 69.
18. Ibid., p. 68.
19. Ibid., p. 96.
20. Ibid., p. 77.
21. Updike, *Assorted Prose*, p. 146.
22. Updike, *Rabbit, Run*, p. 107.
23. Ibid., p. 197.
24. Ibid., p. 121.
25. Ibid., pp. 126–27.
26. Ibid., p. 254.
27. Ibid., p. 91.
28. Ibid., p. 125.
29. Ibid., p. 247.
30. Ibid., p. 128.
31. Ibid., p. 125.
32. Ibid., p. 141.
33. Ibid., p. 143.
34. Ibid., p. 220.
35. Ibid., p. 244.
36. Ibid., p. 231.
37. Ibid., p. 251.
38. Ibid., p. 254.
39. Ibid., p. 197.
40. Ibid.
41. Updike, *Hugging the Shore*, p. 858.

42. John Updike, *Rabbit Redux* (Greenwich, Conn.: Fawcett Crest, 1971), p. 39.

43. Ibid., p. 47.

44. Ibid., pp. 98, 103.

45. Ibid., p. 113.

46. Ibid., p. 28.

47. Ibid., pp. 122–23.

48. Updike, *Picked-Up Pieces*, p. xv.

49. Updike, *Rabbit Redux*, p. 231–32.

50. Ibid., p. 49.

51. Ibid., p. 175.

52. Ibid., pp. 324–25.

53. Ibid., p. 341.

54. Ibid., p. 352.

55. Ibid.

56. Ibid., p. 153.

57. John Updike, *Rabbit Is Rich* (New York: Knopf, 1981), p. 375.

58. Ibid., p. 33.

59. Ibid., p. 47.

60. Ibid., p. 354.

61. Ibid., p. 112.

62. Ibid., p. 417.

63. Ibid., p. 161.

64. Ibid., p. 231.

65. Ibid., p. 208.

66. Ibid., p. 127.

67. Ibid., p. 50.

68. Ibid., p. 97.

69. Ibid., p. 189.

70. Brendan Gill, *Here at the New Yorker* (New York: Random House, 1975), p. 49.

11. PETER DE VRIES AS A HUMORIST OF BACKSLIDDEN UNBELIEF

1. Douglas M. Davis, "An Interview with Peter De Vries," *College English* 28 (April 1967): 526.

2. Ibid., p. 525. Mel Brooks makes this same distinction but for opposite effect, thus revealing himself to be a satirist rather than a humorist. "Tragedy is when I cut my finger. Comedy is when you fall in a sewer pit and drown."

3. Ibid.

4. Roy Newquist, "Interview with Peter De Vries," *Counterpoint* (Chicago: Rand McNally, 1964), p. 153.

5. Quoted by Ben Yagoda, "Peter De Vries: Being Seriously Funny," *New York Times Magazine*, June 12, 1983, p. 55.

6. Davis, p. 525.

7. Peter De Vries, *Through the Fields of Clover* (Boston: Little, Brown, 1961), p. 88.

8. Peter De Vries, *Mrs. Wallop* (Boston: Little, Brown, 1970), p. 163.

9. Newquist, pp. 150–51.

10. Peter De Vries, *Forever Panting* (New York: Penguin, 1982), p. 176.

11. Peter De Vries, *The Glory of the Hummingbird* (Boston: Little, Brown, 1974), p. 172.

12. De Vries, *Mrs. Wallop*, pp. 306–7.

13. De Vries, *The Glory of the Hummingbird*, p. 115.

14. De Vries, *Mrs. Wallop*, p. 168.

15. Ibid., p. 249.

16. Peter De Vries, *Madder Music* (New York: Penguin, 1977), p. 206.

17. Ibid., p. 6.

18. Ibid., p. 147.

19. Ibid., p. 220.

20. Ibid., p. 119.

21. Peter De Vries, *The Vale of Laughter* (Boston: Little, Brown, 1967), p. 148.

22. Ibid., pp. 210–11.

23. Peter De Vries, *The Cat's Pajamas* and *Witch's Milk* (New York: Popular Library, 1968), p. 54.

24. Ibid., p. 112.

25. Ibid., p. 98.

26. Ibid., p. 38.

27. Ibid., pp. 140–41.

28. Ibid., pp. 136–37.

29. Ibid., p. 18.

30. Ibid., p. 37.

31. Ibid., pp. 60–61.

32. Richard B. Sale, "An Interview in New York with Peter De Vries," *Studies in the Novel* 1 (Fall 1969): 366.

33. De Vries, *The Cat's Pajamas*, p. 127.

34. Ibid., p. 150.

35. Ibid., pp. 139–40.

36. Ibid., p. 144.

37. Ibid., pp. 144–45.

38. Ibid., p. 212.

39. Ibid., p. 210.

40. Ibid., p. 208.

41. De Vries, *The Glory of the Hummingbird*, p. 137.

42. Peter De Vries, *The Blood of the Lamb* (Boston: Little, Brown, 1961), pp. 8–9.

43. Ibid., p. 34.

44. Peter De Vries, *Comfort Me with Apples* (Boston: Little, Brown, 1956), p. 109.

45. Ibid., p. 5.

46. Ibid., p. 99.

47. Ibid., p. 9.

48. Peter De Vries, *The Tents of Wickedness* (Boston: Little, Brown, 1959), p. 11.

49. Ibid., p. 5.

50. Ibid., pp. 101–2.

51. De Vries, *Comfort Me with Apples*, p. 18.

52. De Vries, *The Tents of Wickedness*, p. 120.

53. Ibid., p. 51.

54. George Eliot, *Middlemarch* (New York: E. P. Dutton, 1930), vol. 1, p. 171.

55. De Vries, *Comfort Me with Apples*, p. 59.

56. Ibid., p. 60.

57. Ibid., p. 84.

58. Ibid., p. 101.

59. Ibid., p. 35.

60. De Vries, *The Tents of Wickedness*, p. 113.

61. De Vries, *Comfort Me with Apples*, p. 141.

62. Ibid., p. 267.

63. Ibid., p. 14.

64. Ibid., p. 167.

65. De Vries, *The Tents of Wickedness*, p. 68.

66. Ibid., p. 96.

67. Ibid., p. 212.

68. Ibid., p. 22.

69. De Vries, *Comfort Me with Apples*, p. 101.

70. De Vries, *The Tents of Wickedness*, p. 223.

71. De Vries, *Comfort Me with Apples*, p. 16.

72. Ibid., p. 68.

73. De Vries, *The Tents of Wickedness*, p. 115.

74. De Vries, *Comfort Me with Apples*, p. 101.

75. Ibid., p. 89.

76. Ibid., p. 181.

77. Ibid., p. 185.

78. Ibid., p. 187.

79. Ibid., p. 276.

80. Ibid., p. 29.

81. Ibid., p. 201.

82. De Vries, *The Tents of Wickedness*, p. 25.

83. Roderick Jellema, *Peter De Vries* (Grand Rapids, Mich.: Eerdmans, 1966), p. 21.

84. De Vries, *The Tents of Wickedness*, p. 247.

85. Ibid., p. 264.

86. Ibid., p. 267.

87. Ibid., pp. 267–68.

88. Ibid., p. 51.

12. THE COMEDY OF UNCONDITIONAL ELECTION AND IRRESISTIBLE GRACE

1. Peter De Vries, *Through the Fields of Clover* (Boston: Little, Brown, 1961), pp. 23–24.

2. Ibid., p. 17.

3. Ibid., p. 167.
4. Ibid., p. 18.
5. Ibid., p. 146.
6. Ibid., p. 237.
7. Ibid., p. 150.
8. Ibid., p. 162.
9. Ibid., p. 158.
10. Newquist, p. 150.
11. De Vries, *Through the Fields of Clover*, pp. 217–18.
12. Jellema, p. 24.
13. De Vries, *Through the Fields of Clover*, p. 201.
14. Ibid., p. 7.
15. Ibid., p. 16.
16. Ibid., p. 28.
17. Ibid., p. 179.
18. Ibid., p. 46.
19. Ibid., p. 16.
20. Ibid., p. 209.
21. Ibid., p. 203.
22. Ibid., p. 240.
23. Ibid., p. 245.
24. Ibid., p. 246.
25. Ibid., p. 247.
26. Ibid., p. 275.
27. James Bowden, *Peter De Vries* (Boston: Twayne, 1983), p. 161.
28. De Vries, *The Blood of the Lamb*, pp. 207–8.
29. De Vries, *The Vale of Laughter*, p. 215.
30. Ibid., p. 267.
31. Peter De Vries, *Reuben, Reuben* (New York: Popular Library, 1964), p. 184.
32. Ibid., p. 234.
33. De Vries, *The Blood of the Lamb*, p. 151.
34. Ibid., p. 57.
35. Ibid., pp. 24–25.
36. Ibid., p. 73.
37. Ibid., pp. 51–52.
38. Ibid., p. 108.
39. Ibid., p. 165.
40. Ibid., pp. 166–67 and 241.
41. Ibid., p. 176.
42. Ibid., p. 197.
43. Ibid., p. 181.
44. Ibid., p. 182.
45. Ibid.
46. Ibid., p. 209.
47. Bowden, p. 76.
48. De Vries, *The Blood of the Lamb*, pp. 242–43.
49. Ibid., p. 243.

306 / NOTES TO PAGES 267–279

50. Ibid., p. 246.

51. Ibid., p. 236.

52. Ibid., p. 191.

53. Ibid., pp. 191-92.

54. Ibid., p. 237.

55. Barth, *Church Dogmatics*, IV, 3, i: 431–32.

56. De Vries, *The Blood of the Lamb*, p. 238.

57. Peter De Vries, *The Mackerel Plaza* (Boston: Little, Brown, 1958), p. 8.

58. Ibid., p. 7.

59. Ibid., p. 6.

60. Ibid., p. 27.

61. Ibid., p. 8.

62. Ibid., p. 174.

63. Ibid., p. 4.

64. Thomas J. J. Altizer, ed., *Toward a New Christianity: Readings in the Death of God Theology* (New York: Harcourt, Brace and World, 1967), p. 306.

65. Langdon Gilkey, *Naming the Whirlwind: The Renewal of God-Language* (Indianapolis: Bobbs-Merrill, 1969), p. 131.

66. De Vries, *The Mackerel Plaza*, p. 30.

67. Ibid., p. 77.

68. Ibid., p. 78.

69. Ibid., p. 61.

70. Ibid., p. 63.

71. Ibid., p. 18.

72. Ibid., pp. 83–84.

73. Ibid., p. 17.

74. Ibid., p. 102.

75. Ibid., p. 76.

76. Ibid., p. 112.

77. Ibid., p. 116.

78. Ibid., pp. 186–87.

79. Ibid., pp. 225–26.

80. Ibid., p. 164.

81. Ibid., p. 208.

82. Ibid., p. 167.

83. Ibid., p. 198.

84. Ibid., p. 217.

85. Ibid., p. 218.

86. Ibid., p. 245.

87. Ibid., p. 254.

88. Ibid., p. 257.

89. Ibid., p. 259.

90. Ibid., p. 258.

91. Ibid., p. 257.

92. Ibid., p. 260.

93. Ibid., p. 259.

94. Ibid., p. 260.

INDEX

106003

IRETON